For Maynard —

With all good wishes — and hopes
for an end in sight on the biography!
Howard

ALEXANDER POPE AND THE TRADITIONS
OF FORMAL VERSE SATIRE

Alexander Pope

AND THE TRADITIONS OF
FORMAL VERSE SATIRE

by Howard D. Weinbrot

PRINCETON UNIVERSITY PRESS
PRINCETON, NEW JERSEY

Publication of this book has been aided by a grant from the
Paul Mellon Fund of Princeton University Press
This book has been composed in Linotype Baskerville

Clothbound editions of Princeton University Press books
are printed on acid-free paper, and binding materials are
chosen for strength and durability

Printed in the United States of America by
Princeton University Press, Princeton, New Jersey

For Lawrence, Richard, and Wendy Weitzner

Contents

CONTENTS

Preface

JOSEPH ADDISON's discussion of *Paradise Lost* offers a fine example of characteristic eighteenth-century eclecticism. He is aware that his inheritance includes epic poems and criticism of them, and in his *Spectator*, No. 321 (1712), says that he will select from the different approaches, while exercising his own powers: "as the greatest Masters of Critical Learning differ among one another, as to some particular Points in an Epic Poem, I have not bound myself scrupulously to the Rules, which any one of them has laid down upon that Art, but have taken the Liberty sometimes to join with one, and sometimes with another, and sometimes to differ from all of them, when I have thought that the Reason of the thing was on my side." Addison might also have cited Milton's practice as an epic poet who joined with his predecessors while exercising his own talents. In 1688 Dryden wrote these lines for the engraving of Milton in the fourth edition of *Paradise Lost*:

> Three *Poets*, in three distant *Ages* born,
> *Greece*, *Italy*, and *England* did adorn.
> The *First* in loftiness of thought Surpass'd;
> The *Next* in Majesty; in both the *Last*.
> The force of *Nature* cou'd no farther goe:
> To make a *Third* she joynd the former two.[1]

The canon of Pope's formal verse satires reflects a comparable attitude toward distinguished ancestors. So far as I can tell, the anxiety of influence is normally not packed in the psychic baggage of the British man of letters during the

1 *The Spectator*, ed. Donald F. Bond (Oxford: Clarendon Press, 1965), 3: 170; *The Works of John Dryden*, vol. 3, *Poems 1685-1692*, ed. Earl Miner and Vinton A. Dearing (Berkeley and Los Angeles: Univ. of California Press, 1969), 208. See also Spenser's remarks on his own use of earlier epics in the beginning of his "Letter of the Authors," prefaced to *The Faerie Queene* (1590). The British balanced constitution also was a unifying force—of the monarchy, oligarchy, and democracy.

PREFACE

Restoration and the eighteenth century—or in that of Horace, Persius, Juvenal, or Boileau. Rather, they approach their extensive patrimonies the way the wise and faithful servants do in the Parable of the Talents: they accept the challenge to invest and use their collective wisdom in productive ways and gain rewards accordingly.

Part of this challenge implies an active contest with successful authors in one's past. Longinus is working within a tradition already enhanced by Pliny the Elder and Quintilian when he describes Plato's attitude toward Homer in this way, though Virgil's adaptation of Homer could have served as well. Plato's style would not have been so brilliantly metaphoric "had he not been ambitious of entering the Lists, like a youthful Champion, and ardently contending for the prize with Homer. . . . The Attack was perhaps too rash, the Opposition perhaps had too much the Air of Enmity, but yet could not fail of some Advantage; for as *Hesiod* says, *Such brave Contention works the Good of Men.*" This well-known section from *On the Sublime*, xiii. 4, reflects and is congenial with a cast of mind prevalent from the later seventeenth to the mid-eighteenth century, and still familiar through much of the later eighteenth century. In 1794 T. J. Mathias argues that the writer aware of his past is engaged in "an honourable contest for the mastery" with his earlier mentors. Win or lose, as the *Encyclopédie* already had put it in 1765 regarding Boileau's method of satiric composition, the modern can only benefit: "il a joûté contre [Horace] parce que dans ce genre de combat on peut être vaincu sans honte."[2]

---

[2] Longinus adds that "even a Defeat, in such a competition, is attended with Honour." See *Dionysius Longinus on the Sublime*, trans. William Smith, 2nd ed. (1742), pp. 38-39; Mathias, *Pursuits of Literature*, 6th ed. (1798), p. xxviii; *Encyclopédie* (Neufchâtel, 1765), 8: 568. The article, on "Imitation," cites several classical and modern sources for imitation as contest, and argues that Virgil's *Aeneis* is the product of such a combat with Homer. K. K. Ruthven offers interesting remarks on "Imitation and Originality" in *Critical Assumptions* (Cambridge: Cambridge Univ. Press, 1979), pp. 102-34.

x

The concept of literary transmission as amiable combat contradicts the naive view that imitation of an earlier author denotes wholesale acceptance of his values. William King already is commonplace when, in 1709, he says that "An Imitator and his Author stand much upon the same Terms as *Ben* does with his Father in the Comedy [Congreve's *Love for Love*]. '*What th'of he be my Father, I an't bound Prentice to'en!*'" Pope, Swift, Johnson and other major imitators would not have been bound to any author, much less, in the former two cases at any rate, to one whose political and much moral behavior they found repugnant. Edward Young's *Conjectures on Original Composition* (1759) distinguishes between imitation of nature, which deserves the highest praise, and imitation of authors, which deserves less praise (p. 9). The modern must imitate Homer's method, not his work (p. 21), and do so without "Too great Awe" (p. 25) that would hinder the efforts to find one's own voice. Though Young wrongly regards Pope as an imitator of authors, he nonetheless captures an essential aspect of Pope's theory: "Imitation is inferiority confessed; Emulation is superiority contested, or denied; Imitation is servile, Emulation generous; That fetters, this fires" (pp. 65-66). Samuel Johnson read all this shortly after its appearance and perhaps then, but certainly on 30 September 1773, said that "he was surprized to find Young receive as novelties, what he thought very common maxims."[3] There thus was disagreement regarding which authors were emulators; there was not disagreement regarding the need for emulation. Boileau, Pope, and others apparently knew that one way to destroy the past as a guide to the present is inordinately to revere it and to render oneself poetically impotent because unable to walk in such holy paths. Their more productive way was to incorporate and build upon the

[3] King, *The Art of Love: In Imitation of Ovid De Arte Amandi*, p. xxxix; Johnson, in *Boswell's Life of Johnson, together with Boswell's Journal of a Tour to the Hebrides*, ed. George Birbeck Hill, rev. L. F. Powell (Oxford: Clarendon Press, 1934-50): the *Journal*, 5 (1950): 269 and 269n.

best in the authors of a usable heritage, and even "to differ from all of them, when I have thought that the reason of the thing was on my side."

Such incorporation and differing are the bases for the arguments within. The progress of formal verse satire from, roughly, Horace to Pope is not one of rediscovery of the Ur-satirist Horace, whom Pope imitates and with whom he is supposed to have spiritual, moral, and literary kinship. It is a progress of benevolent cannibalism, or in T. S. Eliot's metaphor, of tradition being absorbed, altered and transmitted by a receptive individual talent. The Abbé le Monnier made a similar and already conventional point when commenting on Persius in 1771: "Perse avoit lu son Horace lorsqu'il a fait ce vers. . . . Juvénal avoit lu ses deux devanciers. . . . Boileau est venu ensuite, qui a lu ces trois satiriques, & s'est approprié leurs pensées."[4] And, an English commentator might have added, Pope followed thereafter, read all four satirists, and profited accordingly. By the time Pope began his career as a formal verse satirist, he thus had a pool of poems and conventions supplied not only by the recently resurrected Horace, nor even by the nationally appropriate Juvenal, but also by Persius, whose continuing popularity peaked during the 1730s. Pope was able to select what was useful for his purposes and to criticize what he thought pernicious in the Roman satirists and in Boileau, their most impressive scion and a prior model of the synthesizing satirist—one whose Horatian bias ultimately was uncongenial for Pope's temperament and political needs. Pope is most indebted to Horace in the *Epistles to Several Persons* (1731-35), and mingles his satiric modes far more, and with symbolic proportions, in the *Epistle to Dr. Arbuthnot* (1735) and imitations of Horace and Donne (1733-38). The growing Juvenalian emphases in "Donne" and other poems are further heightened in his overwhelmingly

[4] Eliot's "Tradition and the Individual Talent" (1919) appears in his *Selected Essays* (New York: Harcourt, Brace & Co., 1950), pp. 3-11; le Monnier, *Satires de Perse* (Paris), p. 153, regarding *Satires* v. 10-11.

Juvenalian *Epilogue to the Satires* (1738). James Ackerman observes that Palladio learned to "find himself by knowing others";[5] that eloquent remark applies as well to Pope, who culminates the several satiric traditions before him and probably is their last and best resting place.

I can only speculate on why formal verse satire declined later in the eighteenth century, but one reason, I shall suggest, is that the traditions Pope unifies begin to split again. Though Pope was not alone in mingling satiric conventions, his contemporaries and successors were unable, or perhaps unwilling, to follow his example with any distinction. Much formal satire after Pope suggests a version of the dissociation of sensibility, a splintering of satire into either Horatian or Juvenalian roads—or more precisely into those presumed but badly mapped and paved roads. Before going further, however, I should make clear how I shall be using those amorphous terms "Horatian" and "Juvenalian."

The Horatian satirist is likely to be muted in tone and deal with matters of private, biographical, moral, or ethical concern, even when he is writing to a governor of the nation—nil admirari, adultery, friendship, one's good father, one's role in a literary tradition. He lives in a world that includes discourse with the great but is not dominated by them, a world in which those great men are seen to control a difficult and dangerous empire and to deserve our respect. His norms are not only his family's and his own best selves, but the nation's watchful guardians, whom we often have brought before us so that we may perceive and share their wisdom. Horatian satire affirms stability and the triumph of cogent but not haranguing argument between rational men; the epistle and dialogue thus are among its characteristics, for such satire, though sometimes biting, assumes effective communication between and within different levels of society. It shows the reasonable man accommodating himself, but not normally lowering himself, to a fallible

5 The Architect and Society, *Palladio*, 2nd ed. (Harmondsworth, England: Penguin Books, 1976), p. 31.

and treacherous world, with dignity and pride. His weapons include ridicule, irony, grace, poise, normative friendship, self-knowledge, and severity where required; these, together with the exalted allies who shield him, are capable of protecting and affirming the human spirit. By and large, things work or are manageable in Horatian satire and its world of comedy that reflects apparent Augustan solidity after years of confusion.

The Juvenalian approach, if we ignore, as most eighteenth-century commentators did, the elegiac beauty of a poem like the twelfth satire, tends to produce an elevated, tragic, confronting rather than conciliating sort of poem. Its ironies are likely to be dark rather than witty; its tones will protest decay rather than affirm growth; its norms will be long-gone republican heroes or ages, rural non-Roman cultures, or the indignant satirist himself, rather than the mandarins of the imperial city which, by then, often were emblems of corruption. There will be a catalogue of unscrupulous and ambitious foreigners, slaves, or lowborn "Romans" who mingle with and may be indistinguishable from the patricians who once were patterns of virtue. There also will be bad poets, legacy hunters, brutal soldiers, tyrannical emperors, fawning favorites, fickle plebians, corrupt magistrates, unfaithful women, scarcely recognizable men, and a host of other violators of decency, law, and tradition in a collapsing world, for which symbolic protest, anger, and harsh reproach—even of the ruling family—are the responses an honest man must make. As the imitator of Juvenal's thirteenth satire puts it in 1745, his muse will use the "fellest Scorpion's Sting; / Nor spare the Wicked, tho' she wounds a King."[6] Not to be an indignant satirist in such a

---

[6] *The Thirteenth Satyre of Juvenal Imitated*, p. 17. The same poem offers a précis of the typical world of Juvenalian satire:

> Rapes, Murders, Robb'ries happen ev'ry Hour:
> Laws crush the Poor; the Rich elude their Pow'r:
> The Courts are crouded, and the Pleaders hoarse;
> Yet Vice prevails, for who can stop her Course?

(P. 16)

world is worthy of being satirized in its own right. The satirist is likely to be alone, or with a vaguely defined friend of comparable downtrodden stature, rather than part of a family unit, which may exist for others, but not for his isolated and accusatory self engaged in a fierce monologue. Later I shall elaborate upon these apparently warring modes and include the lesser but important contribution of Persius as well, for in several respects he was the satirist Pope and other poets in the 1730s looked to for transitional devices—for, say, Horatian dialogue used in a Juvenalian political world.

Indeed, though other commentators have begun to see and discuss the non-Horatian aspects of Pope's satires,[7] too often their only other candidate for significant influence is Juvenal, and Persius is ignored. Too often, as well, Juvenalian traits are seen as incidental embroidery upon the Horatian fabric, rather than, in some cases, the essential fabric itself, or a thread that cannot be separated from its elements without destroying the cloth. Moreover, too few modern readers of Pope's satires seem to be aware that his contemporaries often regarded their national character as Juvenalian, and Pope as radically un-Horatian while others

---

[7] For some of these, see Howard Erskine-Hill, ed., *Pope: Horatian Satires and Epistles* (Oxford: Oxford Univ. Press, 1964), pp. 12-16 (Erskine-Hill also observes that "It is a commonly held view that Pope's formal satire . . . is . . . conceived according to the Horatian model, and that Samuel Johnson not Pope is the English Juvenal" [p. 12]); Peter Dixon, *The World of Pope's Satires: An Introduction to the Epistles and Imitations of Horace* (Methuen & Co., 1968), pp. 101-3, 202; Rachel Trickett, *The Honest Muse: A Study in Augustan Verse* (Oxford: Clarendon Press, 1967), pp. 98-99; Roger Lonsdale, "Alexander Pope," in History of Literature in the English Language, vol. 4, *Dryden to Johnson*, ed. Roger Lonsdale (Sphere Books, 1971), p. 130. Michael Coffey, however, offers this perceptive, if unamplified, remark: "Pope used not merely the satires of Horace but the full range of the ancient tradition to write the maturest political, social and literary satire in an age in which men of education could appreciate the quality of great artistry." See his *Roman Satire* (Methuen & Co., 1976), p. 97.

saw him as the improving receptacle of previous satiric forms, which he then sent out with his own stamp.

In the following pages, then, I shall salvage something of eighteenth-century French and British views of formal verse satire and satirists, something of the classical Roman and Boileau's French practice of formal verse satire, British and French views of Pope and, most fully, Pope's complex uses of his inheritance in his satires of the 1730s. I shall conclude with related hypotheses regarding Pope's successors and their disjointed, monotonous ways.

In discussing Horatian, Persian, and Juvenalian satire, I hope to reclaim a historical but not necessarily actual view of those poets. Niall Rudd has severely scolded Dryden for his characterizations of Horace and Juvenal in the "Discourse" on satire (1693). So far as those poets are concerned, he concludes, "Dryden's essay is wrong or misleading on almost every major point."[8] No doubt that censure is deserved, and no doubt the many writers quoted within who anticipate or repeat Dryden's errors deserve censure as well; but their fallibility of perception is less important than the fact of their perception and the patterns those perceptions have formed. Horace may not have been a servile court flunky, Juvenal not a brave enemy of corruption, and Persius not a covert satirist of Nero. Generations of readers, however, behaved as if these portraits were accurate and therefore appropriate for certain literary and political purposes. In such a case the historian is obliged not to praise or bury Dryden but to record him and to draw relevant implications for the development of British formal verse satire in the Restoration and the eighteenth century— namely, for that satire commonly based on Roman models, normally spoken on behalf of the satirist or, generally, by him in his own voice or in dialogue with an adversarius, and loosely unified by means of attack upon a single vice or related vices or follies, and praise of the opposite virtue.

[8] *The Satires of Horace: A Study* (Cambridge: Cambridge Univ. Press, 1966), p. 273.

As we shall see, however, some later eighteenth-century satirists fall under this rubric while not wholly accepting its criteria. I must ask for the modern reader's unwilling suspension of disbelief regarding perhaps misrepresented classical satirists—as also for Pope's excesses regarding Sir Robert Walpole and the court of George II. Considering the fruits of Pope's labors, however, those excesses deserve the forbearance of anyone not claiming descent from the great man or his lesser minions.

THE PLEASURE of thanking institutions and individuals deservedly comes at the beginning of a book. The Graduate School of the University of Wisconsin supplied research assistance and funds to complete a semester's leave made possible by the Newberry Library–British Academy Fellowship during the winter and spring of 1978. The libraries of the University of Wisconsin, the University of Chicago, Princeton University, and Yale University, as well as the Newberry Library and the Henry E. Huntington Library were my chief American sources. I am especially grateful to the Huntington Library for a fellowship during the summer of 1977. The British Library, the Bodleian Library, and University Library, Cambridge, were, as always, never less than helpful and generally invaluable, not merely for their collections, but for the friends in those places with whom I was able to confer and, often, argue. The Huntington Library and the Bodleian Library have generously granted permission to quote from their manuscript sources. Maynard Mack both volunteered to read the chapter on *Arbuthnot* and expedited my examination of the Pope manuscripts at the Pierpont Morgan Library. Martin Battestin generously transmitted discoveries gleaned by the gods of Serendipity and Fielding. Edna Steeves and William Kupersmith granted permission to reprint small portions of essays that appeared in their journals: these are, respectively, "Such as Sir Robert Would Approve?: Answers to Pope's Answer from Horace," *Modern Language Studies*, 19 (1979):

5-14; and "The Conventions of Classical Satire and the Practice of Pope," *Philological Quarterly*, 59 (1981): 313-33. The separate sections on Persius will appear as a unified essay titled "Persius, the Opposition to Walpole, and Pope," in *Greene and Centennial Studies: Essays Presented to Donald Greene in the Hundredth Year of the University of Southern California*, ed. Robert R. Allen and Paul J. Korshin (which, at this writing, is not yet published). Thanks are due to Marian Rothstein for help in translating the nuances of French texts, and to Paula Backsheider for arranging to have the University of Rochester's rare copy of the Abbé Yart's *Idée de la poësie Angloise* sent to the University of Wisconsin's Rare Book Room for my use. My manuscript was typed and retyped by several patient secretaries at the English Department of the University of Wisconsin—especially Jane Renneberg Briggs and Cindy Townsend. Joanna Hitchcock and Robert Brown of Princeton University Press were characteristically helpful in many ways, as was Claude Topf Wells in Madison, Wisconsin, who helped with the final stages of copyediting the manuscript. I should, finally, offer blanket thanks to the compilers of two reference books I have consulted often and cited little: J. V. Guerinot, *Pamphlet Attacks on Alexander Pope*, and David Foxon, *English Verse 1701-1750*, a labor for which the word "gratitude" is inadequate.

My pleasantest acknowledgment is to my colleague Eric Rothstein, who generously tolerated a rough draft and offered numerous suggestions for planing, polishing, rearranging, and saving me from myself. After such varied kinds of aid, it should be obvious that all errors, signs of impatience, and failures of intelligence are my own responsibility, and should be so treated, with the proviso that concludes the Preface to Johnson's *Dictionary*: "when it shall be found that much is omitted, let it not be forgotten that much likewise is performed."[9] Or so I hope, if only on Alexander Pope's behalf.

[9] *A Dictionary of the English Language* (1755), sig. C2ʳ.

Editorial Notes

THIS BOOK is designed as a companion volume to my *Augustus Caesar in "Augustan" England* (1978), draws upon some of its findings, and extends some of its implications. I followed its method, as well, of grouping several adjacent references from one paragraph into a single footnote where, in my judgment, I could do so without ambiguity. I thereby hope to ease the process of reading the text. Much supporting and complementary evidence from little-known sources finds its way into these notes, and the reader with limited time and courage may wish to drink sparingly of such nectar. I have omitted the place of publication whenever it is London, and I have sometimes reversed the order of italics and Roman type when reproduction of the earlier typography would have been obfuscating. I have normally translated Latin in the text and offered the original in an accompanying note, except where the translation is from a Restoration or eighteenth-century source. Where contemporary translations of French sources were not available, I have offered my own, either in the text or, with longer passages, in the "Translations of French Passages" at the end of the book. I thus hope to ease the bobbing of heads that more footnotes would require, and to encourage the reader to work with the French where possible.

The source for modern quotations from Pope is the Twickenham Edition, General Editor, John Butt (Methuen & Co.; Yale Univ. Press): vol. 3, i, *An Essay on Man*, ed. Maynard Mack (1950); vol. 3, ii, *Epistles to Several Persons*, ed. F. W. Bateson, 2nd ed. (1961); vol. 4, *Imitations of Horace, With An Epistle to Dr. Arbuthnot, and The Epilogue to the Satires*, 2nd ed., corrected (1961); vol. 5, *The Dunciad*, ed. James Sutherland, 3rd ed., revised (1963); vol. 6, *Minor Poems*, ed. Norman Ault and John Butt (1954).

ALEXANDER POPE AND THE TRADITIONS
OF FORMAL VERSE SATIRE

CHAPTER 1

Horace and Juvenal in the Seventeenth and Eighteenth Centuries

Behold for POPE [the British Genius] tunes the Laurel Crown,
And centers ev'ry Poet's Pow'r in *one*:
Each *Roman's* Force adorns his various Page;
Gay Smiles, collected Strength, and manly Rage.
Despairing Guilt and Dulness loath the Sight,
As Spectors vanish at approaching Light.

S O JOHN BROWN WRITES in the revised version of his *Essay on Satire, Occasion'd by the Death of Mr. Pope* (2nd ed., 1746, p. 26). Such recognition of Pope's eclectic muse was more familiar during the eighteenth than the twentieth century, for his readers then both knew more of their contemporaries' reactions to Pope as man and poet, and of the several Roman, as well as French and English, satirists Pope gratefully used and surpassed. "Ev'ry Poet's Pow'r in *one*" denotes pluralist rather than monist satiric traditions and suggests the complexity of Pope's achievement as a formal verse satirist.

Pope's modern students have achieved handsome results in reclaiming his varied contexts; but they generally accept two related and, I believe, misleading assumptions regarding Pope and the eighteenth century. The first is that his career is "progressively an *Imitatio Horatii*," and the second is that "Horatianism and Augustanism are definitive of the age." With guiding notions like these Pope of course yields to certain "Augustan" preconceptions, and his "central achievement as a satirist" becomes "his perfection of that plain-style Horatian voice." Thus imperfect by definition, Domitian's Juvenal seems to be only an occasional guide to occasional outbursts in Pope, and a strain upon his Horatian bias rather than a deliberate modification of it.

3

Though Juvenal is important as a model in the satirically undistinguished second half of the century, for the most part he is an unnaturalized citizen who never learns the native accents. Nero's Persius seems scarcely to have been known to the English Augustans and can be thrown out of the nest as a useless addition.[1]

Collectively, this is a venerable hypothesis, but it should yield to the more venerable hypothesis of Pope as a synthesizing satirist. As I hope to show, when Pope looked at his Roman satiric ancestors, he saw that Lucilius, Persius, and Juvenal offered him much that Horace did not, and that much of what Horace offered could be used in negative as well as positive ways; when he looked at the ablest formal verse satirist of his immediate background, he saw that Boileau's success was in part based on his ability to combine the strengths of the classical Romans, but that his preponderant Horatianism made him noisome to British taste; and when he looked at that taste as it expressed itself for 130

---

[1] For the "*Imitatio Horatii*," see Reuben Arthur Brower, *Alexander Pope: The Poetry of Allusion* (Oxford: Clarendon Press, 1963), p. 165; "definitive of the age" is in W. B. Carnochan, *Lemuel Gulliver's Mirror for Man* (Berkeley and Los Angeles: Univ. of California Press, 1968), p. 19. "Horatian voice" is in Raman Selden, *English Verse Satire 1590-1765* (George Allen & Unwin, 1978), p. 33. Such rose-colored Horatianism long has thrived, and continues to thrive. See, for example, among other possible citations, many from distinguished critics, Peter Dixon, *The World of Pope's Satires: An Introduction to the Epistles and Imitations* (Methuen & Co., 1968), p. 30, and Howard Erskine Hill, "Augustans on Augustanism: England, 1655-1759," *Renaissance and Modern Studies*, 11 (1967): 74. According to the former, "The first two decades of the eighteenth century had seen Horace established as the type of the satirist," and to the latter, "Imitation [by Pope and others] . . . shows a conscious and thoughtful act of identification by the modern poet with a poet of Augustan Rome." More recently, Harold Weber argues that "Pope does not abandon Horace and, in spite of the tensions that wear his comic pose, he remains true, after his fashion, to the Horatian ideals he so celebrated." "The Comic and Tragic Satirist in Pope's Imitations of Horace," *Papers on Language and Literature*, 16 (1980): 80. For the characteristic attitude toward Persius, see Selden, *English Verse Satire*, p. 11, and see chapter 2, n. 10, below.

4

years or so prior to his own satiric prime, he saw that though Horace recently had increased in popularity, Juvenal came closer to the national character, and that the often read and imitated Persius provided devices and tones of special utility. Before dealing with matters of practice, then, it is necessary both to clear the ground and to make clear that Horace was only one of several options for the eighteenth century; that so far from being definitive of Pope's age, or any other part of the eighteenth century, he often was regarded as smiling gaily when he should have been raging manfully; and that however brilliant and artful he certainly was, he was not the inevitable choice for an opposition satirist of the 1730s, for whom Juvenal and Persius would have supplied more appropriate ground, on which not merely to stand but to fall.

I: Renaissance and Restoration Satire

Most writers and readers during the Renaissance regarded satire as brutal, punitive, biting, and the product of a perceived Persian (rough, obscure) and Juvenalian (severe, exalted) inheritance that lashed, whipped, or burned out man's vices. The satirist's function is medicinal and purgative; he must bite or he can be no satirist. Such satire includes obscurity, ruggedness of verse, violence of tone, and shrillness of pitch in portraying a world overrun by the hordes of stupid, vicious, powerful enemies of God, the state, reason, virtue, and good sense. In 1509 Alexander Barclay praises Lucilius, Horace, and Persius, but calls Juvenal the "prynce" for his sharp and reviling attacks upon "all such as ar unmeke, Prowde, Couetous, Lecherous, Wanton," and comparably sinful offenders in a long catalogue. Thomas Drant's 1566 translation of Horace's satires tells us that "*Horace* was excellent good in his time, a much zelous controller of sinne, but chiefly one that with sharpe satyres and cutting quippes could wel displaie and disease a glosser." Though Horace sometimes laughs at sin, he normally "assaileth fearcely, and ratleth up bitterly" the vices of the age. Drant's arguments to the satires are consistent with this image of blaming, reprehending satire, and consistent with Richard Stanyhurst's attack, in 1582, on the one class of satirists—Ennius, Horace, Persius, and Juvenal —all of whom are "harshe and rough . . . taunting Darcklye certeyn men of state."[2]

Horace was made, or remade, to fit this pattern in part because of the uncertainty regarding the derivation of the word satire and hence the genre's proper tones. There were several candidates for the satiric paterfamilias, and each pointed toward a form that bravely attacked the enemies of virtue. A translation of "Priscus Grammaticus de Satyra," which appears both in Drant's 1566 and 1567 volumes, outlines several candidates. Satire, which "is a tarte, and carping kind of verse," comes from Arabic, where it "doth signifye a glave"—a broadsword or falchion; or it comes from Satyrus, the rude sylvan god, who "With taunting gyrds, & glikes & gibes must bere the lewde" and "Strayne curtesy"; or from "waspyshe Saturne," who is wrathful toward the vicious, whom he cuts down, but is "courteous and friendly to the good." Drant then offers capsule descriptions of the practitioners of the form:

> Lucill (I wene) was parent of this nipping ryme:
> Next huddling Horace brave in Satyr's grace.
> Thy praysed Pamphlet (Persie) well detected ayme,
> Sir Iuvenall deserves the latter place.
> The Satyrist loves Truthe, none more than he,
> In utter foe to fraude in ech degree.[3]

[2] Barclay, trans. of Sebastian Brant, *The Ship of Fools* (Edinburgh and London, 1874), pp. 7-8; Drant, *A Medicinable Morall, that is, the two Bookes of Horace his Satyres, Englished*, sigs. aii^v, aiii^r; Stanyhurst, *The First Four Bookes of Virgil his Aeneis*, in *Richard Stanyhurst's Aeneis*, ed. Dirk van der Haar (Amsterdam, 1933), p. 53.

[3] *A Medicinable Morall*, sig. H8^v. The text is reproduced and discussed in Mary Claire Randolph, "Thomas Drant's Definition of Satire, 1566" *Notes and Queries*, 180 (1941): 416-18, John Peter, *Complaint*

Horace is accommodated not to insinuating but to invective satire which, whatever its derivation, must be pinching, waspish, nipping, and taunting. In such a world Juvenal, the only one of his group to be knighted, "deserves the latter place."

Milton, who thought that toothless satire was a contradiction in terms, also offers a reason for the necessarily noble tones of satire. Like Drant, he bases his argument on genealogy, one perhaps supplied by the theories of Donatus and Thomas Lodge: "a Satyr is as it were born out of a tragedy, so ought to resemble his parentage, to strike high, and adventure dangerously at the most eminent vices among the greatest persons." In such a milieu it is no surprise that Horace often is redefined, indeed with Juvenal's help. As

and Satire in Early English Literature (Oxford: Clarendon Press, 1956), pp. 301-2, and The Works of John Dryden, vol. 4, Poems 1693-1696, ed. A. B. Chambers, William Frost, and Vinton A. Dearing (Berkeley and Los Angeles: Univ. of California Press, 1974), pp. 519-20. John Peter well sums up the substantial influence of Persius and Juvenal and the minimal influence of Horace in the Renaissance, and observes that obscurity and acerbity dominate over "humour." Complaint and Satire, p. 117. Some of the presumed genealogy of satire and its consequences for the form are discussed in Raymond M. Alden, The Rise of Formal Satire in England Under Classical Influence, Publications of the University of Pennsylvania. Series in Philology, Literature, and Archaeology, vol. 7, n. 2 (Philadelphia: Univ. of Pennsylvania Press, 1899), pp. 37-39; Oscar James Campbell, Comicall Satyre and Shakespeare's Troilus and Cressida (San Marino, Calif.: Huntington Library Press, 1938), pp. 24-36; A. Davenport, "The Quarrel of the Satirists," Modern Language Review, 37 (1942): 123-30; Alvin B. Kernan, The Cankered Muse (New Haven: Yale Univ. Press, 1959), pp. 54-61; Robert C. Elliott, The Power of Satire: Magic, Ritual, Art (Princeton: Princeton Univ. Press, 1960), pp. 100-106; C. A. Van Rooy, Studies in Classical Satire and Related Literary Theory (Leyden: E. J. Brill, 1965); and Dryden, Poems, 1693-1696, pp. 514-22, which also supplies a few other bibliographic items, especially on p. 518, n. 21. Many of these studies, like my own, gratefully acknowledge the pioneering work of Mary Claire Randolph, including her unpublished doctoral dissertation at the University of North Carolina in 1939, "The Neo-Classic Theory of Formal Verse Satire in England, 1700-1750."

Dryden, born in 1631, translates the quite different line 51 of Juvenal's first satire, "Such Villanies rous'd *Horace* into Wrath; / And 'tis . . . Noble to pursue his Path." When Horace is not redefined, his seventeenth-century shade generally takes second place to the dominant satirist. Henry Peacham, in words later quoted in Samuel Johnson's *Dictionary* (1755), thus tells readers of his *Compleat Gentleman* (1622) that *"Juvenal*, of Satyrists is the best," and that "In his Satyres [Horace] is quick, round and pleasant; and as nothing so bitter, so not so satyrical as *Juvenal*." Horace's wrathful nobility was apparent to Boileau in 1662 and was magnified in 1696, when an unknown author imitated his seventh satire and suggested that Horace was not the genteel courtier but the Lucilian lasher. Both those satirists were "arm'd with equall spight" in their battles to unmask lurking vice, revenge virtue's cause, and discountenance sinners.[4]

Several Renaissance Latin opinions regarding satiric authors suggest that the weight of European learning was then on Juvenal's side as well. Though Horace was much admired for his lyrics, correctness, and ethics, as Dryden noted, relatively few worthies were listed as his sponsors in satire— chief among them the German Acta Eruditorum of June 1684, Heinsius, and Vossius. On Juvenal's side we see "Quintilian," Porphyrio, Lipsius, Julius and Joseph Scaliger, Farnaby, and Rigaltius, whereas Casaubon thinks that Persius, Horace, and Juvenal are approximate equals. Sir Thomas Pope Blount's useful compilation *De Re poetica* (1694) in-

---

[4] For Milton, see "Apology for Smectymnuus, in *Complete Prose Works of John Milton*, gen. ed., Don M. Wolfe (New Haven: Yale Univ. Press, 1953-73), 1: 916. This is an attack upon Bishop Hall and an affirmation of the exalted "tragic" nature of satire, which must aim high. The passage was known in the eighteenth century and recorded in Thomas Warton's *History of English Poetry* (1774-81), 3: 52; Dryden, *Poems, 1693-1696*, p. 97, lines 78-79; Peacham, *Compleat Gentleman*, 3rd ed. (1661), p. 89. Johnson quotes this for his fourth definition of the adjective "round," but with a significant difference: Horace is "nothing so bitter, so not so good as Juvenal."

cludes many of these remarks; but several had been long collected in the translations of Juvenal by Sir Robert Stapylton (1647) and Barten Holyday (1673, posthumously) written, though not published, about the same time. Stapylton urges the high praise due Juvenal "for instructing us in point of *Manners*" and virtue, for attacking vice, and for being "incomparably the best *Satyrist*," as "the *learned* know." This noble poet uses "inimitable *sweetness* of language and *Majesty* of *Sentences*" to show the loveliness of virtue and the deformity of vice. Stapylton marshalls Quintilian, the Scaligers, and Lipsius against Horace and evokes Plato who, with either ghostly or anachronistic judgment, joins Stapylton in praising Juvenal as a philosopher. Holyday's comparably respected Preface shows much of the same affection for authority, many of the same remarks and conclusions, as well as several of the issues already joined and, we shall see, to be kept alive through subsequent generations of savants, demi-savants, and common readers. He has no doubt, with Scaliger, that Juvenal's ability and morally perverse times allow him to fulfill the potential of the satiric form, that the smiling, jeering Horace is but "some poor Theme-maker" in comparison to Juvenal's "Ardor, his Loftiness, his Liberty," and ability to reform rather than sneer: "*Horace* and *Juvenal*, may seem to differ as the Jester and the Orator, the Face of an Ape and of a Man, or as the Fiddle and the Thunder."[5]

The preference for Juvenal and his mode of satire neither died nor radically diminished after 1660. This may be seen

[5] Dryden observes that Heinsius and Dacier are Horace's chief defenders, but that "*Scaliger* the Father, *Rigaltius*, and many others, debase *Horace*, that they may set up *Juvenal*." See the "Discourse concerning . . . Satire" (1693), in *Poems 1693-1696*, p. 50. For Blount, see *De Re poetica*, pp. 40-45, "Concerning Satyr," and the entries under Horace (pp. 99-104), and Juvenal (pp. 113-18), as well as Lucilius (pp. 124-27), and Persius (pp. 154-60); Stapylton, *Juvenal's Sixteen Satyrs, or, A Survey of Manners and Actions of Mankind*, sigs. A4ʳ, A5ʳ⁻ᵛ; Holyday, *Decimus Junius Juvenalis, and Aulus Persius Flaccus Translated and Illustrated* (Oxford), sig. a2ʳ.

in the voluminous poems on affairs of state in general, and in the works of Robert Gould and John Oldham in particular, each of whom embodies and continues the earlier tradition transmitted through Marston, Hall, and, among others, Thomas Randolph. His *Muse's Looking Glass* (Oxford, 1638), for example, characterizes "Satyre" as using a whip of steel to lash the brand of shame "Even in the brazen forehead of proud sinne"; hence even "greatest tyrants / Have quak'd below my powerful whip" (p. 12). Gould is especially useful as a reservoir and conduit of satiric indignation, since he did not read Latin, and his notions regarding satire therefore came from his knowledge of English poems and translations.[6] Almost any of his several satires shows his use of presumed Juvenalian devices. Here is part of his "Prologue to the following Satyrs," much of which reads like a Restoration version of Pope's *Epilogue to the Satires* (1738).

> To what Prodigious Height of Vice w'are grown,
> Both in the *Court*, the *Country*, *Camp*, and *Town*,
> That 'tis of late believ'd, and fix'd a Rule,
> Who ever is not Vitious is a Fool;
> Hiss'd at by Old and Young, despis'd, opprest,
> If he be not a Villain, like the rest:
> Vertue and Truth are lost—search for *Good Men*,
> Among *Ten Thousand* you'll scarce meet with *Ten*;
> But Fools and Knaves you ev'ry where may find,
> Almost as universal as Mankind.
>
> (2: sig. A4^r)
>
> What *Saty'rist* then can Honestly sit still,
> And, unconcern'd, see such a Tide of Ill,

---

6 Gould, *The Works of Mr. Robert Gould* (1709), 1: sig. A3^v for Gould's ignorance of Latin texts except "in their several Translations." Subsequent citations from this work are given in the text. Renaissance Juvenalianism is easily illustrated in numerous satires, among them the little known (for our purposes) John Bidle, *Virgil's Bucolicks Englished. Whereunto is added the Translation of the two first Satyrs of Juvenal* (1634).

With an Impetuous Force o'erflow the Age,
And strive not to restrain it with his Rage?

(2: sig. A4^v)

Unbrib'd, Impartial, Pointed, and Severe:
That Way my Nature leans, compos'd of Gall;
I must write sharply, or not write at all.

(2: sig. A5^r)

Oldham's death in 1683 evokes several elegiac poems, including those of Thomas D'Urfey and Thomas Andrews, who celebrate his Juvenalian lashing and rage, and Thomas Wood who admires his "boundless Keenest Satyr." Like others, Gould admires Oldham's "Native Sweetness" but insists on the strength of his "Native Sting" and reforming satire that "spar'd no Grievances, or Crimes." Gould also affirms Oldham's and his own satiric style and suggests that a fashionable new mode already is on the horizon.

How vain are those that wou'd obscure thy Fame
By giving out thy Verse was rough and lame?
They wou'd have *Satyr* their Compassion move,
And wit so pliant, nicely soft and smooth,
As if the *Muse* were in a Flux of Love.
But who of *Beaus*, and *Knaves* and Fools wou'd Sing
Must Force, and Fire, and Indignation bring;
For 'tis no *Satyr* if it has no *Sting*.
In short, who in that Field wou'd famous be,
Must think and write like *Juvenal* and *Thee*.[7]

Subtlety and insinuation are reared, but do not mature, in late Restoration England. Hence, Thomas Shadwell tells

[7] For several of these elegies, see the prefatory poems in *The Works of Mr. John Oldham, Together with his Remains*, 7th ed. (1710). Gould's "To the Memory of Mr. John Oldham," sig. Aai^v in Oldham's *Works*, is quoted from Gould's own *Works*, 1: 219. H. P.'s *A Satyr Against Common-Wealths* (1684) is another example of insistence upon "uneasie roughness" in satire, since it is "disagreeable to see a Satyr Cloath'd in soft and effeminate Language" (sig. B1^v).

readers of his imitation of Juvenal's tenth satire (1687), smoothness is not required in his genre, "which ought to have a *severe* kind of *roughness* as most fit for *reprehension*, and not that gentle *smoothness* which is necessary to insinuation." Dryden, whose "Discourse . . . of Satyr" (1693) sometimes is thought a touchstone of assent to the Horatian temper, argues that the nature of Horace's genre demands attacks and wounds, and gives Horace "the Quivers, and the Arrows, as the Badges of his Satire." We should recall that even when Dryden praises temperate satire, he likens it to "the fineness of a stroak that separates the Head from the Body, and leaves it standing in its place." The malefactor may "die sweetly," but the satirist has beheaded him nonetheless.[8]

From at least the earlier sixteenth to the later seventeenth century, most verse satire remains fierce and outraged; though certainly softening toward the end of that period, it is primarily Juvenalian in its conventions and is just beginning to be encroached upon by a partially defanged Horace who nevertheless bears arrows and is an artful executioner of the guilty. Some of the conception of satire was changing along with the received wisdom regarding its genesis. As Joseph Trapp tells his students at Oxford in 1711, the controversy over the derivation is important, since the solution "in a great Measure defines its *Nature*."[9] The resolution of that conflict was to introduce a new gentility to the English lashing mode, which was to be modified but never eradicated.

II: The Changed Derivation and the Comic Form

Though the derivation of satire was inconclusive in the sixteenth century, it generally was associated with the Greek

---

[8] Shadwell, *The Tenth Satyr of Juvenal, English and Latin*, sig. A4^r; Dryden's "Discourse," in *Poems 1693-1696*, pp. 76, 71 (die sweetly).

[9] Trapp, *Praelectiones Poeticae* (1711-19), trans. William Bowyer and William Clarke as *Lectures on Poetry Read in the School of Natural Philosophy at Oxford* (1742), p. 225.

rustic demigod satyrs who whipped or tossed scurrilous invectives at their victims. Numerous seventeenth- and eighteenth-century prints and frontispieces to editions of satires show the satyr scourging sinners—of course for their own good. The publication of Isaac Casaubon's *De Satyrica Graecorum poesi & Romanorum satira* (Paris, 1605), and the new, and probably accurate, derivation of the word were seminal: satire comes, not from the Greek satyr, but the Latin *satura*, "full," with *lanx* understood. As he and his followers, especially Dacier, understood it, the word was not a noun but an adjective; the *satura lanx* signified a full platter of meats or fruits and suggested the variety, limited only by the size of the charger, of the satiric form. Quintilian thus was correct when he said that satire was wholly Roman: it gradually lost its hardness as it moved away from the Fescennine and Saturnian insults made by peasants, became a regular afterpiece in the theater, and was transformed into a separate discourse in different kinds of verse by Ennius and then Pacuvius. Lucilius added some polish by using only one kind of verse, and more "salt" in faulty imitation of the Greek old comedy. The form, according to several commentators, reached its peak in the varied, dramatic, comedic practice of Horace. Satire is not harsh, exalted, tragic, sublime, or punitive—it evolves into a civilized, gently instructive, "low" form that relates man to man rather than separates them through severe punishment or chastisements. Both Heinsius (1612) and Vossius (1695-1701) stress the desirable nonexalted tones of satire. Heinsius, as Dryden translates him, defines satire as including punitive language, but with the essential word "familiar."

Satire is a kind of Poetry, without a Series of Action, invented for the purging of our Minds; in which Humane Vices, Ignorance, and Errors, and all things besides, which are produc'd from them, in every Man, are severely Reprehended; partly Dramatically, partly Simply, and sometimes in both kinds of speaking; but for the most part, Figuratively, and Occultly; consisting in a low fa-

13

miliar way, chiefly in a sharp and pungent manner of
Speech; but partly, also, in a Facetious and Civil way of
Jesting; by which, either Hatred, or Laughter, or Indig-
nation is mov'd.

Some years later Joseph Trapp discusses Vossius's insistence
that satire should correct vices in private with facetious
good-humored language. Vossius thus finds Horace, Lucian,
and Julian superior to Juvenal and Persius. Trapp sees that
the new derivation of the word has influenced literary judg-
ment, and that for followers of the comic muse, "chearful
bantering Humour should . . . not be forfeited for Morose-
ness"; that the style of satire should be "near allied to
Prose," and that in these and all other particulars regarding
satire, Vossius "sets *Horace* for an Example," one to which
Trapp himself "can by no means subscribe."[10]

Both Dryden and Trapp quarrel with the purist and
monist definitions of comic Horatian satire, and Trapp de-
nies the validity of Casaubon's derivation. In 1711, how-
ever, Trapp was on the defensive, for Casaubon's crabbed
Latin now had over one hundred years to be deciphered,
digested, and, by 1687, in part turned into lucid French by
André Dacier, the translator of, and commentator on, the
best known version of Horace in the seventeenth and eight-
eenth centuries, and a man of great scholarly and literary
authority in both France and England. Sections of his
Préface, Englished in works by Gildon, Dryden, and Tom
Brown, put considerable weight behind Casaubon's theory
of *satura lanx* and the consequent movement away from the
rough satyr's song.[11] His enormous number of Remarques

[10] Dryden, *Poems 1693-1696*, p. 77, the original is italicized; Trapp,
Lectures on Poetry, pp. 227n, 226.

[11] For these see Gildon's *Miscellany Poems, Upon Several Occasions
. . . With an Essay upon Satyr by the Famous M. Dacier* (1692), the
appendix to René le Bossu's *Treatise of the Epick Poem, to which are
added an Essay upon Satyr by Mons. D'Acier and a Treatise of the
Pastoral, by Mons. Fontenelle* (1695), and "An Essay on the Satire of
the Ancients" in *The Works of Mr. Thomas Brown, Serious and Comi-*

and notes affirm and reaffirm Horace's wisdom, subtlety, gentlemanly teaching of virtue, affinity with Augustus and the greatest men of that age, clever turns, happy compliments, utility to the state, and other virtues consistent with a type and shadow of the splendors of the age of Louis XIV which, unlike Augustus's, will be eternal in its glories.[12] The Remarque on *Satires*, ii. 1, is a useful example of Dacier's perception of the social and "comic" Horace at work:

> Dans le premier Livre des Satires, Horace a combatu les Vices. Dans celui-ci il refute les fausses opinions des Philosophes. Et comme cette matiere demande plus de force & plus d'érudition que la première, ce Livre est aussi plus fort & plus rempli de savoir que le premier. Mais c'est un savoir qui n'a rien de dur ni de sauvage, & qui est accompagné de tous les agrémens que les Graces mêmes peuvent donner. Dans cette première Satire il y a une plaisanterie continuelle, & qui a été connuë de fort peu de gens. (7: 16)

The "plaisanterie continuelle" so esteemed by Dacier, both reflected and magnified an already venerable French affection for Horace. That bias was justified by the criterion of generic appropriateness, for Dacier knew that the derivation and conception of satire should dictate the tone of satire—and that was familiar and comic, as befits an imitation of the old comedy. Satire

> est un Poëme d'un caractere entierement opposé à celui du Poëme Heroïque, & le stile de l'un seroit fort méchant

---

cal (1707), 4th ed. (1715), 1: 114-26. According to Benjamin Boyce, Brown probably is the translator of the essay in Gildon's *Miscellany*. See Boyce's *Tom Brown of Facetious Memory* (Cambridge, Mass.: Harvard Univ. Press, 1939), p. 38. Dacier also is the source for much of Dryden's "Discourse concerning the Original and Progress of Satire."

12 See André Dacier, *Oeuvres d'Horace en latin et en françois, avec des remarques* (1681-89), 3rd ed. (Paris, 1709), 6: sigs. ai^r-aiv^v, the "Epistre Au Roy." Subsequent citations are given in the text.

pour l'autre. Je suis même persuadé, qu'un Poëte Sati-
rique qui affecteroit la noblesse & la majesté du Poëme
Epique, meriteroit aussi peu le nom de Poëte, qu'un
Poete Heroïque en qui l'on ne trouveroit que la simpli-
cité des Satires. Et c'est en cela que Perse & que Juvénal
sont fort au dessous d'Horace. (6: 307-8; *Satires*, i. 4, 60)

In 1717 the *Journal Litéraire* joins its voice to this Gallic
chorus. Playing a slight variation on Dacier's tune, its editor
argues that Horace is "fort au dessus [superior] de Perse &
de Juvénal" (9: Table des Matiers, "Horace"). Juvenal is
"un aigre [shrill] Accusateur" (p. 26), who declaims and
raises his voice, attacks vice, and uses an offensive obscene
style that shows his own imperfections. Horace, on the con-
trary, is "un Philosophe" who uses the salt, meter, and
methods of the old comedy, and is appropriately low in his
style drawn from the relaxed and popular comic genre
(p. 263).

Père Sanadon makes a similar point in 1728, when he
publishes Horace's odes in poetic and the satires in pedes-
trian prose. Indeed, when there are disputed readings in a
textual crux, one should choose the most "comic" of the
readings, since that is closest to satiric practice: "le langage
de la comédie & de la satire est le même, j'entens de la satire
d'Horace." Juvenal, Sanadon later says, had two of the three
traits of satire—he had rhetoric and poetic flights, but he
lacked urbanity. He was not "un railleur fin & délié, qui sait
emploier à propos une critique délicate." Unfortunately,
"sa critique tient plus de l'invective que de la raillerie." His
satires differ from Horace's, and by clear implication are
inferior to them, because they lack raillery. In 1747 Saint-
Marc is no less confident that there is a harmony between
comedy and satire and that since the origin of satire has
fixed its character, its proper conventions include playful
wit, conversational speech, the turning of the serious into
the pleasant (5: 372), and abandonment of the Persian and
Juvenalian way of imitating the philosophers or the soph-

ists in their vehement invectives against vice (5: 334). This French view of satire as necessarily comic and Horatian lasts well into the middle and later years of the eighteenth century, and appears in remarks by the Abbé Charles Batteux, the Abbé Sabatier de Castres, and *L'Année littéraire*. In 1782, for example, the author of a review of Jean Dusaulx's second edition of *Les Satyres de Juvénal* rejects Dusaulx's notion that Juvenal is superior to Horace. Hyperbole and farfetched figures are the product of decadence of taste and are poor substitutes for the politeness and urbanity of Horace. In Juvenal, to his cost, "la satyre née de la Comédie ne conserva plus dans ses vers aucune trace de son ancienne origine."[13]

To be other than urbane in satire had in fact long been regarded as slightly gauche and socially unacceptable. In 1673 François Blondel scolds Scaliger and Lipsius for praising Juvenal over Horace, insists upon the former's own heaviness of wit and inability to laugh, and is delighted with the wise Horace, who "is not pleas'd as *Juvenal*, to put himself into a Passion incessantly, but contrarily *Discovers Truths by Laughing*." One year later, René Rapin lauds the gaiety of Horace's genius, as well as his wisdom and, as Rymer translates it, "*delicacy* which properly gives the relish to Satyr." Rapin goes on to characterize Horace, to account for "the way of *jest* and merriment" by which he censured, and to elevate him above Juvenal, who is too serious, choleric, eloquent, vain, and ostentatious in attacking vice, and too little "*delicate*, or . . . *natural*," either to give pleasure or conviction, or to render vice ridiculous as he should.

13 Sanadon, *Les Poésies d'Horace* (Paris), 2: 131, 2: 208-9; Saint-Marc, *Oeuvres de M. Boileau Despréaux* (Paris), 5: 333 (the two other references have been cited in the text). See remarks by Batteux in *A Course of the Belles Lettres: or, The Principles of Literature. Translated from the French of the Abbot Batteux, By Mr. Miller* (1761), 3: 143-45, and by Sabbatier de Castres in *Dictionnaire de littérature* (Paris, 1770), "Poètes Satyriques," 3: 276-78 (with liberal borrowing from the comparable entries in the *Encyclopédie*); *L'Année littéraire*, 6: 151.

In 1695 Père Tarteron makes even clearer that Juvenal was not the right sort at all, for he is "de bien mauvaise humeur; il ne sçait pas assez son monde; il n'est point aux tout aîsé à vivre ni homme d'accommodement. . . . C'est un Misantrope chagrin." For Tarteron, as for Ralph Schomberg in 1769, Scaliger's preference for Juvenal over Horace is a sign of bad taste and, the reverend father says, insufficiently high birth that apparently renders him incapable of understanding Horatian beauties.[14]

The association with France, and especially with Dacier, clearly boosted Horace's already growing reputation and helped to free him from an ill-fitting Juvenalian costume. As Charles Gildon says in 1692, since Horace now is justly esteemed, Gildon cannot "better gratify his Admirers, than to let our English World see those hidden Beauties of this great Poet, discover'd by M. *Dacier*, with no less Wit, than Judgment."[15] Dacier's work also must have enhanced the formidable example of Boileau's satires and epistles as well as several native English tendencies that I can only touch on: the attempted, if finally vulgar, increase in sophistication induced by Charles II and his court poets; the polishing of verse begun by Denham, and Waller, encouraged by Dryden, and lent charmingly vapid aristocratic elegance by John Wentworth Dillon (Roscommon) and John Sheffield (Buckingham); the inevitable tiring with one often hectic satiric mode and consequent openness to another; appreciation of the greatness of Horace's verse; the desire to have an apparently idyllic Horatian world of respect and patronage between throne, court, and poet; the Shaftesburyan insistence on the value of ridicule in testing for truth; the influ-

---

[14] Blondel, *The Comparison of Pindar and Horace*, trans. Sir Edward Sherburne (1696), p. 80; Rapin, *Reflections on Aristotle's Treatise of Poesie* (1674), trans. [Thomas Rymer], p. 138; Tarteron, *Les Satyres de Perse et de Juvénal, traduites en françois* (Paris), sigs. bi^r, b3^v; Schomberg, *A Critical Dissertation on the Characters and Writings of Pindar and Horace*, p. 71.

[15] Gildon, *Miscellany Poems upon Several Occasions* (London), sig. A7^v.

ence of the *Tatler* and the *Spectator* papers as a civilizing and softening force in taste, criticism, and style; the growing availability of Horace in several French versions and Brome's (1666), Creech's (1684), and Dunster's (1709) in English; the consequent tendency to imitate Horace; the conviction that the theories of Dacier, among others, brought to the belief that verse satire should in fact be muted in style and tone, and comic and rallying. No doubt this list can be expanded; but even in its present form it suggests a major change from the days when Horace was not as bitter and hence not as good as Juvenal.

Horace and Horatian satire thus were praised by many voices at many times in late seventeenth- and early eighteenth-century England. Such commentators often focused upon the relationship between satiric delicacy and satiric efficacy. The Duke of Buckingham, for example, believes that satire should be polished, not rough, that "Rage you must hide," for "A Satyr's Smile is sharper than his Frown," and that the Horatian combination of laughter and scorn is likely to be more successful than sharp severity. Dryden may have agreed with his lordship, for in the Preface to *Sylvae* (1685) he argues that Horace is superior to Juvenal "if to laugh and rally, is to be preferr'd to railing and declaiming." Thomas Wood probably was aware of these familiar remarks, and he acknowledges Rapin, who taught him that Juvenal was not natural enough, too scolding and ill-natured, insufficiently sporting and merry, and in need of Wood's softening to "render Vice more ridiculous." Henry Higden must also be responding to such observations in the Preface to his *Modern Essay on the Thirteenth Satyr of Juvenal* (1686), an imitation in burlesque verse. "Some Criticks cavil our Author's Humour is too stiff, morose, and over-serious in down-right lashing and chastising Crimes: Whereas a jocular and facetious Leer and Reproof, laughs Vice out of Countenance, and often works a perfect Cure and Conversion." Others have decided that Juvenal's stately gravity does not permit him to "descend from his lofty

Buskins, to Act the least part of the Comick Droll." Higden
claims to take a mid-path, abate some of Juvenal's serious-
ness, add some raillery, and preserve his dignity (sigs. b2ʳ⁻ᵛ).
St. Evremond, less inclined to compromise, rejects the harsh
satirist who defeats his own purposes by putting his reader
into an "ill humour." Do not, he later urges, "follow *Juve-
nal's* footsteps" in portraying the passions so grossly. "I hate
him more than I do" the excesses of Messalina. Horace, in
contrast, "is a perfect Original of Satyrs, Epistles and Fa-
miliar Discourses."[16]

This refrain is repeated well into the eighteenth century,
and even by a severe Juvenalian satirist. Swift's *Intelli-
gencer*, No. 3 (1728), argues that the characteristic English
humor of Gay's *Beggar's Opera* is "the best Ingredient to-
ward that Kind of Satyr, which is most useful, and gives the
least Offence; which instead of lashing, laughs Men out of
their Follies, and Vices; and is the Character which gives
Horace the Preference to *Juvenal*." In the same year Ed-
ward Young also praises Horatian good humor and the effi-
cacy of laughing rather than railing satire. Horace's censure
appears "to proceed from Judgment, not from Passion.
Juvenal is ever in a passion; he has little valuable but his
Eloquence, and Morality." In 1734, Thomas Catesby, Lord
Paget, expresses his mistrust of exalted language and claims
that "even *Horace* himself, as elevated and great a Poet as
he must be allow'd to be in his *Odes*, apears to much more

---

[16] John Sheffield, Earl of Mulgrave, Duke of Buckingham, *An Essay
upon Poetry* (1682), in *Critical Essays of the Seventeenth Century*, ed.
J. E. Spingarn (Bloomington: Indiana Univ. Press, 1968), 2: 290; Dry-
den, The Works of John Dryden, vol. 3, *Poems 1685-1692*, ed. Earl
Miner and Vinton A. Dearing (Berkeley and Los Angeles: Univ. of
California Press, 1969), p. 16 (see also the "Discourse" in *Poems 1693-
1696*, p. 70); Wood, *Juvenalis Redivivus. Or The First Satyr of Juvenal
taught to speak plain English. A Poem* (1683), sig. A3ʳ (Wood's soften-
ing is scarcely perceptible); St. Evremond, *Miscellaneous Essays By
Monsieur St. Evremont*, trans. by several hands (1692-94), "A Judgment
Upon Seneca, Plutarch, and Petronius," 1: 253; "Of the Cleanness of
Expression," 2: 108; "Of the True and False Beauty of Ingenious
Writings," 2: 97.

Advantage in his *Sermones* and *Epistles*," which have less fancy but more judgment and therefore are, we infer, more likely to do their satiric job.[17]

Others shared that concern with the efficacy of satire and joined to it the important matter of genealogy. Philip Francis, for instance, follows Dacier in arguing that Horace really believed that "a Satirist and a Poet were extremely different characters; and that the Language of Poetry was as unnatural to the Morality of a Satire, as a low, familiar Style to the Majesty of an Epic Poem." The muse of satire walks on foot. "If this Criticism be just," he continues, "the Dispute between Juvenal and Horace may with Ease be decided." Juvenal shows all the "natural Horrours" of vice, "commands his Readers in the Language of Authority, and terrifies them with Images drawn in the Boldness of a truly poetical Spirit." That is precisely the trouble. Juvenal is too warm in that task, too poetical, and too much the priest sacrificing a victim to his gods. He seems to enjoy the screams of the slaughtered and appears cruel, whereas Horace is easy, polite, courtly, and corrects our faults by strength of reasoning rather than dogmatic seriousness. "He has this Advantage over the rigid Satirist, that we receive him into our Bosoms, while he reassures with Good-humour and corrects in the Language of Friendship." The true nature of satire thus blends with the expectations and needs of the audience. We willingly allow ourselves to be corrected by the friend who is like us; we resist the exalted and cruel pedagogue or executioner.[18] David Watson later makes some of the same points and adds that Horace excels in "the Extensiveness of his Morals" and the "Delicacy of his Raillery," which are more important than Juvenal's su-

[17] Swift, The Prose Works of Jonathan Swift, vol. 12, *Irish Tracts 1728-1733*, ed. Herbert Davis (Oxford: Basil Blackwell, 1964), p. 33; Young, *Love of Fame, The Universal Passion*, 2nd ed. (1728), sig. A4^r; Paget, *An Essay on Human Life* (1734), 3rd ed. (Dublin, 1736), sig. A4^v.

[18] Francis, *The Satires of Horace. In Latin and English* (1746), 6th ed. (1756), pp. xii-xv.

perior versification "and the Strength and Vigour of his Genius." Horace's special excellence is in fact "what constitutes the very Essence of Satire." Watson praises Juvenal's tragic satire but is confident that Horace's comic mode is "the true and genuine Satire, and best calculated to banish Vice and Folly."[19]

These and similar remarks, including many in praise of raillery and ridicule, offer some support for James Beattie's statement in 1776: "I find that the generality of critics are all for the moderation and smiling graces of the courtly *Horace,* and exclaim against the vehemence and vindictive zeal of the unmannerly Juvenal."[20] As Beattie significantly adds, however, this judgment is foolish, for Horace and Juvenal do not "admit of comparison in this respect," and, in any case, Juvenal's is the more significant and important satiric form. Each of these points already had been made and remade for well over one hundred years.

III: EACH PERFECT IN HIS SEVERAL WAY

Many critics resisted the temptation to praise one satirist above the other, arguing instead that there was room enough on the platter for apples as well as pears, so long as each was the best of its kind. In 1605, Isaac Casaubon insists that the three very different satirists were about equal in quality. One even hears this opinion in Horatian France

[19] David Watson and S. Patrick, *The Works of Horace, Translated into English Prose* (the first edition thus collected is called the "third edition," 1750), 4th ed. (1760), 2: xlvi, 2: 1.

[20] "On Laughter and Ludicrous Composition," in *Essays* (Edinburgh), p. 662. Some commentators after Watson and Beattie also preferred Horace, in part because of his adherence to satire's generic traits. See the hostile review of Francis Hodgson's *Satires of Juvenal* (1807) in the *Edinburgh Review* 12 (1808): "The peculiar province of satire we conceive to be, the follies and petty vices, rather than the crimes of mankind; and that they have been much oftener rallied out of the former, than lashed out of the latter" (p. 51). The reviewer dislikes Juvenal on doctrinal and most other grounds.

of 1681, when Père de la Valterie observes that the two kinds of satire are Horace's, which has an extremely fine and delicate spirit, and Juvenal's, which condemns injustice with harshness, scorn, and detestation. Each of us will like a particular kind, depending upon his particular tastes. M. le Noble makes a similar point in 1706, as does R.D.S.M. in 1734, the Abbé Charles Batteux in 1746, and the Chevalier de Jaucourt in 1765. Somewhat earlier, and across the channel, John Dryden discusses Lucian's blend of satiric modes and notes that there was both laughing Horatian and biting Juvenalian satire from which to borrow: "Some Diseases are curable by Lenitives; to others Corrosives are necessary."[21]

If Horatianism were triumphant by about 1690-1710, one would expect to find Joseph Addison in the forefront of Horace's army. Such is not the case. Addison faces the old problem of whether Horace's or Juvenal's methods "are most agreeable to the End of Satire." The answer is clear: "Both of them, allowing for the different Manner of their Writing, are perfect Masters in their several Ways; in the one shines the *Ridicule*, in the other the *Severe*." Shortly thereafter, Anthony Blackwall praises each satirist for his separate virtues, and Joseph Trapp, often a partisan of Juvenal, argues that bias dictates judgment, that readers "perhaps will allow Both to be best in *their kind*," and that some prefer one kind, some the other: "*there* is all the real Difference between them." Giles Jacob also neutrally re-

---

21 Casaubon, Peter E. Medine, "Isaac Casaubon's *Prolegomena* to the *Satires* of Persius: An Introduction, Text, and Translation," *English Literary Renaissance*, 6 (1976): 288; Père de la Valterie, *Les Satyres de Juvénal et de Perse* (Paris), 2: 194; Le Noble, *Satires de Perse* (Amsterdam), sigs. *3ᵛ, *4ᵛ-5ʳ; R.D.S.M., *Réflexions sur la poësie en general* (The Hague); Batteux, *A Course of the Belles Lettres*, 3: 135, 3: 177-78; de Jaucourt, *Encyclopédie* (Neufchâtel), 14: 700, s.v. "Satire," which borrows liberally from Batteux, as well as Heinsius, Spanheim, and Dacier (14: 697); Dryden, *The Works of Lucian. . . . With the Life of Lucian, . . . Written by John Dryden* (1711), p. 34. The "Life" probably was written in 1696.

marks that *"Horace,* exercis'd his Censure in Jest and Merriment; and *Juvenal* wrote his Satire in a more serious Strain."[22] John Dennis, who long had anticipated Beattie, tells Matthew Prior that however much Dryden's preference for Juvenal rather than Horace has influenced the "Generality of Readers," such comparisons are useless. Dennis shares Boileau's belief that these satirists' works are not *"ejusdem generis,"* and thus are not comparable, Horace's being patterned on the old comedy, and Juvenal's "a new Satire which was of the Tragick kind." Joseph Spence, of course a learned classicist and friend of Pope's, observes that satire is the offspring of tragedy and comedy and thus may partake of either method, so long as the vicious suffer: "she Smiles in *Horace,* looks Severe in *Persius,* and Commanding in *Juvenal.*" In 1739 Thomas Sheridan tells readers of his Juvenal that he abjures the "ill-natured *Comparisons"* between the three great satirists but would "allow to each his several Merit." Not to be outdone in generosity, the anonymous compiler of a mid-century translation of Horace also says that he cannot "see why both of them may not be justly praised, without detracting from the Merit of either: They are both excellent in their Way, *Horace* in *jocose,* and *Juvenal* in *serious* Satire."[23] Later in the century several other men of letters, including Edward Burnaby Greene, Stephen

[22] Addison, *A Dissertation Upon the most celebrated Roman Poets* (in Latin, 1692), trans. Christopher Hayes (1718), pp. 47, 49; Blackwall, *An Introduction to the Classics* (1719), pp. 71-79; Trapp, *The Aeneis of Virgil* (1718), 1: ix; Jacob, *An Historical Account of the Lives and Writings of Our Most Considerable English Poets* (1720), p. xxiv. Jacob's discussions of Gould, Oldham, and Rochester—all derivative— reinforce one's impression of a dominantly Juvenalian satiric inheritance early in the eighteenth century.

[23] Dennis, "To Matthew Prior, Esq: Upon the Roman Satirists" (1721), in *The Critical Works of John Dennis,* ed. Edward Niles Hooker (Baltimore: The Johns Hopkins Univ. Press, 1967), 2: 218; Spence, *An Essay on Pope's Odyssey* (Oxford and London, 1726), 2: 100; [Sheridan], *The Satires of Juvenal Translated,* pp. xi-xii; the "Davidson" edition, *The Satyres Epistles, and Art of Poetry of Horace,* 5th ed. (1750), 2: x.

Sullivan, Edward Owen, George Alexander Stevens, William Henry Hall, Martin Madan, William Boscawen, William Drummond, William Gifford, and Francis Howes, would confirm either of two conventional views. As James Beattie puts it in 1776, "*Satire*, we must observe, . . . is of two sorts, the Comic and the Serious"; or, as the anonymous translator of Persius puts it in 1806, there are three sorts—"the gay, the serious, and a skilful combination of these two."[24]

One reason for these different sorts was the varied genealogy of the two major forms; another was the difference in their respective times and the consequent requirements of their satiric modes. Rigaltius, for instance, notes that "*Horace* is jeering, and so fit for *Augustus* his times; *Persius* grave, and so more fit for leud *Nero*'s days; and *Juvenal* Terrible, and so most fit for *Domitian*'s desperate Age." Dryden offers a similar remark in his poem prefatory to Henry Higden's *Modern Essay on the Tenth Satyr of Juvenal* (1687), repeats it in his "Discourse" on satire, and could have seen it, had his superterrestrial eyesight been keen enough, in a variety of remarks between Steele's in 1710 and George Richards's in 1788. James Beattie offers a paradigm of such observations. Horace and Juvenal

---

[24] For other relevant remarks, see Burnaby Greene, *The Satires of Juvenal Paraphrastically Imitated, and adapted to the Times* (1763), 2nd ed. (1764), p. x; Sullivan, *An Epistle to a Friend at Rome* (1772), p. 11; Owen, "An Essay upon Satire," in *The Satires of Juvenal* (1785), 2: 243-45, 248; Stevens, *A Lecture on Heads, ... To Which is Added An Essay on Satire* (1787), p. 120; Hall, *New Royal Encyclopaedia* (1789), vol. 3, s.v. "Satire"; Madan, *A New and Literal Translation of Juvenal and Persius* (1789), 2: unnumbered p. 3, or sig. O1ʳ of Preface to Persius; Boscawen, *The Satires, Epistles and Art of Poetry of Horace* (1797), pp. x-xi, and *The Progress of Satire* (1798), pp. 7-8; Drummond, *The Satires of Persius* (1799), p. xviii; Gifford, "An Essay on the Roman Satirists" in *The Satires of Decimus Junius Juvenalis* (1802), p. xliii, et passim; Howes, *The Satires of A. Persius Flaccus* (1809), pp. iv-v. Beattie is quoted from *Essays*, p. 662. The 1806 quotation is from *The Satires of Aulus Persius Flaccus*, p. xvi.

had different views, and took different subjects; and therefore it was right that there should be a difference in their manner of writing. Had Juvenal made a jest of the crimes of his contemporaries, all the world would have called him a bad writer and a bad man. And had Horace, with the severity of Juvenal, attacked the impertinence of coxcombs, the pedantry of the Stoics, the fastidiousness of luxury, and the folly of avarice, he would have proved himself ignorant of the nature of things.[25]

The temper of the age could argue for discrimination and equality of satiric kinds; it also could argue for Horace's superiority or, as the practice of Gould and Oldham shows, for Juvenal's.

IV: "ROME'S SATIRIST, THE FOREMOST OF THE BAND": THE ARGUMENTS FOR JUVENAL

Harsh times, we often hear, will produce more interesting, important, and pleasing satire than gentle times. Surely one is more moved by matters of personal, national, and spiritual life and death than by whether one should agree with the stoic view of the world, or with the need to polish one's verse.[26] Juvenal introduced not a mere new or parallel kind

[25] As quoted in Barten Holyday's *Decimus Junius Juvenalis and Aulus Persius Flaccus* (1673), sig. a2ᵛ. For further discussion of Rigault's well-known Preface to Juvenal, see Howard D. Weinbrot, *Augustus Caesar in "Augustan" England: The Decline of a Classical Norm* (Princeton: Princeton Univ. Press, 1978), pp. 154-56. Dryden is in Higden's *Modern Essay*, sigs. A4ʳ⁻ᵛ, and in the "Discourse," *Poems 1693-1696*, p. 69; Steele, the *Tatler*, No. 242; Richards, "On the Characteristic Differences Between Ancient and Modern Poetry" in *Oxford English Prize Essays* (Oxford, 1836), 1: 252-54; Beattie, *Essays*, pp. 662-63.

[26] The phrase "Rome's Satirist" is from J. M., *The Scale: or Woman weighed with Man. A Poem. Inscribed to her Royal Highness The Princess Dowager of Wales* (1752), p. 5. As one might expect, the poem defends woman, reluctantly scolds Pope—"great among the greatest

of satire but a completion of the genre's best possibilities. The Abbé des Marolles, who admires the peerless Juvenal's detestation of vice, thinks that in his own age Horace excelled in satire but did not serve as a model for Juvenal. Robert Stapylton offers a comparable suggestion in his translation of Scaliger's and then Lipsius's praise of Juvenal's exalted satire. "In heate, and in height, and liberty (which is the essence of Satyr) he goes beyond Horace: He touches vice to the quicke, reproves, cries out upon it." Barten Holyday also quotes Scaliger and Lipsius, adds the formidable Rigaltius's opinion to his own, and makes overt that the harsher the time the better the satire is likely to be. Though Horace's lyrics are noble, his satires are dull. Juvenal, he says, did not merely change but perfected satire, whose end is to reform, "whereas a perpetual Grin does rather Anger than Mend." Horace's "gentle" satire was acceptable in his own age, "Yet this amounts but to an art of *admonition* not the bravery of *chastisement*" (sig. a2ʳ).[27]

This Renaissance commonplace enjoyed a long and healthy life. In *The Malecontent* (1684) Tom D'Urfey is willing to allow some earlier satirists to gloss over lesser sins, like pride, fornication, adultery, and legacy hunting; but in his own age the more serious matters of parricide,

---

Names" (p. 7)—and does not regard Juvenal's sixth satire as appropriate for her Royal Highness:

> Rome's Satirist, the foremost of the Band,
> Who paints fair Virtue with a Master's Hand,
> But brutal Lust indelicately draws,
> Leads up the Van in this ungen'rous Cause;
> Attacks alike the Living and the Dead,
> And withers half the Laurels on his Head.
>
> (P. 5)

27 For the Abbé's first remark, see *Les Satyrs de Juvénal en latin & en françois* (Paris, 1653), sig. e1ʳ; for the second, see *Les Satires de Iuvénal et Perse, avec des remarques*, 2nd ed. (Paris, 1658), p. 279. Stapylton italicizes most of this passage from Lipsius: *Juvenal's Sixteen Satyrs* (1647), sig. A6ᵛ; Holyday, *Decimus Junius Juvenalis*, sig. a2ʳ.

conspiracy, rebellion, incest, murder "and such like," re-
quire that the satirist make each stroke so terrible, and the
shame so obvious, that the greatest dolt can understand.
He rejects the notion that "Satyr should tickle till it
Smarts," since there is plenty of time for tickling when the
wound heals. Severe lashing is the proper satiric way, and
"the undaunted *Juvenal* was in this mind," attacking the
vicious, however mighty. That is "a good example for every
just Author" (sig. A1ʳ⁻ᵛ). Dryden also is in the tradition of
those who elevate the satirist of oppressed times. Horace,
appropriately fit for Augustus's relatively mild reign, wrote
satires "of a lower nature" than Juvenal's; but for Juvenal
"Oppression was to be scourg'd instead of Avarice: . . . the
Roman Liberty was to be asserted." Domitian's days needed
a Brutus "to redeem or mend," rather than a Horace "to
Laugh at a Fly-Catcher. This Reflection at the same time
excuses *Horace*, but exalts *Juvenal*." Joseph Trapp simi-
larly urges that Juvenal's is "the more noble Species" of
satire, as does Walter Harte who, by 1730, offers conven-
tional lines on Horace as "the Foe of Fools not Vice," and
on the "courtly ease" that insinuates its way to the heart;
but Juvenal has "a nobler rage" than his predecessors. In-
deed, "What honest Heart could bear *Domitian's* age?"
Much of the thrust of two centuries' reaction, from Rigal-
tius (1616) to Hodgson (1807), is summed up in Beattie's
essay "On Laughter and Ludicrous Composition." He is
aware of Horace's many partisans and of the twin poles of
satire; but like Holyday long before him, he also knows
"that moral disapprobation is a more powerful emotion
than laughter," and so insists that though Horace did well,
Juvenal "might, as a moral satirist, be said to have done
better. Fired with honest indignation at the unexampled
degeneracy of his age, and disdaining" servile expression,
and the "dastardly soul" that implies, he "dragged Vice
from the bower of pleasure and from the throne of empire,
and exhibited her to the world, not in a ludicrous attitude,"
but in her genuine "loathsome ugliness and hideous distor-

28

tion." Laughter is trivial in comparison with "the disapprobation of conscience," which "in every sound mind is the most powerful principle of the human constitution."[28]

So broad-based a reaction seems predictable on several grounds. Readers in the Restoration and eighteenth century were conditioned to regard epic and tragedy as the highest of genres. Among many comparable remarks, for example, Addison's *Spectator*, No. 39 (1711), urges that "As a perfect Tragedy is the Noblest Production of Human Nature, so it is capable of giving the Mind one of the most delightful and improving Entertainments." Charles Gildon reports that for Vossius, Rapin, and Buckingham the epic is "the greatest and most noble in *Poesy*" and, according to Rapin, "the greatest Work that humane Wit is capable of."[29] Tragedy and epic shared a demand for unity of action that was nonetheless capable of great variation. As Gildon says, "the aim and business of the *Greek Tragedy* was, by some fable or other, to teach and inculcate some one moral maxim; which it did, by the lively representation of the passions" of the actors necessary for the fable.[30] On the other hand, he adds in a different work, most English dramatists misuse "*under Plots* . . . which seldom or never are of a Piece with, and so link'd to the main Design, as not to make the Action double, and so destroys that Unity, without which a just Tragedy cannot subsist." The epic also needs such unity, but it is varied with many episodes of, for example, war, voyages, and treaties, which nonetheless should "have a Relation to the *principal Action*, to make a Work that has *Order* and *Proportion*."[31]

[28] Dryden, "Discourse" on satire, in *Poems 1693-1696*, pp. 69, 65-66; Trapp, *Lectures on Poetry*, p. 227; Harte, *An Essay on Satire, Particularly the Dunciad*, pp. 15-16 (Horace), 17 (Juvenal); Beattie, *Essays*, pp. 662, 663-64.

[29] *The Spectator*, ed. Donald F. Bond (Oxford: Clarendon Press, 1965), 1: 163; Gildon, *Complete Art of Poetry* (1718), 1: 270.

[30] *The Laws of Poetry* (1721), p. 149.

[31] *Complete Art of Poetry*, 1: 236, 274.

Dryden's "Discourse" on satire already had used some of
the same language to make several of the same points re-
garding "the Design of true Satire"—not the inadequately
connected Horatian comic way of low familiar speech, but
the exalted, tragic, Juvenalian and Persian way. This satire
should consider one subject and

> be confin'd to one particular Theme; or, at least, to one
> principally. If other Vices occur . . . they shou'd only be
> transiently lash'd, and not be insisted on, so as to make
> the Design double: As in a Play of the *English* [tragi-
> comic] Fashion, . . . there is to be but one main Design;
> And tho' there be an Under-plot, or Second Walk of
> Comical Characters and Adventures, yet they are sub-
> servient to the Chief Fable, carry'd along under it, and
> helping to it; so that the Drama may not seem a Monster
> with two Heads.

The satirist must "give his Reader some one Precept of
Moral Virtue; and . . . caution him against some one par-
ticular Vice or Folly." Other virtues may be recommended
and other vices scourged, but they must be "subordinate to
the first."[32] In this respect the dominant genres were di-
rectly related to Juvenalian and not to Horatian satire
which, Dryden argues with Casaubon as his tutor, lacks
unity.

This notion of unified formal verse satire was important
throughout much of the eighteenth century. The young
perpetrator of *Four Satires* (1737) tells the audience of his
moderately indignant poems that "in the Conduct of my
Satires, I have observ'd Unity of Design, and confin'd my-
self to a single Subject in every one," except the slightly
more flexible first, on national vices (p. vii). Several years
thereafter, William Boscawen finds "regularity of method"
as well as "energy of sentiments and language" lacking in
Horatian but typical of Juvenalian and modern satire.

[32] *Poems 1693-1696*, pp. 80 (true satire), 79 (one theme), 80 (one
precept).

Tragedy and epic of course deal with the most exalted or sublime characters, problems, and language, all of which are again not in the Horatian comic, but the Juvenalian tragic, mode. Scaliger's words in Stapylton's Preface make clear the value of high language. "Juvenal is neate and clear and absolutely the Prince of Satyrists; & . . . exact in all he writes." Horace is "a Jeerer," who wrote "Discourses; inserting some loose sentences in common talke." Juvenal, however, "is furious, he assaults and kils. . . . His verse is farre above Horace, his sentences sharper, and he speakes things more to the life." Juvenal is as superior to Horace as Horace is to Lucilius. Holyday again repeats all this, adding Lipsius's preference of Juvenal "for his Ardor, his Loftiness, his Liberty." No wonder that in 1675 an unknown author turns the tenth satire into noble Pindaric stanzas, since "*Juvenal* was the properest for a *Pindarick* Version, of any Author of that nature." Dryden, as we should expect, makes clear that Horace's low style is "generally grovelling," whereas Juvenal's is lofty and sublime.[33] Horace's "Wit is faint; and his Salt . . . almost insipid," but Juvenal "is of a more vigorous and Masculine Wit" and is "much more Elevated. . . . and more Noble" (p. 63). What-

---

[33] Stapylton's largely italicized words are from Julius Caesar Scaliger: *Juvenal's Sixteen Satyrs*, sig. a6ʳ⁻ᵛ; Holyday, *Decimus Junius Juvenalis*, sig. a2ʳ; anon., *The Wish, Being the Tenth Satyr of Juvenal Paraphrastically rendered in Pindarick Verse* (Dublin), sig. B1ʳ (this remark is from Edward Wetenhall's letter to Viscount Blessinton); Dryden, *Poems 1693-1696*, pp. 64, 63. Subsequent citations are given in the text. Dryden reiterates that "*Juvenal* was the better Satirist," and, "I am sorry to say it, for the sake of *Horace*; but certain it is, he has no fine Palate who can feed so heartily on Garbage" (p. 73). Moreover, Dryden suggests that Juvenal transcends Horace in part because of Horace's own excellence and example. Horace merely had Lucilius to surpass, and did so, by means of elegance of language rather than vigor and sublimity. Horace thus "made way for a new Conquest over himself, by *Juvenal* his Successor" (p. 64). Far later, Francis Howes makes a roughly comparable remark regarding the weaknesses of Lucilius: "the want of preceding models to be surpassed, usually cause first efforts to be imperfect." See his *Satires of A. Persius Flaccus*, p. vi.

ever Horace's other considerable achievements, "we cannot deny, that *Juvenal* was the greater Poet . . . in Satire" (p. 65), and thus should "Ride first in Triumph" in the contest with Horace and Persius (p. 75).

Early and mid-eighteenth-century critics were no less impressed by the difference in the poets' key and the audience's pleasure. As Joseph Warton says in his *Essay on . . . Pope* (1756), "The sublime and the pathetic are the two chief nerves of all genuine poesy," and it was the sublime that an increasingly numerous body of readers sought in literature and found in Juvenal. That satirist, Joseph Trapp tells his students at Oxford, wrote "generally in the Sublime" style, whereas there was some question, nurtured by Horace himself, whether Horace's pedestrian lines were poetry at all. As John Dennis asserts in 1704, Juvenal's satires "are more musical [than Horace's], because they have a greater Spirit in them." Walter Harte admires Horace's "nice" satire, but it is Juvenal, Harte orates, echoing Dryden, who evokes his greatest feeling:

> See his strong Sense, and Numbers masculine!
> His soul is kindled, and he kindles mine:
> Scornful of Vice, and fearless of Offence,
> He flows a Torrent of impetuous Sense.

John Brown's *Essay on Satire* is opposed to the fashionable canting about the value of ridicule, a "sordid maxim, form'd to screen the vile" (p. 12). Frowns, love of virtue, contempt for vice, are necessary to deal with the illnesses of society. Whatever praise Horace receives for his polite but piercing satire (p. 25), Brown's preference, in this poem memorializing Pope's death, lies elsewhere. When the state is in danger, "when Giant-Vice and Irreligion rise," then "Not lofty Epic soars a nobler flight," as satire, thunder, lightning, and indignation ravage the guilty (p. 22). That epic task fell to the last of the Roman satirists, whose "exalted page" reflects "ardent eloquence, and boundless rage."

32

His mighty numbers aw'd corrupted *Rome,*
And swept audacious greatness to its doom;
As headlong torrents Thund'ring from on high,
Rend the proud rock that lately brav'd the Sky.

(P. 26)

Two years later Stephen Barrett published his own *War,
an Epic-Satyr* (1747), and there tells his reader that such a
mixture of genres is both natural and necessary. To prove
this, he says, one need grant a single postulate, "namely,
That K—gs have Vices; and that their Vices are most de-
structive in their Consequences to mankind. It would," he
continues, ". . . be a publick Benefit to have their Faults
shown them, in order to a Reformation" (pp. vi-vii). He
performs this act in, not the comic, but the elevated mode
because, as Thomas Bowles argues in 1758, Juvenal "is a
Writer of the sublimer Kind of Satyre, and seems to propose
the Tragic Stile for his Imitation."[34]

Similar themes appear in Britain and France for at least
the next fifty years. In 1763 Edward Burnaby Greene, bored
with the comparison between the two satirists, nevertheless
insists that "in one respect I must esteem the conduct of
Juvenal preferable to that of Horace." The latter's verse
sometimes is flat, harsh, unpleasing, and "hobling"; only his
"singular delicacy" and "polished strokes" are responsible
for his being admired rather than dismissed. Juvenal, in
contrast, "rushes against vice; he rarely flags from that fire
and spirit" which is as pleasing to the modern English as
the imperial Roman ear. During the same year young Ed-

---

[34] Warton, *An Essay on the Genius and Writings of Pope,* 5th ed.
(1806), 1: vi; Trapp, *Lectures on Poetry,* p. 232; Dennis, *Grounds of
Criticism in Poetry,* in *Critical Works,* 1: 364; Harte, *An Essay on
Satire,* p. 17. See also p. 11 of Brown's *Essay,* and its insistence on the
political, libertarian, function of satire: "Swift to redress an injur'd
people's groans, / Bold SATIRE shakes the tyrant on her throne";
Bowles, *Aristarchus. . . . With a Critical Dissertation on the Roman
Classics* (Oxford), p. 254. See pp. 227-28 for Bowles's discussion of
Horace, and p. 237 for Persius. His judgments are conventional.

33

ward Gibbon reads Juvenal for the first time and, though aware of his weaknesses, finds his strengths far greater; these include noble indignation against vice, and a sublime and polished style "superior to that of most of the Latin poets." Martin Madan is even more emphatic: "As a writer, [Juvenal's] style is unrivalled, in point of elegance and beauty, by any Satirist that we are acquainted with, *Horace* not excepted." Like Shakespeare, Juvenal held "the mirror up to nature." For Dacier, Juvenal is qualitatively beneath Horace because above him in language; Madan's analogy of Juvenal with Shakespeare, suggests that in Britain the same stimulus was likely to evoke a different response, as indeed it did for some readers in late eighteenth-century France. In 1779 Maupetit calls Juvenal back from the underworld, knowing that he was "un poëte si supérieur à Horace, et que tous les savans de l'Europe ont célébré par un concert unanime." Juvenal, however, in his blunt Roman way, insists that he does not wish to be troubled with such visits, and that his subterranean friends mirror his terrestrial style and concerns: "Je me promenois avec Homère, Tacite et Lucain, et ne les aurois pas quittés pour vous entretenir, si vous n'aviez eu que l'intention de brillanter l'antithèse comme tant d'autres."[35]

Pleasure is a good enough reason for preferring one satirist to another; but as we have seen, several readers were partisans of Horace because he wrote genuine satire. One finds partisans of Juvenal, as well as those apparently liking each kind of satire, who make the same argument, though finding their slogan on the other side of the coin. Tom D'Urfey believes in Juvenal's superiority on such generic

[35] Burnaby Greene, *The Satires of Juvenal*, pp. x-xi; Gibbon, "Extraits de mon journal," in *Miscellaneous Works*, ed. John, Lord Sheffield (1796), 2: 117-18 (this edition includes both the French and English versions of the "Extraits," with the English at the foot of the page); Madan, *A New and Literal Translation of Juvenal and Persius* (1789), 1: ii, italics and Roman type are inverted; Maupetit, *Satires de Juvénal* (Paris), pp. xix, xxvij (je promenois).

grounds, as does Joseph Trapp, who maintains that Juvenal
is better in part because some of Horace's *"Discourses . . .
are scarce reducible under either Species of Satire. Juvenal's
are all true Satires."* James Miller pays Horatian gentle rid-
icule very little mind when his *Seasonable Reproof, a Satire
in the Manner of Horace* (1735) defines satire's role as "to
pull down the Reputation of Fools and Coxcombs, to pil-
lory, as it were, Vices and vicious Men in Effigie, to tear the
Fig-leaf Veil from Lewdness, and strip Malice and Envy of
their plausible Disguises." He will "expose egregious Vices
and Follies *in terrorem.*" By 1744 Corbyn Morris is another
who thinks that satire and severity are synonymous, and
therefore that any derivation urging the contrary is wrong
on the face of it, since ridicule and raillery are not satiric by
definition. Raillery will expose "little Embarrassments";
satire will expose the deformity of vice. Raillery must not
sting too deeply or it will seem rude; "But *Satire*, the more
deep and severe the Sting of it is, will be the more excel-
lent." Raillery should be good natured; satire demands "a
generous free Indignation, without any sneaking Fear or
Tenderness; It being a sort of partaking in the Guilt to
keep any Terms with Vices." Morris's conclusion regarding
the satirists depends on criteria opposed to Dacier's comic
genealogy of satire: *"Juvenal*, as a *Satirist*, is greatly supe-
rior to *Horace*; But indeed many of the short Compositions
of *Horace*, which are indiscriminately ranged together, un-
der the general Name of *Satires*, are not properly such, but
Pieces of *Raillery* or *Ridicule.*"[36]

This respect for Juvenal as the true satirist reappears
often after Morris's essay. Nearly sixty years later, for exam-

[36] D'Urfey, *The Malecontent; A Satyr* (1684), sig. A3ʳ; Trapp, *Lec-
tures on Poetry*, p. 232; Miller, *Seasonable Reproof*, sigs. A1ᵛ, A2ʳ (in
terrorem), italics and Roman type are inverted; Morris, *An Essay
Towards Fixing the True Standards of Wit, Humour, Raillery, Satire,
and Ridicule*, pp. 50-51; see also p. 42, which denies that Horace's
"Impertinent," *Satires*, i, 9, is a satire at all, "as the Subject is not *Vice*
or *Immorality.*"

ple, Robert Potter pays tribute to Samuel Johnson as both a critic and man. In a separate section he offers his own dream after having read Warton's *Essay* on Pope and Johnson's *Lives of the Poets* (1779-81). In this fantasy, Warton both exemplifies and supports the Horatian superficial kind of satire and a mindless adherence to the classics. Johnson is the modern, British, Juvenalian figure whose authority carries all before him. Johnson admires Addison, but, he tells Warton,

> his wit, though pleasing and brilliant, wanted the force of that of Pope and of Juvenal, whom with Martial, you strangely pretend to despise. On the contrary, Sir, a smooth silver knife will never penetrate to the core of vice; but it must be the rough edge of more powerful metal wielded with a strong hand. The tickle of Horace and Addison will but make both the reader and offender laugh, and therefore, they seldom rallied follies; and indeed a turn-coat and debauchee, like Horace, could do no more with an ill grace.[37]

In 1802 William Gifford dismisses Horatian ridicule by insisting that laughter at vice is neither feasible nor "the legitimate office of satire, which is to hold up the vicious, as objects of reprobation and scorn" in order to punish them and deter others. Five years later, the perennially sour Percival Stockdale also evaluates the two Roman satirists. He suggests that Edward Young's preference for Horatian

---

[37] Potter, *The Art of Criticism; As Exemplified in Dr. Johnson's Lives of the Most Eminent English Poets* (1789), p. 207. Johnson's satires were associated with Juvenal's on qualitative grounds. Sir John Hawkins's *Life* of Johnson praises its subject's poetry because "in two instances he nearly equalled the greatest of the Roman satyrists." *The Life of Samuel Johnson, LL.D.* (Dublin, 1787), p. 472. Francis Hodgson notes and admires the similarity of melancholic tone in Johnson's *Vanity of Human Wishes* (1749) and Juvenal's tenth satire. See *The Satires of Juvenal*, p. 183. These are some of the many positive references to Johnson's poem in the later eighteenth and earlier nineteenth centuries.

laughing satire is a sign of a minor poet's "vitiated critical judgment" that evoked an "odd stricture on the greatest satirist that ever wrote."[38]

Some readers, even those like Gibbon who admired Juvenal, found his harshness a sign of malignity of spirit, and faulted him as a person. Some, like Dacier, said little about Juvenal but lauded Horace's frequent tokens of friendship and his cementing, civilizing graces. Many others, however, found Juvenalian rage a sign of Juvenalian virtue, of value in its own right and morally superior to the accommodating courtier. This belief even has currency in seventeenth-century France, for in 1681 De la Valterie argues that, more than Horace, Juvenal had the necessary qualities of a satirist: "une âme libre, élevée au dessus de la bassesse des opinions communes, qui ne sçait ce que c'est que la contrainte, la servitude, la complaisance & la flatterie. Il paroist que Juvénal a surpassé en cela Horace." The Augustan poet dares to criticize very gently, whereas Juvenal pursues all the vices of his century with ardor: "il n'épargne personne, & . . . un guerier intrepide, il se presente hardiment au combat." In *The Malecontent* Tom D'Urfey also praises Juve-

---

[38] Gifford, *The Satires of . . . Juvenalis*, p. xlviii. Gifford would of course have dismissed French, or English, praise of Horace as a poet of moral stature: "Virtue . . . has few obligations to his zeal." He is a distinguished critic, "but . . . as an ethical writer, Horace has not many claims to the esteem of posterity" (pp. xlvi-xlvii). Gifford's preference for Juvenal was a familiar, if not universal, later eighteenth-century judgment. See, for example, Alexander Thompson, *The Lives of the First Twelve Caesars, Translated from . . . Suetonius* (1796): "we hesitate not to place him at the head of this arduous department of poetry" (p. 615). See pp. 225-26 for the largely favorable discussion of Horace.

For Stockdale, see his splendidly eccentric "answer" to Johnson's *Lives: Lectures on the Truly Eminent English Poets* (1807), 1: 554. Stockdale wishes that "Young had had the poetical eloquence of Juvenal, as well as his morality, in his eye [for *Love of Fame*]: we should then have had the powerful flow of a copious poetical river . . . not an unequal, and broken current; playing over pebbles, when it should have been rushing to the ocean" (1: 555).

nal's courage in battling and not tickling the corruption in government and elsewhere (p. iv). Dryden would have agreed with such a judgment, for he too objects to the servitude he thinks inherent in Horatian complaisance. Juvenal, Dryden says in the "Discourse" on satire, treats tyranny and its attendant vices "with the utmost rigour: And consequently, a Noble Soul is better pleas'd with a Zealous Vindicator of *Roman* Liberty; than with a Temporizing Poet, a well Manner'd Court Slave, and a Man who is often afraid of Laughing in the right place: Who is ever decent, because he is naturally servile." The author of *Mirth in Ridicule* (1708) continues that evaluation, which is based in part on political purity and in part on admiration for Juvenal's courage. He praises each of those different satirists but prefers Juvenal because Horace merely laughed at the horrid vices of the new slave masters. "*Juvenal* with a more generous Freedom declaim'd against Vice, like a free-born *Roman*, as if he had breath'd an Air of Liberty under the Power of the ancient Consuls" (pp. 3-4). About mid-century, "Sir" John Hill tells a young nobleman that "*Juvenal* will command the most exalted applause" when he and Horace write on common topics. The noble lasher of the wickedest of times should be revered for genius, morals, and gentlemanly severity even while he crushes "under his feet" the vice at which Horace merely laughs. Consequently, Juvenal may be read "with the greatest" advantage of all the Roman satirists[39]—a view shared by the many late eighteenth-century readers and commentators on Juvenal in France and England.

In 1779, for instance, Maupetit blames the tiresome "fades louanges," the insipid flattery, of Horace, and praises the "moral sublime, . . . élévation, véritable noblesse" of Juvenal (p. xxj). As William Gifford puts it in 1802, Juve-

---

[39] De la Valterie, *Les Satyres de Juvénal et de Perse*, 1: 196; Dryden, *Poems 1693-1696*, p. 65; Hill, *Observations on the Greek and Roman Classics* (1753), p. 265. See also his slightly different discussion in the *Inspector*, No. 136, in John Hill, *The Inspector* (1753), 2: 254.

nal's hatred of the Caesars, patriotic republicanism, and *"elevation of language"* contrast sharply with the style of Horace, who was rewarded for praising the court whose heirs later banished Juvenal. Gibbon already had remarked that "love of liberty, and loftiness of mind distinguishes Juvenal from all the poets who lived after the establishment of the monarchy." Horace and his contemporaries "all sing the ruin of their country, and the triumph of its oppressors. . . . Juvenal alone never prostitutes his muse."[40]

In so rejecting prostitution, British commentators also were puffing their own no doubt pristine liberty, and were again placing themselves closer to the Juvenalian side of the satiric spectrum. " 'Tis not without pain," George Turnbull says, following Lord Shaftesbury and others, that "a Lover of Liberty hears the Glory of Arts flourishing ascribed either to an *Augustus* or to *Lewis XIV*." Turnbull is in part responding to a familiar British judgment regarding the native character, one which is overt in Edward Burnaby Greene's observation that Juvenal's "fire and spirit is . . . delightfully striking to an English ear."[41] An eighteenth-century myth of the race held that Britain was the land of liberty, of hardy rough virtue, of independence and hatred of tyranny. In 1737 the author of *Four Satires* thus fiercely banishes "nice Refinements" as well as "warbling Eunuchs" and other effete tokens of a nation "polish'd into Slavery." Britons should be rough, enjoy "cruel Sports, and bloody Sights," and, perhaps in a line suggesting cause and effect, be "Barb'rous still, if Free" (pp. 13-14).

---

[40] Maupetit, *Satires de Juvénal*, p. xxj; Gifford, *Satires of . . . Juvenalis*, p. 267 (elevation), pp. xlvi-xlviii on Horace's style, character, and "political tergiversation" (p. xlvi), and his aim merely "to keep the objects of his satire in good humour with himself, and with one another" (p. xlvii). Juvenal's style, on the other hand, "proves him to have been a sturdy republican, a genuine and unsophisticated patriot, who loved the honour and dignity of his country, above his life" (p. 290n). Gibbon, *Miscellaneous Works*, 2: 103.

[41] Turnbull, ed., *Three Dissertations* (1740), pp. xv-xvi; Burnaby Greene, *The Satires of Juvenal Imitated*, p. xi.

Horace was not appropriate for such a people, or at least not for those satirists who associated him with polish, court, and slavery.

And so he was seen in many words of outrage printed between about 1726 and 1742, when his growing popularity was blocked by the opposition's ploy of painting the court of Walpole and George Augustus with the dark colors of the court of Augustus Caesar. The administration, in turn, often tried to dissociate itself from such tyranny and claimed that the Tory, Jacobite opposition embraced Augustan tyranny. To be politically Augustan was, for the most part, to commit that worst of sins—be un-British. To be politically Horatian was, for many opposition writers, also to support an absolutist philosophy thought banished after 1688, but threatening to reestablish itself through the talents of Sir Robert. To be Juvenalian, and in many cases Persian, was to offer an appropriate pose of the resistance to tyranny, to play the bloody but unbowed soldier in a small army fighting the good fight against a horde of powerful and unscrupulous brutes wishing to destroy the remnants of national virtue. That romantic, self-conscious, and "patriotic" stance is clear in much of Pope's poetry from 1733, especially in the *Epilogue to the Satires* (1738), where he is the "Last of *Britons*" (*Dialogue* ii, 250) as Brutus, or Cato, or Cassius was the last of Romans, battling the despot. It is equally clear in contemporary adaptations of Juvenal by anonymous authors, by Samuel Johnson, Paul Whitehead, and Samuel Derrick, as well as in later imitations, translations, and commentaries scattered through the century.[42] I have dealt with this matter elsewhere, and so

[42] Johnson's *London* (1738), in imitation of Juvenal's third satire, is of course well known. Whitehead's (?) *The State of Rome Under Nero and Domitian* (1739), "By Messrs. Juvenal and Persius," is discussed below, chapter 5, section 1, and is one of the many Juvenalian-Persian imitations enlisted in the patriot cause. The unsigned *Seventh Satyre of Juvenal Imitated* (1745) also is angry at a world in which "bold Corruption holds the golden Bribe" (p. 4), and Samuel Derrick, in his little-read *Third Satire of Juvenal Translated in English Verse*

will quote from only two works that probably both reflect and enhance the complementary movements—the sullying of Horace and solidifying of Juvenal as a darling of the opposition to hateful despotism.

Thomas Gilbert's *The First Satire of Juvenal Imitated* (1740) makes clear that he is imitating—adapting, manipulating, enlisting—his author, whose words are dutifully reproduced at the foot of the page *"that the Reader may see the Liberties I have taken"* (p. 2). One of those liberties is having Juvenal lash the horrors of Walpole (p. 5) and his unprecedentedly tyrannic administration, while contemptible "other Poets haunt the purling Stream, / And spin out Verses softer than their Theme." For this surrogate Juvenal, "Such trifling Subjects would defile my Page, / Whose pointed Lines should glow with manly Rage" (p. 12). He not only lambastes the government, its venal, upstart politicians, and its authors who "fulsome Panegyricks write" (p. 19), but praises Pope who, like himself, is "manly" and is "arm'd for Virtue." Pope is supremely effectual in terrorizing the wicked and reforming the most miserable corrupt ally of a corrupt minister: "Gay modern *Atheists* kiss the Poet's Rod, / Reform their Lives, and tremble at a God." Walpole and his sycophants now confront a Muse who will "Brand their foul Names to each succeeding Age, / And make the Living dread the future Page" (p. 20). Contrast this portrait with that made of Horace in the same year.

The indignant satirist of *Plain Truth, or Downright Dunstable. . . . With Some Critical Thoughts concerning Horace and Virgil* castigates those poets as *"flattering, soothing, Tools,"* who were "Fit to *praise Tyrants*, and *gull Fools*" (p. 13). Horace's flight at Philippi and, with Virgil,

(1755), though far less hostile than Johnson or others, nonetheless must portray an unflattering world in which the good man leaves the city for the country. For discussion of Juvenal later in the eighteenth century, see R. C. Whitford, "Juvenal in England 1750-1802," *Philological Quarterly*, 7 (1928): 9-16.

praise of the later Augustan enslaver insured their own imperial reward. The honest modern reacts with rage, and wishes those scoundrels away.

> In monstrous times, *such Weeds* thrive best,
> They *ornament a Tyrant's Nest.*
> They serve to *lull and blunt the Pain,*
> Of *vilest Crime*, still hide such Stain,
> In Luxury, they thrive amain.
> Of *Tyranny bear up the Train.*
>
> (P. 15)

More men have been lost "By *Horace*' Book" than by any other, or by the vilest strumpet (pp. 15-16).

Though this vignette is especially vitriolic, Horace's political and moral integrity continued to be attacked well into the early nineteenth century in both Britain and France, whereas Juvenal, for all his weaknesses, remained the poet of "freedom." As Charles Abbott, Lord Tenterden, says in 1786, "It is only by the exercise of political satire, that the spirit of jealousy necessary to the support of all mixed governments can be excited, and the general establishment of the constitution protected and maintained." Juvenal and, to a lesser extent, Persius were thought to have spoken out as just that sort of political satirist. Though Juvenal was too late to save Rome's constitution, he earned the respect of those many British subjects who regarded servility as foreign to the native gene pool. "How poor, how trifling are the rules of intercourse with the great, or a smiling expostulation with folly, compared to" Juvenal's deep reflections, "manly and energetic mind," and indignation, Francis Hodgson claims in 1807.[43] Augustus's patronage of letters "could not, in the eyes of Juvenal, redeem the blood through which he waded to the throne"

---

[43] Charles Abbott, Lord Tenterden, "On the Use and Abuse of Satire," *Oxford Prize Essays*, 1 (1836): 189; Hodgson, *Satires of Juvenal*, p. 442. Subsequent citations are given in the text.

(p. 471). Horace's satire is "philosophical essay-writing," Juvenal's "the inspiration of poetry" (p. 491).

Horace's reputation never recovered from these and comparable attacks. He also was maligned in Pope's first *Dialogue* (lines 11-22) of the *Epilogue to the Satires*, and was imprinted on the minds of many contemporaries as the prop of a morally dubious administration under Augustus Caesar and George Augustus. To be sure, Pope and other satirists had the good sense and poetic skill to adapt several of Horace's devices, some of his tones, some literary and "Sabine" values, and many of his satires, and they generally admired his odes, which were, I believe, more important to eighteenth-century Britain than the satires. To adapt devices, however, by no means demands uniform adaptation of values, and if we review the admired traits of Juvenal as then perceived, it will be clear that in many ways he was more useful than Horace for Pope's political purposes. Juvenal was the sublime or tragic satirist appropriate for the worst of times, when the nation and its government were in decline and oppression was rampant; he was appropriate for an audience seeking sublimity in poetry and unified structure in satire; he therefore was closer both to what many regarded as "true" satire and to the free, rough, and even bloody nature of the British nation staunchly refusing to be "polish'd into Slavery"; he would attack even the most exalted of governors if they deviated from public morality; and, together with his ally Persius, he was easily drafted into the opposition to Walpole during the 1730s, when Horace was regarded as one of the *"flattering, soothing, Tools"* of that great man. All of these traits, we will see, strengthen the muscle and help to explain the tone of many of Pope's satires from 1731 to 1738, the years of his great achievement as a formal verse satirist, and of his imitations of Horace, whom he was *"Something Like."*

One may argue that from the end of the seventeenth to the beginning of the eighteenth century Horace is about equal to Juvenal in reputation as a satirist, and that for many readers and writers, especially those in France, Horace was more faithful to satire's comic aims and therefore was more effective as a satirist and more pleasant to be with. One also may argue that Horace made significant inroads in schools, in the gentleman's class with which Pope liked to associate, and among those seeking polish rather than elevation in verse. On balance, however, English, Latin, and even some French commentators on satire for about 130 years before Pope's satiric prime saw Persius and then Juvenal as the model of satiric excellence. The notion of Pope as an eighteenth-century Augustan Horace wants reconsideration if we are to reclaim Pope's genuine achievements in satire.

For the most part I have been dealing with the reputation of Horace and Juvenal as satirists, and the reasons for those reputations from the seventeenth to the early nineteenth centuries. Since such opinions obviously stemmed from specific poems—whether they were accurate is another matter—we need both to reclaim the satiric modes of proceeding as contemporary readers might have understood them, and to enlarge our focus and consider Lucilius and Persius as well, for these four satirists were seen as part of a spectrum within which Pope's own work deserved a place. Since Pope's satires so often concerned the court and its government, it is appropriate to examine the classical satirists and their relationships with their own rulers.

CHAPTER 2

Roman Modes of Proceeding:
Classical Satire and Norms in Government

THE MAJOR VERSE SATIRISTS had many different and some
overlapping traits; one of the latter was a concern with
government as a public institution and thus as a legitimate
object of praise or, in the majority of cases, blame. In so
writing, each satirist also mirrored the perceived political
and social health of his city, republic, or empire, and pro-
vided variously appropriate models for the needs of later
satirists. I shall treat the four, rather than usual three, sat-
irists, since Lucilius's ghostly presence was felt by his Ro-
man and British offspring.

I: LUCILIUS—PARENT OF THIS NIPPING RHYME

In the eighteenth century as in the twentieth, Lucilius's
thirty books of satires survive only in fragments. His high
reputation and role as the father of formal verse satire were
nonetheless appreciable. As his editor Dousa says in 1597,
even the truncated remains "indicate the magnitude of the
loss Rome suffered in the destruction of Lucilius's works."
Many "of the ancients esteemed him"; Lactantius thought
his "verses about virtue" superior to "many written by the
most famous and clever of men; and there are yet other
remarkable things in these fragments which make us real-
ize the keenness of his wit and the eminence of his learn-
ing" (p. 2).[1] As Schrevelius says, borrowing from Lubin,

---

[1] C. Lucili . . . Satyrarum quae supersunt reliquae. Franciscus Jani
F. Dousa collegit, disposuit & notas addidit (1597) in Censorini liber
de die natali . . . et C. Lucilii Satyrarum (Leiden, 1767): "Maximam
profecto jacturam in illius operum interitu literas Romanas fecisse, hae
ipsae quamvis turpiter lacerae fragmentorum Reliquiae quemvis satis
commonefacere possint" [unnumbered p. 157]. "Simul ut ex eo cogno-

"no one ever inveighed against the vicious ways of the Roman people with greater freedom, nor was held in greater honor and veneration" than Lucilius.[2]

Lucilius also was known through the description by each of his distant sons, who agreed upon his severity against vice. Horace was least happy with that ancestral voice. In Horace's *Satires*, i. 4, and i. 10, for example, Lucilius emerges as the excellent, lashing, but unnecessarily severe and prosodically rough satirist who wrote too much too quickly. Had Lucilius lived in our Augustan age, Horace adds, he would have polished his verse in accordance with our greater sophistication. In *Satires*, ii. 1, however, Lucilius has rather a different image—first as the poet who reveals his character in his book, and then as the well-connected satirist whom the state allows to pursue the vicious wherever they may be. Lucilius is to virtue only and her friends a friend.

There is no ambivalence in Persius's or Juvenal's description of Lucilius. Persius's first satire characterizes Lucilius as flaying the city, attacking the specific men Lupus and Mucius, and thus offering now-rejected historical warrant for Persius's own severity (lines 114-15). Juvenal's first satire also tells his readers that he will run in the same course as Lucilius (lines 19-21), and then adds, in an eighteenth-century translation,

---

scerent ii, quibus minus notus Poëta noster, quanti eum veteres aestimaverint, quem Lactantius disertissimus Theologorum dignum habuerit, ut ejus potissimum de Virtute versus ex tot praeclarissimorum ingeniorum scriptis penitus excuteret, quanquam & alia sunt in his Reliquiis non minus illustria, quae ingenii ejus acrimoniam, & doctrinae praestantiam suspiciendam nobis praebant" [unnumbered p. 157; italicized].

2 *D. Junii Juvenalis et Auli Persii Flacci satyrae* (Leiden, 1671), p. 4, note to *Satires* i. 20: "Nemo majore libertate in flagitiosos populi Romani mores unquam invectus est, ac majori in honore ac veneratione habitus." Subsequent quotations from Juvenal and Persius are from this edition.

Sharp as a Sword, *Lucilius* drew his Pen,
And struck with panic Terror, guilty Men;
At his just Strokes the hardened Wretch would start,
Feel the cold Sweat, and tremble at the Heart.[3]

At least three distinct traditions emerged as a result of
these remarks. Several commentators, especially the French,
saw Horace as the culmination of Roman satire and thus
justified in repudiating Lucilian roughness. Hence Cru-
quius says that in *Satires*, i. 10, 64-71, Horace hopes to win
good will for himself and ill will for Lucilius. The earlier
poet wrote a "new kind of satire, very sharp to be sure, but
too harsh and biting towards his fellow citizens." Horace
admittedly is derivative: "nor does he want to beat or even
to wound anyone with poisonous babblings, but only to
deter citizens from vice, with civilized and witty reproof
of their conduct."[4] André Dacier already had noted that
Horace dissociated himself from Lucilian severity. No mat-
ter when Lucilius lived, Dacier urges, "c'est toûjours la
faute du Poëte, quand il prend un sujet qu'il ne peut pas
traiter poliment." In 1693 Dryden argues that Horace "far
excels [Lucilius] in the design" of his satires; and in 1728
Père Sanadon clarifies the ways in which Horace ridiculed
Lucilius's continual mockery. The spirit of these and other
remarks is well exemplified in a comment by the Abbé
Charles Batteux. After offering the usual information re-

---

[3] Henry Baker, *Medulla poetarum romanorum; or the Most Beauti-
ful and Instructive Passages of the Roman-Poets, with Translations in
English Verse* (1737), 2: 329.

[4] *Q. Horatius Flaccus*, ed. Jacobus Cruquius (Antwerp, 1578), p. 352.
"Exorditur ab antiquae Comoediae scriptoribus, ut sibi quidem non-
nihil apud Romanos benevolentiae, Lucilio vero plus comparet inui-
diae; ut qui ad illorum imitationem, nouo quoda modo suam Satyram,
satis quide acute, sed durius, & in ciueis mordacius scripsisset, & quasi
ex professo, nouam poesin fecisset: se vero nihil tale meditari, neq.
sugillare, neq. virulentis blateramentis ait se quemqua velle perstrin-
gere; sed urbana tantum, & faceta moru castigatione ciueis a vitiis
deterre."

garding his author, Batteux adds that "if we believe the judgment that Horace has passed upon this writing, we have no great reason to regret the loss" of the thirty strong but unpolished books. Batteux is so inclined to believe the admired Horace that, he says, "It is to be wondered at that a critic of Quintilian's profound judgment and taste should differ in opinion with Horace in this point."[5]

Horace's opinion also evoked a less flattering response, one related directly to Lucilius's relationship to his government and its governors. Dacier is pleased with Horace in *Satires*, ii. 1, for knowing that Lucilius was not an example to follow, and that he and Trebatius lived under the reign of a monarch opposed to such liberties. British commentators shared Dacier's perception but not his conclusion. Hence in 1763 Thomas Blackwell praises Lucilius because he "attacked Vice wherever he found it." Neither eminent birth nor station could "secure the *base Priest*, th' *immoral Peer*, or purse-proud Plebeian from appearing in their proper colours." Indeed, some of Horace's "*coarse* Expressions" probably were traceable to his study of Lucilius, who wrote "under the high liberty of the *Roman* State." Several years later, Edward Owen argues that the tone of each satirist was a function of the political climate of his respective age. He praises "that full scope and license which the free constitution of the Roman republic gave to [Lucilius's] great abilities." The "freedom of the Roman constitution

---

[5] Dacier, *Oeuvres d'Horace en latin et en françois avec des remarques critiques et historiques* (1681-89), 3rd ed. (Paris, 1709), 6: 616, note to *Satires*, i. 10, 57 (the 3rd ed. is the revised and preferred edition); Dryden, n. 14 to Persius's first satire in the *Satires* of Juvenal and Persius, in The Works of John Dryden, vol. 4, *Poems 1693-1696*, ed. A. B. Chambers, William Frost, and Vinton A. Dearing (Berkeley and Los Angeles: Univ. of California Press, 1974), p. 279; Sanadon, *Les Poésies d'Horace* (Paris), 2: 229; Batteux, *A Course of the Belles Lettres: Or, the Principles of Literature. Translated from the French . . . By Mr. Miller* (1761), 3: 141-42. See also the comment by Algorotti in *Saggio sopra la vita di Orazio*, reviewed as *Essai sur la vie d'Horace* (Venice, 1760), in *Journal Etranger* 7 (1761): 225.

. . . permitted Lucilius to adopt the bolder stile of the old comedy. . . . Horace, however, formed himself in a great measure, upon the model of the new, according to the altered state of Rome from a free republic to an absolute, though mild, monarchy." William Gifford regards the popularity of Lucilius as a covert protest against declining liberty under Augustus. "I suspect," he says in 1802, "that there was something of political spleen in the excessive popularity of Lucilius under Augustus, and something of courtly complacency in the attempt of Horace to counteract it." Shortly thereafter, Francis Howes reiterates the essence of these remarks when he praises Lucilius's "truly republican" severity and boldness. "He lived at a time when the government had not yet made liberty of speech a crime." The political connection also was appropriate for the modern world. As T. J. Mathias observes in *The Pursuits of Literature* (1794), "I know not what a modern French Directory might do with a man of his character [who satirized "even men of high quality, and of consular rank"]; but Lucilius enjoyed respect and impunity in the Roman Republick."[6]

No self-consciously patriotic Briton could prefer an absolute foreign to a native balanced state. Horace's rejection of Lucilian roughness meant a corresponding rejection of Lucilian liberty; Persius's, and especially Juvenal's, greater affection for Lucilius meant affection for freedom. Commentators for hundreds of years thus noted the affinity between Lucilius and Juvenal. Sir Robert Stapylton insists that Juvenal abandoned the pleasant oratorical fictions of Quintilian "to prosecute the bitter but wholesome truths of the Satyrist *Lucilius*," whom he promptly surpassed. Dryden

---

6 Dacier, *Oeuvres d'Horace*, 7: 37n; Blackwell, *Memoirs of the Court of Augustus* (Edinburgh and London, 1753-63), 3: 50, 67; Owen, *The Satires of Juvenal*. . . . Also Dr. *Brewster's Persius* (1785), 2: 242-43; Gifford, *The Satires of Decimus Junius Juvenalis* (1802), p. xliii; Howes, *The Satires of A. Persius Flaccus* (1809), p. v; Matthias, *Pursuits*, 6th ed. (1798), p. xxvi.

observes that both Persius and Juvenal thought Lucilius more useful a model than Horace for their antityrannic satire. Edward Burnaby Greene later adds that Juvenal, like Lucilius, "rushes against vice." Francis Hodgson's remarks are a paradigm of the politically oriented view of the four satirists that begins the nineteenth century. Horace seemed not to understand the severity of a man who "did not spare vice in any of the most conspicuous character; but fearlessly named the object of his reprehension." Juvenal, however, "in whom the spirit of Lucilius, equally ardent, but more refined, seems to have become immortal, has . . . described him in his genuine colours." Though Persius also understood him thoroughly, Juvenal's "was exactly the virtuous indignation of Lucilius, and he knew that from thence arose 'Revenge and Tears' "—that is, revenge upon and tears from the satirist daring enough to attack the powerful and corrupt men around him. The Lucilian-Persian-Juvenalian satirist places himself in harm's way in the cause of virtue and, in Lucilius's case, does so with the blessings of the government. "He was defended by his own connexions. These are a tower of strength to the satirist. He may, so protected, quietly take his stand as upon a safe eminence, and dart at whom he pleases."[7]

Lucilius's apparent method of proceeding as perceived in the eighteenth century, then, was to seek protection from his friends in Rome's free government and to take the liberties to which he was entitled when trying to protect his country from exalted or subservient criminals. A free constitution, the argument runs, makes a free satirist, one moved to anger and not likely to spend his time burnishing hexameters to please sophisticates. Lucilius anticipated and shared the political and satiric severity of Persius and Juve-

---

[7] Stapylton, *Juvenal's Sixteen Satyrs: Or, A Survey of the Manners and Actions of Mankind* (1647), sigs. A7^{r-v}; Dryden, "Discourse" on satire, in *Poems 1693-1696* (n. 5, above), pp. 69-70; Burnaby Greene, *The Satires of Juvenal Paraphrastically Imitated and adapted to the Times* (1763), 2nd ed. (1764), p. xi; Hodgson, *The Satires of Juvenal: Translated and Illustrated* (1807), pp. 310, 331, 310.

nal and, some thought, was misunderstood and intention-
ally maligned by Horace. Whatever that case may be, Hor-
ace was perceived as not only more elegant and sedate than
Lucilius but also more accepting of his age, for he had the
good fortune to live when a poet, prime minister, and
prince were on amiable terms.

II: HORACE AND MAECENAS

Horace's characteristic attitude toward his government may
be seen through the roles Maecenas plays in his satires and
epistles. As virtual prime minister, Maecenas was an exten-
sion and reflection of the Octavian and then Augustan or-
ders. Pope's attacks upon Sir Robert Walpole often include
or mask attacks upon George II. In contrast, Horace's
praise of Maecenas often implies praise for the world Au-
gustus helps to create both in Rome and between Rome
and her poets.

Such support demands the mutual esteem that we find in
Satires, i. 3, where Horace is so close to Maecenas that he
allows his thought or reading to be interrupted by Horace's
friendly chatter and sees that the poet's virtues far out-
weigh his faults. In *Satires*, i. 10, Maecenas again appears
incidentally but crucially in a Horatian apologia, where he
is one of the few whose approbation Horace wishes to have
(as he also appears in *Epistles*, i. 19, 1, as "Maecenas docte"
who understands Horace's true and original contribution
to Latin poetry in his odes and epodes). By *Satires*, ii. 6,
Maecenas has given Horace the Sabine farm and is asso-
ciated with the benevolent power of the gods—"Hoc erat
in votis" (line 1)—as, indeed, he is associated in poetry and
commentary with his master Augustus, who "was attentive
to the wise counsels of his minister, and received infinite
advantages from them," one of which was the reputation of
being Horace's patron.[8]

[8] Latin quotations are from *Quinti Horatii Flacci opera* (1691), ed.
Ludovicus Desprez, 7th ed. (1722). Line references are given in the
text. This contemporary version, like those of Juvenal and Persius, dif-

Maecenas's role in several other poems is more important, for his character makes him virtually an element of structure, especially when he is the person to whom a poem is addressed. Maecenas never speaks, but he is eloquent nonetheless and says a great deal about the myth of normative Augustan life and letters. In *Satires*, i. 1, for example, Horace talks to Maecenas with respect and engages him in a mutual enquiry into the weaknesses of the human situation rather than those of one political administration. No one is content with his lot, and thus each man envies his neighbor, whose job he would nonetheless refuse if it were offered to him. Horace's approach is general not particular, urbane and witty not blunt and angry, and wholly suited to the tones desired by the elegant man next to the man who was turning Rome from brick to marble. As Horace says, "quanquam ridentem dicere verum / Quid vetat?" (lines 24-25): Why can't I laugh while telling the truth? After all, teachers sometimes give tempting treats to children to help them learn their alphabets. The reader thus is like the child, coaxed into learning how to build a civilized language of morality rather than bludgeoned or frightened into abandoning a language of immorality. Horace's own art is the norm of intelligent probing and humorous mockery that includes its author in its objects of satire; the tone of that art is made possible by Maecenas who, like the implied norm, "intra / Naturae finis viventi" (lines 49-50),

---

fers in minor respects from modern editions; larger matters have been checked against the appropriate Loeb text. In attempting to understand Horace's satires, I have been aided by several works, especially Eduard Frankel, *Horace* (Oxford: Clarendon Press, 1957); Niall Rudd, *The Satires of Horace: A Study* (Cambridge: Cambridge Univ. Press, 1966); and of course the many seventeenth- and eighteenth-century commentators and editors whose work inspires both gratitude and vexation. The remarks regarding Augustus, Maecenas, and Horace are from *The Life of Maecenas. With Critical and Historical Notes. Written in French By M. Richer, Translated by R[alph] Schomberg, M.D.* (1748), pp. 58, 84-85. Pages 41-51 are especially concerned with Maecenas and the poets. Richer is commonplace.

lives within nature's limits and desires and uses just what he needs. Indeed, Horace says repeating his key word, *fines*, "sunt certi denique fines" (line 106)—there are sure limits beyond which one should not go. Be neither a miser nor a prodigal. Horace concludes with "Iam satis est" (line 120) —that's enough, or you will think that I have stolen from the manuscripts of the pedantic Crispinus, who bores everyone with lectures about virtue. Maecenas thus is a normsetter in his own right, setting the norm of when to stop writing satire so as not to change instruction for tedium. He knows the lesson Horace is hoping to teach, and thus is dissociated from the child and his treat. In *Satires*, i. 1, then, Maecenas is an adult coinvestigator who helps to imply both the poem's wisdom and its satiric norm.

His role is appreciably more important in *Satires*, i. 5, the journey to Brundusium, which would scarcely be known as a satire unless it were so labeled, for it is a poem of celebration and reunion, not attack. Maecenas the mediator is at the heart of that reunion, since Horace, Virgil, and others are to join him on a mission to Antony in order to reestablish harmony between him and Octavian. The poem begins with "Egressum magna . . . Roma" (I leave great Rome), and ends with "Brundusium longae finis chartaeque viaeque [est]," Brundusium is the end of a long tale and a long road; specifically, the disruption between rulers to be ended by the vigorous and tactful Maecenas. At Anxur they are to meet Maecenas and Cocceius, ambassadors on great matters, veterans at helping friends to smooth rough spots, and friends to the adversaries themselves. Horace's relationship with potential competitors for rule in the republic of letters mirrors the unifying force that Maecenas suggests. Antony and Octavian will be related in the same way that Horace, Virgil, and Rome's other great men of letters already are, and with at least as great rejoicing. At Sinuessa the group meets the virtuous Plotius, Varius, and Virgil, men to whom Horace is as close as can be: "O, qui complexus, & gaudia quanta fuerunt! /

Nil ego contulerim jucundo sanus amico" (lines 43-44).
The embracing, the rejoicing! So long as he is healthy,
there is nothing that brings him more joy than reunion
with a friend! The meeting of literary men accompanying
Maecenas is an emblem of the reunion that Maecenas
brings to Antony. The republic of letters and the republic
of Rome are one, are harmonized, are indeed celebrants of
one another in the symbiosis the poem projects. The me-
diating, ball-playing, god-placating Maecenas is the agent
of a conciliatory Octavian. The gods do not send us their
favors when they are sad; now they are joyous, and so
Brundusium is the end of a long tale and a long road.
Maecenas's imminent meeting with Antony sets in motion
a variety of other reunions: of celebratory poets, of man
and man on the journey, of man and gods, and conse-
quently of the disjointed masters of Rome.

We have seen Maecenas as a moral and political guide;
in *Satires*, i. 6, we see him as a social guide as well. In this
gentle satire on nobility and its burdens, Maecenas again
is a norm—not merely because he upholds the aristocrats'
best values, but because he is the proper representative and
exemplar of the state's best values. He is an aristocrat in
practical as well as social terms—"nemo generiosor est te"
(line 2)—but also believes in meritocracy. The close rela-
tionship between Maecenas and Horace is a warrant for
Maecenas's own good character, since much of the rest of
the world, all socially beneath Maecenas, sneers at Horace's
humble origins and lack of ambition. Maecenas was born
to, and deserves, the world's respect, and thus he passes
that respect to others of whom he approves, whatever their
birth. In the process, Maecenas also aligns himself with
Horace's freedman father, who gave his son the education
and even some of the external trappings of the knight or
senator. Horace's father sees in his son the potential of an
intellectual aristocrat and educates him accordingly. As an
adult, Horace has that judgment seconded when Virgil and
Varius introduce him to Maecenas who, nine months later,

asks Horace to join their group and thus confirms the inherent merit hitherto seen by his father and Rome's other great poets. Maecenas's reach extends to the noblest poets of Rome, to the judgment of the freedman, and to the worth of his son. Maecenas, in fact, understands Horace well enough to know that he wishes to remain a literary aristocrat, without seeking the burdens of public office. For such a choice, "sanus fortasse tuo" (line 98)—you should think me sane, whatever the world, already discredited as a judge of men and merit, may think. Maecenas now is the man of subtle perception who sees worth in others, however different that worth may be from his own; and, we remember, he represents Augustus.

Thus far Maecenas and the court he exemplifies have been defined by what they are and do; Horace has, in part, been defined by his invitation to join the elite corps that Maecenas nurtures as the microcosm of Roman values. Each man also can be defined by what he does not do. Hence in *Satires*, i. 9, we see Horace symbolically placed on the Via Sacra, besieged by an impertinent heretic who accosts him there and seeks admission to the circle that Maecenas embodies. The Impertinent characterizes the stereotypical court of intrigue, bribery, and sycophancy, and tries to get Horace to introduce him to Maecenas, as Virgil and Varius so introduced Horace. Our poet, of course, refuses the bait and in the process shows why he deserves Maecenas's respect, for he makes clear that the minister excludes intrigue, jealousy, and ambition. "Vix credible" (line 52), the Impertinent insists, and affirms his own inadequacy and inability to understand: I'll corrupt his slaves (line 57) to gain entry! Just as the man is leaving, we get further, "external" warrant for his villainy, as the plaintiff in a lawsuit against the social-climbing, uncomprehending outsider sees him, seizes him, and engages Horace as a witness against him. "Sic me servavit Apollo" (line 78) the poet says, implying the distinction between the legal and illegal, the divine and the profane, and thus reminding us that the poet began on the Via Sacra. Apollo both saves Horace from further harassment and affirms the sanctity of Maecenas's court. By rejecting the Impertinent and his vulgar notions, Horace protects Maecenas from potential infection and, in the comic context of the poem, thereby earns the intercession of Apollo on his own behalf.

We see a similar affirmation by negatives in *Satires*, ii. 8, where Maecenas is a guest of honor at the dinner party given by the wealthy and ostentatious Nasidienus, who plies them with the most excessive of delicacies as well as his own tiresome culinary lectures. The poem ends with Maecenas and his friends leaving prematurely and refusing to eat the food so grossly served to them. This satire is not one of Horace's more attractive efforts, and has the stench of snobbery from beginning to end. In its way it shares one aspect of the ethic of the Restoration so-called comedy of wit, in which the wits share the proper social values and punish the Witwouds whose false aspirations make them fair game for brutal treatment. Hence Maecenas's abandonment of Nasidienus and Fundanius's subsequent telling of the tale to Horace are not signs of their callousness, but affirmations of their social standing. Maecenas, as representative of the best Augustan values, is out of place in the home of affectation and affluent bad taste; Horace shows this by having Maecenas realize the nature of his host and refuse to stay and share a meal with him. Since Horace is part of Maecenas's circle, the tale of Nasidienus's dinner obliquely defines Augustan, Maecenian, and Horatian traits.

Finally, *Epistles*, i. 7, suggests yet another aspect of the relationship between the two men, which now is so rich and enriching that it allows denial of the great man's requests. Horace again expresses the deepest gratitude to Maecenas, from whom he nonetheless can be independent, and whose invitation to return to Rome and visit, Horace can refuse. In *Satires*, ii. 3, 312-13, Damasippus criticized the poet for rushing off to accept Maecenas's last-minute dinner invita-

tion, even when Horace had to abandon his own guests. Now, however, Horace knows that Maecenas will grant his request for seclusion because he has his friend's welfare at heart, and, perhaps as important, because he is capable of understanding Horace's position and the nature of human change and decay. Horace thus makes clear that there are certain gifts that Maecenas can give—the Sabine farm and all the secondhand splendor of being associated with the Augustan court—and certain gifts that he cannot give. If you want me back with you, Horace tells his patron, return my health, my youth, the joys of departed mindless prattle, decorous laughter, and the ability to drink away the night. Since Maecenas cannot restore those gifts of nature, he cannot legitimately call his friend back to Rome, for he needs the country to soften and soothe the human pains that fall to his share. As for Maecenas's material gifts, from one Horace is proud to call ruler and father, Horace will gladly return them if he wishes; but of course Maecenas does not so wish, and recognizes Horace's needs and values. The great man understands that small men need small things (line 44), and that Horace would lose too much in regaining the elaborate bustle of Rome. In his final line Horace respects his own and his patron's state of being, and clarifies the gulf and the bridge of understanding between them: it is fit that each man should measure himself by his own rule.

This fine epistolary poem shows Horace's willingness to restore any land that may also imply a mortgage on his inner life; it assumes that Maecenas would never ask for such a restoration; and it portrays the patron and client, the court's embodiment of Augustan values and the literary celebrant of them, communicating in a tender but firm way, as the courtier is educated and recognizes the poet's wisdom. By being so good a student, Maecenas is shown to have earned the titles "rexque pater" (line 38) that Horace offers, and that also redound upon Augustus himself, on the principle of *ad exemplum regis*. The words *urbane* and

57

civilized are inadequate for such a poem, one that evoked Scaliger's praise, Dacier's concurrence, and David Watson's recognition of the dignified relationship between its humble writer and exalted recipient. This friendship clearly is only a part of the ambience of respect between poet and government. Virgil, Varius, and Plotius, after all, shared Horace's joy in the journey to Brundusium, and each, in his poems at least, offered a comparable ideal that endeared readers for hundreds of years to what seemed the perfect union between two centers of value. Lewis Maidwell is happily commonplace when, in 1707, he praises Horace as one of "the characters *of Good, and Great Men, who have bin Renon'd . . . for doing Service to their* Country, *and conferring Benefits on Mankind.*"[9] Horace's service to his country meant service to his dynasty, ruler, prime minister, and government in general. His next great successor was less able to serve in these ways, for satire under Nero begins to be satire in opposition; it begins a retreat into either the self or the country, a retreat made necessary by the corrupt city and its governors. Persius was leagued with Juvenal as inheritor of Lucilian freedom and enemy of tyrants, and was far more popular and useful than his modern students believe. The standard view that Lucilius and Persius "were not used directly as models by the English Augustan satirists" wants reconsideration.[10] The evi-

---

[9] For Scaliger and Dacier, see Dacier's *Oeuvres d'Horace*, 8: 366-67; Watson, *The Satires, Epistles, and Art of Poetry of Horace* (1743), pp. 242-43; Maidwell, *Comitia lyrica: sive carmen panegyricum. Inque, ad exornandas magni Godolphini laudes, omnes omnium odorum modi ad Horatio delegantur. . . . Paraphras'd in English, By Mr. Tate, Servant to Her Majesty* (p. 21). Maidwell is an enthusiast for Horace, Augustus, and his "Principal Favorites" (p. 22).

[10] This view has been stated by Raman Selden. See *English Verse Satire 1590-1765* (George Allen & Unwin, 1978), p. 11. For other views, however, see William Frost, "English Persius: The Golden Age," *Eighteenth-Century Studies*, 2 (1968): 77-101; and especially Cynthia Dessen's study of Benjamin Loveling's *First Satire of Persius Imitated* (1740): "An Eighteenth-Century Imitation of Persius, Satire I," *Texas*

dence regarding Persius is substantial and requires ample display.

III: Perceptions of Persius

Persius generally has been considered far less attractive than Horace or Juvenal and thus far less important as a contributor to the history of British satire. The few modern studies of Persius's relevance for the eighteenth century suggest an advanced case of anorexia, a willful starvation and withdrawal of nourishment rather than a healthy leanness. Most earlier readers also placed Persius beneath Horace and Juvenal, though still in their qualitative group, and of great interest and significance. His dark, rough, grave poems were essential for the ongoing Renaissance view of what satire should be, and his other conventions mingled well with those of Juvenal to create a satirist of immediate utility for Pope and the opposition to Walpole —the biting, hostile, somber, virtuous outcast who attacked a society rotting from the top down.

Studies in Language and Literature, 20 (1978): 433-56. Some of Persius's apparently political qualities, and their consequent utility for the opposition to Walpole, are discussed in this useful essay as well. For more classically oriented studies, see Cynthia Dessen, *Iunctura Callidus Acri: A Study of Persius' Satires*, Illinois Studies in Language and Literature, 59 (Urbana: Univ. of Illinois Press, 1968); J. C. Bramble, *Persius and the Programmatic Satire: A Study in Formal Imagery* (Cambridge: Cambridge Univ. Press, 1974); and Niall Rudd, "Imitation: Association of Ideas in Persius," in *Lines of Enquiry: Studies in Latin Poetry* (Cambridge: Cambridge Univ. Press, 1976), pp. 54-83. There are several useful overviews of classical satire. See Ulrich Knoche, *Die Römische Satire* (Göttingen: Vandenhoeck & Ruprecht, 1957); *Satire: Critical Essays on Roman Literature*, ed. J. P. Sullivan (Routledge & Kegan Paul, 1963); Dietmar Korzeniewski, ed., *Die Römische Satire* (Darmstadt: Wissenschaftliche Buchgesselschaft, 1970), Wege der Forschung Band 138; Edwin S. Ramage, David L. Sigsbee, and Sigmund C. Fredericks, *Roman Satirists and Their Satire: The Fine Art of Criticism in Ancient Rome* (Park Ridge, N.J.: Noyes Press, 1974); and Michael Coffey, *Roman Satire* (Methuen & Co., 1976).

Some of his attraction can be documented in the list of English translations from 1616 to 1817: Holyday (1616), Dryden (1693), Eelbeck (1719), Sheridan (1728), Senhouse (1730), Stirling (1736), Brewster (1741-42), Burton (1752), Madan (1789), Drummond (1797), anonymous (1806), Howes (1809), and Gifford (1817).[11] Oldham acknowledges his debt to Persius for the Prologue of his *Satyrs upon the Jesuits* (1679); F. A. imitates the third satire in 1685; Tom Brown tries his hand at the Prologue and part of the first satire in 1707; six different imitators emerge between 1730 and 1740; Thomas Neville imitates most of the satires in 1769; Edward Burnaby Greene follows suit in 1779; an unknown author applies the fourth satire to Pitt in 1784; William Gifford's *Baviad* (with its title-page motto from Juvenal, i. 1-4) massively expands the first satire in 1791; and George Daniel's *Modern Dunciad* performs a similar

[11] These are, respectively: Barten Holyday, *Aulus Persius Flaccus His Satires Translated into English* (Oxford, 1616; rpt. with his Juvenal in 1673); John Dryden, et al., *The Satires of Decimus Junius Juvenalis. . . . Together with the Satires of Aulus Persius Flaccus* (1693); Henry Eelbeck, *A Prosaic Translation of Aulus Persius Flaccus's Six Satyrs* (1719); Thomas Sheridan, *The Satyrs of Persius* (Dublin, 1728); John Senhouse, *The Satires of Aulus Persius Flaccus, Translated into English Prose* (1730); John Stirling, *A. Persii Flacci, Satirae: or, The Satires of A. Persius Flaccus. . . . For the Use of Schools* (1736); Thomas Brewster, *The Satires of Persius* (1741-42; printed individually from 1733); Edmund Burton, *The Satyrs of Persius* (1752); Martin Madan, *A New and Literal Translation of Juvenal and Persius* (1789); Sir William Drummond, *The Satires of Persius* (1797); anon., *The Satires of Aulus Persius Flaccus; Translated into English Verse* (1806); Francis Howes, *The Satires of A. Persius Flaccus* (1809); William Gifford, *The Satires of Aulus Persius Flaccus* (1817, in vol. 2 of his Juvenal). This list should be supplemented with the several editions of Holyday's Persius (5th ed., 1650), Dryden's Juvenal and Persius (7th ed., 1754), and Brewster's Persius (2nd ed., 1751), which was reprinted in *D. Junii Juvenalis et A. Persii Flacci Satirae Expurgatae: In Usum Scholarum* (1784)—this includes Johnson's *London* (1738) and *Vanity of Human Wishes* (1749)—and in Edward Owen's *The Satires of Juvenal. . . . Also Dr. Brewster's Persius* (1785). William Gifford's Persius appeared in 1821 as well.

task in 1814.[12] Persius also was commented upon in numerous encyclopedias, manuals, discussions of Roman satire, and Latin editions of his works, and often was translated in France, where he again was regarded as the least exalted of the elevated three. No doubt this is a partial list, since the voluminous miscellanies and collected poems must harbor other individual efforts. One may say, erring on the side of conservatism, that from the earlier seventeenth to the earlier nineteenth century in Britain, Persius enjoyed a minimum of thirteen complete translations, two nearly complete groups of imitations, eleven imitations or translations of individual satires, and much commentary, controversy, and pedagogical application. Multiple English, Continental, and Latin editions, many known in Britain, would swell this list substantially. Reclamation of Persius's conventions and reputation suggests that his influence must have been virtually inevitable, and inevitably in the direction of Juvenal and Pope.

The eighteenth-century's Persian inheritance probably begins in 1605 with Isaac Casaubon's *Prolegomena* and edition of the satires, which, together with his revolutionary *De Satyrica Graecorum poesi & Romanorum satira* became loci classici of the study of Persius and formal verse satire. To Casaubon goes the credit for permanently forcing Persius into the same circle as Horace and Juvenal, vigorously

[12] For these, see Oldham, *Some New Pieces* (1684), with its separate pagination and title page for *Satyrs upon the Jesuits*, 3rd ed. (London, 1685), sig. A2ʳ; F. A., *The Third Satyr of A. Persius, In Way of a Dialogue, or Dramatick Interlude* (1685); Brown, *The Works of Mr. Thomas Brown, Serious and Comical*, 4th ed. (1715), 1: 75-76; the different imitators are discussed in chapter 4, section IV, and chapter 5, section I, below; Thomas Neville, *Imitations of Juvenal and Persius* (1769); [Edward Burnaby Greene], *The Satires of Persius Paraphrastically Imitated and Adapted to the Times* (1779); anon., *The Fourth Satire of Persius Imitated, and Much Enlarged, In Application to the Right Honourable William Pitt* (1784); William Gifford, *The Baviad. A Paraphrastic Imitation of the First Satire of Persius* (1791); George Daniel, *The Modern Dunciad. A Satire. With Notes Biographical and Critical* (1814).

resisting Scaliger's attacks upon him, and establishing Persius's reputation as a dominantly political satirist. From Dacier and Dryden to Drummond and Howes, most roads lead to and from Casaubon.[13]

His *Prolegomena* insists that the three Roman satirists must be examined with respect for their different individual contributions and for their "nearly equal . . . diverse virtues," each of which he describes in familiar terms.[14] Casaubon's defense implies that he prefers Persius to his brother-satirists, but he nonetheless concludes modestly "that there is no one of these who was not superior to the rest by a certain virtue peculiar to himself; and, again, that there was no one who was not inferior to the rest for some reason" (p. 294).

Obscurity was one of the points on which Persius needed defense. Casaubon turns that apparent fault into an asset and characterizes Persius as courageous and clever in the face of political intimidation: "in Persius what spirit? What ardor? What stimulus? For indeed his outspokenness was so great that he could not be induced even by fear of death to spare Nero" (p. 293). Since Persius was neither

[13] André Dacier's edition and translation of Horace, probably the best known such version in the seventeenth and eighteenth centuries, includes a "Préface sur les Satires d'Horace, Où l'on explique l'origine & le progrès de la Satire des Romains; & tous les changemens qui lui sont arrivez." Dacier quickly announces his indebtedness to "le savant Casaubon." See *Oeuvres d'Horace* 6: 1, et passim. For brief discussion of contemporary knowledge of Dacier, see Howard D. Weinbrot, *The Formal Strain: Studies in Augustan Imitation and Satire* (Chicago: Univ. of Chicago Press, 1969), pp. 60-68. For Dryden's use of him in particular, see the notes to the "Discourse" on satire, in *Poems 1693-1696* (n. 5, above).

[14] As translated by Peter E. Medine, in "Isaac Casaubon's *Prolegomena* to the *Satires* of Persius: An Introduction, Text, and Translation," *English Literary Renaissance* 6 (1976): 288. Subsequent quotations are given in the text. Casaubon's distinction between satiric kinds already was becoming commonplace. "Description in Horace," for example, "is humbler, in Persius grander, in Juvenal often sublime" (p. 294).

foolhardy nor courted the separation of body from soul before its proper time, he intentionally wrote obscure verse "out of fear of that most cruel and bloodthirsty of tyrants against whom" his satires were written. The source of this wisdom was his tutor Cornutus, "who as an old man repeatedly whispered to him the words, 'be obscure.' Although Probus, or whoever is the writer of the life, does not say this explicitly, he nevertheless reports matters from which we ought to infer this much" (p. 296). These and comparable remarks would echo throughout the next two hundred years.

After 1605, in fact, nearly everyone agreed that Nero was Persius's main target in several of his six satires. Though most modern scholars remain unconvinced, British translators from Holyday to Howes, from 1616 to 1809, tell readers that, as Senhouse argues, Persius "aims particularly at [Nero] in most of his Satirs." This opinion appears in France as well, and even though the formidable Pierre Bayle, later joined by the Abbé le Monnier in 1771, characteristically doubts that received truth, he admits his is a minority opinion. "I should never have done," he says, "if I undertook to quote all the Authors who imagine that" Persius attacks Nero's unfortunate taste and poetry by citing four lines from his presumed, and bad, tragedy. These commentators also tend to follow Casaubon in explaining Persius's obscurity. As Holyday says, difficulty in reading Persius proceeds in part "from the want of Libertie, which in his desperate times, was altogether lost." Far later, Senhouse confirms that "the Fear of his Safety under *Nero*, compell'd him to this Darkness in some Places" (sig. A4ʳ). In 1736 John Stirling offers a similar commonplace to his schoolboy audience: though Persius aimed at Nero in most of his satires, he was "prudent enough not to arraign him openly and plainly."[15]

---

[15] Senhouse, *The Satires of . . . Persius* (n. 11 above), p. 1. Subsequent citations from Senhouse are given in the text. Bayle, *A General Dictionary, Historical and Critical*, trans. John Peter Bernard, Thomas

For some critics, the veil of obscurity extended beyond the grave. According to M. Selis in 1776, Persius's satires appeared after his death because only in that way of self-censorship could he be secure in attacking Nero. He thus joined caution to courage; he had the wisdom not to circulate his work, and he died in his bed. Since Cornutus had comparable affection for his own life, he refused to edit the satires, surrendering them instead to Caesius Bassus. Selis is confident that Persius's consistent attacks upon Nero are clear enough for haters of the tyrant to recognize them, and obscure enough for the tyrant not to understand them. No courtier would dare explicate such satire in order to illumine his master's darkness. Apparently, for courtiers as well as poets, it was necessary to be obscure in such matters, under pain of losing one's life.[16]

Nero was a target owing to his own corrupt taste and character, and to their influence on his subservient aristocrats, for as a bad poet, the emperor encouraged a perverse emulation of incompetence. According to Senhouse, in Satire One *"Persius* covertly strikes at *Nero,* some of whose Verses he recites with Scorn and Indignation. He also takes notice of the Noblemen and their abominable Poetry, who in the Luxury of their Fortune, set up for Wits and Judges" (p. 6). John Stirling adds that "as a Friend to true Learning," Persius sharply lashed "the corrupt and degenerate Taste both of the Poets and Orators of his Time" (sig. A3^r), and especially the poetry of Nero. Persius thus appeared to Pope's ancestors and contemporaries as a poet

---

Birch, John Lockman, et al. (1734-41), 7: 327. Subsequent references are cited in the text. See also the Abbé le Monnier, *Satires de Perse* (Paris, 1771), pp. xix-xxi. Le Monnier is aware of, and comments upon, Bayle in several places—pp. xvii-xviii, for example. Holyday, *Aulus Persius Flaccus His Satires* (n. 11 above), sig. A3^v. Subsequent citations from Holyday are given in the text. Stirling, *The Satires of A. Persius Flaccus* (n. 11 above), unsigned sig. A3^r, counting the title page as A1^r. Subsequent citations from Stirling are given in the text.

[16] *Satires de Perse, Traduites en François, avec des remarques* (Paris, 1776), pp. xxviii (*sagesse*) and 116 (*peine de la vie*).

concerned with the decay of letters and with the imperial cause of that decay. "Indignation breaks out more and more because they would make such base and affected Verse," Eelbeck observes of Satire One.[17]

These cultural and political poses evoked a variety of related satiric conventions, four of which are especially useful for our purposes: disguise, dialogue, the nature of the adversarius, and irony.

John Stirling discusses the consequence of Persius's politically enforced obscurity—disguise, or what we might call the use of a persona for the poet, and a historical label or analogue for his victim. Persius, Stirling claims, "was oblig'd to strike at [Nero] under borrowed Names, the better to evade his cruel Resentment" (sig. A3ʳ). Comparable remarks pervade the criticism of Persius throughout the seventeenth and eighteenth centuries. According to Dryden, such role playing begins in the Prologue itself, which hoped to conceal its author's name and station. "He liv'd in the dangerous Times of the tyrant *Nero*; and aims particularly at him, in most of his Satyrs: For which Reason, though he was a *Roman* knight, and of a plentiful Fortune, he wou'd appear in this Prologue, but a Beggarly Poet, who Writes for Bread." In 1728 Thomas Sheridan observes that in Satire One "It is very probable that *Persius* levels at *Nero* under this covert Name" of Polydamus. Sheridan also joins previous commentators and anticipates later ones in saying that in Satire Four Persius "levels at *Nero* under the name of *Alcibiades*, for presuming to undertake the Administration of publick Affairs, without sufficient Qualifications for so great an Undertaking."[18] Just two years thereafter, John Senhouse offers virtually the same argu-

---

[17] *A Prosaic Translation of Aulus Persius Flaccus's Six Satyrs*, p. 15, n*. Subsequent citations from Eelbeck are given in the text.

[18] Dryden, *Poems 1693-1696*, p. 255; italics and Roman type have been reversed; Sheridan, *The Satires of Persius*, 2nd ed. (1739), pp. 6, 60, respectively; italics and Roman type have been reversed in the second quotation.

ment and traces its provenance to Casaubon, who "made it apparent, that the Sting of this Satir was particularly aim'd at *Nero*" (p. 97).

The many shifts of speaker were another reason for the apparent obscurity of Persius. According to Casaubon, because of satire's "affinity with the plots of drama, it is complicated by the shifts of personae" (*Prolegomena*, p. 297). De la Valterie dutifully concurs in 1680 and says that since satire is a species of comedy, there are frequent changes of voice in Persius's poems. The first satire, for example, is "un Dialogue perpetuel." These shifts were thought to have been largely sorted out by the eighteenth century, and so readers knew who was speaking to whom. The dialogue between them, however, is quite different from that of Horace and the Pope of *Fortescue* and *Arbuthnot*, where dialogue is an emblem of dialectic, of the thrust, counterthrust, and resolution of argument in which speakers grow and change. Instead, Persius offers unchanging characters enunciating noble or ignoble set pieces, and, often, with general rather than particular targets. Edward Burnaby Greene observes something along these lines when, in 1779, he says that Horace portrays "*living* Characters" in action, whereas Persius is busy " 'teaching the passions to move' in the higher circle of *Personification*," and that his dialogues were closer to "the spirit of Epic Poesy" than to the conflict between "the human puppets of the *Horatian Drama*." More than forty years later, William Gifford would complain that Persius "drew his ideas of mankind from the lessons of his preceptor, and looked upon human actions in the abstract; not modified and controlled by conventional circumstances, but . . . independent of all extrinsick influence."[19]

---

[19] Abbé de la Valterie, *Les Satyres de Juvénal et de Perse* (Paris, 1680), 2: sig. Liii^r. The translation of Persius is dedicated to Boileau; Burnaby Greene, *The Satires of Persius Paraphrastically Imitated*, pp. xxvii-xviii; Gifford, *The Satires of Aulus Persius Flaccus*, p. xvi. Subsequent citations from this edition are given in the text.

I suspect that Burnaby Greene and Gifford have over-
stated the degree to which disembodied voices palaver in
the thin air of Persius's poems; but there is a satirically
and aesthetically sound reason for such relatively nonter-
restrial conflicts: namely, the participants are so morally
distant that they cannot hear or influence one another.
Eighteenth-century readers knew that the Monitor who
tried to dissuade Persius from writing shared the values of
Nero's court and courtiers. John Aden accurately points
out that Persius is the only one of the three Roman sati-
rists to use a corrupt and uneducable adversarius, one who
is unchanging in his support for values that a decent man
would abandon.[20] Since the satirist cannot "refute" some-
one incapable of understanding his own folly, Persius in-
vites his readers to see the adversarius discredit himself—
a device, we will see, that Pope turns to excellent use in his
Epilogue to the Satires (1738).

As a result of the impenetrable dullness before him,
Persius sometimes must retreat behind the protection of
both masked and revelatory irony. Henry Eelbeck observes
that the fourth satire's apparent attack upon Alcibiades
really is "an Ironical Oration, vehement and very sharp,"
that labels Nero an unprepared ruler "intirely ignorant,
either to condemn the Guilty, or to defend the Innocent"
(p. 43, n*). The sixth satire includes "A Satyrical Irony in
the Person of some third Speaker" (p. 80, n*). In 1752
Edmund Burton praises the politics and political irony in
Satire One, for the satirist could not openly attack his
emperor as a bad poet. Indeed, most auditors praised
Nero's verse, "it being his constant custom to bribe people

---

[20] *Something Like Horace: Studies in the Art and Allusion of Pope's
Horatian Satires* (Nashville, Tenn.: Vanderbilt Univ. Press, 1969), p. 6.
Aden also observes that in this respect "Pope more nearly resembles
[Persius] than he does either Horace, whom he ostensibly imitates, or
Juvenal, with whom he has very little in common at all" (p. 6). Juve-
nal's ninth satire approaches the use of an uneducable adversarius, but
is more like an exchange of monologues than a dialogue.

into an approbation of his ridiculous writings."[21] Hence, Burton says, in a passage that illuminates Persius's use of political opposition, disguise, and irony,

> The following five lines [from line 59] are beautifully couched under a strong irony, and the greater pains we take to discover their beauties, the greater will be the pleasure which results from a true knowledge of their meaning. By the word *Iane* [Janus] we are to understand *Nero*, as by the word *patricius sanguis* [blue-blooded patricians] following, is meant the *Roman* nobility. By this subtle irony *Persius* seems to be paying *Nero* a great compliment; whereas those three lines mean quite the reverse of what they seem to import. (P. 20)

Commentators and readers also were interested in the man behind "Persius" and found that he was both like and unlike his satiric mask. Barten Holyday praises Persius's prudent bravery, political virtue, consequent anger at those without it, and the punishment he must therefore inflict. Such a reincarnation of Brutus and his now-dead Roman virtues shall take his purer fire and burn out "th' envenom'd fogges of vice" from their seat of infection,

> And then inflame
> Them, that they may be lights to their Owne shame;
> Which, as a Comet, may affright the earth
> With horror, at its owne prodigious birth;
> And, with its darting tail threatning dread
> Vengeance, point-out to wrath each guilty head.

F. A., in 1685, relates Persius's bravery to the poet's own virtue, which must overcome all. He thus has the tutor, thought to be a persona for Persius in the third satire, tell his student: "*Dare* to be good;—and *Vertue* be thy Guide; / No way to daring Vertue is deny'd."[22] Henry Eelbeck, on

---

[21] *The Satyrs of Persius* (n. 11, above), p. 19. Subsequent citations are given in the text.

[22] For Holyday, see *Decimus Junius Juvenalis, and Aulus Persius Flaccus Translated and Illustrated* (Oxford, 1673), p. 341, "An Apos-

whose list of *"Encouragers and Subscribers"* Dr. Arbuthnot appears in 1719, characterizes Persius as scorning the vulgar opinion of his Monitor, who discouraged his writing of satires. He would vigorously soldier on, "notwithstanding all the Vengeance that might befal him either from *Nero* the Emperor, or any Nobleman at *Rome"* (p. 3). And, as Senhouse insists, Persius, who "is of a free Spirit, breaks through all these Difficulties, and boldly arraigns the false Judgment of the Age in which he lives" (p. 7).

Prudent bravery, good taste, and animosity to bad taste, clearly bring with them other important traits of personal and literary character. In the first satire Persius describes himself as a teller of harsh truths (lines 56-57, 120-23) and a man whose petulance and spleen (line 12) burst forth in response to miserable art, for he knows true passion and can be moved only by it (lines 90-91). This indignation easily can be, and was, praised as necessary for the opponent of imperial vice. It also could be seen as unpleasant. In his *Poetices* (1561) Julius Caesar Scaliger labels Persius "morosus." By 1674 René Rapin tells readers in France and England that Persius is grave, vehement, obscure, and "speaks not but with *sadness*, what by *Horace* is said with the greatest mirth imaginable, whom sometimes he wou'd imitate; his moroseness scarce ever leaves him, . . . and he never sports, but after the most serious manner in the world." Boileau calls Persius "un Philosophe chagrin"; the Abbé Batteux regards him as grave, serious, and "ever melancholic"; the *Encyclopédie* thinks him "un peu triste," as indeed does Edward Burnaby Greene, who remarks Persius's "gloom of severity" due to the collapse of learning and morals in his age.[23]

---

trophe of the Translator to his Author Persius." The original is italicized. For F. A., see *The Third Satyr of A. Persius*, p. 3.

[23] Scaliger, *Poetices septem libri* (Lyons, 1561), p. 323 ("Persii vero stilus, morosus"); Rapin, *Reflections on Aristotle's Treatise of Poesie* [trans. Thomas Rymer] (1674), p. 139; Boileau, *Oeuvres de M. Boileau Despréaux*, ed. M. de Saint-Marc (Paris, 1747), 1: 116; Batteux, *A Course of the Belles Lettres* (n. 5, above), 3: 155; *Encyclopédie, ou*

Persius clearly had his faults, which clearly did not in-clude political sycophancy. A look at his practice further supports the hypothesis that Persius easily could have been a model for opposition poets using the rhetoric of freedom against tyranny.

IV: PERSIUS AND NERO

Several parts of Persius's small canon suggest utility for eighteenth-century political and literary satire. In Satire Two, for example, Persius offers at least a hint of political causation regarding the decaying mass around him. Mes-sala was the republican hero who fought against Octavian, was defeated, and then joined his cause; he accepted but quickly abandoned the office of first prefect of Rome, be-cause he feared that it provided tyrannical powers. Now, however, we see a picture of Messala's bleary-eyed offspring (line 72) and are invited to accept the norm of what such a man cannot give—namely, not wealth and profit, but a pure mind and honorable soul. The reference to Messala evokes a contrast between noble republican and debased imperial values.

Perhaps such decline is responsible for the situation in Satire Five, where Dama goes from slave to master, from unreliable surety for a loan, to judge, witnesser of deeds, and probably landowner and slaveholder in his own right. You can't make a *Roman* so quickly, Persius complains, as he sees the consequences of such "libertas" (line 173)— the denial of genuinely Roman character traits. Perhaps as well this decline explains the insubordination and in-version of values in Satire Six, where Persius's heir scolds him for being too profligate with money that should ulti-mately go to him when Persius finally has the good man-ners to die (lines 61-74).

Dictionnaire raisonné des sciences des arts et des métiers (Neufchâtel, 1765), 14: 701, s.v. "Satyre," by the Chevalier de Jaucourt; Burnaby Greene, *The Satires of Persius*, p. xxxiv.

These nods and starts, however, had taken greater direction in Satires One and Four, poems consistently seen as covert attacks upon Nero for his abuse of politics and letters, and for his consequent bad influence upon aristocrats and others beneath him. The change from the relationship between Horace and Augustus to Persius and Nero is striking. Horace is essentially social and respectful toward Augustus's court, since it holds several norms to which he can relate; Persius is essentially private because there is no one in Nero's court to whom he can relate; with the exception of his old schoolmaster in Satire Five, Persius himself is the only guide to decent values. For Horace, one must be resolutely independent in an admirably interdependent world—of court and letters, for instance. For Persius "nec te quaesiveris extra" (*Satires*, i, 7): don't look to anyone outside yourself. That remark is a function of his stoicism; it also is a function of the unreliable world in which he lived.

Indeed, the first satire begins with Persius's self-conscious statement of the vacuity of life: Oh the troubles of man. How great the emptiness in human matters. This line may in part be parodic, but it immediately sets the tone for Satire One: the speaker is alone and promptly is challenged by a Monitor who wonders if anyone will read such stuff. No one, Persius replies, or perhaps one or two. What a pity, the Monitor adds. Not at all, says Persius, revelling in his distance from the wells of Roman poetry now defiled, for he scorns the fear that Polydamas, thought to be Nero, will place the miserable poet Labeo above him. He also has a secret that he is bursting to tell, has no one to confide in, but will have to let out sooner or later. "Quid faciam?" (line 12) he complains in words that Juvenal would later use. What can I do? I have a splenetic wit and I must laugh out loud.

Persius has established several conventions and themes in his first twelve lines: a very dim adversarius who represents literary court values that are debased; a satirist in isolation and in a moral and poetic, though not organized political, opposition; a satirist whose nature forces him to laugh at what the rest of the world, as exemplified in the unteachable Monitor, finds acceptable.

Bad taste and the poets' desires to cater to that taste with bad art are everywhere. Polydamus was a covert Nero; the patricians are overt enough in their vulgarity. The *Titos* (for Titienses), one of the three original Roman tribes and those who puffed themselves on their lineage, listen with indecent pleasure to the licentious verse produced for them. The poet who needs praise from such putative sons of Romulus is beyond contempt. Persius, like others among us, may speak like a philosopher but acts like a man, and so he tells his Monitor that he can indeed be tempted by praise; however, not from the mob of those now offering it, whose indiscriminate "euge" and "bene" (line 111) are anything but the truth from those patronizing patrons.

I have suggested ways in which Persius was different from Horace. I suspect that he was aware of some of those differences and played upon them, not only in his contrast between private, social, and sophisticated versus debased poetic worlds, but also in the development of Roman poetry and the attitudes toward Roman government and tradition. For instance, in *Satires*, i. 10, Horace insists that had Lucilius been living in the Augustan age, he would have polished and thus improved his poems. Horace respects while criticizing his satiric grandfather. Persius's Monitor talks as if he too were Augustan: now we have highly polished numbers, as smooth as the finest marble. Yes, Persius replies, uniformly smooth and lofty, so that generic distinctions collapse, and men not fit to write pastorals babble on with epic or tragic themes and even teach such miserable poetic lingo to their children, thus infecting the next generation (lines 63-82). The desired polish of the Augustans has become the conventional and unthinking imposition and propagation of one badly executed literary kind. Yet again, Persius is cut off from the poetic world of his day and emerges as normative in his isolation.

That poetic world, however, remains ominous and powerful. In Horace's *Satires*, ii. 1, Trebatius tells Horace that whether he is right or wrong in attacking some of his victims, he had better be careful, since they may get together and cool off his person or career. Enraged at such potential intimidation, Horace is all the more resolute in pursuing his course; he warns any such ne'er-do-wells that he is well-connected and that in any confrontation, they will lose. Augustus is Horace's and hence satire's friend and is the trump card that wins the day.

For Persius, matters are not so easy, and he again makes clear his difference from the Horatian world by echoing part of it. The Monitor tells Horace—be careful that the doors of the best people don't grow cold toward you, and then adds: don't you hear the barks of the dog? Since Persius cannot take the unusually blunt Horatian way of refutation and affirmation, he retreats to irony: all right, I'll draw everything as white as can be in the future. Everyone and everything will be marvellous! My satire will disappear. But that, he then adds, was not the way of lashing Lucilius or laughing Horace, who attacked Rome and its inhabitants. Can't I say one word? The secret that Persius had been keeping in since his first speech now emerges and substantiates the decline of Rome and poetry. Lucilius lashed the *urbs*; Horace laughed at the individual *amicus*; Persius has difficulty satirizing anyone: "discedo" (lines 107-21). I'll leave, leave writing satire that is. His secret that everyone in Rome is an ass is told to a ditch! Though he concludes with a plea for the right sort of reader, the rest of the poem suggests that such readers are scarce. In a comparable situation, Horace was able to name several elevated and important men in his audience, Maecenas among them, who would set the balance right. Persius had no such names and no such allies.

The explanation for this disappearance of norms has already been suggested in the perceived attack on Nero, one that implies a degradation of values extending from the throne to the patricians to the plebeians, from figurative

and literal father to son. The Messala of the republic is
dead; the decadent Messala of the empire is alive. Persius's
oblique hints are collected and gathered into one clear
statement: "Haec fierent, si testiculi vena [pars: Loeb text]
ulla paterni / Viveret in nobis?" (lines 103-4)—a genteel
version of which might be, Would such stuff be written if
the manhood of our fathers still flowed in our veins? In-
stead, we have a poetically castrated race, whose interior
includes not republican blood but bones without marrow.
These Persian lines upon bad poetry were especially telling,
since they follow the Monitor's recitation of verses the
eighteenth-century commentators thought were written by
Nero himself, whose testiculi were known to help place
their attached member in unorthodox places.

Satire Four offered a related and frequently taken inter-
pretation: the description of Alcibiades as an inept, un-
ready, and luxurious ruler, one known for his homosexual-
ity, was another submerged attack upon Nero, and a lament
for the degradation of *ad exemplum regis*: "The fourth
Satyr is levelled at *Nero* and the young Nobility who re-
sembled him in their Vices," Edward Manwaring says in
1737.[24] The speaker remains alone in a collapsing world

[24] *An Historical and Critical Account of the most Eminent Classical
Authors in Poetry and History* (1737), p. 116. The importance of the
notion of *ad exemplum regis* for the eighteenth century is made clear
in Swift's hostile "On Reading Dr. Young's Satires, Called the Univer-
sal Passion," where we hear that

> all antient Sages
> Decree, that *ad exemplum Regis*,
> Thro' all the Realm his *Virtues* run,
> Rip'ning, and kindling like the Sun.

See *The Poems of Jonathan Swift*, ed. Harold Williams, 2nd ed. (Ox-
ford: Clarendon Press, 1958), 2: 392. The poem was written in 1726
and published in 1734. The problem was treated more bluntly in 1736
by the author of *An Essay on Preferment* (Dublin, 1736). After detail-
ing the dangers self-seeking favorites can inflict on the throne and the
nation, the angry good man cries:

> Yet let us trace this Evil to its source,
> It falls upon the Prince with double force,

and finds his sole norm in Socrates of the distant past. The somber, solitary, pessimistic Persius offered a poetic milieu, a government, and norms far different from those of the congenial Horace talking to his wise Maecenas and, through him, the yet wiser Augustus.

During the Restoration and eighteenth century, then, there was one nearly unchallenged view of the widely read Persius: he was the brave, prudent, serious satirist who attacked moral, political, and literary vice, especially as exemplified by the tasteless, wicked, bribing Nero and his court. Since open attack would have meant death, he resorted to masks, irony, a self-refuting, self-condemning, and uneducable adversarius, and the obscurity his friend and tutor urged upon him; he even refused to have his satires published until after his death, thus assuring that he could be prudently satirical during his lifetime. The decay around him both angered and saddened him, but did not affect his personal ethics, family life, or religious views, all of which were excellent, in spite of the severity and occasional vulgarity in his poems. Though probably not as great a satirist as Horace or Juvenal, he was their moral superior and certainly in their approximate qualitative rank.

For many eighteenth-century readers, Persius and Juvenal shared the lamentably ineffectual opposition to a Caesar and his evocation of the decline of Rome and letters. And for many, Juvenal was the satiric, emotional, and rhetorical fulfillment of the epic in which a lone soldier fights the wicked legions headed by Domitian or another suitable emblem of exalted vice. Here, however, the battle

---

Who chose the minister, and durst not trust,
An upright Servant, daring to be Just;
But chose a Sycophant to keep him blind,
And lull him into his Lethargy of Mind.

(P. 12)

The poem ends with praise of Swift, and was reissued in 1744 as *An Epistle on Preferment, Inscribed to the Rev. Dr. Swift.*

is lost, not merely because the good are outnumbered by the bad, but because the Roman family that once nourished Roman values has ceased to function in the old ways.

V: JUVENAL, THE REPUBLIC, AND THE CAESARS

Juvenal's sixth satire is rightly regarded as a satire against women. His hostility, however, is not addressed so much to licentious women or even to foolishly dense men, as in Boileau's marginally comparable poem; it is addressed to woman as part of the downward evolution of Roman society and values, a retrogression enhanced and possibly caused by behavior of the upper reaches of Roman society in general, and the bad example of the male and female part of the Caesarean household in particular. The poem has an introductory passage berating the folly of Postumus, who wishes to marry in an era long distant from the Saturnian days of virtue, when women actually were chaste. It also has a coda in which the satirist protests the tragic reality of the world he is portraying. Within these confines, however, the poem is framed by two definitive acts by two different wives of the Emperor Claudius.

The first concerns Messalina's unfailing sexual appetite. Juvenal has just discussed the indiscreet conduct of Eppia, a senator's wife who ran off with a gladiator. His low place on the social scale, ugly face, and presumably crass spirit did not inhibit her actions, nor detract from the solid pleasures for which she left her senatorial home. If that troubles you, Juvenal then tells Postumus and his larger audience, look at what Claudius, one of the apotheosized rivals of the gods, had to put up with from his wife Messalina. She would go from his bed to the whorehouses of Rome where, after a full night's work for a full night's pay, she would leave still unsated. She returned to Caesar's pillow with all the smells and stains of the stews on her body. The imperial house and the whorehouse have become interchangeable, as the emperor's own wife commutes be-

tween Caesar's and pander's palace and trades the dignity
of one for the seminal fluids of Rome's phallic dregs in the
other.[25] Juvenal may even imply that Claudius's son Britan-
nicus himself, then heir to the throne, was the fruit of such
liaisons (lines 122-24). The pollution in such a scene is not
merely personal; it is essentially an attack upon the center
of value that Horace saw as benevolently Augustan. The
principle of *ad exemplum regis* often is behind a discussion
of the positive or negative traits of the monarch and his
circle: if Messalina is a whore who violates the duties of
queen, wife, mother, and friend, then other Roman women
follow suit.

Consequently, from the introduction of Messalina at line
116 through most of the remainder of the poem, we see
women breaking every social, moral, and familial bond
Juvenal can conjure up in this his longest poem and, by
extension, his longest attack upon the moral debility of the

----

25 The unpleasant possibilities of such a scene are suggested in Wil-
liam Popple's manuscript translation of the sixth satire:

> With glowing Cheeks and with disorder'd face,
> She mounts the Royal-Bed and scents the place;
> And on Great-Caesar robb'd of his repose,
> The filthy Leavings of a Stew bestows.

See Douce MS. 201, Bodleian Library, Oxford, folio 64. I am grateful
for permission to quote from this manuscript. For another adaptation
of this section, see *The History of Insipids, A Lampoon, By the Lord
Roch——r. With his Farewell: 1680 Together with Marvell's Ghost.
By Mr. [John] Ayloff* (1709). "Rochester's Farewell" includes a savage
attack on the Duchess of Mazarine, and a possible "source" for Dry-
den's *MacFlecknoe* (1682), lines 29-30: "Lewd *Messaline* was but a Type
of thee, / Thou highest last degree of Lechery." See pp. 12-13. Pope
owned a copy of this poem, and wrote on its title page: "Probably by
the LdDorset." See Maynard Mack, "Pope's Books: A Biographical
Survey with a Finding List," in *English Literature in the Age of Dis-
guise*, ed. Maximillian E. Novak (Berkeley and Los Angeles: Univ. of
California Press, 1977), p. 286.

For varyingly useful modern overviews of Juvenal's satires, see Gilbert
Highet, *Juvenal the Satirist* (Oxford: Clarendon Press, 1954), and
J. Gérard, *Juvénal et la réalité contemporaine* (Paris: Société d'Edition
"Les Belles Lettres," 1976), and its extensive bibliographies.

empire. Juvenal, indeed, reminds us that his initial statement that female virtue can be found only in Saturnian days was a smoke screen: he characteristically invokes the republican past as the norm against which the empire should be judged. All three families he cites were heroes of the republic. Blind Metellus was often thought to have lost his sight when saving an image of Pallas Athene from fire in the temple of Vesta, the chaste goddess of the hearth, the emblem of the Roman family as communal unit and as the state, whose shrine was the most sacred in Roman religion.[26] Such patriotic and spiritual echoes were intended, fruitlessly one suspects, to shame the granddaughters of Lepidus, blind Metellus, and Fabius Gurges, who could not have imagined the excesses of modern patrician women.

Near the end of the poem, Juvenal describes several different abuses of the marital bed that suggest the decay of the Roman family—not merely in the modern sense of family, but of historical lineage, of the *gens* from which the state's highest officers were culled. Poor women, he says, bear their children; not so for the wealthier sort who have abortions and murder the race in the womb. Upon second thought, this is just as well for the husband, since his child may turn out to be an Ethiopian. Moreover, there are many supposititious children taken from fountains, at which children were abandoned, and transported by Fortune to the best families, where they are given good names, and whence they unworthily become priests of religion and of Mars. Women, alas, do wrong even when they wish to "love" their husbands, for Caligula's wife Caesonia drove him mad by giving him a love potion (lines 614-16).

By invoking the imperial family, the aberrant Caligula

[26] See Desprez, ed. (note 8, above), pp. 180-81n, and M. Aemilius Lepidus (and the Lepidus family), Caecilius Metellus, and Fabius Gurges in Louis Moréry, *Le Grand dictionaire historique* (Lyons, 1674), 8th ed. (Amsterdam, 1718). Martin Madan, *A New and Literal Translation of Juvenal and Persius*, 1: 265-66, and Hodgson, *The Satires of Juvenal* (n. 7 above), p. 433, give more concise notes.

and his foolish wife, Juvenal signals that the last part of the frame is about to be set in place. "Quae non faciet, quod principis uxor?" (line 616). Who will not follow when Caesar's wife leads? The statement of *ad exempla reginae* could not be clearer, and so we see a reintroduction of Claudius, now with a new and more deadly wife, Agrippina the younger, who fed her princeps poisoned mushrooms and killed him. This was, however, less horrible than Caesonia's actions, since in his madness Caligula demanded fire, sword, torture, and the consequent bloody deaths of many innocent eminent men. The Emperor Claudius, though, was the victim not only of his wife but of himself. Since Agrippina the younger was Claudius's niece, she could not legally marry her uncle, and so Claudius changed the law. To satisfy her ambition he adopted her son L. Domitius Ahenobarbus, better known thereafter as the Emperor Nero, and removed his own son Britannicus from immediate succession. When Agrippina later seemed to back Britannicus's claim to the throne, Nero had her killed. Agrippina, then, the great-granddaughter of Augustus, incestuously married her uncle, who manipulated the law on her behalf, placed her son ahead of the rightful heir, and suffered matricide in return. The consequences of Claudius Caesar's violation of order through a version of uxoriousness are plain and include regicide through Agrippina's culinary expertise.

It seems reasonable to say that such behavior is less than normative. Perhaps that is why at this point Juvenal mentions neither Claudius's name nor rank, and describes him in uncomplimentary terms. At the beginning, the Emperor Claudius was one of the "rivales Divorum" (line 115); now he is an insignificant murdered old man packed off to the hereafter with his palsied head and blubbering lips. Claudius has helped to create the world that finally destroys him as emperor, as man, and as simple object of compassion or respect.

Because other women will do what the empress has done,

79

the following paragraph is nearly anticlimactic, as murder moves down the social ladder. Juvenal is frighteningly matter of fact in saying that it has long been regarded as quite proper indeed for a mother to slay her step-son; but now wealthy young men with estates had better look out, since a mother will gladly poison the pastries she has baked for him. The nourishing Roman mother has been replaced by the poisoning Roman mother. "Quae non faciet quod principis uxor?" She merely expands upon the actions of the empress, trading pastry for mushrooms and a son for a husband. In lines Pope may have recalled for the beginning of the second *Dialogue* of the *Epilogue to the Satires* (1738), Juvenal assures his readers that this all has external warrant and is verifiable. Pontia, he tells us, poisoned her two children at dinner and would have poisoned seven if that was the fruit of her womb. No, this is not satire exceeding limits and breaking into the higher flights and acts of tragedy and fantasy; it is a statement of satiric truth, one that uses the collapse of Roman womanhood as a sign of the collapse of republican virtue and then of the empire itself. Even within the frame of the poem an emperor's first wife is a whore, and his second wife is an incestuous murderer who soon is killed by her unworthy son indebted to her for his throne.

Juvenal's sixth satire is a world of closure, of no exit from the decline, collapse, and abysmal conduct everywhere. The norms are found in a Saturnian golden age or more realistically in distant republican heroes. Tom Brown is correct when, in his dialogue between Juvenal and Boileau, he has the Roman satirist sternly tell his French imitator that the sixth satire offers no living norms whatsoever.[27]

This brief analysis of Juvenal's satiric mode of proceeding as regards contemporary norms and government can be expanded. Satire One is the impassioned description of a

---

[27] *The Works of Mr. Thomas Brown* (n. 12 above), 2: 90.

world running down; Satire Three portrays an urban scene so uniformly corrupt that Umbricius must leave and seek out morally republican enclaves in the country; Satire Five extols the "new man" Cicero as a genuine patriot and father of his nation, whereas the noble Octavian, the future Augustus, was a butcher at Philippi, when Brutus, Cassius, and Roman liberty died. In Satire Nine, Edward Manwaring says, Juvenal "makes it no wonder the Nobility should be mimics, when the Prince [Nero] is a Fidler."[28] As Johnson's *London* (1738) denotes, such poems and their devices were given political interpretations during the seventeenth and eighteenth centuries.

Several points should emerge from this review of Roman satiric conventions used to praise or blame respective governments. In spite of Persius's use of some Horatian techniques, his satire includes more of Juvenal's declining world than Horace's stable one, and thus includes more bitterness than equanimity. Horatian dialogue is transmuted by this Juvenalian spirit of hostility to an adversarius who wishes only to gain official praise, even at the expense of truth and virtue. The choice of satiric options, including those apparently in the fragments of Lucilius, thus was heavily weighted on the side of a satirist portraying himself as the brave, often outnumbered, hostile enemy of daring vice performed or inspired by those highly placed in the state. Perhaps of equal importance, however, was that there were these several options available for a sympathetic and synthesizing individual talent. The first great such exemplar was Boileau, whose own practice would be rendered suspect to his later English colleagues.

28 *An Historical and Critical Account* (n. 24 above), p. 109.

CHAPTER 3

Boileau: "As *Horace* did before me, so will I"

T HE SATIRES OF Horace, Juvenal, and Persius were well edited and annotated and were propagated through much of seventeenth-century Europe. The dominant British taste was for the sublime Juvenal and obscure Persius, though Horace, once regarded as harsh and biting, was beginning to be thought more elegant and polished than he had seemed under the shadow of the Juvenalian umbrella; by the later seventeenth century his temperate voice had established itself as a clear alternative to Juvenal's. In France, on the other hand, the process of Horatianizing had begun earlier and lasted longer, so that the primary satiric model was Horace with generous dollops of Juvenalian anger and Persian solemnity added as required—fairly near, that is, to reversing the British paradigm. In each case contemporaries assume that modern satire has a pool of satiric poetry behind it. Some of these poems are more pleasing than others; some proceed in different ways from others; some are morally dubious; but all are necessary for the modern to know so that he can vary his voice with his intention, record the echoes as they rebound from Rome's marble walls, keep the past alive in the present, and preserve both continuity and opportunities for comparison and contrast. Louis XIV, after all, was greater still when the French saw him as a veritable Augustus in good taste and patronage of the arts; and Louis XIV was yet more ominous when the English saw him as a veritable Augustus in his absolutism and desire for universal monarchy. For the former, Horatian respect and civilized discourse are appropriate, though of course at times one must raise one's voice to deal with the aberrant rascals that even the best of states may have. For the latter, Juvenalian outrage and angry protest are appropriate, though of course at times one must lower one's voice to deal with the lesser threats that even the worst of states may have. Both views require the pooling of conventions for full satiric coherence, and as we have seen, Persius himself has something of each earlier and later mode, together with his own solemnity of vision, that of the *philosophe chagrin*, as Boileau called him.

Until Boileau wrote his satires and epistles between 1658 and 1700, however, there was no great modern satirist able to turn those conventions to his own use and thus establish the beachhead through which later writers could pass on the way to Parnassus. Rochester's talent was essentially one of gilded misanthropy and self-hatred. He flirted with Horatianism in the "Allusion to Horace" (1675) but left the affair unconsummated when he returned to his more agreeable and less virtuous muse. Robert Gould was committed to what he thought the stridently outraged voice of Juvenal in English garb. Oldham tried Horace in small doses but gained his essential praise and dispraise for his severe, stabbing, Juvenalian satires and attacks upon the Jesuits and their alien supporters. Dryden lowered the decibels and burnished the knives of Restoration satire; but his satiric talent was mock-heroic, ratiocinative, and allegoric, and fell outside of the classical paths, while his translations were excellent efforts that mirrored, more than created, developing fashions. Tom Brown's "Essay on English Satire" (1707), for example, alludes to Dryden's "Discourse" on satire prefaced to his translation of Juvenal and Persius, but does not mention Dryden's own satires.[1] Boileau, I believe, is the man to whom we must turn for an early model of how to make a synthesized, modern, formal verse satire.

[1] *The Works of Mr. Thomas Brown*, 4th ed. (1715), 1: 27-32 for the "Essay," pp. 27-28 for the allusion to Dryden. Brown discusses Rochester, Dorset, and Oldham, "who are the greatest *Satirists* of the English" (p. 29).

BOILEAU

I: The Syncretic Satirist

Boileau's discussion of classical satire in his *Art Poétique*
(1674) and its English versions illustrate both his mingled
inheritance and his foreign readers' attempts to adjust that
recipe for their own taste. Lucilius, the first Roman satirist,
held the mirror to the Romans and their vices, showing
the virtuous on foot and the vicious in a carriage. Horace
added his playful wit to this satiric bitterness, so that no
fool escaped with impunity. Unhappy the man who was
drawn into their verse! Persius was obscure, forceful, and
witty, and was more concise in words than in meaning.
In these portraits Lucilius and Horace each have been
given four lines and Persius two; Juvenal is given eleven,
or more than the first three combined.

> Juvénal, élevé dans les cris de l'Ecole,
> Poussa jusqu'à l'excès sa mordante hyperbole.
> Ses ouvrages, tout pleins d'affreuses véritéz.
> Etincelent pourtant de sublimes beautéz;
> Soit que sur un Ecrit arrivé de Caprée,
> Il brise de Séjan la statue adorée:
> Soit qu'il fasse au Conseil courir les Sénateurs;
> D'un Tiran soupconneux, pâles adulateurs:
> Ou que, poussant à bout la luxure Latine,
> Aux Portefaix de Rome il vende Messaline.
> Ses Ecrits pleins de feu partout brillent aux yeux.[2]

Boileau has captured one essential view of the libertarian
Juvenal, the enemy of tyrants, the exalted teller of frightful
truths. Immediately thereafter he adds: "De ces Maîtres
sçavans, disciple ingénieux, / Regnier seul parmi nous
formé sur leurs modeles" (1: 209). Even though Juvenal
seems the dominant satirist, it is "leurs modeles" collec-
tively upon which Regnier forms himself, and for which
he is praised.

[2] *Oeuvres de Boileau Despréaux*, ed. Charles Brosette (Geneva, 1716),
1: 208. Subsequent quotations from this edition are cited in the text.

The *Art Poétique* was Englished by Sir William Soames, with Dryden's additions and modernizings, in 1683, and turned that couplet away from Regnier and toward what the young student himself should be doing.[3] Soames, however, also changes "ces Maîtres" to "such a Master" (p. 25), and since Juvenal comes immediately before this line, he seems to be Soames's referrent. This Juvenalian putsch— either a careless oversight or a conscious adaptation—was corrected in the second edition of 1708, where we see the more accurate "To imitate such masters be your aim." This is the same version that also appears in "Ozell's" Boileau of 1712, a further polishing of Soames.[4]

The English vacillation about whom to follow suggests a return to a reasonable rendering of Boileau's meaning, though it also suggests that some readers may have thought

[3] Tonson offers this remark in his Advertisement to *The Art of Poetry*, . . . *Made English by Sir William Soame, Bart. And Revis'd and Alter'd by Mr. John Dryden*: "I saw the Manuscript lye in Mr. *Dryden's* Hands for above Six Months, who made very considerable Alterations in it, particularly the beginning of the 4th *Canto*; and it being his Opinion that it would be better to apply the Poem to *English* Writers, than to keep the *French* Names, as it was first Translated, Sir *William* desired he would take the Pains to make that Alteration, and accordingly that was entirely done by Mr. *Dryden*." See *The Annual Miscellany: for the Year 1694. Being the Fourth Part of Miscellany Poems*, 2nd ed. (1708), sig. A2^r.

[4] For these, see *The Art of Poetry, Written in French by the Sieur de Boileau, Made English*, p. 25 in the 1683 version, p. 17 in the 1708 and 1710 versions, and *The Works of Monsieur Boileau. Made English from the last Paris Edition, By Several Hands* (with *Le Lutrin* and probably other works by John Ozell), 2nd ed. (1736), 1: 104. Subsequent citations to Boileau's English *Works* are from this edition and are given in the text. The French and first English version—with Juvenal as apparent Master—were quoted with approval in Peter Motteux's *Gentleman's Journal: Or The Monthly Miscellany. By Way of Letter to a Gentleman in the Country* 1 (October 1692): 7. Pope owned and annotated the 1683 *Art of Poetry*, as well as the 1716, Geneva, *Oeuvres de Boileau* (n. 2 above). See Maynard Mack, "Pope's Books: A Biographical Survey with a Finding List," in *English Literature in the Age of Disguise*, ed. Maximillian E. Novak (Berkeley and Los Angeles: Univ. of California Press, 1977), pp. 239, 240.

Juvenal the basic model of satire. More important, how-
ever, is the combined addition and subtraction in the final,
Ozell, version, where we hear that "In what [Juvenal]
Writes there's something of Divine" and "In all he Writes
appears a noble Flame" (1: 104). Both divinity and nobility
are missing in Boileau's description of Juvenal, and of Lu-
cilius, Horace, and Persius. Boileau had in fact hinted that
Juvenal may have gone too far or, almost as bad, that he
went as far as he could with rhetorical bitterness: Juvenal
"Poussa jusqu'à l'exces sa mordante hyperbole." In
Soames's first version, we read that Juvenal did in fact go
too far (p. 24); in the revised Soames and Ozell versions,
this appears merely as "*Juvenal*, with Rhetorician's Rage, /
Scourg'd the rank Vices of a wicked Age" (1: 103). In the
Art Poétique in England between 1683 and 1712, then,
Juvenal loses his suggestion of excess and gains nobility and
divinity.

The balanced examination of satirists, with tilting to the
side that taste dictated, was not limited to the *Art Poétique*
or to theoretical pronouncements. Readers of Boileau in
France and Britain throughout the seventeenth and eight-
eenth centuries comment on his mingling of satiric traits
and praise him for, in one poet's terms, having "such a
Genius . . . / As tickles us at once and bites." John Dennis,
for instance, knows that Horatian and Juvenalian satire
are very different; one includes pleasantry, the other fire.
Since Boileau has both, he "is equal to either of the *Roman*
satirists." Dryden similarly argues that Boileau is "a living
Horace and *Juvenal*," while Joseph Trapp in 1711 and Ed-
ward Young in 1728 say much the same thing. Far later,
young Vicesimus Knox also thinks that "Boileau seems to
have blended with judgment the manner of Horace and
Juvenal." In the year that saw the publication of *Lyrical
Ballads*, when a new world was supposed to have dawned
upon the waiting multitude, T. J. Mathias makes this fa-
miliar observation: Boileau "alternately assumes the char-
acter of the three great Romans. . . . He is their true and
lawful brother," and part of our important "fraternal

league" with them. The youngest brother nonetheless retains his originality while advancing morality: he "is the just and adequate representative of Horace, Juvenal, and Persius united, *without one indecent blemish.*"[5]

French readers were even more attracted to Boileau's magnetic force, and both praised and blamed him for his collection of previous satiric conventions. One detractor accused him of merely translating Horace and Juvenal for his own purposes, but so far from denying such a claim, Boileau admitted and gloried in it. In 1685 Jacques Pradon sarcastically tells Boileau that "Vous étes mon Horace, mon Perse, mon Juvénal, & je vous trouve seul dans ces trois hommes." Fifteen years thereafter, Pierre Henry observes that Boileau joins the salt of Horace to the spleen of Juvenal. The author of *Remarks on the Letters concerning England and France* (1726) adds that "we equal M. *Despreaux* to the Antients, that is, to *Horace* and *Juvenal*"; and in 1749 the Abbé Yart says, "Lorsque Boileau représente Perse & Juvénal, il imite la précision de l'un & l'énergie de l'autre."[6]

Such remarks could only have pleased Boileau, for syn-

---

[5] *The Second, Fourth, and Seventh Satyrs of Monsieur Boileau Imitated* (1696), sig. A6^v, the original is italicized; Dennis, *The Advancement and Reformation of Modern Poetry* (1701), in *The Critical Works of John Dennis*, ed. Edward Niles Hooker (Baltimore: The Johns Hopkins Univ. Press, 1967), 1: 226; Dryden, "Discourse" on satire, in The Works of John Dryden, vol. 4, *Poems 1693-1696*, ed. A. B. Chambers, William Frost, and Vinton A. Dearing (Berkeley and Los Angeles: Univ. of California Press, 1974), p. 12; Trapp, *Praelectiones Poeticae* (1711-1719), trans. William Bowyer and William Clarke as *Lectures on Poetry Read in the Schools of Natural Philosophy at Oxford* (1742), p. 236; Young, *Love of Fame, The Universal Passion*, 2nd ed. (1728), sig. A4^v; Knox, "On Satire and Satirists," in *Essays Moral and Literary* (1778), 2: 152; Mathias, *Pursuits of Literature*, 6th ed. (1798), pp. xxviii, and p. 69 note f (without blemish).

[6] Pradon, *Nouvelles Remarques sur tous les ouvrages de Sieur D* * ** (The Hague [Lyons]), p. 14; Henry, *Le Pour, et le contre de marriage, avec la critique du Sr. Boisleau* (Lille, 1700), p. 68; *Remarks on the Letters*, p. 51; Yart, *Idée de la poësie Angloise, ou traduction des meilleurs poëtes Angloises . . .* (Paris, 1749-56), 2 (1749): 90n.

thesizing was important to him as a man and as a satirist. The epigram under his engraving in several editions of his works was encouraged by Le Verrier and probably written by Boileau himself. Its final couplet is: "J'ai sceu dans mes Escrits docte, enjoué, sublime, / Rassembler en moi Perse, Horace, et Juvénal." Or as the English translator puts it, while misarranging the important order of the first line, *"Learned, Sublime, & Gay, in all he writes: / He Persius, Horace, Juvenal unites."*[7] Boileau tells Le Verrier that the French lines are his "fidèle portrait," and he tells Brosette, with comparable approval, "Suppose—que cela fust vrai, *docte* respondant admirablement à Perse, *enjoué,* à Horace, et *sublime* à Juvénal."[8] He also was pleased that his readers would see his works edited "avec des notes, et surtout avec la conférence et la parallèle des endroits d'Horace et de Juvénal" that he had imitated. The major editions by Brosette (1716) and Saint-Marc (1747), among others, emphasize those points of common thought and borrowing from the masters, while also insisting that Boileau borrowed only to repay in French gold equal or superior to rusty ancient coins. This mingling need not be limited to overt borrowing of design or detail; it also could

7 The French is quoted from the lines beneath the Drevet engraving in *Oeuvres de Boileau Despréaux . . . avec des remarques & dissertations critiques,* ed. M. de Saint-Marc (Paris, 1747), 5: 165; see 2: 408 for another version. The English is from the lines beneath the frontispiece in *Works* (n. 4 above), volume 1.

8 Boileau to Le Verrier, in *Oeuvres de Boileau,* ed. Saint Marc, 5: 165. See also *Les Satires de Boileau commentées par lui-meme et publiées avec des notes par Frederic Lachèvre: Reproduction du commentaire inédit de Pierre le Verrier avec les corrections autographes de Despréaux* (Courmenil, 1906), p. ix. For Brosette, see *Correspondence entre Boileau Despréaux et Brosette,* ed. Auguste Laverdet (Paris, 1858), p. 47. The epigram was not always treated with respect. Isaac Disraeli observes: "The inscription under Boileau's portrait, describing his character with lavish panegyric, and a preference to Juvenal and Horace, is unfortunately known to have been written by himself." *An Essay on the Manners and Genius of the Literary Character* (1795), p. 116n.

be, and commonly was, an adaptation of an earlier satirist's tones. Brosette and Saint-Marc both report of Satire Eight, concerning man, for example: "Cette SATIRE est tout à fait dans le goust de *Perse*, & marque un Philosophe chagrin, & qui ne peut plus souffrir les vices des Hommes." Saint-Marc adds that this is what Boileau himself said. In spite of relatively few overt echoes, Persius was indeed extremely influential for Boileau. As Le Verrier writes, with Boileau's approval and corrections of his manuscript, "J'ay souvent ouy dire à l'autheur que dans tout ce qu'il avoit pris de ces trois Poëtes, rien ne luy avoit plus réussi que ce qu'il avoit imité de Perse."[9]

Other borrowings were more obvious. The notes to Brosette's edition of Boileau record thirty-four imitations of Horace (eighteen to the *Satires*, twelve to *Epistles*, one to *Epodes*, one to *Odes*, two to *Ars Poetica*), thirty-three of Juvenal, and seven of Persius. Boileau's twelve satires also are indebted to the structure or governing ideas of his Latin predecessors: Horace provides inspiration or precedent for Satires Three, Seven, Nine, and perhaps Four; Juvenal evokes Satires One, Five, Six, Ten, and perhaps Eleven; and Persius influences Satire Eight. Only Satires Two and Twelve apparently lack classical sources, though Two has Horatian echoes. As Saint-Marc says of Boileau, the French moderns not only have borrowed from Ariosto, but have taken all that suited them in Horace, Persius, and Juvenal (1: 106). A look at Boileau's own practice in matters of tone and conventions confirms this, and confirms his, shall we say, Sabine bias.

II: Boileau's Mingled Practice and Horatian Sympathies

Boileau's excellent third epistle, to M. Arnauld, starts in medias res, as if we have just been made privy to an intelli-

[9] Brosette, *Oeuvres de Boileau*, 1: 129; Saint-Marc, *Oeuvres de Boileau*, 1: 116; Le Verrier, *Les Satires de Boileau commentées par lui-même*, p. 70.

gent and ongoing dialogue between old friends. This device
immediately establishes a social context in which the poet
praises Arnauld and subtly establishes his own complicity
in the fraud that all of us, and poets in particular, need to
get by in life. "Yes, ARNAULD, thou dost easily perceive /
The Fraud of those whose Art is to deceive" (2: 29). We
are only too capable of being our own worst enemies, and
of refusing to change merely because we will be upbraided
for changing (2: 31). Hence we fear the judgments of oth-
ers, remain powerless over our own wills, and continue in
paths we know lead nowhere but to unpleasant places we
already have been. The speaker includes himself in the
human situation, as indeed the social Horatian epistolary
satirist must, for his paradoxical argument on authority
includes an admission of weakness. The Horatian thereby
gains our favor by being like his fallible but morally decent
reader, whose faults he often forgives because they are part
of the baggage of mortality. "Shame" both forces and re-
flects vice, and is, everyone knows, hateful and to be rooted
out; yet notice that Boileau treats Shame as if it were a
communicable disease from which he too suffers and whose
ravages he must tolerate while resisting.

> Ev'n I my self, who thus against it Rhyme,
> Its mighty Pow'r by sad Experience know,
> Compell'd to what I blame so much, to bow:
> Conscious of both the Folly and the Harm,
> My self, in vain, I with weak Virtue arm.
> Thus am I always Sliding, and in Doubt,
> I've always in the Slough of Vice a Foot,
> For one gets in, so soon as t'others out.
>
> (2: 36)

Boileau's Horatian poem includes the satirist in its objects
of satire and its norms of satire, for in spite of continued
defeats, the speaker nonetheless pulls his foot out of the
Slough of Vice and avoids the Slough of Despond. Such a
man has the perceptive and sympathetic Arnauld, "Doctor

of the Sorbonne," as his friend and guide, one for whom
knowledge of the world does not deny faith in an after-
world and includes awareness of the reason for the mess in
which we find ourselves.

This point suggests another aspect of Boileau's Horatian
guise—namely, a theory of causation that absolves the rul-
ers from any blame for making the world which requires
satire. Persius, Juvenal, and Pope know just whom to
blame, and worry those at the center of government. For
Boileau, we are corrupt not because of any maladministra-
tion or immorality by the crown, but because in Adam's
fall we sinnéd all.

> 'Tis [shame] who dost undo us all, who first
> The Race of Man in *Adam*'s Ruin curst:
> By thee our Father fell, and fondly proud
> Of a false Blessing and mistaken Good,
> He durst not his deceitful Consort blame;
> And parted with his Paradise thro' *Shame*.
>
> .   .   .   .
>
> From *Adam*'s Fall we all our Evils date,
> He lost with Innocence his happy State:
> And by his wandring in forbidden Ways,
> His Race, of cruel Woe a Tribute pays.
>
> (2: 33, 34)

Boileau faces and accepts his and our weakness, while fight-
ing them with the help of the social and moral channels
that a letter to a sympathetic, sharp-eyed theologian im-
plies. He also places the fault for human error in the per-
spective of the fall of man and its example of how dreadful
the inability to conquer our shame can be. Boileau's epis-
tolary satiric world is ordered; it provides a way out, as it
were, and keeps its norms functioning before us, one of
which is the pleasant speaker and poet who is threatened
but not defeated.

Boileau's protection of his norms thus denotes protection

of his king, who remains beyond the range of blamable causation. This is clear in Boileau's sixth satire, which imitates those parts of Juvenal's third satire (the danger and difficulty of life in Rome) that Boileau omitted from his first satire. Such partition gives us a less ominous and massive world than Juvenal's far longer and grimmer poem, though the French effort is more enclosed, offers no escape, and thus makes one even more frantic than Juvenal's downtrodden poor Roman who leaves while he can. Boileau is Juvenalian in many other ways—his speaker is alienated from his urban environment; he seems to be the only one in Paris with either sense or virtue; he is victimized and must speak out or burst. Yet Boileau lowers the tone of his original and, as Saint-Marc notes, turns some of its indignation into comedy,[10] as perhaps he must if he is to eliminate the temporal cause of corruption. His satire is directed at the noise and discomfort of Paris, at the city as city, not, as in Juvenal, at the city as emblem of decadent empire. In Juvenal's poem, for example, Rome is overrun by offensive aliens who submerge the values that once made Rome great. Aliens have no place in Boileau's poem because Paris, though disadvantageous in several ways, remains the center of a thriving French universe. Johnson was far closer to Juvenal when he turned his *London* (1738) into an antiadministration poem. Juvenal's virtuous impoverished Roman is crushed to death by the marble from an overturned broken cart—his body is crushed as the spirit of Rome already had been crushed. In Boileau the burdened cart "runs against a Coach, and breaks a Spoke, / And overturns it with a furious Shock" (1: 196). This causes a massive traffic jam, as coach is blocked by coach, the line lengthens, a drove of oxen appears, mules bray, horses press in upon the crowd, soldiers futilely try to restore order, and the bedraggled poet is set upon, soiled, drenched by rain, and finally escapes an angrier and dirtier

[10] *Oeuvres de Boileau,* 5: 372.

man. Boileau's city is the frustrating, horrifying, vibrant, and passionate force that repels and attracts the poet who does not leave it, whereas Juvenal's is the (cinematic) Frankenstein monster destroying those who created it. This difference in intention was noted in Maupetit's 1779 translation of Juvenal. The Roman poet is superior to Boileau in his two imitations, Maupetit argues, not only because Juvenal has more spirit, but also because he demonstrates more of a fund of irrepressible tenderness for his country.[11]

Another of Boileau's Juvenalian poems shows how the Roman is put into Gallic dress and also how certain clear Persian devices can blend with the Juvenalian framework. Boileau's tenth satire draws deeply upon Juvenal's fiercely misogynist sixth satire. Unlike his distant brother, however, Boileau gives us a poem that is a dialogue rather than a monologue or diatribe, and thus he suggests a Horatian or, yet more, Persian exchange. Boileau at once invokes both Juvenal and his own recalcitrant friend Alcippe who, unlike the perceptive Arnauld of Epistle Three, is both grumpy toward the speaker and dim regarding himself.

> "When you have said your worst 'twill be no more
> "Than *Juvenal*, whose Vein you thus adore,
> "Had told us with his utmost Spite before.
>
> . . . .
>
> "How far beyond your Railery is this?
> "These Words have in his Mouth an *Emphasis*.
>
> (1: 254)

This "emphasis" is different from Boileau's and is wasted on his friend, who still needs a lecture he must have read, in more violent form, in a poem some sixteen hundred years old. Boileau's Satire Ten thus opposes two essential targets—the obvious one is the varied discomforts the woman is pleased to inflict upon the man in the married

---

[11] *Satires de Juvénal* (Paris, 1779), p. 70.

state. Such a wife's characteristic traits may include infidel-
ity, coquettishness, avarice, vanity, gaming, penuriousness,
jealousy, hypochondria, bookishness, pride in ancestry, re-
ligious hypocrisy, carnality with her confessor, censorious-
ness, lechery, drunkenness, smoking and, one is made to
feel through the piling on of portraits, any number of other
vices from an infinitely expandable catalogue of woman's
malfeasance. Such a Juvenalian technique pushes hard in
the direction of closure within a world that encircles one
like a python caressing its intended meal. However abun-
dant this catalogue may seem, it therefore scarcely begins
to describe the female condition:

> 'tis in vain
> To think of all for thousands still remain.
> Three Quarters of 'em are untouch'd at least,
> I'm tir'd, and will excuse you of the rest.
>
> (1: 298-99)

The satire's other chief target is the blandly uncompre-
hending adversarius who rushes into the marital state not
knowing he is a bull being led to the slaughter, or at least
not believing the advice that Boileau's speaker, with his
announced Juvenalian precedent, offers and offers. The
satire on woman therefore also is a satire on man, who is as
necessary to his spouse as the masochist to the sadist or the
male to the female praying mantis. Woman is vilely in-
corrigible, and man is stupidly uneducable. If womankind,
and Alcippe's own wife in particular, is so dreadful, why
Alcippe will simply divorce her, return her dowry like the
jolly good sort he is, and go on his single way. Worse and
worse, Boileau tells the hopeless youth. She won't go! "And
can you think she'll quit the dear Delight / Of Teazing,
Plaguing and the Sweets of Spite" (1: 300)? No—she wants
the strife of marriage as much as the strife of suing him to
get more than her dowry. The dolt had better keep "the
Plague of Plagues, your Wife" (1: 302).

In Boileau's blackly comic satire, the grim marital situa-

tion is part of the human situation, and is not peculiar
to seventeenth-century France, not a function of the Bour-
bon Louis XIV, and not politically emblematic, as Al-
cippe's opening remarks make clear. Again we hear about
the ultimate cause in our "Grandsire *Adam*" (1: 259).
Juvenal is essentially different in portraying his world of
female aberration. The portraits not only are uglier and in
some cases obscene; we remember that they also portray
woman and the family, once the respected center of a
matriarchal and powerful republic, in the gravest state of
collapse under the Emperor Nero, and that Messalina, the
Emperor Claudius's wife, was a royal volunteer in the
stews. Sexual morals during the Sun King's reign in Ver-
sailles may have lapsed from the strictest virtue on rare
occasions. If so, however, such uncommon events went un-
celebrated in Boileau's satire, which, in this sense, is un-
Juvenalian.

It is in another sense as well. Juvenal's poem is a ha-
ranguing monologue; Boileau's poem is a dialogue that is
disproportionately on Boileau's side, but a dialogue none-
theless. Horace's technique also was different, for his ad-
versarius was rarely quite so incapable of learning. Persius,
on the other hand, did offer a model in his first satire, in
which a corrupt and morally unchangeable second speaker
remains stolid from beginning to end. Though I am not
suggesting direct influence in this case—Alcippe is ignorant
rather than hostile—I am suggesting that Persius's conven-
tion of the uneducable adversarius was in the pool of de-
vices from which Boileau could draw when composing his
modern poem.

Such grafting of the new to the old is present, in subtler
ways, in Boileau's eighth satire, avowedly in the taste of
Persius. Again we have the dense adversarius whose pride
refuses to let him see, and whose theological knowledge,
unlike that of Arnauld in the third epistle, is a hindrance
not a help to his humanity and his ability to help others.
In this sense one part of Persius's world is more enclosed

than Juvenal's, for it offers no education in spite of the
exchange between its characters. Communication is an
empty gesture. Moreover, that dark world includes disillu-
sion that Horace avoids by mocking many of his own aspi-
rations and by finding norms in the political state, and that
Juvenal avoids by indignant exclamatory brilliance and
nostalgic republicanism that recreates Rome in the country-
side and country of his own mind. Persius's darkness is
well captured in Boileau's eighth satire, as translated by
Oldham in 1682, corrected by Ozell in 1712 and, by the
way, neither captured nor sought in Rochester's imitation,
his *Satyr against Reason and Mankind* (1679).

> 'Tis Man, 'Tis Man alone, that worst of Brutes,
> Who first brought up the Trade of cutting Throats,
> Did Honour first, the barbarous Term devise,
> Unknown to all the gentle Savages;
> 'Twas not enough, his Hand was taught by Hell,
> To Knead Salt-Petre, and to sharpen Steel.
> Farther to Plague the World, he must ingross
> Huge *Codes* and bulky *Pandects* of the Laws,
> With Doctors Glosses to perplex the Cause.
> Where darken'd Equity is kept from light,
> And under Heaps of Authors buried quite.
>
> (1: 219)

Here is the *philosophe chagrin* Boileau saw. We now may
understand in part, at least, what Le Verrier means when
he reports he had often heard it said that of all Boileau
had borrowed from the three satirists, nothing had been
more successful than what he had imitated from Persius.[12]
   One of Boileau's essential satiric techniques, then, is the
mingling of the varied conventions of his Latin predeces-
sors while exercising his own original genius. As Brosette
says, when Boileau imitates he either corrects his author's
thoughts, places them in a new context, gives them more

[12] *Les Satires de Boileau, commentées par lui-même*, p. 70.

energetic expression, or adds new images. "Il disoit quelque fois, en parlant de ces sortes d'imitations," Brosette continues, *"Cela ne s'appèle pas imiter; c'est joûter contra son original"* (1: 2n). As Saint-Marc later adds, however much the young Boileau had his head filled with Horace and Juvenal, he soon learned what they could teach him, used nature as his real model, and then was their equal and sometimes their superior (5: 294-95).

III: "As *Horace* DID BEFORE ME"

Though the evidence for mingling is clear, the weight of the borrowed satiric materials is on the Horatian side. Since Boileau and most of his contemporaries had learned the lessons of Casaubon and then Dacier, that is how they were likely to view the dominant voices of satire, whose beginnings lay in the slightly off-color Greek old comedy, and whose perfection came in the Roman Augustan age. Satire is essentially comic in origin and hence its conventions, Saint-Marc insists, demand Horatian playful ridicule. "Il en est tout autrement de la *Satire emportée*: c'est celle de *Perse* & de *Juvénal*. Ces deux *Poëtes*, livrés à leur humeur chagrine, préférèrent d'imiter *les Philosophes* ou les *Sophistes* dans leurs invectives véhémentes contre les Vices, à marcher, ainsi que *Lucilius* & qu' *Horace*, sur les pas des anciens *Comiques Grecs"* (5: 333-34). Boileau himself, therefore, should be scolded when he temporarily forgets that satire emerges from comedy (5: 392) and must be conversational and not oratorical, or "poetic." Some lines of sublime eloquence may be placed in satire, though with reserve. Satire Eight, unfortunately, is too much "une *Invective Oratoire"* without enough conversational tone (5: 392). At times, that is, Boileau ignores the rules of his Horatian comic genre and lets the Juvenalian element intrude too much.

At most other times, though, Boileau's art better controls his passions and he does what he should. Satire Six is based on Juvenal's eighth satire, on false honor; but the French version is appropriately different, for, Saint-Marc tells us, it lowers Juvenal's tones. *"Despréaux* n'a point renchéri sur *Juvénal*. L'Expression Latine a tout autant d'*Energie* que l'Expression Françoise; & le mérite de nôtre *Poëte* est d'avoir changé la nature de ce qu'il empruntoit à *Juvénal*, & d'avoir fait, d'un trait extrêmement sérieux, une idée plaisante & même très-plaisante" (5: 372). As Saint-Marc and others saw Boileau, he has turned Juvenalian invective into something like Horatian ridicule.

This may have been necessary in order to satisfy Boileau's expectations of satire; it was also necessary to accommodate satire to the "Augustan" myth that Louis XIV's court and stable of writers were pleased to promulgate. Horace had his Augustus, who had his Maecenas, who spread the imperial largesse to those who saw and praised the imperial virtues. Louis XIV was perhaps greater than Augustus, for he had the good fortune of being French, Christian, and even more sympathetic to modern letters. Boileau was of course an "ancient" in the noisy quarrel between the ancients and moderns; but on politics, ethics, religion, and science he was resolutely modern, and so told his enemy Perrault.[13] Accordingly, he was a warm supporter of his king, who provided Boileau with a pension, read, praised, and copied his satires at court, let it be known that he thought Boileau a worthy nominee for the Académie Française, allowed several poems to be addressed to him, and finally appointed Boileau Historiographer Royal in order to give him ample time to chronicle innumerable acts of Bourbon wisdom and courage during so long and fruitful a reign.

Louis's faith was amply justified. Epistle Eight, dedicated to the king, for instance, is so effusive that with little alteration it could have been transplanted to Pope's later *Epistle to Augustus* (1737) as a parody of George II. Since Louis

[13] See, for example, his letter to Perrault in 1700, in *Oeuvres complètes de Boileau*, ed. A. Charles Gidel (Paris, 1883), 4: 209-21.

has rewarded Boileau, the poet admits, the malicious crowd may wrongly think his praise purchased. In fact, Louis's great and numerous conquests make it too hard for Boileau to soar as he should, for the king's thousand virtues are difficult for any one to sing, much less a satirist biased toward blame. Fortunately, the problem can be resolved.

> My Zeal, the want of Genius, shall supply;
> As *Horace* did before me, so will I.
> With Vapours He, as well as I, was vext,
> And with a double Muse alike perplext.
>
> .   .   .   .
>
> Him, in my Verse, to Copy, I pretend
> *Calliope* provok'd, may be my Friend,
>
> .   .   .   .
>
> [Horace] Cou'd move fair *Glycera* with tender Lays,
> And strike the sounding Lyre in *Caesar*'s Praise.
> Follow his bright Example. Can'st thou find,
> O Muse a Better, to improve thy Mind?
> Thus to my self, I say, and take the Lyre,
> Strike the rebounding Strings, and to his Song aspire.
> The Rocks methinks are list'ning when I play,
> And Dancing Woods my pow'rful Notes obey;
> My Verse comes flowing like a mighty Stream,
> When *Horace* is my Guide, and *Lewis* is my Theme.
>
> (2: 88-89)

The English resisted the flood with a dike of rage and ridicule. As the patriotic author of *A Satyr Against the French* (1691) fumes upon hearing Louis's name,

> my *Satyr* boyls with Rage,
> *Lewis* [*is*] *the Plague* and *Firebrand* of the Age,
> Whom Nature in an angry Humour hurld
> Down as a fit Fiend to vex the Christian World.
>
> (P. 27)

Three years later, Edmund Arwaker published his *Epistle to Monsieur Boileau, Inviting his Muse to Forsake the French Interest, and Celebrate the King of England* (1694). Arwaker mischievously urges Boileau no longer "To make the *worst* appear the *best* of Men," and to stop confusing appearance with reality. In Boileau's adulatory verse Louis sees

> Not what he is, but what he wants to be.
> And he must all his boasted Glories own,
> Not from himself deriv'd, but thee alone;
> Whose Muse so well does his mean Deeds rehearse,
> That he becomes Immortal in thy Verse.
>
> (P. 3)

Why not sing William, a monarch worthy of celebration? Arwaker asks. If Boileau should "a servile Labour chuse / Where *Arbitrary Pow'r* enslaves thy Muse" (p. 7), William really has no need for French verse in any case, since his own victories and English poets will do the job quite well enough.

Boileau's *Ode sur la Prise de Namur* (1692) was especially galling in its overpraise of Louis's achievements, and it evoked controversy and reply in France and England. Matthew Prior's *English Ballad, on the Taking of Namur* (1695) bluntly states that Boileau is so far from being a Pindaric eagle, that he is a vulture who "only flies / Where sordid Interest seeks the Prey." In fact, "Give *Boileau* but Five Hundred Pieces, / And *Louis* takes the Wall of Jove" (p. 2).[14] After Blenheim an anonymous patriotic Englishman also writes to Boileau, taunting him—while granting

---

[14] For further discussion of the relationship between Boileau and Prior—one far more admiring than this exchange suggests—see Charles Kenneth Eaves, *Matthew Prior: Poet and Diplomatist* (New York: Columbia Univ. Press, 1939), pp. 97, 137. Prior wanted his English lines to face and answer Boileau's French: "I do not pretend it is an exact answer, nor do I care; 'tis only sense to those who understand the original" (p. 97).

his genius—and calling his a "Servant Muse." Tom Brown's
Works a few years later include an epistolary dialogue be-
tween Juvenal and Boileau, in which Juvenal berates his
French disciple for finding so many norms. He bitterly con-
cludes that "Your sordid Interest has made you a Traytor
to *Satyr*." The author of an epistle from Paris "To the
Reverend Dr. Ayscough at Oxford" (1728) probably would
have agreed with the indignant shade of indignant Juvenal.
Though Boileau *"like* the *Ancients* writ" in style, he ap-
parently was unlike them in spirit. He "Permission gain'd
inferior *Vice* to blame, / By lying Incense to his *Master's
Fame.*"[15] Pope's own imitation of the first satire of the sec-
ond book of Horace (1733) labels Boileau a court toady
who puffs his master at the expense of truth.

All this, I suggest, is in response to one logical outgrowth
of Horace as the apparently dominant guide for Boileau—
the Juvenalian often is present, often is important, and
often is subservient to support for the virtues of the reign-
ing monarch, who is the benevolent font of benevolent
power and emulation. The moral posture of Juvenal and
Persius is supported by very different assumptions about
the nature of imperial government and of living norms
which, if extended to France, would of course have been
more dangerous and obnoxious than they were in the British
court so victimized by the opposition to Walpole. Indeed,
after a while Boileau's insufficient Juvenalian salt was no-
ticed by French taste as well as English, for later in the
eighteenth century the philosophes attacked Horace's com-
plicity with Augustus's imperial designs. Such disfavor was
bound to spill over into evaluation of Boileau, and bound
to cause his reputation some harm when he was compared
with a more Juvenalian satirist, with, for example, someone
like the antiauthoritarian Rochester.

Early in the eighteenth century such a comparison in

---

[15] "Servant Muse" is in *A Letter to Monsieur Boileau* (1704), p. 1;
Brown, *Works*, 2: 90; "To . . . Dr. Ayscough," in Timothy Scribble
[Ashley Cowper], *The Norfolk Poetical Miscellany* (1774), 1: 281.

France would have found Boileau the easy victor. In his satires, the *Journal Litéraire* says, there is not a single word that might alarm the most scrupulous modesty. For all Rochester's spirit, the *Journal* argues, he is cruel, pitiless, and licentious, and even in the relatively modest and successful *Satyr against Reason and Mankind*, based on Boileau, one sees that the poet Rochester can please decent men but does not wish to and that, because of this defect, Boileau's satires are superior to the English satires.[16] By the late eighteenth century, however, a new generation of critics regard energy and sublimity as far more important than scrupulous modesty. Specifically, in 1786-87 France saw an acrimonious controversy regarding the merits and value of Boileau's several kinds of poetry and influence on French literature. The hostile side included the Marquis de Ximenez and the Chevalier Michel Cubières de Palmézeaux; the sympathetic side included Pierre Claude François Daunou, Charles Michel Marquis de Villette, and Jean François de la Harpe. Cubières-Palmézeaux deals with Rochester in his "Lettre à M. le Marquis de Ximines, sur l'influence de Boileau en littérature" (1787). He chides Boileau for his poetic frigidity, uncomfortable rules, deaf ear, generally constraining influence, harsh personal satire coupled with sycophancy, and merely imitative genius, among other cardinal sins. In the process, he insists that Boileau lacks both the ease and controlled casual air of Horace, and the sublime, captivating anger of Juvenal. Rochester then becomes a measure of Boileau's inferiority, as the eighth satire falls under Cubières-Palmézeaux's hand and examination:

il n'en est point de plus riche; il n'en est point qui puisse être creusé avec plus de fruit, et qui offre un champ plus

[16] *Journal Litéraire*, 9 (1717): 170-71. This is from article 10, "Dissertation sur la poësie Angloise," and is an interesting precursor of the Abbé Yart's more important, and substantial work the *Idée de la poësie Angloise.*

vast à la réflexion: voyez comme son début est sec, insignifiant et même trivial:

> De tous les animaux qui s'élevent dans l'air,
> Qui marchent sur la terre, et nagent dans la mer,
> De Paris au Perou, du Japon jusqu'à Rome,
> Le plus sot animal, à mon avis, c'est l'homme.

Oh! que le Juvénal d'Angleterre, oh! que l'impetueux Rochester entre en matière d'une manière bien plus vive, lorsqu'il traite le même sujet!

> Infortuné d'être homme et d'avoir pour prison
> Le corps d'un animal si fier de sa raison,
> Que ne m'est-il permis d'en changer tout à l'heure! etc.

Comparez ces deux satyres, M. le Marquis; vous verrez dans celle-ci déborder tout le fiel d'une misanthropie sublime, et telle que l'inspire ordinairement aux âmes énergiques la passion de la vertu, vous verrez dans l'autre, *qu'une chèvre a l'esprit mieux tourné que n'a l'homme; qu'un docteur,* meme de Sorbonne, *est moins savant qu'un âne,* et cent autres lieux communs exprimés, je l'avoue, en vers très harmonieux et très-précis, mais qui ne laissent rien dans la tête ni dans le coeur.

He concludes with the lamentation: "Le voilà nôtre véritable satyrique! Le voilà nôtre Lucilius, nôtre Juvénal, nôtre Rochester!"[17]

---

[17] See *Boileau jugé par ses amis et par ses ennemis, ou le pour et le contre sur Boileau* (Paris, 1802), pp. 59-61. For a reasonably full list of the authors and works in the controversy, see Boileau, *Oeuvres complètes precedées d'un discours sur les caractères et l'influence des oeuvres de Boileau* [by P.C.F. Daunou] (Paris, 1809), 1: cxxviii-cxxxiii. Boileau and his reputation have been discussed at length in John Richardson Miller, *Boileau en France au dixhuitième siècle,* Johns Hopkins Studies in Romance Literature and Language, Extra Volume 18 (Baltimore: The Johns Hopkins Univ. Press, 1942). For more recent discussions of Boileau, see Julian Eugene White, *Nicolas Boileau* (New York: Twayne Publishers, 1969), Bernard Beugnot and Roger Zuber, *Boileau: Visages anciens, visages nouveaux 1665-1970* (Montreal: Les Presses

Rochester as the maverick in a royal court, a gadfly to authority, an unpolished, unregulated author associated with Juvenal's hostility to the empire and man's vicious nature, and the product of English "freedom" clearly was congenial to the republican spirit of Cubières-Palmézeaux. He cannot bear to read the fawning *Ode sur la prise de Namur* (pp. 52, 67), and he finds Boileau in general a man who flatters the great and successful of the age (p. 51). For a moment, at least, the English Restoration poet John Wilmot Earl of Rochester was an ally in an eighteenth-century aristocratic French republican's effort to overthrow the literature of the Ancien Régime. He served as that ally because he was one of the several Juvenals of England, in contrast to the essentially compliant and unsatiric Horatian that Boileau had come to seem for many on either side of the channel. The lesson, learned far earlier than 1786, was not wasted on Pope, the opposition to Walpole, and any other satirist engaged in a real or fancied battle against tyrants. Polite and comic satire can have little place in a poem made by indignation. That force often was invoked in British satire and was at least as representative as the muted voice of Horace or the somber voice of Persius. Indeed, Pope and others would follow Boileau's lead, if not his entire path, in mingling the satiric conventions available to them, though as we shall see, they also used those conventions in their purer forms as well.

---

de l'Université de Montréal, 1973), and Gordon Pocock, *Boileau and the Nature of Neo-Classicism* (Cambridge: Cambridge Univ. Press, 1980). Beugnot and Zuber provide a bibliography of works by and about Boileau that is fuller than Pocock's.

CHAPTER 4

British Modes of Proceeding: National Character and Satiric Forms

CLASSICAL SATIRES not only offered British writers Horatian, Persian, and Juvenalian modes of proceeding; as Boileau's example shows, they also allowed mingling of modes that are important for Pope's satiric art. Each kind was often used and exists in relatively discrete proportions.

I: HORACE REDIVIVUS

There was a large body of poetry that was designed to recreate the perceived sense of union between poet and society or poet and self that Horace so brilliantly captures. Any brief discussion of these manifold efforts can only be suggestive; however, we can isolate a few shared assumptions of the British (and French) Horatian kind, one of which is the political wisdom of those who rule the nation. André Dacier well sums up this attitude when he describes the many virtues of Augustus and then tells Louis XIV that these are his majesty's own principal traits.[1] Since Walpole's administration lacked a Dacier to sing it, it encouraged humbler workers in the journalistic and poetic fields. On 8 January 1726, its *London Journal* thanks Bubb Dodington for his adulatory verse *Epistle to . . . Walpole* (1725), and observes that in the Augustan age Horace was "exquisitely adapted to the Politeness of a Court" and was able to endear his patron Augustus "to the *Roman* People." The epistolary poet—like Dodington—should show the statesman's "worthiest Sentiments rising to his View in their full Lustre," and thereby, the *Journal* says on 5 Feb-

---

[1] *Oeuvres d'Horace en latin et en français*, 3rd ed. (Paris, 1709), 6: sig. aij^r.

105

ruary, both attain and teach others to attain "the Smiles of the Great Man." One important Horatian mode, then, included celebration of the state and its government's authority, each closely related to a real or implied plea for patronage, and often aware of the Augustan analogy.

A related mode is not so blatant in its design, but does share Horace's faith in a nation capable of controlling itself and its politics, and therefore avoiding Juvenalian *saeva indignatio.* The author of *Virtue, an Ethic Epistle* (1759) knows that several leaders function as norms and link man with God. Though there is abundant folly in the world, the speaker argues that paragons like Home, Gardener, Grenville, and Townshend will help to give virtue her day and establish honor, however long it takes.

> Those Charms strength'ning in the radiant Round
> Of rolling Ages which no Time shall bound,
> By Heaven's high Council, and eternal Laws,
> All strong for Virtue and her sacred Cause,
> Are fixt by Necessity; and, soon or late,
> The unfading Garland crowns her purer State.
>
> (P. 10)

Much Horatianism is not overtly political and, like these examples, in fact often appears in the essay or epistle, a form which, even in its occasional scolding, is traditionally less angry and more social than the harsher satire. In the anonymous *Design and Beauty. An Epistle* (1734), for instance, we are introduced to a world in which a polished speaker addresses Highmore regarding the poem's subjects and their source in an actively concerned and benevolent deity. "Design," we read, is "that Particle of heavenly Flame, / Soul of all Beauty, thro' all Arts the same." Such order has its exemplars in poetic, plastic, and graphic arts, in ancient and modern rhetoric, and in the nature we all imitate. "Truth and Order animate the Muse" (p. 1) in this world of the triumph of ethical and artistic imperatives. "Various Arts proceed, for human Wit / But imitates the

Plan by Nature set." Aberrations from nature thus are laughable, not ominous—"As *Cibber*'s Odes to *Handel*'s Music set." The poem is well strewn with words like *extend, compass, bring, fit, aptitude, true, noblest, more perfect,* and *nourished* (p. 2), all given coherence by the pattern of the successful, harmonious poet himself:

> True Poets are themselves a Poem, each
> A Pattern of the lovely Rules they teach;
> Those fair Ideas that their Fancy charm,
> Inspire their Lives, and every Action warm;
> And when they chaunt the Praise of high Desert,
> They but transcribe the Dictates of their Heart.
> Thus is *Apollo*'s Laureat Priest endow'd,
> Himself a Temple worthy of the God.[2]
> Such *Homer, Solon, Phineus* are enroll'd;
> Sages, and Lawgivers, and Prophets old:
> All Poets, all inspir'd; an awful Train,
> Seated on *Pindus*' Head, apart from the Profane.
>
> (Pp. 9-10)

Since the epistolary, Horatian, satiric form preserves its roots in comedy, it tends to be patient and forgiving, hoping to bind man to man rather than to punish malefactors. Hence the 1738 version of *Three Epistles in the Ethic Way. From the French of M. de Voltaire,* offers competent poems in which harsh satire is always held in check, and "The social forms aspiring jointly rise" (p. 46). In this world even "Sir *R*—— only happy lives, / Not in the wealth he has—but what he gives!" (p. 7). Such poems at their best avoid self-satisfied conquests over trivial matters, or compla-

---

2 Pope's muted epistolary influence suggests the tone of this work and is overt in this line. Compare Pope's *Epistle to Burlington* (1731): "Bid Temples, worthier of the God, ascend" (line 198). For other discussion of epistles and Pope, see Howard D. Weinbrot, *The Formal Strain: Studies in Augustan Imitation and Satire* (Chicago: Univ. of Chicago Press, 1969), pp. 129-38, and the beginnings of chapters 6 and 8 below.

cent affirmation of the government's status quo. They could also easily fall into those traps, however, and represent the flaccid side of the Horatian mode, which can be as tiresome as the mannered hostility of Juvenalian outrage, and apparently designed not to tax the abilities of a dim ten-year-old baronet learning his social graces. Here is part of Benjamin Stillingfleet's *Essay on Conversation* (1737), whose fluid couplets are at home in a world of conventional human beings wishing to get on with like-minded colleagues.

> Would you both please and be instructed too,
> Watch well the Rage of Shining to subdue;
> Hear every Man upon his favourite Theme,
> And ever be more knowing than you seem.
>
> (P. 8)

> But if your Temper to Extremes should lead,
> Always upon th' indulging Side exceed;
> For tho' to blame most lend a willing Ear,
> Yet Hatred ever will attend on Fear.
>
> (P. 13)

Such Horatian satire was also applicable to the self, and it suggests again a world of acceptably manageable folly that requires a decent man's self-discipline to effect a cure. "The Duty of Employing one's Self. An Horatian Epistle" (1748), is a gentle reproach of the idle, including a typical Sir John, who is unoccupied and miserable until he bestirs himself to get drunk at midnight. The poem's speaker knows better, keeps busy, has learned how to purge his unpleasant spleen, and actively embodies the successful good man doing his duty in a friendly domestic setting. Rather than rage, he will work off his anger in sweat. If the time, men, and manners seem dreadful,

> I take my horse.
> One mile reforms 'em, or if aught remain
> Unpurg'd—'tis but to ride as far again.

Thus on my self in toils I spend my rage;
I pay the fine, and this absolves the age.[3]

Depravity cannot be objectively verified and labeled so that
it can be fought on the beaches, hedgerows, and commons;
it is a function of internally created malaise and is a form
of error for which one must be fined through purging
physical exercise. One need not break or flap a butterfly so
long as one has a good hunter-jumper willing to take the
bit.

Celebration, patronage, confidence in the state's gov-
ernors, its satirists, and their values; verbal polish, informal
tones, concern with the pleasantries of the world, epistolary
dialogue, optimism concerning the gods and their affection
for man and the speaker's nation—these are a few of Hor-
ace's traits as seen in several variously Horatian poems.
We would of course have to add concern with literary mat-
ters, the values of retirement, apologia, and autobiography
in any list pretending marginally to represent Horace in
eighteenth-century Britain.[4] As some of these examples sug-
gest, Pope adapts several Horatian traits for his own *Epis-
tles to Several Persons* (1731-35), in which the satirist and
his values triumph by means of wit, moral suasion, and an
educable nation or adversarius. He also rejects many other
Horatian conventions, however, since their "comic" geneal-
ogy made them useless, or worse, under an administration

---

[3] Robert Dodsley, ed., *A Collection of Poems. By Several Hands*
(1748), 3: 63. This poem, by E. Rolle, is preceded by the same author's
"Life Burthensome, Because we know Not How to Use it. An Horatian
Epistle."

[4] Some of this work has begun, especially on Horace in France. See
Jean Marmièr, *Horace en France, aux dix-septième siècle*, Université
de Rennes, Faculté de lettres et de sciences humaines publications
(Paris: Presses Universitaires, 1962). See also Marmièr's *La Survie
d'Horace à l'époque romantique* (Paris: Marcel Didier, 1965). Reuben
Brower's *Alexander Pope: The Poetry of Allusion* (Oxford: Clarendon
Press, 1959), includes a chapter on "The Image of Horace," and there
are of course numerous studies of Pope's use of Horace's "image" or of
particular poems.

that Pope thought tragic. Cibber becomes ominous not laughable, and Sir Robert's wealth brings corruption not happiness. The poems I have cited are a small sample of the Horatian abundance of the first half of the eighteenth century; they also suggest that some of Horace's perceived conventions were foreign to Pope's satiric aims. Neither the Juvenalian nor related Persian modes offer paradigms for Pope's satires; but they do provide devices and tones more readily adaptable for the needs of many eighteenth-century satirists, and for the presumed native temperament.

II: JUVENAL AND BRITISH SURLY VIRTUE

Joseph Trapp could not have shocked his students at Oxford when he told them in 1711 that their countrymen were splendid satirists—"I mean in that Species of it in which *Juvenal* writ: For the *Horatian* Satire is but little affected among us." In 1755 Thomas Blackwell complains that, unlike Horace, "the greater part of the modern Satyrists seldom afford us a smile." He also laments that Horace is so little read and seems to be caviar available for very few. By 1779 Edward Burnaby Greene observes that Dryden decided "the preference of Juvenal over Horace on the *general* management of Satire," and adds, as if in approval: "Juvenal is undoubtedly most adapted to the disposition of *our English* multifarious Writers." Early in the nineteenth century a translator of Persius (1806) claims that though Juvenal's elevated tones "have been imitated with considerable success by several, ... where shall we find, with the exception of Pope's beautiful imitations, the same rivalry with Horace?" Shortly thereafter, Thomas Denman adds that Juvenal's satires "are peculiarly consonant to the habits of thinking which have long prevailed in England."[5]

[5] Trapp, *Praelectiones Poeticae* (1711-19), trans. William Bowyer and William Clarke as *Lectures on Poetry* (1742), p. 236; Blackwell, *Memoirs of the Court of Augustus* (Edinburgh and London, 1753-63), 3: 64, 73 for how little understood Horace is "by the Majority of *Latin*

Several of the *Essays Moral and Literary* (1778) of Vice-
simus Knox provide further evidence for this British bias.
Though his "On Satire and Satirists" offers familiar praise
for all three great satirists, it also insists that "the English
seem to have copied the manner of Juvenal rather than of
Horace. Our national spirit is indeed of the manly and
rough kind, and feels something congenial with itself in the
vehemence of the sullen Juvenal" (2: 150). In other essays
he expands upon his perception of the national spirit and
warns against deviating from it.

The Englishman's character, he argues in "Classical
Learning Vindicated," is like "the disposition of an old
Roman"—presumably a pre-Caesarean republican. "He has
a natural generosity, and a love of independence" as well as
"a gravity of Temper, better adapted to mental and moral
improvement than any other; because more capable of
fixed attention"; he thus flourishes under sympathetic clas-
sical tutelage. The French mind, however, wanders more,
has less dignity than the English or Roman, and would
stunt domestic moral growth if it were to replace classical
learning in contemporary England (2: 22). Knox's Franco-
phobia soon takes on literary consequences, for in "On the
Grave and Gay Philosophy" he associates Horace with
French luxury and corruption, and Juvenal, by extension,
with sturdy British gravity: "an increase of wealth and our
imitation of French and Asiatic manners, have greatly al-
tered our natural disposition. We begin to relish none but
the gayer kind of philosophy. Horace, were he English,
would at present be more read than Juvenal, and Lucian

Scholars." Blackwell also observes that Pope could be both severe and
Horatian (3: 66-67), and that Dryden preferred Juvenal to Horace (3:
73); Burnaby Greene, *The Satires of Persius Paraphrastically Imitated
and Adapted to the Times*, p. xx; 1806 translator, *The Satires of Aulus
Persius Flaccus*, pp. xxv-xxvi; Denman, *Monthly Review*, second series
55 (1808): 247. The attribution is in Benjamin Christie Nangle, *The
Monthly Review Second Series 1790-1815: Indexes of Contributors and
Articles* (Oxford: Clarendon Press, 1955), p. 148.

than Seneca" (2: 121). In "On Preaching and Sermon Writers," Knox adds that the English, in their "characteristic solidity," have "delivered harangues unequalled in the schools of Athens" (2: 158). On the one side, in these essays, are fidelity to the English character, manliness, roughness, vehemence, generosity, independence, gravity, improvement, discipline, solidity, superiority in moral harangues, Seneca, and Juvenal. On the other side, are a lapse from the national character, French learning and intellectual flightiness, luxury, gaiety, Lucian, and Horace.[6]

The French themselves saw a strain of roughness, vigor, skepticism regarding institutions, and Juvenalian liberty in their violent cross-channel neighbors, whom they often regarded as inspired madmen, or worse. Some French perceptions of the British temper were responses to the English language which, René Rapin argues in 1674, "is proper for great expressions," and thus is suitable for a nation that excells in tragedy because it "delights in cruelty." Such a view is consistent with Jacques Bernard's in 1710. His *Nouvelles de la république des lettres* depicts English spirits who are searching and bold, and who vigorously speak and write against received opinions.[7] These genuine skeptics attack everyone and are attacked in turn, both in conversation and "dans la plupart des livres qu'on écrit sur des points ou de Théologie ou de Métaphysique" (March, pp. 346-47). In 1717 the *Journal Littéraire* carries the discussion into specific authors and works. Its "Dissertation Sur la poësie Anglaise" complains that *Absalom and Achitophel's* transparent attacks upon the king and his court

---

[6] Such remarks again make one doubt whether Horace wrote satire that "men of the seventeenth and eighteenth centuries . . . could confidently approve and which they would have liked to live by." See P. K. Elkin, *The Augustan Defence of Satire* (Oxford: Clarendon Press, 1973), p. 156.

[7] Rapin, *Reflections on Aristotle's Treatise of Poesie*, trans. [Thomas Rymer], p. 122; *Nouvelles* (Amsterdam), "Essai sur l'usage de la raillerie & de l'enjouement dans les conversations. . . . Traduit de l'Anglois," p. 346.

were part of Dryden's "malignité odieuse" and "dégoûtante obscénité." During the reign of Charles II there were all too many English satiric poets who distinguished themselves by bloody satires against those in the court and the town. Their only discretion was to use the first letter of a name or word and fill in the blank with ellipses; yet even then they might give away the name by placing it at the end of the couplet, thus forcing the spoken to evoke the unspoken rhyme. The practice of using first and last initials of well-known peers was comparably revealing, while protecting the poet, since the severe punishments for libel specified in the law of *scandalum magnatum* demanded explicit spelling-out of a name. English law cannot shield royal or noble persons from satire by their inferiors. Hélas, the *Journal* continues, such harshness and general immodesty are everywhere in English satire. The poems of Oldham, "appellé par quelquesuns le *Juvénal Anglois* . . . sont à la verité bien fortes & même violentes, mais il y forte manque du tour & de l'exactitude, de sort qu'il n'est pas rangé par les Anglois même parmi leur Poëtes du premier rang." Even Pope's *Rape of the Lock*, an acknowledged masterpiece, is immodest at times in its equivocations, which in France one would avoid with care in a piece "dediée à une Dame, & destinée à divertir le beau Sexe" (9: 174-75).

These themes of political, literary, and emotional excess typify much French criticism of British satire in the eighteenth century, and appear often in the *Journal des Savants* and other places. In 1745, for example, the *Journal Etranger* finds itself mapping terra incognita for a French audience unfamiliar with the term "Satirique d'Etat." It expresses something "plus connue en Angleterre qu'en France, ou du moins envisagée différemment. La forme du Gouvernement rend licite dans l'une quelquefois même utile, une genre d'écrire justement proscrit & méprisé dans l'autre" (2 [April 1755]: 207). A relevant implication of such national and literary character is made clear by Montesquieu in 1748. He observes that one can tell the character of a nation through its literary productions. England, with its tradition of liberty and checks upon absolutism, produces "satirical writings that are sharp and severe, and we find amongst them many Juvenals without discovering one Horace."[8]

The Abbé Yart's important *Idée de la poësie Angloise* (1749-56) also supports the hypothesis of British Juvenalian satire and its consequent political bias.[9] All of Yart's third volume (1753) is devoted to commentary on Pope, and at several places it provides useful insights into his satiric methods. The French, Yart says, have authors like Corneille, la Fontaine, and Molière who equal or surpass the ancients. Is it not possible that a nation as laborious and learned as England also has poets of such surpassing achievements? "Il y a des morceaux dans Shakespear, dans Milton, dans Addison, dans Pope, dans Swift, dans Gay,

[8] See Jacqueline de la Harpe, *Le Journal des Savants et la renommé de Pope en France au XVIIIᵉ siècle*, University of California Publications in Modern Philology, vol. 16 (Berkeley: Univ. of California Press, 1933). She observes, for example, that though the French always admire the genius and energy of the English, they also regret the consequent "pédantisme, et la bizarrerie, ou . . . la vulgarité et se servent d'expressions considérées trop communes et basses en France pour être matière à littérature" (p. 207). See also de la Harpe's *Le Journal des Savants et l'Angleterre 1702-1789*, University of California Publications in Modern Philology, vol. 20 (Berkeley: Univ. of California Press, 1941).

The *Journal Etranger* is discussing an "Essai sur les différentes espèces du ridicule. London 1754." This is Joseph Warton's *Adventurer*, No. 133, 12 Feb. 1754. Montesquieu, *The Spirit of the Laws*, trans. Thomas Nugent, 5th ed. (1773), 1: 467. Joseph Warton quotes Montesquieu's judgment and cites several of Dorset's verses in hopeful confutation. See *An Essay on the Genius and Writings of Pope* (1756), 5th ed. (1806), 1: 48-49.

[9] The full title is *Idée de la poësie Angloise, ou traduction des meilleurs poëtes Angloises qui n'ont point encore paru dans nôtre langue, avec un jugement sur leurs ouvrages, & une comparison de leurs poësies avec celles des auteurs anciens & modernes, & un grande nombre d'anecdotes & de notes critiques* (Paris). Citations to this eight-volume work are given in the text.

dans Tomson, qui méritent autant nôtre estime que tout ce que l'antiquité a jamais produit" (3: xxv). Part of this distinction stems from the English character and satiric temper. Yart notes, for example, that the English are consistently "plus hardis"—bolder, more impudent—than the French poets (2: 7-8). Such energy can be expected from them: "leur Pays est l'asyle de la Satyre; la liberté y dégénéré presque toujours en une licence effrénée; chaque semaine est marquée par des feuilles de toute espèce, où la Religion, la Gouvernement, les Princes, les Magistrats, le Clergé, sont attaqués sans ménagement" (2: 132). English thought, like its satire, is excessive and has too much liberty, too much boldness—so much so that in Yart's translations and commentaries he will suppress or refute what is too free (3: xxv-xxvi). Indeed, some English ideas and language are so extraordinary "qu'ils en ont beaucoup que n'étoient jamais entrées dans l'esprit humain" (3: xvij). In speaking of the first few lines of Pope's epistle to Cobham, Yart laments "que la Langue Angloise permette à un Auteur aussi élégant que Pope d'insérer ces vilains mots dans son Poëme" (3: 208n). There, as elsewhere, Pope treats certain matters "d'une manière trop Angloise" (3: 217n). Pope is not alone in such bizarre literary conduct, for Prior's parody (in 1695) of Boileau's *Ode sur la Prise de Namur* "est si outrée, qu'il ne m'est pas permis d'en citer plus de six strophes sur seize" (5: 68).

Yart's summing up of English national traits further suggests their connection with English literary traits. The English are opinionated, somber, rude, uneven, gloomy, and nearly always "chagrine & mécontente." From this stems (a clearly un-Horatian)

haine des Anglois pour leurs Rois & pour leurs Ministres. Ils portent depuis long-temps, avec une répugnance insurmontable, le joug de l'autorité: non contens d'avoir changé sous chaque regne les loix fondamentales du Royaume, ils ne soummettent qu'avec peine à celles qu'ils ont établies depuis un siècle. Ils prêtent, souvent sans examen, à leurs Rois & à leurs Ministres, des projects d'ambition, d'usurpation, de tyrannie; & leurs Poëtes, tels que ceux dont on a imprimé les Ouvrages dans un immense Recueil, intitulé *Affaires d'Etat*, irritent encore l'orgueil de leur Nation, & son amour pour l'independence. (4: 243)

At its best, this political fervor exercises itself against "des Rois despotiques & des Ministres injustes" (4: 247) and on behalf of a beloved country, for English poets offer great praise as well as blame for many aspects of national life— true patriotism, taste in the useful arts, ardor for commerce, zeal for public works, and love of the poor have not always received such just acclaim and honor as they have in England. In what must be one of the highest compliments the Abbé Yart—of the Académie Royale des Belles-Lettres, Sciences, & Arts de Rouen—could pay, he adds that the spirit of Athens and Rome seems to have left the tombs of their citizens to be resurrected in England. "Leurs Poëtes, témoins Pope & Gay, sont plus enflammés que les nôtres de l'amour de la Patrie, passion qui peut seule après la Religion en sauter le sublime. Passons donc les défauts de leurs moeurs & de leur style en faveur de leurs vertus héroïques & de leurs grandes idées" (4: 247). This verbal portrait of a rough and politically surly state and literature thus concludes by emphasizing the grandeur of English ideas and the heroism of English virtues ("témoins Pope & Gay") in resisting despotism, traits specifically denied to Horace and associated with Juvenal in his Roman and British guise. The many commentators who thought Juvenal the characteristic model for British satire based their observations on poems and conventions in ample supply.

III: Facit Indignatio Versum

Earlier eighteenth-century satirists who looked back on their satiric tradition were likely to see the numerous offspring of harsh Renaissance satire, sometimes clothed in more elegant, and subtle, dress from about 1680. Tom Brown's "Short Essay on *English* Satire" of 1707 portrays a largely brutal satiric world scarcely changed by the recent acceptance of Horatian smiles and characterized instead by satire as an avenging angel who hacks and hews offenders. As Defoe's example in 1702 shows, this satirist may be suppressed but will "answer with *Juvenal*" that it is difficult not to write satire in such times. Though Oldham imitated Horace as well as Juvenal, later satirists tended to join Thomas Gilbert, who heard and used an "invective Tongue" and who invoked Oldham as a guide whose "pointed Wit" provided "Curses, for the lowest Scoundrel fit." Oldham's "Keen Genius" shall "Improve my Rage, and stab in every Line" until the miscreant is destroyed.[10] Indeed, the earlier view of a morally collapsing world, an offended God, exalted enemies and venal flunkies massed against the isolated, angry good man—all this could have been seen through the *Craftsman*'s own dark glasses during the 1730s. Such formulaic fury had long been available and was long to continue. As a simple sign of the exuberant continuity of one such pose, let us look at a few adaptations of Juvenal's "Si natura negat, facit indignatio versum," and "Nam quis iniquae / Tam patiens urbis, tam ferreus, ut teneat se?" (*Satires*, 1, 79, 30-31): "If Nature cou'd not, Anger would indite," and "To view so lewd a Town, and to refrain, / What Hoops of Iron cou'd my Spleen maintain?"[11] The aggressive affirmation and aggres-

---

[10] Brown, *The Works of Mr. Thomas Brown*, 4th ed. (1715), 1: 34-35; Defoe, *Reformation of Manners, A Satyr*, p. 4; Gilbert, *The World Unmask'd. A Satire* (1738), pp. 24, 21-22; William Whitehead's *Essay on Ridicule* (1743), p. 14 (see below), and the anonymous *Modern Virtue. A Satire* (1746), p. 14, also invoke a stabbing Oldham as a guide.

[11] The first satire is quoted, respectively, from *D. Junii Juvenalis et A. Persii Flacci Satirae* (1684), ed. Ludovicus Prateus (1736), and The Works of John Dryden, vol. 4, *Poems 1693-1696*, ed. A. B. Chambers, William Frost, and Vinton A. Dearing (Berkeley and Los Angeles: Univ. of California Press, 1974), pp. 99, 95, lines 121, 44-45.

sive interrogatory are staples in the good man's fight against omnipresent evil.

For generations such satirists, lacking the peripheral vision to see their neighbors in the trenches, tirelessly took up the cudgels in defense of the threatened motherland. In 1700, for example, Sir Richard Blackmore is faced with numerous hostile, poetic insects and locusts destroying the nation, and so his *Satyr against Wit* stridently asks: "Who can forbear, and tamely silent sit, / And see his Native Land undone by Wit?" Just two years later Defoe also describes a land so threatened with its own vice that God's vengeance is imminent. The satirist wonders

> How long may Heaven be banter'd by a Nation
> With broken Vows, and Shams of Reformation,
> And yet forbear to show its Indignation?
>
> (P. 5)

By 1719 some poets thought that Pope's *Homer* was a sign of literary decay. The incensed author of *Three Satires* thus cries out:

> Who can his just *disdain* or *rage* with-hold?
> Who that true sense of the prepost'rous deed
> Provokes, wou'd not to *rigid* terms proceed?
>
> (P. 6)

Life was not much better in 1732, when the author of *Verres and his Scribblers* sides with the opposition to Walpole, sees vice everywhere, and begins his poem with a familiar exercise in the rhetorical figure erotesis:

> And shall I then for ever silent stand?
> And let th' illiberal, servile, scribbling Band
> Pass unchastis'd? Who that has Ink, or Gall,
> Can bear unmov'd these courtly Witlings Brawl?
>
> (P. 1)

This enormous collection of noxious insects and locusts, of insolent, loud, noisy, factious scandalous enemies to

virtue, truth, and freedom, shall be resisted by the poet, for
"Indignation fires the Muse" (p. 4).

Administration writers were not so dull that they could
not see and adapt a useful convention. Though they gen-
erally preferred not to portray a declining world that
would reflect on the first minister himself, they excepted
opposition satirists. The anonymous perpetrator of *Modern
Patriotism, or Faction Display'd* (1734) is tired of waiting
for some manly poet to "lash the desperate Folly of the
Age," and so, "Impatient of delay! I snatch the Pen, / To
scourge the wicked ways of guilty Men" (p. 3). Like his
opponents, he is a lonely hero fighting the armies of dark-
ness, pointing "unpolish'd Rhymes," and insisting that
"what Art, or Nature, to the Muse deny, / An honest In-
dignation shall supply" (p. 5). The ministerial writer of
A Satire (1734) asks Walpole to aid him "with a just in-
dignant Rage, / To scourge the great Disturbers of our
Age" (p. 4).

Thomas Gilbert returns us to an opposition author who
frequently attends the indignant muse. In 1737 he writes
"An Epistle to . . . Henry Bathurst" which praises *"Juve-
nal*, whose manly spirit glows / With sharp-edge'd satyr
against virtue's foes"; his Preface to *The World Unmask'd*
(1738) characterizes Walpole's measures as so "destructive
to the interest of his country" that Gilbert ". . . could not
help expressing his indignation against him";[12] in 1740 he
writes a highly political imitation of *The First Satire of
Juvenal* in which the speaker proclaims: "What honest
Spirit can his Spleen contain, / Nor dare to lash the Vices
of this Reign?" (p. 7); and in such a reign "Vice is sacred
held among the Great, / And Virtue spurn'd by Ministers
of State" (p. 11). In short, as the anonymous *Man of Hon-
our* exclaims in 1737, under such a wicked dispensation

[12] As in Gilbert's *Poems on Several Occasions* (1747), pp. 105, 123.
The World Unmasked was corrected and revised for this edition; its
Preface is italicized. Gilbert's debt to the Juvenalian Pope is obvious
throughout his poems.

119

"shall the Muse be silent? Heav'n forbid!" (p. 4). Heaven
was glad to comply, and so in *The Modern Englishman*
(1738), a poem attributed to Pope in the Dublin edition,
"angry Truth proclaims [Britain's] injur'd Cause." The na-
tion "fill'd with Folly, Fraud, and Vice," is aided by Apollo
(p. 3) to "Rouze honest Satire! scourge a guilty Land"
(p. 6), as corruption spreads, Guilt rules, and "Flattery,
Fraud, and Knavery, seem no Crimes" (p. 17). In 1739
Paul Whitehead is so angry that "Fierce Indignation boils
within [his] Veins" as he looks around him. Since this is
the worst of all possible times, Satire must spread her
wings and fearlessly attack her prey, "tho' lurking ne'er
so high." In such a world Juvenal's own line must be used:
"If Nature could not, Anger would indite."[13] Anger indites
again in William Whitehead's *Essay on Ridicule* (1743)
when Whitehead argues that smiles are inadequate for
dealing with the high crimes around him:

> 'Tis Indignation swells th' exalted Stile,
> Learns the bold Verse with *Roman* Rage to glow,
> The Stab of Oldham, or thy Scourge, *Despreaux*.
>
> (P. 14)

These Juvenalian outbursts against vice were by no
means limited to the first half of the century. We see them
in *Covent-Garden: A Satire* (1756)—"YES, while these eyes
can see the light, / This pen, tho' *weak*, shall wage the
fight" (p. 14)—and T. H. Delamayne's *The Senators*
(1772)—"honest indignation swells my breast, / And all th'
insulted Briton stands confest" (p. 2)—and T. J. Mathias's
Preface to *The Shade of Alexander Pope on the Banks of*

---

[13] The attribution to Whitehead is uncertain. *The State of Rome,
under Nero and Domitian: A Satire. . . . By Messrs. Juvenal and Per-
sius*, 2nd ed. (1739), p. 5. The image of the satirist as Abdiel was made
overt by Tobias Smollett in *Advice: A Satyr* (1746), though used with
obvious irony. Pitt, the Friend says, is "the unshaken *Abdiel* yet un-
sung"; but the Poet wonders if Pitt's name and Abdiel's virtue "ever
dwelt together" (p. 4 and note).

the Thames (1799), where the satiric poet feels not "malice, but indignation and resentment against vice and wickedness" (p. 12). The Juvenalian option was plainly natural for the demands of angry, elevated satire that often was in personal or political opposition, and often was opposed to Horatian complaisance and support for the government. Pope is in this tradition when he claims to wield "the last Pen for Freedom," and fears that "Truth stands trembling on the edge of Law" (*Dialogue* II. 248-49). Juvenal's satires were commonly printed with Persius's and, through much of the seventeenth and eighteenth centuries, were commonly regarded as cousins-german in the battle against a variety of ills. This related Persian mode was especially useful during the 1730s, when the war of the wits against Walpole was most fierce and most revealed the bitter and eclectic genius of British formal verse satire. These angry modes also remind us that a "Horatian Epistle" which "absolves the age" is not likely to be a good soldier in an opposition army of the 1730s.

IV: PERSIUS AND OPPOSITION

As early as 1685 an angry adapter of Persius struck what would become a familiar pose. The tutor, confident of the power of "daring *Vertue*," speaks to his student and hopes that the "Great *Sovereign* of the Skies" will vouchsafe "To scourge the Pride of Tyrants" by showing them the face of goodness and the felicity they have lost. So punished, they will "*turn pale*, and pine away, and dye."[14] Whether this satire was read in the 1730s is doubtful, and irrelevant, for it nevertheless shows Persius's lashing and contemplative mode, and makes plain that he was known to poets as well as commentators for his dialogue, praise of virtue, insistence on close human relationships, and immediate involvement in the resistance to tyranny.

[14] F. A., *The Third Satyr of A. Persius, In Way of a Dialogue, Or Dramatick Interlude*, pp. 3-4.

Several of these traits were blended with Persius's melancholic and, in this case, marginally political mode in John Lord Hervey's unsigned *A Satire in the Manner of Persius: In a Dialogue Between Atticus and Eugenio. By a Person of Quality* (1730, 1739).[15] Atticus is at first indignant regarding man, and his young friend Eugenio is sadly disillusioned: "I thought Men worthless, now I've prov'd 'em so" (p. 10), he laments. Since Atticus already has that knowledge and knows of the "Senate's sinking Fame" and Britain's mere "Shew of Freedom dwindled to a Name," lashing the wicked age is appropriate (p. 6). After this Juvenalian remark, Atticus offers quasi-stoical advice and urges Eugenio to laugh at men's follies before he weeps at their faults. If the wicked prosper,

> submit, for Prudence lies
> In suffering well—'Tis equally unwise
> To see the Injuries we won't resent,
> And mourn the Evils which we can't prevent.
>
> (P. 8)

Eugenio cannot take this sound advice and regretfully says that he is immune from disappointments, because immune from the vain hopes of joy: "Repuls'd, I strive; betray'd I trust no more" (p. 9). After hearing more of Eugenio's complaints, lashing of the world, and reluctant acceptance of the miserable human condition—"What Joy for Truth, what Commerce for the Just?" (p. 14)—Atticus praises his friend's early wisdom and refusal to be seduced by secular tinsel. He consoles us with a Christianized stoic vision and an orthodox answer to a familiar question regarding the existence of evil, for man's sight cannot see God's plan:

[15] According to Robert Halsband, this poem was "composed by Hervey during the 1720's," and was published in 1730 and 1739. I have not seen the 1730 version, and I quote from that of 1739. The "Christian stoic point of view," Halsband argues, "is not characteristic of [Hervey's] thinking." *Lord Hervey: Eighteenth-Century Courtier* (New York: Oxford Univ. Press, 1974), p. 235, n. 38.

undeserv'd he ne'er inflicts a Woe,
Nor is his Recompence unsure, tho' slow.
Unpunish'd none transgress, deceiv'd none trust,
His Rules are fix'd, and all his Ways are Just.

(P. 17)

The manner of Persius is reflected in the stoical but bitter personal and political tones of the educated and aristocratic speakers appropriate for the highest born and most academic of the three great Latin satirists.

Hervey's commitment to the administration made it difficult for him to portray too corrupt a political world, and so most of the poem laments the human, not Walpolean, situation. But Walpole's literary enemies were quick to realize that the general could be made particular, Zeno could be altered to Cobham, the tyrants of the mind could be replaced by the tyrants of the court, and Nero could evoke George II, Walpole, or both. Historical parallels were popular with the opposition in part because of the legal camouflage they supplied.[16] At least five such minimally disguised efforts suggest that, in varying degrees, the opposition was leagued with Juvenal and Persius and generally found Horace irrelevant or antithetical to its purposes. Indeed, as the "progress" of these poems suggests, the imitations become harsher, more overtly political, more Juvenalian, and more indebted to Pope as the decade advances.

The first is a relatively muted anonymous adaptation of the fourth satire and its attack upon Nero. In *Advice to an Aspiring Young Gentleman of Fortune* (1733) that un-

[16] See, for example, *The Art of Poetry* (1741):

Old *Roman Names* your Characters suit best;
Secure, as if in *Roman* Armour drest.
Happy the Author whose Performance shines
With living *Nero*'s, living *Catilines*!

(P. 9)

Such mock-historicism was one of the opposition's frequent, and transparent, techniques.

pleasant emperor has been replaced by his modern equiva-
lent, the author's "*garter'd* Friend . . . / To whom an
injur'd Nation Vengeance owes." The court is a place "of
well-invented Lies" where the "Dangers of *Excise*" must
be slurred over (p. 5), the corrupt rich thrive, purchased
coronets abound, and flattery, not achievement, will "fit
you for *Preferment* in a trice" (p. 10). It is best, the honest
speaker urges, to leave the ticklish helm of government "to
——*y*'s saving Hand" (p. 10). That line supports replace-
ment of Walpole with Pulteney, is hostile to the gartered
knight, and commissions Persius as a Roman officer in the
opposition's British army.

One year later the pseudonymous Griffith Morgan
D'Anvers is less subtle than his predecessors. D'Anvers's
*Persius Scaramouch: Or, a Critical and Moral Satire on the
Orators, Scriblers, and Vices of the present Times* (1734)
imitates Persius's first satire and dedicates it to Pulteney,
without benefit of nonobfuscating dashes. D'Anvers, in
dialogue with Orator Henley, immediately opposes the
"ministerial Crew of profligate Scriblers" (p. iii) who try to
defame Pulteney, aligns himself with Juvenal, who also had
to say "*Semper ego auditor tantum nunquamne reponam?*"
(p. iii), and labels himself "a Man of a true old *British*
Spirit and Integrity." D'Anvers alludes to, and approves of,
Pope's earlier and potential attacks on the administration,
and offers his own political and moral enemies "a little
present and gentle Chastisement"; but he is assured that
their miserable characters "will be transmitted to Posterity
with all the Infamy they deserve, by a Person of as great
a Genius as this, or perhaps any other Age hath produc'd"
(p. iv).

For some, the mask of Persius has a partially downturned
tragic mouth; for many others it has bared teeth and satyr's
horns by which the administration was not amused. *Persius
Scaramouch,* for instance, mocks Sir Robert as inviting
hacks to "caper nimbly o'er [his] Stick," and to sing "Not
to their own, but to his Honour's Notes" (p. 7). Similarly,

"W—p—le's Gold and Coxcomb's Praise" have also al-
lowed "worthless Scriblers" to usurp the laureateship (p.
13). Juvenalian qualities in the Persian poem, however,
consist of more than opposition to and attacks on the
Robinocracy by a nonaristocratic speaker; they also include
both personal bitterness of tone and a cultural theory of
causation, each related to the political climate induced by
Walpole. Hence the main speaker stresses his *"British
Mind"* (p. 9), his refusal to compromise with corruption
(pp. 9, 11, 13, passim), his persecution because of his pov-
erty and virtue (pp. 9, 17), and his consequent anger, gall
(p. 9), and spite (p. 19). This imitation could have as its
motto the Juvenalian tag, "Difficile est Satyram non Scri-
bere" *(Satires,* 1, 30). Among the several reasons he must
write, one far transcends personal deprivation: wherever he
looks he sees decay. "How ripe for Ruin is the present
Age!" the poem begins (p. 9), in a more than free rendering
of Persius's *"O Curas hominum! O quantum est in rebus
inane!"* to which D'Anvers's facing line refers. Commons,
peers, courts of law, bishops, and most groups in society
are corrupt in a world where "Who can be wickedest Men
seem to strive" (p. 11). The reason for such ruin is made
clear in the attack on the poet laureate appointed by the
prime minister. Men strive to be bad poets as well, it seems.

> Some *Cibber's* Works peruse, and some rehearse
> Thy Flights *Blancoso* in *Miltonick* Verse.
> No wonder therefore, if the younger Fry,
> Unable to distinguish, read and try
> To write pert Nonsense, like the *London* Spy.
>
> (P. 15)

British natives, like British virtues, are banished, "since
Frenchmen, like a mighty Flood, / O're-spread the Land"
(p. 17), and "belie our Father's Reins" (p. 17). Pope again
must be the scourge who "roastedst well the Witlings of
our Isle" (p. 19). When Henley tells D'Anvers that a surly
Welshman like himself will never get past the great man's

door, where only courtiers and Henleys prosper (p. 17), D'Anvers must retreat to the privacy of his closestool for release from his spleen and spite. There he "Shall tear some Trifler's Works whene'er I sh—te" (p. 19).

By 1739 one Mr. Dudley, with better control of his bowels, had also turned the *First Satire of Persius* to opposition use. His translation is dedicated to the Society of Ancient Free Catonians, since there is a "near Affinity . . . in the respective Characters and Principles of our Satirist" and Cato. Each man enjoyed an abstemious severity in the cause of virtue and freedom: "If *Cato* scorn'd and detested *Caesar* on Account of his Tyranny and Usurpation; *Persius*, animated with the same Godlike Spirit, disdain'd to be the Slave of *Nero*, and held that Monster of Impiety in a like Abhorrence" (p. iv). The Argument of the poem also indicates that Persius hated the bad taste of Nero and his nobles, and emphasizes that Nero was "*the Patron of every mean Pretender*" to wit (p. 9), a man, the reader might suspect, perhaps something like Sir Robert. This Persius assumes the familiar pose of noble adversary of the horde of bad, court-encouraged poets, even though his prudent friend urges him to "desist. Invidious Truths conceal" (p. 11). For Dudley's Persius, if "none dare their Follies to disclose," his own "warm indignant Zeal" shall act: "Be mine the Province," he claims as protector of poetic virtue. "What can I do? My Spleen is too severe, / Such sordid Scribblers urge the scornful Sneer" (p. 11). In so responding, he is consciously in the great tradition of Lucilius, who "lash'd the latent Vices of the State" (p. 25), and of a "subtle" but, in this context, vigorous and potent Horace, who slyly and politely destroyed foibles. "Shall I be cow'd, / Nor dare to whisper what they spoke aloud?" (p. 27). Clearly not, though Dudley is threatened with hanging by his ungentle adversarius (p. 25).

Even fuller antiministerial suggestions in the first satire were not to wait long before being plucked from the politicized classics. In 1740 Benjamin Loveling published his

First Satire of Persius Imitated, the third known version in six years, and abandoned even the pretense of being deliberative, general, or stoic. He offers sheer opposition propaganda that clarifies the *"Obscurity"* of the poem by means of cleverly attacking the court and administration and praising Pope and the opposition. Loveling's Persius is a product of what the commentators long had taught. He ridicules *"Bad Poets . . . Bad Orators, and . . . the depraved Taste of* Rome, *in admiring the wretched Performances of* Nero *and his* Nobles" (sig. A1ʳ). His modern counterpart implicitly compares the reigns of Nero and of George, for he dislikes "what *Cibber* sings" and *"Grubstreet* Swans [who] delight the Ear of Kings" (p. 5). "Gazetteers" are the mere *"Beings of a Day"* (p. 9), and though he purports to admire George II, he knows that he himself is the lone soldier fighting barbarism (p. 7), that his adversarius thinks it grand to be *"By Kings rewarded, and by Nobles prais'd"* (p. 9), and that he himself can be praised by such paragons of taste only if he writes a birthday ode, those "Songs by the Court and vulgar Great admir'd" (p. 11). Predictably, certain opposition leaders have no place in such a world.

> *Stair* and *Cobham*, Names to *Britain* dear,
> Names which the Virtuous and the Wise revere,
> Sick of the Fool's and Parasite's Resort,
> Retire, illustrious Exiles from a Court!
>
> (P. 13)

The poem is punctuated with references to stage licensing, Fanny, poor Jenkins's lost ear, echoes of Pope's satires, and celebration of that satirist as "sworn Foe to Knave and Fool" who assailed Timon, Chartres, Peter, Ward, and Balaam (p. 19). The imitation has plucked the fig leaf of obscurity from Persius's satire upon "Nero," and left itself covered only by the shadow of Cobham's opposition seat at Stowe, a world far different from the one Loveling sees in Walpole's London:

Feign but a Senate where Corruption reigns,
And leads her courtly Slaves in golden Chains,
Where one directs three hundred venal Tongues,
And owes his Grandeur to a People's Wrongs;
To ——'s Favour can the Bard pretend?
No Hints he cries, the Minister's my Friend;
And for the *Sock* the Stage is never free,
For draw a Blockhead ——'s Death! the Dog means me!

(P. 15)

In contrast, "Tis Noise and Froth that *Young* or *Blackmore* sings, / Tho' both were favour'd with the Smiles of Kings" (p. 17). By now this modern Persius is unwilling even to pretend to keep his harsh satire in the secure privacy of his book. His heroes are not Lucilius and Horace, but Dryden and the hostile Pope, and his poetical enemies are all those, including Boileau and Prior, who praise kings.[17] By 1740 Loveling's Persius has eschewed even the transparent irony of earlier masks, and insists on speaking out. His satirist will remain undaunted in the cause of virtue, and "Yes, I will sneer the Follies of Mankind" (p. 19). As we soon shall see, the indignant opposition Persius who blends well with Juvenal is made even more overt in Paul Whitehead's *The State of Rome, Under Nero and Domitian* (1739), presumably written "By Messrs. Juvenal and Persius."

This review of an English, opposition Persius makes clear that his imitators in the 1730s become more hostile to Walpole as the decade advances; along the way, they also become more Juvenalian and allied with Pope, the frequent parent of their invective and one probable source for how "Persius" should write. Since Pope's imitations of

[17] Pope was often invoked by other satirists as the lonely warrior defending decency against its powerful enemies. See *The Wrongheads. A Poem Inscrib'd to Mr. Pope. By a Person of Quality* (1733), p. 3; Paul Whitehead, *The State Dunces. Inscrib'd to Mr. Pope* (1733), pp. 2-5; Thomas Gilbert, *A View of the Town* (1735), p. 18, and Whitehead's (?) *State of Rome*, pp. 5, 9. See also chapter 4, section IV, and chapter 10, section II, below.

Horace and presumably Horatian dialogues often supplied that image, such uses of Persius also invoke and support the hypothesis of mingling satiric conventions that Pope received, enhanced, and transmitted, but, unlike Boileau, with more weight given to the genre's tragic than to its comic implications.

V: Examples of Mingled Forms

Satire as a genre of mingled conventions probably would have been acceptable not only in France and England, but in classical Rome, for her satirists seem to have regarded themselves as sibling rivals rather than warring chiefs. We recall that each Roman satirist looks back to Lucilius in some form as the master who originated the genre and, as Horace argues, did not sufficiently polish his verse in his poetically rude age. Francis Howes puts a comparable modern case in 1809: "the want of preceding models to be surpassed, usually cause [sic] first efforts to be imperfect." Persius was able to add his own adaptations of Horatian dialogue and insinuation as well as echoes of specific scenes and lines. Juvenal both alludes to Lucilian wrath, and elevates yet further Persius's raised voice. The Abbé le Monnier notes this satiric symbiosis in 1771, when he comments upon part of Persius's Satire Five: "Perse avoit lu son Horace lorsqu'il a fait ce vers. . . . Juvénal avoit lu ses deux devanciers. . . . Boileau est venu ensuite, qui a lu ces trois satiriques, & s'est approprié leurs pensées."[18]

Awareness of the comparison as well as contrast between the satirists was part of Renaissance and later seventeenth- and eighteenth-century awareness of classical satire. William Coward considers both such concord and discord in

[18] Howes, *The Satires of A. Persius Flaccus*, p. vi; le Monnier, *Satires de Perse* (Paris), p. 153. Ralph Cohen has discussed a version of "mingled forms" in his "On the Interrelations of Eighteenth-Century Literary Forms," in Philip Harth, ed., *New Approaches to Eighteenth-Century Literature* (New York: Columbia Univ. Press, 1974), pp. 33-78.

his *Licentia Poetica Discuss'd* (1709). He knows Horace's and Juvenal's separate ways of reforming manners and clearly prefers the drolling to the hectoring mode. Part of that preference is based on Horace's ability to combine the harshness of Lucilius with what he calls the sweetness of Juvenal. Coward cannot excuse Juvenal's frequently blunt style, which is "beyond that which a true Satyrist ought to use. Hence the old commentators say, *Horatii Satyra*, inter Lucilii *Satyram*, & Juvenalis est media; Nam & Asperitatem habet, qualem Lucilius, & Suavitatem qualem Juvenalis, tho' I cannot deny *Juvenal* to be an excellent Satyrist in the *General*." Père Sanadon makes a similar point in 1728: "Plus judicieux & plus châtié que Lucile, [Horace] tient le milieu entre les bouillantes invectives de Juvénal & la brièveté obscure de Perse." For Lewis Crusius, on the other hand, one reason Juvenal is the best of the Roman satirists is his ability to combine their greatest strengths for his own purposes: "He is elegant and witty with *Horace*, grave and sublime with *Persius*, and to both their characters has added the pomp of his own eloquence, which makes him the most entertaining, as well as the clearest writer of the three." Crusius later adds that Juvenal's gross expressions may have been learned from, or at least have precedent in, Lucilius's satires. According to the *Biographia Classica* of 1740, assiduously following Dryden's "Discourse" on satire, Juvenal is better than Horace in part because Horace had only one predecessor from whom to borrow. He refines Lucilius's verse, but writes humble satire and limits his desires "only to the Conquest of *Lucilius*." Horace thus "made way for a new Conquest over himself by Juvenal his *Successor*" (2: 211), who was able to use Horatian refinement and wit together with his own sublime verse. Later in the century, Vicesimus Knox observes that Juvenal added perspicuity to the Persian fire already available to him. In 1806 a translator of Persius wisely backs away from a definition of satire but does observe that it falls into three classes—"into the gay, the serious, and a skilful combination of these two." Horace exemplifies the first kind, while "Persius and Juvenal have scantily blended this with the more dignified and moral."[19]

Other commentators admired Persius for one of the same reasons that Coward admired Horace and Crusius admired Juvenal: namely, his blend of satiric modes. Isaac Casaubon well summarizes the satiric tradition and its individual talents. Though Horace certainly imitated Lucilius, Persius "was the first of all to enrich, correct, and change for the better Roman satire of this kind," which "had been ambiguous" in its structure. Persius's imitations of Horace thus always show "his own judgment everywhere," and in turn provided a model of unity for his successors. Juvenal, for instance, "approved of the strategy of Persius, and did not confusingly . . . embrace various arguments in the same poem; but in the manner of Persius in his satire he usually added a 'single underlying type'" of argument. Bolingbroke, however, turns the criterion of mingling against Persius who, he argues in a letter to Aaron Hill on 25 October 1747, "might have done something of both" Horatian sneering and Juvenalian lashing at Vice "if he had studied to be intelligible, instead of affecting obscurity." Several years thereafter, Edward Owen also describes Persius as an at least partially failed model of mixed satiric modes. Persius had a "middle character" as a satirist, "for he fettered and cramped himself by a close imitation of Horace, while his genius naturally led him to the Great and Serious, which Juvenal afterwards attained."[20] Owen's

---

[19] Coward, *Licentia Poetica Discuss'd: Or, The True Test of Poetry. Without which It is Impossible to Judge or Compose, A Correct English Poem,* p. 73, note c; Sanadon, *Les Poésies d'Horace* (Paris), 1: sig. aij^v, the original is italicized; Crusius, *Lives of the Roman Poets* (1726), 3rd ed. (1753), 2: 80, 83; Knox, "On Satire and Satirists," *Essays Moral and Literary* (1778), 2: 149-50; 1806, *The Satires of Aulus Persius Flaccus,* pp. xvi, xxv.

[20] Casaubon, in Peter E. Medine, "Isaac Casaubon's *Prolegomena* to the *Satires* [1605] of Persius: An Introduction, Text, and Translation," *English Literary Renaissance,* 6 (1976): 291-92; Bolingbroke, *The Works*

ability to see the shades of satiric gray extends to Juvenal and Horace as well. In parts of the first satire Juvenal "descends from the TRAGIC tone of satire, and assumes the COMIC, with somewhat of the gaiety and humour of Horace" (1: 2-3); and in the ninth satire, we hear, Juvenal adds a touch of the railleur and Horatian "irony and grave banter" (1: 190); in the tenth, he and Horace share the excellent trait of *"oblique* satire" (1: 222).

At least two later authors argue that only such mingling can influence the often depraved British audience. William Whitehead's *Essay on Ridicule* praises the intention but mocks the achievement of those satirists who use either the lash of vengeance or the smile of ridicule. In the one case "The hardy Felon quite contemns the Law"; in the other, "laughing Satire weakens" the case because "Crimes turn Frolics" (pp. 13-14). There is a better way, one of course wholly infused with British good nature and drawn from native as well as imported models. Whitehead thus urges the satirist to adopt Cervantes's gravity, Lucian's gaiety, Butler's drollery, Garth's politeness, Rabelais's jest—"without his Ribaldry"—Phillips's pomp, Gay's ingenuous style, *"Arbuthnot's* various, *Swift's* unweary'd Smile." When so mingled, satire can in fact improve life and work its proper end, and we will "See Vice, attended by his captive Train, / Confess its Justice, while he bites his Chain" (p. 20).

The poet behind *Modern Virtue* (1746) is not so optimistic as Whitehead. The "Friend" in his dialogue agrees that satire in corrupt Britain is useless, whether delivered in Oldham's stabbing or Young's smiling verse (pp. 14-15). The "Author" himself at first thinks that success will follow if he redoubles his Juvenalian effort, but he then concedes that the more likely path to success, if any, is by adding another choice—to be "Sublimely grave, or whimsically gay" while attacking court or 'change, empress or

---

of the Late Aaron Hill, Esq. (1753), 2: 415; Owen, *The Satires of Juvenal* (1785), 2: 244; subsequent references to this work are cited in the text.

bench, and keenly pursuing vice "With *Rabelais*'s Jest." He will thereby continue to point at *"Folly*'s gay Plume" and "Each Frenzy mortify, each *Vice* confound" (pp. 23-24). In both theory and practice, the best way to write effectual satire again is to combine the high and low styles and to engage the enemy, whether he is vicious or foolish.

Such overlapping satiric method was also seen by prose commentators upon Horace and Juvenal. John Hill's *Inspector* for 12 June 1751 fully acknowledges the apparent conflict between Horatian and Juvenalian methods and their respective devotees; but Hill thinks it wrong to suppose Juvenal wholly concerned with lashing vice and agrees instead with the elder Scaliger, that "he takes in by the Way . . . little Follies, and forgetting Acrimony of Style, often reproves . . . with great Humour and Pleasantry." Throughout Juvenal's work there is "a great deal of extreme good Humour; and if you behold him sometimes frowning and threatening, you may at other times see him smiling and jesting."[21] A similar view appears in William Henry Hall's *New Royal Encyclopedia* (1789). Hall reports the commonplace that Horace is jocose, and Juvenal serious, and then adds that they "both agree . . . in being pungent and biting; and from a due consideration of these authors, who are masters in this art, we may define satire to be, a free and often jocose, witty, and sharp poem, wherein the follies and vices of men are lashed and ridiculed in order to their reformation" ("Satire," vol. 3). Perhaps the author of *Modern Manners* (1793) shared this inclusive definition of satire when he gave himself the name of Horace Juvenal, and called Pope "the prince of *Satire*" (p. 26).

We recall that relatively "pure" Horatian and Juvenalian poems were not in short supply. But if Horace could be thought Juvenalian and Lucilian; if Persius could be Lucilian and Horatian; if Juvenal could be Lucilian, Horatian,

---

[21] As quoted in the *London Daily Advertiser, and Literary Gazette*. The numbering of the *Inspector* here, and in the collected volumes of 1753, is different. This number, for example, is omitted in 1753.

and Persian; and if many poets and commentators could argue that some such mingling was the best way to succeed, can there be any wonder that the practice of modern satirists should be affected? We will see this development at its best in Pope; that his was not an isolated case is evident to readers of the imitations of Persius, and of Edward Young's "original" *Love of Fame, The Universal Passion* (1725-28), whose Preface sings Horatian laughing satire but admits that the angry Juvenal also has his moral and rhetorical contribution.[22] Young's Satire Six, against women, invokes Juvenal's "severer rage! / To lash the ranker follies of our age," and proceeds to show how women are dissolving the established order—"Naked she stalks o'er *law* and *gospel* too" (pp. 143-44)—to such a degree that " 'Tis not a world, but Chaos of mankind" (p. 145). The Juvenalian

[22] Quotations are from the 2nd ed., 1728, which is the first collected edition and the first to include the useful Preface. See sigs. A4^{r-v} for Young's remarks on Horace and Juvenal. Subsequent citations are given in the text. I have discussed Young at greater length in *The Formal Strain*, pp. 95-128. See also Raman Selden's remarks on Young in his *English Verse Satire 1590-1765* (George Allen & Unwin, 1978), pp. 122-28. Swift criticizes Young's poem in "A Copy of Verses Upon Two Celebrated Modern Poets," and especially in "On Reading Dr. Young's Satires, Called the Universal Passion," each probably written in 1726 and published in 1734. For the relevant comments in the latter poem, see *The Poems of Jonathan Swift*, ed. Harold Williams, 2nd ed. (Oxford: Clarendon Press, 1958), 2: 391-92.

For another example of inept mingling of modes, see *The Modern Englishman. A Satire* (1738; 2nd ed. appears in 1743 as *The Characters of the Age: Or The Modern Englishman. A Satire*). The poem includes the stock Juvenalian baggage—"Contagious Ills spread dire Disease around; / Search! search the Cause! deep probe the fatal Wound" (p. 3) —and portrays a world ripe for the lash of "poignant Satire" (p. 11). Once the poet invokes his favorite peer, however, "Envy dies, Ambition sleeps in Peace, / Self-interest falls, and public Factions cease" (p. 18). The power of "L——" to effect an instant cure renders the poet's earlier gloom and judgment suspect; and the Horatian's faith in the wisdom of his recipient-aristocrat seems like an ill-worn costume. The work was, oddly, attributed to Pope in a Dublin edition that had "London" on its title page.

outburst, however, is inconsistent with the poem's domi-
nant Horatian convention of a world in which stable, in-
telligent governors embody the nation's best values and
defeat the threat of evil. The wicked older sort of courtier,
for example, can only revive "*Walpole,* when men forget
to copy thee" (p. 166); Queen Caroline's appearance on
the scene immediately banishes the disorder that Young
had urged was a threat to the survival of the race (p. 155).
He has not faced the aesthetic or logical implications of
the Juvenalian intrusion in a Horatian world, and like
other satirists inept at mingling modes, threatens the in-
tegrity and coherence of his poem. The use or abuse of dif-
ferent conventions thus not only can help to explain part
of an author's intention but can serve as a touchstone of
quality. As Swift notes, Young has distinct and inade-
quately related layers of satire.

The flaw is magnified in Thomas Newcomb's *The Man-
ners of the Age* (1733), which at 587 apparent pages may be
the longest satire of the eighteenth century; it has the sig-
nal advantage of leaping from page 208 to 409 with the
turn of a leaf. In his earlier poem *Bibliotheca* (1712) New-
comb had insisted that "Stubborn Folly" is best arraigned
"by a candid and easy Rebuke," by smiles, and good humor
rather than severity (sigs. A3^{r-v}); but he knows that in a few
instances, when opposing the worst offenders, he must
transgress that otherwise sound rule (sigs. A4^{r-v}). Newcomb
uses both gentle and severe strokes in his subsequent effort
as well. The thirteen satires in *Manners* are filled with hor-
rible imprecations—of how the vile age must be stung,
lashed, whipped, poisoned, scourged, and otherwise pun-
ished with terms as familiar to satirists as to Kraft-Ebbing.
His world is filled with an endless number of scoundrels,
and only he himself, nobly fearless in his heroic costume,
can defeat them and defend virtue:

> In vertue's cause, if others dread the fight,
> Let satir arm—the muse assert her right;

The goddess on her sacred throne maintain,
Scourge of the base, and terror to the vain.
Say then, who first shall feel her venom'd sting?
(Sat. 1, p. 8)

Yet each satire is dedicated to a different successful Whig potentate or fellow traveler—Walpole is fourth in line— and each finally develops Young's vitiating tone of respectability, generalized character, harmless attacks, and glib success in defeating the world's evil.[23] Moreover, the Juvenalian posturing emerges as shadow without substance. In Satire Ten Newcomb tells Sir William Yonge that "Half won by you, my conquests are but small" (p. 463), and in Satire Thirteen he urges the most toothless of attacks: "Be fond to praise, and cautious to offend" (p. 562). *Love of Fame* located its Juvenalian declamations in a few major places; *Manners* comes close to alternating a Horatian pose of comfort in highly placed triumphant allies with a Juvenalian pose of the satirist as surrogate Abdiel at Thermopolae. The latter convention seems no more than ritual invoked, though its presence is powerful evidence of the need for that ritual. Like Edward Young, Newcomb fails to unify his satiric kinds and writes an unsuccessful tribute to his own timidity.

These instances of improperly used but nonetheless significant Juvenalian devices in Horatian poems can easily be multiplied and extended to Horatian-Persian and Persian-Juvenalian examples as well—as the imitations of Persius make clear. Young and Newcomb, however, may have had an extrapoetic and noncongenital reason for their apparent errors of strategy: both were ministerial allies and were ideologically and prudentially committed to the sort of

---

[23] Newcomb was aware of the political implications of his *Manners*, since the poem was reprinted in his admittedly partisan *Miscellaneous Collection of Original Poems . . . Written Chiefly on Political and Moral Subjects. To which are added, Occasional Letters and Essays, formerly published in Defence of the present Government and Administration* (1740).

success their poems portrayed. Nearly all of the best satirists were on the other side and had greater room for maneuver and manipulation of conventions potentially hostile to one another. One such poem is worth discussing in this context, for it shows the intrusion of Juvenalian devices in Horatian poems. Moreover, this poem is a useful transition to the larger issue of how Pope and his satire were perceived by his contemporaries, for these Juvenalian devices stem from Pope's precedent.

The unsigned *Epidemical Madness: A Poem in Imitation of Horace* (1739) is an extremely free imitation of Horace's *Satires*, ii. 3. Here Damasippus the Stoic proclaims the madness of the world but, after scoring several points, nonetheless is dismissed by the more perceptive satirist who sees his adversarius's own madness and banishes stoicism as a serious option. The modern poem, however, opens with a dialogue between the Poet and his Friend that is adapted from Horace, *Satires*, ii. 1, as infiltrated by *Fortescue* (1733) and the *Epilogue to the Satires* (1738). The Friend solemnly says: "You write so seldom, and are so severe, / That you are hated almost every where" and are wished dead (p. 3). The Poet himself is aware that his satire is ineffectual and that he may as well retire to his rural pleasures while awaiting death. This Friend is very different from the several adversaries who inhabit Pope's own dialogues, for he bluntly states that the Poet is not in a rural bliss but in wretched exile, and since he will be abused by the town even if he is silent, "take a Friend's Advice, and lash it still; / Let Envy snarl, and Guilt say what it will." "Really!" the surprised poet responds, as if aware that the traditional role of Persius's dissuading adversarius has been changed and that an encourager of satire now rejects Fortescue's earlier advice that the poet not write.

> *Fr.*—Yes! on my Word you may depend,
> Since I without a Fee advise my Friend.
> *Po.* Then to your Council I'll again give Way,

And epidemic Madness will display.
  Know,—with the *Stoicks* I at last agree,
And own that all are touch'd in some Degree.

(P. 4)

Thereafter the poem becomes a somber, almost Persian catalogue of the varied kinds of pandemic madness. Many are perfectly conventional targets—lust, avarice, martial fame—but several are related to the greatest form of madness, one at the heart of the nation.

  Not *Bedlam* stinks with greater Madness than
  The Manners of a great imperious Man;
  Who, if not homag'd more than God's ador'd,
  And for the Boon with humbler Grace implor'd,
  Will on superior Merit turn his Back,
  And treat a Patriot worse than any Quack.

(Pp. 5-6)

The "mad ambitious Man" rises at the cost of others, his nation, and harmony, while he himself actually opens the way "To Tyranny and universal Sway." In the process he insures that he will "live the Curse of Human Race" (p. 6). The satirist responds to this, and to other examples of madness, by saying: "I wonder that we do not all run mad: / But that we do not am extremely glad" (p. 10). Well might he wonder, for as he looks around him, he sees politically manipulated and bribed Dunces helping to make a world in which *"Credit, Trade, and Reputation sinks, / And worse than* Newgate *with Reproaches stinks"* (p. 15).

For Horace, madness is part of the human situation but, ultimately, is subhuman and part of rejected stoicism; for the *Epidemical* author, madness is all too present, is at least in part a product of the administration's political debauchery, and is resisted by the few who know that Virtue only adorns one's name. In that view "alone there's all that *sober* lies, / And he's a Mad-man that the Truth denies" (p. 16). The presumed imitation of Horace is infused with the Juvenalian spirit of Pope. Its world is one of political and moral decay, of an exiled poet forced to do further combat with Virtue's tormentors, and it assumes, as its Greek tag on the title page suggests, that all sorts of evils flourish among men. By 1739 such replacement of Horatian sense, method, and outlook with Juvenalian outrage and hostility was commonplace, especially among opposition authors. Equally commonplace was the view that though Pope was sometimes Horatian, he was also, qualitatively, the chief native architect of such satiric displacement and of mingling of modes. These efforts sometimes won praise and sometimes condemnation; but they were never ignored.

※※

CHAPTER 5

Responses to Pope

MANY READERS IN THE eighteenth century, as in the twentieth, thought that Pope perfectly captured Horatian wit, style, and tones. In 1735 even Thomas Bentley, Richard's nephew, unhappily reported the generous words spoken about Pope's imitations of Horace: "if any body has a mind to taste HORACE, they need only read *them*. A Cartload of Commentaries will signify nothing without 'em. There's more *Wit* in 'em, than in HORACE's Original Sermones." Joseph Spence had much the same to say, but with more pleasure at the success of his friend's efforts. In *Polymetis* (1747) Spence reports that his reading of Pope's imitations helped to reveal Horace's true aims, for Pope's education at home allowed his mind to play directly upon the poems without being hindered by the ponderous and intrusive commentaries inflicted on university students. George, Lord Lyttelton, probably would have agreed, for in the fourteenth of his *Dialogues of the Dead* (1760), between Boileau and Pope, Pope says, "we both followed Horace," and Boileau admits that "you hit the *Manner* of Horace, and the sly Delicacy of his Wit more exactly than I, or than any other Man who has writ since his time." Several years thereafter Vicesimus Knox enthuses that Pope "imbibed the very spirit of Horace" in his "liberal imitations."[1] Shortly thereafter, the poet of *Party-Satire Satirized*

---

[1] Bentley, *A Letter to Mr. Pope, Occasioned by Sober Advice from Horace*, p. 15; Spence, *Polymetis: Or, an Enquiry concerning the Agreement Between the Works of the Roman Poets, and the Remains of the Antient Artists*, 2nd ed. (1755), p. 287; Lyttelton, *Dialogues of the Dead*, p. 112 (followed Horace), p. 116 (sly delicacy); Knox, "On Satire and Satirists," in *Essays Moral and Literary* (1778), 2: 151. Spence's remark in *Polymetis* is quoted approvingly by Thomas Tyers. See his *Historical Rhapsody on Mr. Pope*, 2nd ed. (1783), pp. 56-57. Lyttelton's

(1779) reviews some of the unattractive qualities of irrational modern political satire and asks when he can expect "To see another *Dryden*, or a *Pope?*" (p. 8). Whenever it will be, it can happen only after tiresome moderns are aware that in Pope, Britain had a satirist who could sting and draw laughs, and who thus was Britain's *"Horace* of her own"* (p. 23).

Such contemporary judgments nonetheless describe only a small part of Pope's satiric bias. That Pope adapted and revealed some Horatian conventions—dialogue, delicacy, and wit, for example—is true on the face of it; that he was basically "Horatian," or imitating Horatian values, however, is less true by far. In fact, many of the events and much of the direction of Pope's career and character, even before his political opposition of the 1730s, point to an un-Horatian road and destination.

I: LIFE AND LETTERS

"William Ayre's," perhaps Edmund Curll's, *Memoirs of the Life and Writings of Alexander Pope* (1745) implies several of the reasons for this lack of congruence with the courtly Horace near the center of the Augustan world. Pope "was not made for Courts; he had nothing insinuating nor fawning about him, neither could he flatter any Body: His Person was not such as is sought out to make a Figure, and his Constitution would not have supported the Fatigue of Attendance: His Religion excluded him from all Offices of Trust and Profit, and he rather wanted somebody

---

remark is part of the tug-of-war regarding Pope's affinities with or differences from Boileau. Warburton, *The Works of Alexander Pope, Esq.* (1751), 4: xi-xii, and Joseph Warton, *Essays on the Genius and Writings of Pope* (1756, 1782), 5th ed. (1806), 1: 94-96, 2: 257, see Boileau as Pope's analogue or model. Percival Stockdale is characteristically outraged at such stuff—"it is impossible that your assertions can be true," he tells Warton. *An Inquiry Into the Nature and Genuine Laws of Poetry* (1778), p. 67. See also *Memoirs of the Society of Grub-Street* (1737) 1: vi, for Pope as "an English *Boileau.*"

to humour him than to humour others; so that he was cal-
culated for the private Life he led."[2]

Pope's lack of insinuation was made clearer than ever
after the appearance of the *Dunciad* in 1728, a satire re-
garded as excessive even by some of his friends and ad-
mirers. In spite of many literary quarrels, Pope had gen-
erally been thought of as the successful author of a variety
of poems in different and unthreatening genres, and as an
editor of Shakespeare, and a translator of Homer. He had
now moved into the center of ugly personal combat in a
genre of dubious respectability. In 1723 Pope is praised for
his perfectly easy, soft, and almost "Female" lines written
with "good Diction"; by 1730 the budding Boy-Patriot
George Lyttelton sends Pope an epistle from Rome, lament-
ing the harshness and bad diction of the great poet's new
verse. Lyttelton regards Pope as the heir of Addison and
Congreve, and thinks him capable of restoring and con-
tinuing British genius in a land of liberty. As Lyttelton
strews flowers on Virgil's tomb, that shade conveniently
arises and asks his foreign visitor to bring Pope this mes-
sage:

> No more let meaner Satire taint thy Bays,
> And stain the Glory of thy nobler Lays:
> In all the flow'ry Paths of *Pindus* stray,
> But shun that thorny, that unpleasing Way.[3]

---

[2] Ayre, 2: 95. This work was attributed to Curll in [J. H.], *Remarks
on 'Squire Ayre's Memoirs of the Life and Writings of Mr. Pope. In a
Letter to Mr. Edmund Curl, Bookseller* (1745): "give me leave to ask
you, whether it was, as *Edmund Curl*, your proper identical Self, or in
your assum'd Person of *William Ayre, Esq*; that you was thus impor-
tun'd to write these Memoirs?" (p. 17). One suspects that those tepid
Memoirs are not scandalous enough to be Curll's. George Sherburn
thought that Curll might be Ayre's publisher. See the *Correspondence
of Alexander Pope*, ed. Sherburn (Oxford: Clarendon Press, 1956), 3:
19, n. 3

[3] "Female lines," *Poems on Several Occasions*, pp. 110, 126; Lyttelton,
An Epistle to Mr. Pope, From a Young Gentleman at Rome, p. 5. Sub-
sequent quotations are cited in the text. For another comment on

Pope is wrongly forcing his genius from its proper "soft, engaging Muse," and is courting "the least attractive of the Nine" (pp. 6-7). He should celebrate the glories of his free nation, "Where Honours on distinguish'd Merit wait, / And Virtue is no more a Foe to State." That once was Virgil's song, and if it now becomes Pope's, "Immortal and unblam'd thy Name shall live," defeat black Envy, and gain the praise of Patriot and poet (p. 8). Alas, Pope could not so sing, as Lyttelton himself would soon appreciate, since the British world his Virgil described was rapidly passing, and Pope's movement into literary opposition also signaled his movement into political opposition.

One essential aspect of Pope's self-defense both before and after the *Dunciad* was his insistence upon the brave and masculine spirit chained within his warped body. The *Rape of the Lock* (1712-17) and the epistle *To a Lady* (1735) portray an avuncular male narrator familiar with the psychological quirks of the female mind. Warmer passions find themselves romantically arrayed in poems as different as the early pastorals (1709), the *Elegy to the Memory of an Unfortunate Lady* (1717), and *Eloisa to Abelard* (1717). As one detractor of *Sober Advice from Horace* (1734) says, that poem shows Pope sending Horace out to rut.[4] Other poems include a more important kind of mascu-

---

Pope's "harmonious Lays," see James Miller, *Harlequin Horace: Or, The Art of Modern Poetry* (1731), pp. 6-7. The *Epistle to Bathurst* (1733) excluded Pope yet more from certain "polite," normally administration circles. See, for example, anon., *The Muse in Distress. Occasion'd by the Present State of Poetry* (1733), dedicated to Sir William Yonge:

> The *Twitt'nham* 'SQUIRE, grown petulant and bold,
> Forgets the Notes with which he charm'd of old;
> To *Spleen* he prostitutes his noble Art,
> Alike a Bigot in his Verse and Heart.
>
> (P. 12)

For further response to *Fortescue*, see chapter 7, section III, below.

4 Anon., *Sawney and Colley, A Poetical Dialogue* [1742], pp. 20, 20n. See also Thomas Bentley's *Letter to Mr. Pope* (n. 1 above), which

line pose—namely that of the isolated soldier defending
Virtue and Truth, even at the cost of his life if necessary.
Pope refuses to pay a version of Danegeld to those he
thought the new, domestic barbarians. Instead, he will
draw "the last Pen for Freedom," praise the "Last of *Brit-
ons*," and like them be willing to "Fall, by the Votes of
their degen'rate Line!" (*Dialogue* II. 248, 250, 253).

This Juvenalian pose in a poem *"Something like Hor-
ace"* was useful in the *Epilogue to the Satires* and else-
where for several reasons, two of which I think especially
important. On biographical grounds, Pope must have felt
the need to counter the frequent attacks that portrayed him
as sexually minuscule and thus, by an inscrutable chain of
cause and effect, unworthy of serious consideration as a
poet, much less as an imitator of an apparently all too
experienced rake like Horace. *The Female Dunciad* (1728),
for example, offers us a ditty in which Pope tells a woman
who rallied him on his ugliness:

> You know [where] you did despise,
> (T'other Day) my little Eyes,
> *Little Legs*, and *little Thighs*,
> And some *Things* of *little Size*,
> You know where.
> (P. 6)[5]

---

claims that Pope has "published a most obscene thing, worse than any
Bacchanalian Song made for a Bawdy-house" (p. 4). Bentley seems
fascinated, if not pleased, with Pope's obscenities in this imitation.

[5] The passage, from a rondeau by Voiture, was translated by Pope
in June of 1710 and presented to a woman who was tormenting him.
See the *Correspondence of Alexander Pope*, 1: 90, and Dustin H. Grif-
fin, *Alexander Pope: The Poet in the Poems* (Princeton: Princeton
Univ. Press, 1978), p. 44. *The Female Dunciad* is of course not in-
tended to be slyly sympathetic, and it may have been written by Curll.
See J. V. Guerinot, *Pamphlet Attacks on Alexander Pope 1711-1744*
(New York: New York Univ. Press, 1969), pp. 142-44, and *The Dunciad*
in the Twickenham edition, p. 210. There is a fuller discussion of the
episode in Emile Audra, *L'Influence française dans l'oeuvre de Pope*
(Paris: H. Champion, 1931), pp. 325-27. For yet another attack on Pope

Edward Ward's *Apollo's Maggot in his Cups* (1729) is ruder still, for it shows Apollo and a group of drunken muses making Pope into a thing halfway between a monkey and a man. Ward exchanges the Biblical God's fecund earth for building materials that include rubbish, urine, and feces, all molded into a disproportioned, deformed creature that lacks the distinguishing mark of his sex. To remedy that oversight, the muses "dab'd on just an Inch of Stuff, / Enough to show the Gender" (p. 19). By 1742 the author of *Sawney and Colley* trundles out a very old saw when he claims that Pope was "As impotent in *Spite* as *Love*" (p. 7).

Replies to such insults were necessary for Pope's personal dignity and for his ability to set his manliness against the sexual irregularities of Horace and Hervey. In the second satire of the first book, which became Pope's *Sober Advice*, Horace wonders why in the world a sane man would endanger himself through adultery with aristocratic ladies, when there were professionals and boys who would offer more pleasure and less danger. Joseph Spence says that Horace's "debauchery, made him still the more agreeable to Maecenas." Tobias Smollett's *Advice. A Satire* (1746) shows a corrupt modern behaving like Horace in keeping "two boys array'd in white," and "Worthy to feel that appetence of fame / That rivals *Horace* only in his shame!" (p. 9). Pope's own poetry insisted on normal sexuality and on bravery in the face of the enemy, for Horace, as Pope's *To Augustus* observes (see the note to line 204), abandoned Brutus and his own shield and fled before Octavian's army at Philippi. Pope also implicitly contrasts himself with Lord Hervey, who shared one of Horace's vices, and whom the opposition long had described as the bisexual betrayer of manhood.[6] The "Master up, now Miss" and "vile An-

---

for his non-Horationism, see *A Letter to a Friend in the Country* (1740), where a speaking ass berates Pope for thinking he was "born to copy *Flaccus*" (p. 20).

[6] Spence, *Polymetis*, p. 21. For a use of *appetence* comparable to Smollett's, see *Paradise Lost*, XI. 618-21. Donald Korte's "Tobias Smol-

tithesis" (lines 324-25) of Sporus in Pope's *Arbuthnot* thus evoke Pope's own contrast and insistence "That, if he pleas'd, he pleas'd by manly ways" (line 337) presumably different from Hervey's and Horace's. Pope was glad to rival Horace, but not in his shame.

Pope's indignation was of course noticed by several of his friendly readers. In 1733, for example, the patriot behind *The Wrongheads*, inscribed to Pope, makes plain both his hero's role in the task of defending Virtue, and the indignation the good man feels in his battle against the many evil men; the latter shall neither receive applause nor avoid censure because "*Pope* forbids" and is "fir'd with honest rage" (p. 3). Thomas Gilbert also was a sympathetic reader of Pope, and also saw so much vice about him that he scarce knows "what vices first deserve my rage." He lays out several of these for our inspection, and then links Pope, rage, Oldham, and by obvious extension, Juvenal:

O *Pope*, thou scourge to a licentious age,
Inspire these lines with thy severest rage;
Arm me with satire keen as *Oldham* wrote
Against the curst *Divan*, with poignant thought.

---

lett's 'Advice' and 'Reproof,' " *Thoth*, 8 (1967): 45-65, discusses Smollett's debt to Pope's "Sporus" for these and other lines attacking homosexuality. There are attacks on Hervey's sexuality in, among other places, Caleb D'Anvers [William Pulteney], *A Proper Reply to a late Scurrilous Libel; intitled, Sedition and Defamation display'd* (1731), and [William Sherwin], *A Most Proper Reply to the Nobleman's Epistle to a Doctor of Divinity* (1734), p. 19. See chapter 8, below, for discussion of Pulteney's work. See also *Lord Hervey and His Friends*, ed. Giles Stephen Fox-Strangways, 6th Earl of Ilchester (John Murray, 1950), pp. 296-98, which reprints verses about Hervey sent to Stephen Fox in 1734. Robert Halsband discusses relevant aspects of Hervey's reputation in *Lord Hervey: Eighteenth-Century Courtier* (New York: Oxford Univ. Press, 1974), especially pp. 111, 118 (Hervey as a "*Master and Miss*"), 138-39, 165-66. For further relevant discussion of Pope and Hervey, see Camille A. Paglio, "Lord Hervey and Pope," *Eighteenth-Century Studies*, 6 (1973): 348-71.

Comparable words, tones, and recognition of satiric geneal-
ogy and satiric offspring appear in the works of James
Miller. In 1739, for example, he characterizes Pope's art
and a dominant non-Horatian satiric strain of that decade.

> A righteous Rage at our degen'rate Days,
> Arm'd *Pope* with his *own* keen *Iambick* Lays,
> To scourge th' enormous Folly o' the Times,
> And make the Vicious tremble at his Rhimes.
> With like Success, but not with like Desert,
> Our *Sock* and *Buskin Bards* have ap'd his Art;
> Each *Vice*, by turns, flies, bleeding from *his* Stroke.[7]

Other commentators aware of Pope's rage also were
aware of his consequent elevation. The author of *The State
Weather Cocks* (1734) consecrates his verse to Pope, and
prays:

> Cou'd I but reach thee in thy lofty Flight,
> I wou'd not then despair to hit the Wight.
> So high you soar, that how shall I pretend,
> With callow Wings, to follow thee, my Friend.
>   (P. 4)

By 1737 the author of an imitation of Horace's second ode
of the fourth book also uses the metaphor of flight for
Pope's satire and insists that he is like "some Heav'n-
instructed Bard." As such a bard, he opposes enemies of
God as well as the state and must abandon smiles for savage
and soaring indignation—as John Brown observes when
celebrating Pope's "lofty" traits in 1745.

> When fell Corruption dark and deep, like Fate,
> Saps the Foundation of a sinking State:
> When Giant-Vice and Irreligion rise,

7 Gilbert, *A View of the Town: In an Epistle to a Friend in the
Country* (1735), pp. 2, 18; Miller, *The Art of Life. In Imitation of
Horace's Art of Poetry*, p. 14.

On mountain'd Falsehoods to invade the Skies:
Then warmer Numbers glow thro' SATIRE's Page,
And all her Smiles are darken'd into Rage:
On Eagle-wing she gains *Parnassus'* Height,
Not lofty EPIC Soars a nobler Flight.[8]

We have already seen some of the ways in which Pope
influences the several imitations of Persius, and how as the
1730s progress Persius becomes more angry and less stoic.
This movement is exemplified in Paul Whitehead's un-
signed *The State of Rome, Under Nero and Domitian: A
Satire. Containing, A List of Nobles, Senators, High Priests,
Great Ministers of State, &c. &c. &c* (1739).[9] This bitter
poem pretends to be written "By Messrs. Juvenal and Per-
sius" and imitates scattered sections of Persius, *Satires* 1 and
4, and Juvenal, 1, 3, 7, and 8, whose patchwork of support-
ing Latin is reproduced at the foot of the page. The amal-
gamated, fiercely indignant satirist asks, "What Ribs of
Iron can my Gall contain?" (p. 4) as he sees the political
and consequent literary corruption around him. He thus
seeks support from Pope and alludes to his satires as an-
other natural ally in the resistance to a government he
thinks so corrupt that "No social Virtue meets one Friend
at Court" (p. 7). Accordingly, in this emotive rhetorical
monologue, Messrs. Juvenal and Persius virtually become
the angry, elevated Alexander Pope, and proclaim with
him, in lines stemming from the *Epilogue to the Satires*
and the *Epistle to Dr. Arbuthnot,*

Spread, Satire, spread thy Wings, and fearless fly
To seize thy Prey, tho' lurking ne'er so high.

(P. 5)

Here *Sporus* live—and once more feel my Rage,
Once and again I drag thee on the Stage;

[8] *An Ode to the Earl of Chesterfield, Imploring his Majesty's Return.
In Imitation of Horace. Ode II. Book IV*, p. 8; Brown, *An Essay on
Satire. Occasioned by the Death of Mr. Pope*, 2nd ed. (1746), pp. 20-21.
[9] Quotations are from this 2nd ed. (1739) and are cited in the text.

Male-Female Thing, without one Virtue made,
Fit only for the *Pathick*'s loathsome Trade.

(P. 9)

Walpole's "servile Court," his manipulation of George II
(p. 14), and the nation's degradation appear in uncompli-
mentary Roman dress. Britain is a land in which an abso-
lute Nero refuses to accept advice (p. 16), and which, like
an overlarge fish long out of water, stinks and is rotting just
below its surface (p. 17). Satire here can only play for high
stakes.

Pope's detractors also saw that he soared his way out of
Horace's flat and into Juvenal's elevated satiric kingdom.
Soon after Lady Mary imprudently published the *Verses*
to Pope, an unfriendly anonymous writer described Sap-
pho's world, "When *Rome* was lash'd by JUVENAL's sharp
Lines" and "Each conscious Breast apply'd them to his
Crimes." In 1739 the poet behind *Characters* attempts to
dissuade Pope and Paul Whitehead from further disgorg-
ing "a Stew of Satire on the State" (p. 5). The Augustan
Horace himself lost half his reputation when he fell into
satire. Worse yet, he tells his presumed audience, you too
will be as ineffectual as the satirist of Domitian:

> you from *Juvenal* would snatch the Rod,
> And scour along the Path in which he trod;
> Who, banish'd from the State he could not save,
> Did live but little better than a Slave.

(P. 11)[10]

[10] Lady Mary is scolded in *Advice to Sappho. Occasioned by her
Verses on the Imitator of the First Satire of the Second Book of
Horace. By a Gentlewoman* (1733), p. 3. See also *Characters: An Epistle
to Alexander Pope Esq; and Mr. Whitehead*, pp. 9-10; *Scriblerus Maxi-
mus. The Art of Scribling, Address'd to All the Scriblers of the Age*
(1733), pp. 2, 16-17; and *A Proper Reply to a Lady, Occasioned by her
Verses address'd to the Imitator of . . . Horace* (1737), pp. 3-7. The
author of *Characters* assumes the Juvenalian pose of indignant enemy
of vice. Pope himself is "a specious Knave; / A Tool, to Envy, and

Many of these remarks, whether friendly or hostile, implicitly recognize that Pope is using Horatian conventions for Juvenalian ends and is mingling satiric modes. Other commentators were explicit. On 31 July 1738, for example, Aaron Hill praises the second dialogue of the *Epilogue to the Satires* because it "carries the acrimony of *Juvenal*, with the *Horatian* air of ease and serenity. It reaches *heights* the most elevated, without seeming to design any *soaring*. It is raised and familiar at once." The author of a poem prefaced to Pope's imitation of Donne's fourth satire (1733) also praises Pope's ability to censure folly and impertinence in the tones of both major predecessors:

> So *Juvenal*, in keen Remarks of Old,
> *Rome*'s tainted Manners elegantly told;
> With such just Boldness *manly Horace* writ,
> And baffled Folly, by his vig'rous Wit.

(P. 4)

In 1740 one "Lorleach" observes that Pope has "Rais'd *Horace* up" and changed his courtly ridicule of faults into bitter, if useless, attacks upon vice. Shortly thereafter, Colley Cibber facetiously cites Pope as an example of the independence and superiority of modern to ancient literature. In the process, he characterizes one of Pope's essential techniques:

> Nay even our *Pope*, who tho' from *Horace*,
> He plainly Plans of Satire borrows,
> In new-mill'd Coin the Loan repays,
> And mends the Weight of *Roman* Lays;
> In stronger Strokes, and Tints of Nature,
> His Fools and Knaves enrich the Satire,
> And sound his Sense in more harmonious Metre.[11]

Ambition's Slave" (p. 7). Truth, however, will reveal "a *Garter* or a *Star*, / Without a Blemish, and without a Scar" (p. 13).

[11] *The Works of the Late Aaron Hill, Esq.* (1753), 1: 293, Hill to Pope, 31 July 1738; see also Pope's *Correspondence*, 4: 112. Pope's

We remember that in his *Essay on Ridicule* (1743) William Whitehead recommends a blend of satiric kinds for the best of British satire. His model for such verse is presumably Pope himself, "Who bids all *Greece* at once revive" and who "Shares every Art that every Muse can give" (p. 2). We also remember that John Brown's *Essay on Satire* (1745) praises Pope for his ability to unify all three Roman satiric kinds, to exemplify the *"British* Genius," and to satirize both vice and folly. *"Each* Roman's force adorns his various Page," which offers "Gay Smiles, collected Strength, and manly Rage" (p. 26).

This view of Pope as a satirist was not merely a function of the party rage of the Walpole years, for it was affirmed in apparently neutral observations at home and abroad throughout the later eighteenth century. William Warburton, to whom Brown's poem was dedicated, plays a variation on this theme in 1751, when introducing Pope's imitations of Horace. Warburton states the facts of Pope's eclectic satiric mode, and he insists that anyone seeking either a paraphrase or "a faithful Copy" of Horace's genius or mode of writing will be disappointed.

> Our author uses the Roman Poet for little more than his canvas: And if the old design or colouring chance to suit his purpose, it is well: if not, he employs his own, without scruple or ceremony. Hence it is, he is so frequently serious where Horace is in jest; and at ease where Horace is disturbed. In a word, he regulates his movements no further on his Original, than was necessary for his concurrence, in promoting their common plan of *Reformation of manners.*

Had it been his purpose merely to paraphrase an ancient satirist he had hardly made choice of Horace; with

---

blend of satirists also is noted in *The Impertinent: Or, a Visit to the Court. A Satyr. By Mr. Pope,* 2nd ed. (Dublin, 1737), p. 4; Lorleach, *A Satirical Epistle to Mr. Pope,* p. 4; Cibber, *A Rhapsody Upon the Marvellous: Arising from the First Odes of Horace and Pindar* (1741), p. 7.

whom, as a Poet, he held little in common, besides a
comprehensive knowledge of life and manners, and a cer-
tain *curious felicity* of expression, which consists in using
the simplest language with dignity, and the most orna-
mented, with ease. For the rest, his harmony and strength
of numbers, his force and splendor of colouring, his grav-
ity and sublime of sentiment, would have rather led him
to another model. Nor was his temper less unlike that of
Horace, than his talents. What Horace would only smile
at, Mr. Pope would treat with the grave severity of Per-
sius: and what Mr. Pope would strike with the caustic
lightning of Juvenal, Horace would content himself in
turning into ridicule.[12]

Recognition of Pope as temperamentally un-Horatian
and as the poet of mingled satiric forms was reinforced in
Owen Ruffhead's *Life of Pope* (1769). Ruffhead borrows
some of Warburton's words and expands this parallel to
include Young's and Pope's satires on women: "What
Young smiles at, POPE treats with the grave severity of Per-
sius; and what POPE strikes with the caustic lightning of
Juvenal, Young contents himself with turning into ridi-
cule" (p. 278). By 1797 Joseph Warton had come to a simi-
lar conclusion regarding Pope and his Roman models.
Anyone, he says, aware of Horace's poems and their indebt-

---

[12] *The Works of Alexander Pope*, 4: 51. This passage was often read
and discussed. For one hostile response, see the first of three unpub-
lished "Dialogues between a certain R.R. Doctor of D——y. and A
Critic" (ca. 1760), folios 123-32, which examines Warburton's com-
ments and Pope's *Fortescue*. The other two dialogues concern "M͏ʳ
Pope's first Epistle [of the *Essay on Man*], to the Lord Bolingbroke,"
and "On the Second Satire of the Second Book of Horace Imitated by
M͏ʳ Pope." All three efforts attack Warburton's commentaries and,
often, Pope's verse. The critic concludes that Pope is a lamentably
uninventive poet (folios 161ʳ-62ʳ). See Douce MS. 201, the Bodleian
Library, Oxford. I am grateful for permission to quote from these
manuscripts. Late in the century William Boscawen applauds Warbur-
ton's distinction between Pope and his brother-satirists. See *Satires,
Epistles, and Art of Poetry of Horace* (London, 1797), p. xvi.

edness to the old comedy immediately sees that in his imitations Pope "has assumed a higher tone, and frequently has deserted the free colloquial air, the insinuating Socratic manner of his original: and that he clearly resembles in his style, as he did in his natural temper, the severe and serious Juvenal more than the smiling and sportive Horace."[13]

Just one year later William Boscawen, a careful student of classical satire, published *The Progress of Satire*. Like several of his predecessors in this task, he considers the historical and psychological nature and origin of satire, its movement through time and different subspecies, and its achievements in the three Roman exemplars. From these, he argues, Britain gains her laws for satire but adapts them in her own way, for she is "Free as her sons, and varying as her clime" (p. 8). Nonetheless, her dominant direction is in the Persian-Juvenalian mode of bold flight that brands statesmen or kings, and engages in the factious strife of political satire. In all the pantheon of British satirists, one stands out above his distinguished colleagues; he does so not only because of his special talent, but because he is both the harbor of previous satiric forms and the embarkation point for subsequent ones. He unifies and naturalizes Roman strains, and sends them into the world in their British costume. Pope's fine ear, exquisite taste, masculine sense, and literary polish are all brought to bear upon his synthesizing yet analytic voice.

> Each softer charm that grac'd th' Horatian lyre,
> Sublim'd by Juvenal's more vigorous fire,
> Breathes in thy numbers, with prevailing art
> Steals on the sense, and wins th' enraptur'd heart.
> Each graceful form the Sons of Satire choose
> Springs from thy various, thy accomplish'd Muse.
>
> (P. 10)

---

[13] Ruffhead's *Life of Alexander Pope* and its indebtedness to Warburton are discussed by W. L. MacDonald, in *Pope and his Critics: A Study in Eighteenth-Century Personalities* (J. M. Dent, 1951), pp. 256-60; Warton, *The Works of Alexander Pope*, 4: 61n.

Lest we should be puzzled by Boscawen's points, his note yet further clarifies the clear meaning. In note (z) he observes that though there were examples of "these different species of Satire prior to the writings of Pope, . . . our subsequent satirists, in these different branches, have in general, taken him for their model" (p. 10), a model that includes Horace sublimed by Juvenal. Persius's translator in 1806 also describes Pope's "various" muse, for he imitates both Juvenal's "stately oratory, and caustic declamation" and Horace's "airy, . . . playful, and facetious" tones.[14]

The Abbé Yart could not know whether Boscawen was correct in determining Pope's satiric influence, but in 1753 he saw that Pope had two important traits: he mingled satiric kinds and typified the British, Juvenalian satiric character. The passionate oration in *Fortescue*—"What, arm'd for Virtue"—evokes this comment: "Ne semble-t-il pas que c'est Juvénal qui tourne à sa manière ces pensées d'Horace."[15] All of *Arbuthnot*, he argues, is Juvenalian in its fragmentary composition, for each man wrote a section immediately after he was prompted to do so by some outrage. The opening itself immediately recalls Juvenal, who "a presque toujours ce ton vif, brusque, & bouillant, qui est si original & si naturel" (3: 102n). The attack on Hervey shows that when Pope was irritated "*facit indignatio versum*" (3: 159n), though in this attack Pope was being too English which, we infer, is almost to say too Juvenalian, and pushes too far in his hostility and language (3: 162n). Pope had not only the pride of a hero but the magnanimity to forgive his enemies (3: 165n).

These links between Pope and Juvenal are riveted in the repetition of some important words in French discussion of satire. The English genius, Yart claims, is profound but

14 *The Satires of Aulus Persius Flaccus*, p. xxv.

15 *Idée de la poësie Angloise, ou traduction des meilleurs poëtes Angloises* (Paris, 1749-56), 3: 69n. Subsequent citations are given in the text. All of volume 3 (1753) concerns Pope and is indispensable for an understanding of eighteenth-century Anglo-French relations.

"est presque toujours outré" (3: 170n); Pope himself was "un Philosophe, chagrin & sévere, un Poëte vif & outré; & en un mot, un Anglois" (3: 239). Now compare a remark about Juvenal in *L'Anée Littéraire* for 1782, chonologically distant yet in ways verbally close to Yart: "Dans la décadence du goût, le Rhéteur *Juvénal*, nourri d'hyperboles & de figures outrées, . . . substitua à la politesse & à l'urbanité du favori d'*Auguste*, un ton dur & chagrin, une emphase pédantesque, & la satyre née de la Comédie ne conserva plus dans ses vers aucune trace de son ancienne origine" (p. 151). Both *outré* and *chagrin*, which had characterized the English mind and Pope's satiric art, find a congenial home in a negative remark about Juvenal who, like his subsequent emulators, took the tragic not comic satiric path.

Moreover, Yart characterizes *Arbuthnot* as a model of formal verse satire in the mingled way. This poem, he says, offers "des morceaux admirables, ecrits avec la force & la véhémence de Juvénal, la légèreté & la finesse d'Horace, la précision & la noblesse de Perse. M. Pope semble avoir affecté en quelques endroits de prendre non-seulement le ton & les Dialogues de ce dernier Poëte, mais encore son air mystérieux, & son obscurité, pour derober aux yeux de ses ennemis dangereux ou puissans, les traits qu' il leur lançoit" (3: 96-97).

Several other readers noticed some of the same traits in Pope but were neither kind nor merely descriptive in their judgments, since for them being like Juvenal or Pope was more than a simple failure of taste.

II: "In every Respect, the reverse of *Horace*"

Horace long had been praised for his devotion to friends and patrons. In contrast, critics of Pope often focused on his presumed ungrateful attacks on Addison and, especially, Chandos, maliciously thought to be Timon in Pope's

Epistle to Burlington (1731). The author of an epistle to
Chandos (1732) makes plain that such ingratitude could
only be offered by a wretch, adder, daemon, or like disgrace
to humankind. This unpleasant and hysterical portrait is
one of the several sallies against a poet who violated every
canon of Horatian friendship.

> Ah! hapless *They* on whom, unknown you *smile,*
> Whose yielding *Hearts* thy *Flatteries* beguile;
> *Themselves* they soon shall see with wild *Surprize*
> Adorn'd, as *Victims,* for the *Sacrifice*:
> So *Addison*——Peace to his gentle *Shade*!
> Was to thy *treach'rous* Merit once *betray'd*—
> So *Ch—nd—s,* gen'rous *Lord,* is taught to know
> That to *oblige,* is to *exasp'rate* you——
> The same shall ev'ry worthy *Patron* see,
> And *B—rl—ngt—n* Himself be stabb'd by *Thee.*[16]

[16] "An Epistle, Humbly inscribed to his Gr—ce the D—ke of
Ch—nd—s. 1732," in Timothy Scribble [Ashley Cowper], *The Norfolk
Poetical Miscellany. To which are added Some Select Essays and Letters
in Prose. . . . By the Author of the Progress of Physick* (1744), 1: 366-
67. For some of the many references to Pope's ingratitude, here to
Addison, see *Characters of the Times; Or, An Impartial Account of
the Writings, Characters, Education, &c. of several Noblemen and
Gentlemen, libell'd in a Preface to a late Miscellany Published By
P-pe and S-ft* (1728), pp. 29-30, 45; Smedley, *Gulliveriana: Or A Fourth
Volume of Miscellanies . . . published by Pope and Swift* (1728), p.
ixj; Thomas Newcomb, "A Poet's Gratitude," in *A Miscellaneous Col-
lection of Original Poems* (1740), p. 223; Colley Cibber, *A Letter From
Mr. Cibber, To Mr. Pope* (1742), p. 17. The presumed attack on
Chandos drew even graver response. See the offensive frontispiece to
Ingratitude: To Mr. Pope . . . (1733), in which Pope is urinated upon
for his behavior to Chandos and Addison (pp. 8-9). Leonard Welsted
attacks Pope in *Of Dulness and Scandal. Occasion'd by the Character
of Lord Timon. In Mr. Pope's Epistle to the Earl of Burlington* (1732).
He is answered by the unsigned *An Epistle to Mr. Pope* (1732), which
praises its subject as "Immortal POPE" (p. 4) and criticizes Welsted as
"His Lordship's Fool, or Poet, or what not, / A Pimp, to the Right Hon-
ourable Sot" (p. 7). *The Man of Taste. A Comedy. As it is Acted By a
Summer Company near Twickenham* (1733) is a reissue of *Mr. Taste,
The Poetical Fop* (1732) and, on its title page, tells Pope to stop criti-
cizing Chandos "Because he takes not Nature for his Guide." After all,

Pope's alleged disloyalty also extended to his country, as his choice of both spiritual and secular gods indicates. Historians and administration apologists agreed that, in the words of the *London Journal* of 8 January 1726, Horace helped Augustus "to confirm his new Empire, by endearing Him to the *Roman* People," a claim that ministerial writers were not likely to make about Pope on behalf of his own Augustus and court. Thomas Bentley, among many others, in fact reverses the argument, claiming that Pope's praise of Bolingbroke is "almost treasonable!" and that Bolingbroke himself is an impossible guide. "Can you think the Christian Religion true . . . and not fear being *damned* with him . . . to *everlasting Torments?*"[17] Pope is inviting the loss of British liberty and the acquisition of Popery. This common charge was summed up in *Plain Matter of Fact: or, Whiggism The Bulwark of these Kingdoms* (1742), written by an unnamed Lover of his Country. He knows that the horde of opposition scribblers "take *their Instructions* from a *Romish Satyrist,* as *he* from that arch Enemy of our Constitution" Bolingbroke, who well supplies "French *Lewis D'ores*" in place of sound and modest British half-pence (p. 13).

Much of this scarcely controlled rage was political, much personal. There must have been little difficulty recruiting troops to fight the author of the *Dunciad,* a poem that threatened the livelihoods of its victims and included imagery designed to offend their otherwise chaste imaginations. The *Daily Journal* for 28 May 1728 prints this comment from a poet outraged by "the most filthy and indecent Instances of the *True Profound,* that ever defiled the *English* Language." Pope, he says,

---

"in thy Form we see / That Nature may mistake as well as he." Even some of Pope's advocates thought that he attacked Chandos. See the anonymous *A Proper Reply to a Lady* (n. 10, above), p. 7. The presumed Chandos-*Taste* connection surfaces late in Pope's career, as in *Sawney and Colley* (n. 4 above), pp. 14, 14n.

17 *A Letter to Mr. Pope,* pp. 12, 11.

> is dwindled to a Boghouse Wit,
> And writes as filthy Stuff, as others sh——.
> Who reads *P*——*e*'s Verses, or *Dean Gully's Prose*,
> Must a strong *Stomach* have, or else no *Nose*.[18]

Even the smoother turn of Pope's Horatian verse displeased the remaining noses and ears of certain readers. Indeed, once Pope's satiric career begins in earnest, several hostile commentators insist that whatever his parent poem might be, he was not a Horatian satirist, especially and paradoxically in the imitation of Horace. The simplest argument dismisses Pope as a copier who is both inept and necessarily beneath the original Horace. In 1733 Lord Hervey claims that Pope "ne'er could think" and, like a schoolboy, begs sense from his author. Pope's "best Works" are linked to ancient authors; his more original satires bring him "eternal Shame." Hervey was referring to Pope's Homer as well as Horace. One year later, the author of "A Sequel to Tit for Tat" (1734) limits himself more clearly to *Fortescue* and has Lord Hervey, as a speaking Gold-Finch, claim that Pope merely is "a bare-fac'd *Plagiarist*" who "Pretends to vaunt with borrow'd Wit" yet is mocked by "every Cit" for his indiscriminate bespattering of the living and dead, including his own patrons (p. 11).[19]

The wide and elevated range of Pope's satiric targets also made him a dubious Horace. In 1739 Patrick Guthrie's (?) *Candour: Or, An Occasional Essay On The Abuse of Wit and Eloquence*, praises Pope's divine talent but explodes at works like the *Epilogue to the Satires*, in which the satirist spares neither church nor throne, flatters the people in order to induce rebellion, threatens to subvert the state and restore anarchy (p. 3), and foolishly praises Bolingbroke. "See the State-Cripple halt to touch thy Shrine" (p. 5),

---

[18] As in Smedley's *Gulliveriana* (n. 16, above), p. 316.
[19] *An Epistle from a Nobleman to a Doctor of Divinity*, p. 7. The "Sequel" is in the *Court Oracle: A New Miscellany* (1734). Much of the "Sequel" borrows from Hervey's *Epistle*.

Guthrie orates. Other critics also complained that Pope's scattergun satire hit their political allies, but they were not nearly so kind, if Guthrie may be so called. The poet of *One Thousand Seven Hundred Thirty Nine* (1740) sees Pope peevishly flinging "His Dirt, on Players, Poets, Peers, and Kings," writing ironic praise, as in *To Augustus*, and swelling his poem with slander and names only in order to make it sell (pp. 5-6). By 1742 Lord Hervey had long been victimized in *Arbuthnot* and was less willing than ever to see excellence in Pope's satires. In his unpleasant *Letter to Mr. C——b——r, On his Letter to Mr. P——* he insists that though his wee enemy may be a *"good Copyist"* (p. 22), he is also a scurrilous name-caller and as much a satirist as "a drunken Scold of an Apple-woman" or "a foul-mouth'd Hackney-Coachman" (p. 11). In summing up, Hervey offers a paradigm of what a Horatian satirist is not: Pope is "at best a *second-rate Poet*, a *bad Companion*, a *dangerous Acquaintance*, an *inveterate, implacable Enemy, no body's Friend*, a noxious *Member of Society*, and a *thorough bad Man"* (p. 25).

Other responses left even less to the reader's imagination, and bluntly stripped the Horatian mask to reveal Pope's sadistic leering face beneath. As early as 1716, for example, John Dennis's "True Character of Mr. Pope" responds to a lost imitation of Horace in which Pope "libels" Horace and Dennis. According to Dennis, perhaps a partial witness, "the Difference between *Horace*, and such an Imitation of him, is almost Infinite." Pope, like other minor poets in England and France, is "in ev'ry Respect, the reverse of *Horace*, in Honour, in Discernment, in Genius."[20] Lady Mary and Lord Hervey would have agreed with this distant

[20] See E. Parker, *A Complete Key To the New Farce, call'd Three Hours after Marriage. With an Account of the Authors* (1717), pp. 11, 14. For this account of Pope, see also "A True Character of Mr. Pope and his Writings," in *The Critical Works of John Dennis*, ed. Edward Niles Hooker (Baltimore: The Johns Hopkins Univ. Press, 1967), 2: 107.

ally, for their *Verses Address'd to the Imitator of the First Satire of the Second Book of Horace* (1733) sharply distinguishes between the Roman wit, sense, and satire of Horace, and the English rage, ribaldry, and scandal facing it. "On one side we see how *Horace* thought; / And on the other, how he never wrote." Pope's imitation is as burlesque an image of Horace as Pope's body is of man—"at once Resemblance and Disgrace" (pp. 3-4). With only a slight diminution of vulgarity, their lady- and lordships epitomize Horace's and Pope's satiric styles.

> *Horace* can laugh, is delicate, is clear;
> You, only coarsely rail, or darkly sneer:
> His Style is elegant, his Diction pure,
> Whilst none thy crabbed Numbers can endure;
> Hard as thy Heart, and as thy Birth Obscure.
>   If *He* has Thorns, they all on Roses grow;
> Thine like rude Thistles, and mean Brambles show
> With this Exception, that tho' rank the Soil,
> Weeds, as they are, seem produc'd by Toil.
> *Satire* shou'd, like a polish'd Razor keen,
> Wound with a Touch, that's scarcely felt or seen.
> Thine is an Oyster-Knife, that hacks and hews;
> The Rage, but not the Talent to Abuse;
> And is in *Hate*, what *Love* is in the Stews.
>
> (P. 4)

A comparable attack appears in 1735, when Thomas Bentley's *Letter to Mr. Pope* uses the fancied anonymity of *Sober Advice from Horace* as the sting in the tail to punish Pope for, finally, being un-Horatian. Pope, he says, originated "this new way of writing" imitations, and did so *"to get upon the Back of* HORACE*"* in order to "abuse every body you don't like with Impunity!" But the author of *Sober Advice* misfires: "You," he tells Pope, "are a *Rasor*, he a *Wedge*." Pope can please in spite of his unpleasant satire; the *Sober* imitator "blasphemes and talks bawdy," and thus, Bentley says in a revelatory turn, that associates the "two" disliked satirists, is "closer to his Master POPE, than his Master HORACE" (p. 4).

In the same year the correspondent of *An Epistle to Alexander Pope* also praises his numbers while being tired of his spleen and frothing. Pope's pretensions of sharing Parnassus with his satiric ancestors are outrageous, for they—Horace must be meant—did not abuse "gentle Dames," or specific persons, but aimed high, at Vice (p. 1). Unlike Pope, they were loyal to the state, grateful for help, and not mercenary. The author quotes a presumed Pope who consistently talks this sort of foolishness.

> "See this old Cloak, 'twas *Horace*'s of Old,
> "Patch'd thus by *Bentley*, worth its Weight in Gold;
> "In this I domineer, repeat old Saws,
> "And sell 'em to the Crowd, *Apollo*'s Laws."
>
> (P. 2)

The dazzling foe of the state and reason also must be a foe of Horace, and thereby takes "from thyself the Poet's Crown" (p. 6).

Three proministerial poems by Thomas Newcomb in about 1739-40 further chart the great divide separating the imitator and his parent poet. In his *Supplement to One Thousand Seven Hundred Thirty-Eight. Not written by Mr. Pope* (Dublin, 1739), Newcomb's speaker A, tells Pope, B, that "Your old friend *Horace*, never wrote so keen, / As when he felt his muse quite free from spleen." He rarely gave "hard words" and always lashed gently whenever he "touch'd a sore" (p. 12). Poor B, however, is a prisoner of his own distorted personality, is no longer capable of praise, and "wou'd methinks be honest——if I durst" (p. 24), as the un-Horatian, ungenerous lasher cannot be. Newcomb's "An ode of similies, on some late imitations of *Horace*. The *Latin* printed on one side, and the English on the other" (1739) is also an obvious response to Pope's Horatianizing strain. At least "the *Roman* side," of the book is successful, though the rest is unrecognizable to a

puzzled Horace, who must wonder how Maecenas can be
turned into Bolingbroke:

> Those who deserv'd the ax and rods,
> In thy own lov'd *Octavius'* days,
> Make pious hero's, saints, and gods,
> In *British* verse, and *Tw*——*am* lays.
>
> Thy patriots all in virtue nurst,
> For generous actions were renown'd;
> His, by his country scorn'd, or curst,
> Are traitors first, and after crown'd.[21]

In another effort, Newcomb's muse is able to evoke the
indignant voice of Horace, who insists that he and Pope
were enemies not allies. "Pert, meddling bard!" Horace's
spirit grouses, "must I arise / From bliss each year, and fix
my name" to lies about "*St. John*'s worth, and *Walpole*'s
shame?" (p. 52). Such Tory misrepresentations are heretical
violations of Roman decorum and praise of true national
heroes. Horace never sang a traitorous, immoral man, nor
libeled or satirized a friend, nor was ungrateful to benefac-
tors, nor exalted a driveling priest-ridden monarch like
James, nor verbally punished the nation's true friends. Hav-
ing "Horace" commit such sins in London today may cause
Britain to treat his memory with scorn. Such misconcep-
tions must stop.

> 'Twou'd blast the wreath that *Phoebus* gave,
> At my fair fame and honour strike;
> Cou'd it be wrote upon thy grave,
> That * * * * and *Horace* thought alike.
>
> .   .   .   .

---

[21] T[homas] N[ewcomb], *A Miscellaneous Collection of Original
Poems*, pp. 49, 51. Italics and Roman type are reversed in the title, as
in the title of Newcomb's next work quoted, "*Q. Horatii Flacci* ad
Curionem epistola: Or, an epistle from *Horace* in *Elizium* to *Curio* in
England, faithfully translated into *English* from the *Elizian* copy."
Page references are cited in the text.

If you quote me——I must protest,
And swear, your sense is none of mine.

(Pp. 54-55)

Other writers shared the political annoyance of these sev-
eral commentators. The author of "Modern Characters"
(1739), for instance, returns to an essential distinction be-
tween the old and new Horace. Among other un-Horatian
traits, Pope claims to see good and not satanic evil in Bol-
ingbroke's circle, while also failing to see the true noble
spirit of the administration: "Is this to imitate the glorious
Roman, who would scorn to be the *Dupe* of the *Seditious*,
or be borne away with the destructive Tide of Faction?——
But even this *Inversion*, or rather Prostitution of the celes-
tial poetic Art, is owing to the persuasive *Poison*, of the
Grand Incendiary."[22] Yet again, the basic role of Horace as
a satirist sympathetic to the government makes his pose
recognizably alien from Pope's, whose satire, in the words
of *A Letter To a Friend in the Country* (1740), is the libel-
ing of a braying ass who oddly thinks himself "born to copy
Flaccus" (pp. 20-21).

The ministerial press both shared and encouraged such
differentiation between Pope's appearance and Horace's
reality, while making clear the dangers should Pope con-
tinue in his misguided ways. The administration well
knew that by claiming a particular satiric ally, or by modi-
fying or denying the relevant conventions, writers could
take political sides. The *London Journal* for 8 January
1726 notes that Horace's epistles conferred a positive im-
mortality upon their recipients. On 14 September and 19
October it argues that real persons must not be named in
satires. Its successor, the *Daily Gazetteer*, was equally in-
sistent on Horatian general satire, which on 12 June 1737
it relates to the practice of comedy: "Tho' *Dryden* now

[22] *A Hue and Cry After Part of a Pack of Hounds, Which broke out
of Their Kennel in Westminster. To which is added, Modern Charac-
ters, By Another Hand*, p. 28.

and then had a Bob for the Court, yet it was general Satyr —not meant at any particular Person." Once the vicious old comedy was deservedly "put down by Publick Authority," comedy took the proper path, and had "nothing to do with this Description of the Vices and Follies of the Great." In fact, Horace is an authority for censorship of such comedy, as he is again on 16 July (see also 4 June), when the administration reminds us that those who libeled "Persons of high rank" could have been cudgeled to death under Augustus's reinstituted Law of the XII Tables, and that such a law would have salutary effects under George Augustus as well. Now contrast the same newspaper's response to Pope's imitation of Horace's first epistle of the first book, where Bolingbroke replaces Maecenas, particular replaces general satire, disaffection replaces affection for the court, and, in the terms I have been suggesting, significantly mingled satiric conventions replace the Horatian archetypes.

On 27 March 1738 the *Gazetteer* suggests that Pope may not know how to write satire at all, "for would any one, who, pretends to have no other Aim but the encouraging of Virtue, and discountenancing of Vice in his Writings, make Choice of such a Patron" as Bolingbroke? He does not deserve Pope's praise, is not the good man he describes, and—unlike the recipient of the usual Horatian epistle— "was endeavouring to subvert the Laws and Constitution of his Country, and to introduce in the stead of it, Tyranny and absolute Power. . . . Oh! admirable Poet!" it ironically proclaims, you have ". . . made a very proper Choice of a Person to go down to Posterity in the same Bottom with." There is further fretting about such epistolary non-Horatianism on 6 April (see also 13 April), when we hear about "several Imitations of the *Epistles* and *Satires* of *Horace*," adapted to modern characters and circumstances. Those who once were props of an admirable court, have been replaced by opponents of the court: "I cannot but observe that in these Performances, the Friends to the present *Government* are continually the Subject of his *Satire*, as they who are the avowed Enemies to their Country are thought worthy of his Panegyricks." This, the speaker says, is so obvious that he need not quote from "Mr. P——'s late Writings," though he does mention the offensive praise of Bolingbroke. The *Gazetteer* implies that Pope's satiric tone and kind are not Horatian, since those are affirmative and comic, whereas Pope is harsh and negative toward the state. Hence, "I am very far from approving the Method which this great Author has given as an Example for the Wits, of modernizing the old *Roman* Satire into temporary Invective." Moreover, on 9 January 1739 it berates Pope's *Epistle to Augustus* (1737) as an absurdly non-Horatian effort that attacks all levels of society and government "in a *Lump*." The "very Cream of the Jest" in *Augustus* is that Pope "pretends to imitate *Horace*" and has even foolishly printed "the Verses of that *fine, courtly Satyrist*, with his own *Billingsgate*. But how ridiculous is the *Comparison*." Pope actually refuses to acknowledge George II as "his lawful King, and to give the Government the slender Security of his Oath for good Behaviour."

Annoyance with Pope's mingled but ever more hostile phase, however, was as nothing in comparison with the *Gazetteer*'s response to the Juvenalian *Epilogue to the Satires*, which evoked threats of death, a frenzy of quotation, and the sterner dissociation of savagely railing Pope from comically rallying Horace. The *Gazetteer* for 26 May 1738 repeats the familiar ministerial complaint that Pope sees only bad in the court and good in the opposition. In so doing, its anger perfectly catches his and like-minded satirists' Juvenalian pose of the isolation of the good man in a decaying world of unprecedented evil at its worst—as Juvenal claims in line 149 of his first satire. If opposition complaints are true, we hear,

> there never was a People so degenerated and sunk so low in Vileness and Infamy as we; for I think, according to this account of the Matter, there are not above ten or a

dozen wise and honest Men in the Nation, and those all within the Circle of their own Friends and Acquaintances; as for all the Rest, they have very fairly and plainly treated them as a parcel of Knaves or Fools, without either common Sense or common Honesty.

It is indeed a most extraordinary thing, and what can't have its Parallel in any History, that all Degrees and Orders of People in a Nation that once was famous for Wisdom, Knowledge, and Virtue, should all of a sudden undergo so strange a Transformation, as is imputed to them in these Writings; that *the Soldier, the Churchman, the Patriot, and the Man in Power, should all think it a Shame not to be corrupted; that all our Nobles should beg to be Slaves; that the Ambition of our Fools should be to be Rogues; that the Wit of Cheats, and Courage of a Whore, should be what Thousands should make the Objects of their Envy and Adoration; that all in general should look up with Awe and Reverence at Crimes that escape and triumph over the Laws;* and *in fine, that while Truth, Worth and Wisdom, are daily decry'd, nothing should be esteem'd Sacred but Villany.*

Since this Juvenalian satire is unacceptable, on 27 October the *Gazetteer* again urges a new version of the Law of the XII Tables, in which Pope could be "clubb'd, or rather bastinadoed" for his defamation of virtually everyone in the government.[23] In contrast, Horace "never took the Liberty to turn Persons of Consular Dignity into Ridicule," though as a courtier he at least had the unexercised right to do so. In making this argument, Walpole's writer not only ignores Horace's proud affirmation of his humble status as

---

[23] Such ongoing threats to reinvoke Roman laws did not go unnoticed, as the discussion of *Fortescue* in chapter 7 suggests, and as Stephen Barret makes clear in his *War, an Epic-Satyr. Setting forth the Nature of Fr—ch Policy. And the True Cause of The Present Commotions in Europe,* 2nd ed. (1747). It is as unreasonable, Barret claims, "for modern Authors to be judg'd by Rules laid down two or three thousand Years ago; as for *English* men to be try'd by the Laws of the *Twelve* Tables" (p. iv).

a freedman's son, in *Epistles*, i. 20, for example; he also invokes a surprising ally, Lucilius. In *Fortescue* and its advertisement, Pope claims that he is like Lucilius because he has exalted friends of his own and, more important, because he is a friend to virtue. Though the *Gazetteer* does not specifically mention that claim, it implicitly debunks it and puts the authors of the opposition and of the *Craftsman* in their miserably subordinate class. Only a social upstart, as well as a hunchbacked midget incapable of writing true satire, could be such a libeler:

> If *Horace* cou'd have given Way to a more Libertine Wit, which was not consistent with the Probity of his Mind and the Extent of his Knowledge, he was himself a Courtier and a Favorite, and might have been the Freer with his Fellows; but what wou'd have become of a Scribbler, who ply'd for Business at the Pillars before the Booksellers' Row, much frequented by such Gentry in old *Rome*, if he, like *Caleb D'Anvers*, had bely'd and vilify'd the Principal Ministers of State? If *Lucilius* the Satyrist, made free with *Metellus* and *Lupus*, Men of Quality, he was himself the same, and being on a Par with them as to Rank and Birth, he was intitled to those Liberties in his Speech of them, which a *Bond man* or a *Freed man* would not have been privileg'd in, but have been turn'd over to the *Lictors*, for the Correction which was injoyn'd by the Laws. There is no Instance in any good Author, Antient or Modern, of the Insolence and Brutality of our pretended *Ralliers* and *Satyrists*. . . . But this, and every thing else reasonable and commendable, is thrown away on such Libellers and Lampooners as our Modern Raillers and Satyrists, who can no more judge of such Things without Wit, than they can add a Cubit to their Stature [Matthew, vi. 27], or turn a Curve Line into a Right.

This *Gazetteer* grants an essential premise of Lucilian satire as then perceived—a free satirist should have the protection of the state when he attacks highly placed vice; but it adds a corollary that banishes Catholic Pope from that franchise. One must be an old boy to attack an old boy, as the curve-lined satirist was not.

Walpole's partisans wished to invoke and encourage Horatian optimism and friendship, while discouraging Juvenalian and Persian gloom, invective, and indignation. They also looked to Boileau as an acceptable model for mingled satire. On 27 October 1738 the *Gazetteer* praises that severe satirist who "lays it down as the only Excuse for such Poems, that they must not offend the *State* nor *Conscience*," and even he "gave such offence to Persons of Virtue and Honour, that the Duke de *Montausier* . . . said of him, . . . In a well-govern'd State he would be sent to the Gallies." As we have seen, the case was altered from an opposition point of view, and Boileau, like his best mentor Horace, was unacceptable to Pope precisely because he did not offend an offensive state.

This review of some personal and political response to Pope's satire reinforces several points: his mingling of satiric modes was perceived by friends and foes and praised or blamed according to the reader's own predilection; the trend of this mingling—indeed the satiric trend of the 1730s—was toward greater use of the Juvenalian and Persian than Horatian conventions; and this trend was consistent with Pope's and Britain's native character. From Dennis in 1716 to Boscawen in 1798, numerous commentators agree that whatever the apparent similarity between the satirists in the reigns of Augustus Caesar and of George Augustus, the differences are substantial. "Your sense is none of mine," Newcomb's ministerial Horace tells Pope; "you from *Juvenal* would snatch the Rod," the author of *Characters* insists; "Each *Roman*'s force adorns his various Page," Brown says; Pope treats some folly "with the grave severity of Persius," Warburton and Ruffhead claim; Pope's is a "various . . . Muse," Boscawen says at the end of the century. Pope thus is being both individual and traditional in his synthetic and increasingly dark satiric practice.

Nonetheless, by writing the *Epistles to Several Persons* Pope adheres to another tradition—the use of the satiric epistle as the defining Horatian social, poetic form, one that separates Horace from his brother-satirists in Rome. We must turn to Pope's own epistles if we wish to see his most genuine version of "Horace," and perhaps see why even the most attractive values of that great satirist had to be abandoned or radically modified as Pope and the 1730s progressed.

𝕏𝕏𝕏

Pope's *Epistles to Several Persons*:
A System of Ethics in the Horatian Way

THE HORATIAN SATIRIC POEM has identifying marks that are different from most identifying marks of poems by Persius or Juvenal. Isolating Horatian satiric conventions, however, is slightly more difficult than isolating Juvenalian conventions, because Horace wrote both satires and epistles subsumed under the genre of satire. These offspring of common parents chose different methods to reform folly. As Lodovico Dolce observes in 1559, in "the satires it was Horace's intention to remove the vices from the breasts of men, and in the epistles to plant there the virtues." This view was repeated many times thereafter and was enshrined in André Dacier's widely known discussion of the difference between the two forms. In Horace's first book of satires, Dacier writes, "il travaille à déraciner les vices; & . . . dans le second il s'efforce d'arracher les erreurs & les fausses opinions." In the epistles, however, "il s'attach à y donner des preceptes pour la vertu, & à allumer dans nos coeurs l'amour qu' elle merite."[1] Satire removes errors so that epistles can encourage virtue.

This fluid but real distinction between the subspecies of Horatian satire was known in theory and practice through much of the eighteenth century.[2] Most, but certainly not

---

[1] Dolce, *Discorso sopra le epistole* appended to his translation of Horace, as in Bernard Weinberg, *A History of Literary Criticism in the Italian Renaissance* (Chicago: Univ. of Chicago Press, 1961), 1: 143; Dacier, *Oeuvres d'Horace . . . avec des remarques critiques et historiques*, 3rd ed. (Paris, 1709), 8: sig. Aiiij^r; the original is italicized.

[2] For a mid-century French reaction, see Saint-Marc's comment on Boileau's third epistle, on shame: "Le sujet de cette Pièce est beau; mais il est plus propre pour une *Satire*, que pour une *Epître*. . . . *L'Epître Morale* est proprement un Ouvrage didactique qu' il faut orner & qu' on peut egaïer: mais dont le fonds doit être nécessairement

all, verse epistles I have seen (the generalization can be extended to verse essays as well) are gentler in tone, less fervid in their hostility to vice, and not so angry or apocalyptic as satires against individuals, nations, or the human condition. The convention of sometimes episodic communication between civilized gentlemen was a powerful deterrent to raising the voice, and it was enhanced both by Horace's and by Pope's precedent. Those poets who looked directly at Pope's epistolary poems, rather than for an excuse to squabble with their tormentor, are useful guides to his aims. James Bramston's *The Man of Taste, Occasion'd by an Epistle of Mr. Pope's On that Subject* (1733) creates a foolish speaker who deals with the modish rather than traditional vision of taste. He is proud of his folly, speaks lines that undercut his own authority, and thereby reinforces the reader's sense of superiority. The poem holds up implicit norms of widely accepted good taste, against which the fop's innovations are judged and ridiculed. The clear and gentle victory of civilization over ridiculous barbarity emerges as early as the frontispiece, where a moronic dandy wearing a long bow tie points to his garden, parterre, and cupola, radically out of proportion and topped with an owl. The landscape includes a building in front and to the right of a mountain crowned by a winged donkey. Pope's Sir Balaam is an apt hero for a man so mindlessly proud of his braying Pegasus and lumpish Parnassus; and so our enthusiastic beau wishes to view a "broad Sir *Balaam* in *Corinthian* brass" adorning Cheapside with "His magisterial Paunch and griping Face" (p. 12).[3] Bramston has

---

un assemblage de raisonnemens Philosophiques suffisament poussés. C'est ce que l'on cherche en vain ici." *Oeuvres de M. Boileau Despréaux* (Paris, 1747), 5: 475. See also Francis Howes, *The Satires of A. Persius Flaccus* (1809): Horace's "*Epistles* are composed in a very different vein [from that of his satires], and the humour which they contain is seldom of the satiric kind" (p. xx).

3 Bramston's poem evoked a mate, perhaps by Thomas Newcomb: *The Woman of Taste. Occasioned by a late Poem, Entitled, The Man of Taste. . . . In two Epistles, from Clelia in Town to Sapho in the*

adapted some of Pope's epistolary devices—the restrained mockery of bad taste and security in the triumph of good taste—so that virtues need not be planted, so much as given richer soil for deeper roots.

William Thompson's *Sickness. A Poem* (1745) also indicates that Pope's epistles were regarded as in a moral and philosophical mode. Thompson characterizes a few central techniques of Pope's Horatian pose and uses language that could have been Dacier's. Though Thompson is referring directly to the *Essay on Man* (1733-34), that poem was written in four epistles and, we shall see, shared much of the ethical system of the *Epistles to Several Persons* (1731-35).

> To root excesses from the human-breast;
> Behold a beauteous pile of ethicks rise;
> Sense, the foundation; harmony the walls;
> (The Dorique grave, and gay Corinthian join'd)
> Where Socrates and Horace jointly reign.
> Best of Philosophers! of Poets too
> The best! He teaches thee thyself to know
> That virtue is the noblest gift of heav'n:
> "And vindicates the ways of GOD to Man."
> O hearken to the Moralist polite!
> Enter his school of truth; here Plato's self
> Might preach; and Tully deign to lend an ear.[4]

> (Pp. 61-62)

Readers as well as poets knew epistolary conventions and were not always pleased with significant deviations from them. In spite of its title, the *Epistle to Dr. Arbuthnot*

Country (1733). The woman is the female counterpart of Bramston's fop and is meant to be disapproved of by the superior audience, who of course will reject the narrator's mindless activities, deceptions, cheating of tradesmen, affectation, and the like. Lines from Bramston also appear on the title page of *The Modern Poet. A Rapsody* (1736).

[4] These lines, among others from Thompson's poem, were reprinted in [John Serle], *A Plan of Mr. Pope's Garden. . . . To which is added A Character of all his Writings* (1745), pp. 28-29.

(1735) violated such expectations and gave Pope's enemies a desired stick with which to beat him. Hence a self-interested author wrote "The 17th *Epode* of Horace *Imitated. A Palinody to Mr. Pope, by one of the Heroes of the Dunciad, occasion'd by his Epistle to Dr. Arbuthnot.*" That hurtful and misnamed poem shows Pope revelling in his victims' pain, spurning their friendship, and frustrating their chances to gain literary employment. You "Epistles into new Invectives turn," the angry speaker claims. Thomas Bentley was comparably indignant on comparable grounds—violation of received generic distinctions, which produced too severe a poem: "The Epistle to Dr. Arbuthnot is improperly called an *Epistle*. 'Tis a *Satire* throughout. Horace made a difference. His Epistles to his polite Friends are not stuffed with Bills of Complaint [as Pope calls his poem in its Advertisement] and cruel Descriptions, like Mr. Pope's."[5]

Pope's imitators and detractors both make plain that the Horatian epistle should largely exclude invective and complaint, include discourse with polite friends, and show manageable folly not rampant vice. Indeed, Pope himself must have shared much of this view of the Horatian letter, for in the summer of 1729 he tells Broome that "for the future he intended to write nothing but epistles in Horace's manner," and he later claims that his epistles to several persons are part of his longer "system of Ethicks in the Horatian way."[6] The precise meaning of this phrase remains Delphic, but when placed next to the continuing distinction be-

---

[5] "Palinody," in *Mr. Pope's Literary Correspondence. Volume the Second* (1735), p. 42. The poem also criticizes Pope's praise of Bolingbroke and the obscenities in *Sober Advice from Horace* (p. 44). The volume is one of Curll's efforts. For Bentley, see *A Letter to Mr. Pope, Occasioned by Sober Advice from Horace* (1735), p. 4.

[6] Pope's remark is in a letter from Fenton to Broome, in *The Correspondence of Alexander Pope*, ed. George Sherburn (Oxford: Clarendon Press, 1956), 3: 37. The "Horatian Way" is in Bateson's edition of the *Epistles to Several Persons*, p. xvi, and Pope to Swift, 28 November 1729, *Correspondence*, 3: 81.

tween satires and epistles, it does imply that Horace's "way" of pursuing, describing, and encouraging ethical conduct was more properly performed in mildly satiric epistles than harsher satires.

As we have seen, the epistolary satirist is likely to be in a social world whose communication is played out before us. The receiver of Horatian epistolary wisdom is often a highly placed aristocrat who serves both to modulate the poet's tone and to suggest that in so civilized a world even a busy governor can take the time to be educated by a contemplative poet. The norms in such poems thus are characters who are named and known, and who personify the deservedly thriving or at least properly functioning state, even though man is persistently foolish and requires satire to keep him on his moral guard. This epistolary satirist also assumes and shows the harmony between the satiric norms and the gods, and in a comic and tautological way he suggests that providential intervention remains possible for those who deserve it. He surely does see a world of nasty activities, but in the epistles there is little danger that an aberrant passion or person will become a significant threat to the nation. The epistolary writer attacks follies that are not consequences of the monarch's bad examples but are unevictable squatters in the human breast. His readers and perhaps even victims are likely to agree that such folly is wrong, deserves scolding, and no doubt will be scolded by an audience that no doubt again will need reminding of its lapse from ideal behavior, while remaining confident in its protection by the gods and guides whom the satirist evokes. Pope's *Epistles to Several Persons* share and develop Horatian conventions and subdue or nearly exclude the Persian and Juvenalian. In those modes one is more likely to see a real or metaphorical monologue and withdrawal into nostalgia or the self, norms drawn from antique heroes, a skeptical or bluntly unbelieving attitude toward the gods, and a sense of symbolic protest against encroaching universal darkness, rather than belief in the ability of small fingers to plug large dikes. Pope's four ethic epistles embody his most genuine and most successful use of the Horatian satiric voice.

I: HORACE'S CONVENTIONS IN POPE'S EPISTLES

The affectionate social world of Pope's epistles is announced at or near the beginning of each work. *Cobham* starts with a cohesive "Yes" between Twickenham's poet and Stowe's Lord Viscount. *To a Lady*, presumably to the humble Martha Blount as Pope's "dear Madam" (line 151), begins with the more garrulous "Nothing so true as what you once let fall." Shortly after the beginning of *Bathurst*, Pope and the briefly disagreeing baron conclude that "We find our tenets just the same at last" (line 16). And as early as line 23 of the epistle *To Burlington*, Pope generously tells the earl that "You show us, Rome was glorious, not profuse." There is no irony here, as there is in Pope's satiric imitation of Horace's epistle *To Augustus* (1737) where the notion of a respectful letter is turned on its end. As the ethic epistles show, each recipient is or becomes a proven norm, and one aspect of such a norm is dialogue with the poet and willingness to join him in inquiry and education.

To Bathurst is most pronounced in its nonetheless subtle use of epistolary dialogue as an emblem of dialectic, one that ends in community between the peer, poet, and God. At the beginning, for example, there are two theological views—the benevolent Christian one, which sees human values as descending from Heaven to Nature to Pope, and the malevolent pagan one, which sees those values going from Jove to the harshly laughing Momus to Bathurst.[7] As

---

[7] I am indebted here to Earl R. Wasserman's reading of *Bathurst*, in *Pope's Epistle to Bathurst: A Critical Reading with an Edition of the Manuscripts* (Baltimore: Johns Hopkins Univ. Press, 1960), pp. 11-57, especially pp. 19-20. I do not share Wasserman's sense of the ultimate unhappiness of the poem, of its "satiric venom" (p. 43), and of "every possible horror" in the portrait of Sir Balaam (p. 53). See also Howard

the poem develops, Pope shows his adversarius the implications of his view, since without some form of explanation, anchor, and model, the world and its uses of money remain inexplicable and dangerous. "Why take it [the world], Gold and all" (line 80) is one possible response, that of withdrawal. "All this is madness" (line 153) is another. By about two-thirds of the way through the poem, however, Bathurst rejects those options, sees the true workings of providence in the world, becomes an active model of benevolence, and in spite of a cautionary "yet," sees his own changed character as a moral norm:

> Oh teach us, BATHURST! yet unspoil'd by wealth!
> That secret rare, between th' extremes to move
> Of mad Good-nature, and of mean Self-love.
> (Lines 226-28)

> Who copies Yours, or OXFORD's better part,
> To ease th' oppress'd, and raise the sinking heart?
> Where-e'er he shines, oh Fortune, gild the scene,
> And Angels guard him in the golden Mean!
> (Lines 243-46)

The social nature of the poem thus expands while the relationship between Pope and Bathurst becomes more intense. The initial distinction of Jove–Momus–Bathurst versus Heaven–Nature–Pope disappears in favor of the direct line God–Bathurst–Man of Ross. Pope can step aside because Bathurst comes to share his view of a benevolent Christian God, and because as a baron his model is more important than a poet's. Hence immediately after we see that the copier of Bathurst's (or Oxford's) generosity will

---

Erskine-Hill, *The Social Milieu of Alexander Pope* (New Haven: Yale Univ. Press, 1975), where Bathurst's conclusion is called "savagely near-negative" (p. 265), and the poem in general includes a "dark world and desperate ironies" (p. 294). For an overview of some of Pope's techniques in his several epistles, see Lawrence Lee Davidow, "Pope's Verse Epistles: Friendship and the Private Sphere of Life," *Huntington Library Quarterly*, 40 (1977): 151-70.

be protected by angels, we also see the activities of John Kyrle, Man of Ross. In the poem's world, rather than the real world of chronology, Bathurst's example and teachings filter down to his social inferiors, as do, in a destructive way, the models of the empressses Messalina and Caesonia in Juvenal's sixth satire. The unified relationship between Pope and Bathurst moves to the unified relationship between God and Bathurst, and then to the pedagogical relationship between Bathurst and British society: "Oh teach us, BATHURST . . . / That secret rare." In this sense the Man of Ross is one of Bathurst's students and "copies" him, just as Bathurst once was Pope's student and learns to "copy" God's plan.

As a member of the House of Lords, Bathurst of course has a role in government, and thus he functions as a check upon the monied forces who threaten the kingdom. "At length Corruption, like a gen'ral flood, . . . / Shall deluge all" (lines 137-39), but in the meanwhile justice is alive and is exemplified in the multipurposed portrait of Sir Balaam. Pope need not thump his tub because he still can insinuate and bring Bathurst into the satiric process. The poem ends with the tale of Balaam, which answers the question that Pope poses to his rapidly tiring lord:

> Say, for such worth are other worlds prepar'd?
> Or are they both, in this their own reward?
> A knotty point! to which we now proceed.
> But you are tir'd—I'll tell a tale. 'Agreed.'
>
> (Lines 335-38)

The largely monosyllabic, non-Latinate, colloquial speech is perfectly adapted to the Horatian poet's masking of serious issues behind friendly patter to a busy aristocrat. It also cements the already firm bond between them, as "we now proceed" to cut or unravel the knot.

Sir Balaam is an aspiring, monied, Walpolean, negative analogue of the Man of Ross, just as lordly Buckingham is a negative analogue of Bathurst; the City Knight em-

bodies the vices of the wrong use of riches, an aggrandize-
ment of family and self associated with the godless vision
of Sir Robert and the devil. Earlier in the poem Pope fears
that paper money "bribes a Senate, and the Land's be-
trayed" (line 34). In the providentially ordered world that
Bathurst comes to accept and perpetuate, however, Sir
Balaam is "In Britain's Senate," does take "a bribe from
France" (lines 393, 396), and the land is not betrayed—
quite the opposite. Ministerial allies prove unreliable in
Commons and Lords; the court is comparably unreliable,
being motivated by greed not principle; and the opposition
forces presumably maintain their ground in defense of the
nation. Hence "The House impeach him; Coningsby ha-
rangues; / The Court forsake him, and Sir Balaam hangs"
(lines 397-98). Impeachment is "the judicial process by
which any man, from the rank of peer downwards, may be
tried before the House of Lords at. the instance of the
House of Commons" (*OED*). Commons requests the proc-
ess; Lords, represented by the Whig Thomas Earl Con-
ingsby—who had moved Robert Harley's impeachment in
1715—also includes the opposition Bathurst, who presum-
ably shares in the impeachment proceedings, as he now can
since he himself is a moral norm; even the court of George
II, no doubt aware that it will acquire a fortune, abandons
Sir Balaam to his fate. For whatever reasons, justice at all
three levels is done and seen to be done in a poem that
affirms social coherence, the existence of an afterworld, the
need to behave well here in order to deserve a happy here-
after, the wisdom of narrator and educable adversarius, the
spreading role of virtue in the world, the existence of evil
that is held in check by the splintering of the monied inter-
ests, the intransigence and triumph of the forces of virtue
in private and public life, and the active intercession of
providence in human affairs. The return to order is so
complete that even the apparently victorious devil, with
Balaam and his family in tow, is defeated and made an
agent of God's will: he rids the world of a Walpole aide,

shows the danger of such an alliance based on the wrong use of money, and shows Bathurst that, whatever misguided pagans might think, virtue is not just a word but a concept of active benevolence that has its pattern in heaven and heavenly workings. All this generally is delivered with temperate language suitable for the decorum that Lords flatter themselves is part of their public posture.[8]

These comforting points, for Pope if not Sir Balaam, affirm both the optimism and the basis for optimism of Pope's Horatian voice: the benevolent Christian God is actively at work on behalf of man who obtusely makes His job harder. In fact, each of the *Epistles to Several Persons* affirms God's intrusion in the short- and long-range workings of our lives. "Know, God and Nature only are the same" (line 154), Pope tells Cobham. Atossa's money "wanders, Heav'n directed, to the Poor" (line 150), he informs his lady. "Hear then the truth: ' 'Tis Heaven each Passion sends . . .' " (line 161), he assures Bathurst, as he assures Burlington that "Good Sense . . . only is the gift of Heav'n" (line 43). Pope the Horatian is committed to a system of ethics with a merciful, intrusive God on our side, a God whose mysterious workings can be understood if only man will hear the truth that Pope writes to us, to viscounts, earls, barons, and dear madams. In this as in other respects these poems draw upon the precepts of theodicy in the *Essay on Man*, with which they once were affiliated. Pope himself, Warburton, and modern commentators have discussed the relationship between Pope's four epistles called the *Essay on Man* and his four epistles sometimes called the *Moral Essays*. Miriam Leranbaum, for example, shows that each larger work was once thought of as a first and second book of a common unit called "Ethic Epistles," that the

---

[8] See, for example, Charles Towneley Strachey, Lord O'Hagan, as amiable Aristarchus in his receipt to make a House-broken Lord: "we humour an extempore autobiographer, but we hate a fervent tub thumper, especially those well supplied with moral indignation." See "A Welcome to the Upper House," London *Times*, 27 April 1978.

eight epistles are related, and that, as one instance, *Bathurst* is "part of a unit springing from and directly related to" the second and fourth epistles of *An Essay on Man*.⁹

One major similarity is the shared belief that the world was created and is held together by God's gift of a ruling passion and by his felicitous *discordia concors*, a harmonious reconciliation of warring contraries on man's behalf.¹⁰

⁹ Miriam Leranbaum, *Alexander Pope's Opus Magnum 1729-1744* (Oxford: Clarendon Press, 1977), p. 36 (common unit), p. 100 (Bathurst in the unit); see also p. 102. Bateson prints Pope's table-talk concerning the related parts of his *"Opus Magnum"* in the *Epistles to Several Persons*, pp. xx-xxii. For further discussion of Pope's scheme, see George Sherburn, "Pope at Work," in *Essays on the Eighteenth Century Presented to David Nichol Smith* (Oxford: Clarendon Press, 1945), pp. 50-51, and *Joseph Spence: Observations, Anecdotes, and Characters of Books and Men Collected from Conversation*, ed. James M. Osborn (Oxford: Clarendon Press, 1966), 1: 128-43. Warburton discusses the related works in *An Essay on Man. Being the First Book of Ethic Epistles. To H. St. John L. Bolingbroke. With the Commentary and Notes of Mr. Warburton* (1743), the unique copy of which is at the British Library. Warburton's notes also appear at the appropriate places in his edition of *The Works of Alexander Pope, Esq.* (1751).

¹⁰ The *discordia concors* has been abundantly discussed by Leo Spitzer, "Classical and Christian Ideas of World Harmony," *Traditio*, 2 (1944): 409-64, and 3 (1945): 307-64; Maynard Mack, in the Twickenham *Essay on Man*, pp. xxxiv-xxxv; Earl R. Wasserman, *The Subtler Language: Critical Readings of Neoclassic and Romantic Poems* (Baltimore: Johns Hopkins Univ. Press, 1959), pp. 53-57, on *Windsor Forest*, and more recently, with healthy correctives of his predecessors, by Brendan O Hehir, *Expans'd Hieroglyphicks: A Study of Sir John Denham's Cooper's Hill* (Berkeley and Los Angeles: Univ. of California Press, 1969), pp. 165-76. Wasserman discusses the *discordia concors* in Pope's *Epistle to Bathurst*, pp. 33-40.

Pope's contemporaries no doubt recognized *Burlington's* theological assumptions; but as the Timon controversy shows, they responded at least as much to the known characters portrayed. See, for example, *The Review* (1744):

> Is *B–rl—gt–n* for private Virtues shewn?
> So private—they are really still not known.
> Let him enjoy his Taste in any soil,
> It may produce a House, but not a *Boyle*.
> (P. 8)

"ALL subsists by elemental strife" Pope tells us in the *Essay* (1: 169). In the psychological and moral sphere one finds that "Passions, like Elements, tho' born to fight" are mixed, softened, united (2: 111-12), and thereby "Make and maintain the balance of the mind" (2: 120); and in the political sphere one sees that "jarring int'rests of themselves create / Th'according music of a well-mix'd State" (3: 293-94). This concept has often been used and abused, but it remains essential for our understanding of Pope's several epistles and their consistently optimistic conclusions in the face of a consistently foolish nation.

The solid theological base of the epistles suggests explanations for the apparently incoherent world about us. In *Cobham* man at first appears to be a jumble of warring traits, scarcely more perceptive than a parrot, hopelessly differing from himself as well as others, and coloring the world he sees with his own uncertainties (lines 19-27). The piling on of words and phrases like *chance, Notions, guess, varying, differs, varies, whirls, shifting eddies, hurries all too fast, In vain, no more, you lose, is lost,* and *Tir'd we yield* suggests uncertainty, indecision, and fallibility. Soon, however, we are told to "Know" the stability of God and Nature (line 154), and shortly thereafter to

> Search then the Ruling Passion: There, alone,
> The Wild are constant, and the Cunning known;
> The Fool consistent, and the False sincere;
> Priests, Princes, Women, no dissemblers here.
> This clue once found, unravels all the rest,
> The prospect clears, and Wharton stands confest.
>
> (Lines 174-79)

The dramatic shift to words like *constant, known,* and *consistent* assumes knowledge of the principle of the ruling passion in the *Essay on Man*. God, aware that we would otherwise be plantlike clods, gives us a motivating force that is ours at birth, leaves us only at death, and helps to define our humanity. Wharton thus is comprehensible when we realize that his "ruling Passion was the Lust of Praise" (line 181) and that all his misguided actions were aimed in that direction. "Nature well known, no prodigies remain, / Comets are regular, and Wharton plain" (lines 208-09). Cobham too is "plain," since a viscount no less than a duke is infused with a ruling passion. The final lines of the poem thus show the brief positive character of Cobham balancing Wharton's as the object of satire. The satiric norm uses God's gift on behalf of his country, and also suggests one way in which politics function in the epistles.

> And you! brave Cobham, to the latest breath
> Shall feel your ruling passion strong in death:
> Such in those moments as in all the past,
> 'Oh, save my Country, Heav'n!' shall be your last.
>
> (Lines 262-65)

Heaven remains actively involved, concerned, and a legitimate source of power to be used in man's and virtue's aid. Since God is the source of constancy, His association with Cobham denotes an ally unbribable by Sir Robert and thus lends strength and moral respectability to a vigorous loyal opposition. Immortal God and mortal man are reconciled in "patriot" concerns.

The other epistles offer even more striking instances of the ruling passion and a perceivable *discordia concors* operating in the fallen world. In *Bathurst*, for example, these ruling passions are labeled as part of the process of God's reconciling force. Why, we are led to wonder, is both collective and individual man so wildly inconsistent in his ruling passions? "The ruling Passion conquers Reason still" (line 156), as it must if it is to do its divinely ordained job of motivating man. Heaven itself sends our passions and directs them to different ends, Pope tells us as he quotes from a version of his *Essay on Man*, 2:205-6:

> "Extremes in Nature equal good produce,
> "Extremes in Man concur to gen'ral use."

Ask we what makes one keep, and one bestow?
That Pow'r who bids the Ocean ebb and flow,
Bids seed-time, harvest, equal course maintain.
Thro' reconcil'd extremes of drought and rain,
Builds Life on Death, on Change Duration founds,
And gives th' eternal wheels to know their rounds.

(Lines 163-70)

Paternal penury and filial prodigality are explicable—indeed almost comforting, since the father is "but a backward steward for the Poor" (line 174) and is all too rectified by the flood of money to come from the son.

In the epistles, God tends to work in a leisurely fashion, through generations, or seed-time and harvest time, as the *discordia concors* plays itself out in natural rhythms. The man, like Bathurst, who wishes to "ease, or emulate, the care of Heav'n" (line 230) must act more quickly and prod the backward steward while restraining the overflowing streams. The golden mean (line 246) is the norm the best men should try to put into effect as the earthly counterpart of the *discordia concors*. God supplies prodigals because He knows that man will abuse his ruling passion of acquisition; He supplies misers because He knows that other men will spend too much and dissipate their wealth. But one can spend and acquire in moderation—as do both Bathurst and the Man of Ross in their different spheres—and therefore "ease" God's job. Those who seek gold do so in spite of God's wisdom in hiding it beneath the earth (lines 9-11), and condemn themselves to the mines (lines 111-12, 133-34). Those who disperse it properly take on the Biblical qualities so prominent in the portrait of the endearing Man of Ross who, for example, like Moses bids the waters flow from the dry rock, and like the good Samaritan brings health to the ill. Secular figures thus are normative to the degree that they ease or emulate the providential norm, which is man's ultimate guide and friend, is joined by poet and peers, and is embodied not only in specific

183

persons and their actions, but in specific places as well—
as *To Burlington* shows.

This Horatian epistle again begins with a puzzle and
ends with certainty. " 'Tis strange," Pope tells Burlington,
"the Miser should his Cares employ, / To gain those Riches
he can ne'er enjoy" (lines 1-2). This strangeness and insta-
bility finally give way to a nobly growing world of "Impe-
rial Works, and worthy [of] Kings" (line 204). The steps
along the way in this poem, the last ethic epistle in the
final printed version, again show God intervening in man's
world, and helping the aristocrat and didactic poet to un-
derstand and improve that world.

The plans of Palladian baths that Burlington has just
published certainly will be imitated, distorted, and de-
graded in our fallen world; but Burlington himself remains
unsullied and knows that even before taste, one must have
"Good Sense, which only is the gift of Heav'n" (line 43).
Pope again relates his norm to a providential pattern of
which the speaker and the epistle's recipient are a part, for
each has the gift of good sense that is manifest in Pope's
directions to other would-be architects of house and garden.
In Pope's epistolary social world one must consult not only
the real client but "the Genius of the Place in all" (line
57). By subjecting himself to nature, the architect subjects
himself to God and insures harmony. The Genius of the
Place is an active partner; it "tells the Waters or to rise, or
fall," "Joins willing woods, and varies shades from shades,"
and "Paints as you plant, and, as you work, designs" (lines
58, 62, 64). With a method that incorporates heavenly Sense
and respect for nature, one may even produce a work
worthy of Cobham's Stowe, the patriot and seat in tune
with Heaven and Pope's version of political virtue. By
proper following, one learns to "advance, start . . . strike,"
so that nature *shall* be one's creative partner:

> Still follow Sense, of ev'ry Art the Soul,
> Parts answ'ring parts shall slide into a whole,

> Spontaneous beauties all around advance,
> Start ev'n from Difficulty, strike from Chance;
> Nature shall join you, Time shall make it grow
> A Work to wonder at—perhaps a Stow.
>
> (Lines 65-70)

Man, the Genius of the Place, Time, and God as manifest in Heaven's Sense—all are present in the harmonious relationship of parts and whole.

This normative passage, however, quickly is under pressure, as Pope's earlier lines regarding the feared degradation of Burlington's plans begin to be acted out. Villario abandons his pleasant but too formal gardens as he grows tired of them and himself, and prefers a plain field (line 88). Sabinus's son destroys the vistas his father creates, and "The thriving plants ignoble broomsticks made, / Now sweep those Alleys they were born to shade" (lines 97-98). The violation of the Genius of the Place in the last line also is a violation of Sense and of Heaven's order. Timon's villa now appears and is part of the downward antisocial progress in which architect and client cut themselves off from man, nature, and God: "his building is a Town, / His pond an Ocean, his parterre a Down" (lines 105-6). Lack of order in architecture brings personal discomfort, as his innovations merely improve "the keenness of the Northern wind" (line 112) and signal separation from God. Timon's genius is foreign to the place in which he builds. It reduces him to "A puny insect, shiv'ring at a breeze" (line 108) and nature to a grotesque imitation of art, as "Trees [are] cut to Statues" (line 120) and "Gladiators fight, or die, in flow'rs" (line 124). Under such a dispensation, literature becomes the backs of unopened foreign books (lines 133-40), and his chapel an exercise in pride and genteel, decadent religion (lines 141-50). The social world culminating in the service of man to his loving God collapses at Timon's villa, where we see neither human nor spiritual nor even culinary pleasures. The portrait ends with the dinner, "A solemn Sacrifice, perform'd in state" (line 157) because its rush, empty forms, and pretense are emblems of the villa's spiritual isolation and its effect upon its inhabitants, who are "In plenty starving, tantaliz'd in state" (line 163). The starvation of body and soul causes Pope, like Maecenas at a dinner long before him, to leave the unnourishing place that rejects the providential coherence Burlington embodies, and Pope then immediately reintroduces, together with another confident, imperative *shall*:

> Yet hence the Poor are cloath'd, the Hungry fed;
> Health to himself, and to his Infants bread
> The Lab'rer bears: What his hard Heart denies,
> His charitable Vanity supplies.
> Another age shall see the golden Ear
> Imbrown the Slope, and nod on the Parterre,
> Deep Harvests bury all his pride has plann'd,
> And laughing Ceres re-assume the land.
>
> (Lines 169-76)

Each paragraph has its own explicit return to order: in the short run the extravagant vulgarity and disruption of Timon's villa nonetheless provide employment and thus family unification for the lower classes. This economic order suggests a spiritual order unintended and unachieved by Timon, but induced by the watchful God who is responsible for the happy consequences of the oxymoron "charitable Vanity." The second paragraph indicates the consequent triumph of divine Sense and the Genius of a place designed for and ultimately returned to agriculture. Here gold is redefined from the "gilded clouds" (line 147) on the ceiling of an irreverent chapel, to the color of the nourishing grains, and Ceres laughs because the scene is pleasant, harmonious, productive, and superior to the sterility of Timon's land.

Return of the providential norm again, as in *Bathurst*, evokes a return of the secular norm; aristocrats imitate

divine Sense, and the gentry imitates the aristocratic sense
of those who plant like Bathurst or build like Burlington
(line 178). The poem now offers continuity between father
and son on their land, willing aid to their neighbors, ten-
ants, and livestock, and service to the nation that denotes
the long-term investment of which a forest is an apt symbol.
The father's "rising Forests" provide "future Buildings, fu-
ture Navies," and "his plantations stretch from down to
down, / First shade a Country, and then raise a Town"
(lines 187-90). The epistle's final compliment springs from
the word *raise*, as Burlington himself is reinvoked as the
raiser of "falling Arts" (line 191), erector of new buildings,
and culminator of a great historical tradition recreated in
modern Britain. He shall "Jones and Palladio to themselves
restore, / And be whate'er Vitruvius was before" (lines
193-94)—namely, architect to Augustus so that George Au-
gustus will put Burlington's plans to work. The monarch
is introduced as a norm for the only time in the ethic
epistles, and his presence may partially explain why this
first of the poems to be separately published is the last in
the collected series and ends the unit with the word *Kings*.
Unlike the "Imitating Fools" (line 26) who wrongly adopt
Burlington's drawings at the beginning of the poem, the
king grasps not mechanical rules but "th'Idea's of your
mind" (line 195), and so extends the Platonic line from
Vitruvius, to Palladio, to Jones, to contemporary Britain.
He thus gives the nation harbors for commerce, temples
for worship, dikes and breakwaters for control of the sea,
rivers for navigation and irrigation, and the ocean in
proper subordination. "These Honours, Peace to happy
Britain brings, / These are Imperial Works, and worthy
Kings" (lines 203-4).[11]

[11] Since Pope refers to "Kings" and does not mention George II, I
can only speculate that in 1731 he still hoped that Burlington could
educate George Augustus as Vitruvius (line 194) educated Augustus
Caesar. Whether George II wished to take the hint is another matter,
and Pope may have been thinking of the Prince of Wales when, in a

By extension, the king has worked with the Genius of the Place—here the genius of Britain herself—and is the master architect following God's own blueprint. *Bathurst* shows the satirist providing a norm that is emulated by those beneath him; *Burlington* provides a norm that is emulated by those above him. In so doing, the king also is emulating the providential pattern already seen to be at work in spite of man's bungling. In *Burlington,* George II apparently knows what Pope has learned through his own knowledge of God's plans: " 'Tis Use alone that sanctifies Expence, / And Splendour borrows all her rays from Sense" (lines 179-80). In this perhaps most Horatian of Pope's satires, the poet, aristocrat, development of architecture, king, nation, and God are perfectly and beautifully in tune.

This union is possible because all of the dangers in the poems, the objects of satire themselves, are routed or forced to retreat. There are dangers aplenty here, but like Timon, they never triumph. Similarly, recognizable and nasty political enemies are treated with the derision and condescension their cheek and failure deserve. "Poor Avarice" (*Bathurst,* line 47), embodied in the outrageously penurious Edward Wortley Montagu, is to be pitied. Pope is writing to an opposition grandee who still has power and can affirm and exercise contrasting values. Even the hated, rich, corrupt and corrupting Peter Walter is likened to an upstart of the past, whose fate was obvious: "Glorious Ambition! Peter, swell thy store, / And be what Rome's great Didius was before" (*Bathurst,* lines 127-28). That is, buy

---

note to the poem in 1735, he described "public works which become a Prince" (p. 155n). In either case, the poem preserves its Horatian core by linking poet, aristocrat, and monarch. For useful discussion of this passage, see Martin C. Battestin, *The Providence of Wit: Aspects of Form in Augustan Literature and the Arts* (Oxford: Clarendon Press, 1974), p. 40. The passage also is discussed in Irvin Ehrenpreis, *Acts of Implication: Suggestion and Covert Meaning in . . . Dryden, Swift, Pope, and Austen* (Berkeley and Los Angeles: Univ. of California Press, 1980), p. 99.

leadership of the nation, if your speculator's ambition so demands, and be a murdered corpse two months later. Political concerns and threats abound in the ethic epistles, and especially in *Bathurst*, but these targets are subordinated to more general human concerns and are always defeated.

The benevolent Horatian world of Pope's epistles to several persons thus includes aristocrats with the power to make positive changes in their world and themselves, an educable adversarius, reasonably effective satirist, an actively involved and clearly perceivable divine pattern that spreads to human beings wishing to emulate it, a social world of cherished ongoing personal relations, and an opponent capable of being defeated or held at arm's length. For the most part I have discussed these traits in the three epistles addressed to men. Several of them appear as well in the poem *To a Lady*, worth discussing in its own right, as a Horatian epistle and, to some degree, as a poem designed to be compared and contrasted with the very different satires of Juvenal, Boileau, and Edward Young.

II: *To a Lady*

To a Lady both shares and plays variations upon the conventions of its brother epistles to lords, while deviating sharply from the antifeminist satires to which it has wrongly been linked.[12] For example, Pope immediately es-

---

[12] See the unsigned *Sawney and Colley, A Poetical Dialogue* (1742), where "ev'ry *Woman*"—Pope is presumed to claim—is "a *very Whore*" (pp. 10-11). The author then applies this maxim to Pope's mother (p. 11n). See also the less hostile "An Epistle to Mr. Pope. Occasion'd by his Characters of Women," in Timothy Scribble [Ashley Cowper], *The Norfolk Poetical Miscellany* (1744), 2: 65-72; and Owen Ruffhead, *The Life of Alexander Pope, Esq.* (1769), pp. 289-91.

For some modern essays on *To a Lady*, see Reuben Arthur Brower, *Alexander Pope: The Poetry of Allusion* (Oxford: Clarendon Press, 1959), pp. 265-81; Rebecca Price Parkin, "The Role of Time in Alexander Pope's *Epistle to a Lady*," *ELH*, 32 (1965): 490-501; Irvin Ehren-

tablishes a pleasant relationship between himself and his lady, whereas Juvenal and Boileau speak to a man whom they warn away from women. Even Young's fifth and sixth satires (1727) in *Love of Fame* (1725-28) frequently are apocalyptic in tone, for women are a threat not only to man and Britain but to the propagation of the race, and thus, the heaviest artillery must be directed against them. In contrast, Pope attempts to educate rather than to lash woman, who is as foolish as her tyrant man. Indeed, Pope urges woman to improve so that she in turn can improve man's life. *To a Lady* suggests that man and woman are mutually dependent; though the battle of the sexes is endless, its hostility is reduced in the amiable example of the lady herself. Juvenal has no contemporary norms; Boileau has very few and all are held at an emotional distance; Young's are patently the creation of preferment seeking. Juvenal and Boileau are consistently punitive toward women in almost all levels; Young commonly is punitive, though also didactic, and assumes the possibility of correction; Pope is punitive only toward types (though particular women often were intended) while nonetheless proclaiming the general attractiveness of the sex. Since men are drawn to women because of their weaknesses, each side is fallible in the sexual equation.

> Ladies, like variegated Tulips, show,
> 'Tis to their Changes that their charms we owe;
> Their happy Spots the nice admirer take,
> Fine by defect, and delicately weak.

(Lines 41-44)

---

preis, "The Cistern and the Fountain: Art and Reality in Pope and Gray," in *Studies in Criticism and Aesthetics, 1660–1800: Essays in Honor of Samuel Holt Monk*, ed. Howard Anderson and John S. Shea (Minneapolis: Univ. of Minneapolis Press, 1967), pp. 158-70; Frank Brady, "History and Structure of Pope's *To a Lady*," *Studies in English Literature*, 9 (1969): 439-62; and Felicity Nussbaum, "Pope's 'To a Lady' and the Eighteenth-Century Woman," *Philological Quarterly*, 54 (1975): 444-56.

Pope thinks little of either person in such a liaison, as is evident through the name he gives to the woman to illustrate his point: " 'Twas thus Calypso once each heart alarm'd" (line 45) as she bewitched several Odysseuses she kept from their higher duties. But Pope does not seize the opportunity to belabor woman or to snarl at seducible man sailing off his proper course. Instead, he states but cannot eradicate one of the painful mysteries of a male-female relationship. By using the first person he also includes himself in the human, courting situation, one from which Juvenal and Boileau were immune. Calypso is "ne'er so sure our passion to create, / As when she touch'd the brink of all we hate" (lines 51-52). The Abbé Yart was more perceptive than Warburton or Ruffhead when he said of this poem: "Il n'a point écrit, comme Boileau, dans le dessein d'imiter Juvénal & d'outrager les femmes: il n'a eu d'autre projet que de dévoiler la nature."[13]

The poem, then, is social in its relationship between author and reader as well as author and recipient of the epistle. The respect and friendship between the two latter begin and permeate the poem. Pope takes his topic sentence from the lady and praises the apparent accuracy of her casual perception about her own sex. "Nothing so true as what you once let fall, / 'Most Women have no Characters at all' " (lines 1-2). The metaphor of the gallery tour allows Pope frequently to consider her opinion and reaction, and at one point again shows him endorsing her responses and adapting them as part of his own epistolary satiric techniques. Seeing the apparently soft Silia storm and rave, "You tip the wink, / But spare your censure" because Silia is not drunk, merely enraged at a pimple on her nose (lines 33-34, 36). At times, Pope's rhetorical questions engage his

---

[13] *Idée de la poësie Angloise, ou traduction des meilleurs poëtes Angloises* (Paris, 1749-56), 3 (1753): 239. See also the remarks in the *Journal Etranger*, 2 (1755): 209, which reproduces much of Joseph Warton's *Adventurer*, No. 133 (1754), and its preference for Boileau, Pope, and Johnson, above Horace and Juvenal.

friend in implied dialogue (lines 59-60, 93-94, 115, 219); at others, she or a comparable nonce-adversaria enters the poem with observations or remarks of her own (lines 157, 160) which, though not brilliant, are not less so than those of Lord Bathurst in the epistle addressed to him. In each case we have an essentially decent and educable adversarius, whose normative relationship with the speaker reflects social and religious union. Pope and his lady project the poem's one healthy exchange between man and woman. As we will see, the roles of Pope as Horatian satirist and Pope-and-the-lady as a norm of social harmony are even clearer when set against the portraits of the disharmonious and destructive Atossa, and the excessively "artistic" queen, whose portraits also highlight their inadequacy and the lady's excellence.

Atossa is a sad paradigm of changeable women who, like all their sex, share the important trait of contrarities, in this case bad contrarities. The lady herself, on the other hand, sat for "The Picture of an esteemable Woman, made up of the best Kind of Contrarieties" (p. 45), as Pope's argument puts it. The best woman, like the best state or the best mind, is a harmonious blending of reconcilable opposites. Servility and dominance are irreconcilable; submission and sovereignty within the family are positive and can be blended, so that the wise woman "by submitting sways" (line 263). This oxymoron suggests the ultimately harmonious *discordia concors* familiar in the other epistles; unreconcilable opposites suggest discord. Hence in Narcissa "Now Conscience chills her, and now Passion burns; / And Atheism and Religion take their turns" (lines 65-66). Philomede is "Chaste to her Husband, frank to all beside, / A teeming Mistress, but a barren Bride" (lines 71-72). Flavia will "die of nothing but a Rage to live" (line 100), and Simo's mate divides her life between "the Church and Scandal" (line 105).

Atossa embodies all such women for she is "Scarce once herself, by turns all Womankind!" (line 116). Accordingly, she also embodies several different aspects of the satire on woman and Pope's techniques in *To a Lady*. She is, we see, a microcosm of the parodic *discordia concors* of unpleasant and unreconcilable contrarities in an antisocial world. She must be superior to all persons and emotions: "Love, if it makes her yield, must make her hate" (line 134), and "Oblige her, and she'll hate you while you live" (line 138). No wonder that in spite of her years and reading, she is "The wisest Fool much Time has ever made" (line 124). Her death in "unrespected age" (line 125) shows both her own disruption and God's benevolent reshaping of at least part of her will:

> Atossa, curs'd with ev'ry granted pray'r,
> Childless with all her Children, wants an Heir.
> To Heirs unknown descends th'unguarded store
> Or wanders, Heav'n-directed, to the Poor.
>
> (Lines 147-50)

The final line shows Pope leaning on his strongest ethical staff in his Horatian epistles, one which, Warburton said "he never loses sight of, and which teaches, that Providence is incessantly turning the evils arising from the follies and vices of men to general good."[14]

Moreover, Atossa exemplifies the kind of satire and satirist anathema to Pope at all times, and especially here. He always insists upon the presence of moral norms even, as in the *Dunciad*, if they are submerged by numbers. In the epistle he makes plain that "If Folly grows romantic, I must paint it" (line 16)—as he does in his portraits of foolish not vicious women, who largely hurt themselves. As we have seen, he also draws a normative relationship between himself and his lady, and soon will draw the lady's own splendors to counterbalance the romantic folly in most of the poem. Atossa, in contrast, offers normless satire of which she herself is a part, and which results in isolation

[14] *Works of Alexander Pope*, 3: 203. Subsequent references are cited in the text.

and anger, not the harmony and peace Pope's poems evoke. She

> with herself, or others, from her birth
> Finds all her life one warfare upon earth:
> Shines, in exposing Knaves, and painting Fools,
> Yet is, whate'er she hates and ridicules.

(Lines 117-20)

With such evident self-hatred, we are not surprised that Atossa causes her own death by causing her own sickness. She is "without one distress / Sick of herself thro' very self-ishness!" (lines 145-46). The lady, on the other hand, whether subject to "Spleen, Vapours, or Small-pox, [is] above them all" (line 267). In each case physical health mirrors spiritual health. The lady is healthy, in part, because she is "Mistress of herself" (line 268) and because she has the guiding voice of the social, Horatian satirist to help her. Atossa is suicidally ill because she depends only on her inadequate, isolated, and warring self that is incapable of affectionately medicinal satire.

With the exception of the tepid portrait of tepid Cloe, Atossa culminates the catalogue of foolish women—but she does not exemplify highly placed vice. Atossa is probably intended to be Katherine Darnley, Duchess of Buckingham, and is so severely treated because her high example might influence those below her. Pope rejects the option of the duchess's influence by soon moving to a portrait of the queen, who is both unlike Atossa, and is a realistic playing out of one misguided desire of women: "ev'ry Lady would be Queen for life" (line 218).

Like many other passages in the epistles, the discussion of Queen Caroline has political implications that are present but not allowed their full satiric potential. Pope is surely unhappy with Queen Caroline as an ally of Walpole and friend of Lord Hervey; but his main target here is not queenly sway used in a bad cause; it is what happens to the woman herself who actually is a queen. We have so far seen two kinds of satiric portrait painters: Pope painting folly to reform it, and Atossa to punish it—and herself in the process. Now we see another portrait, that drawn with the brush of panegyric:

> One certain Portrait may (I grant) be seen,
> Which Heav'n has varnish'd out, and made a *Queen*:
> The same for ever! and describ'd by all
> With Truth and Goodness, as with Crown and Ball:
> Poets heap Virtues, Painters Gems at will,
> And show their zeal, and hide their want of skill.
>
> (Lines 181-86)

Warburton understood much of Pope's point when he said that "This is entirely ironical, and conveys under it this general moral truth, that there is, in life, no such thing as a perfect Character; so that the satire falls not on any particular *Character* but on the *Character-maker* only" (3: 206n). False panegyric is no better than false satire. The epistles, we recall, celebrate the golden mean as the essential way for human beings to ease or emulate the care of heaven, which does not use artificial varnish, or make human beings perfect, or let them last forever. Those women who try to turn themselves into a "Sex of Queens" (line 219) all too soon realize that they are not unchangeable, that their beauty and power decay, that public life leaves them "like Tyrants, old and friendless grown" (line 227) and unmourned in death.

The portrait of the queen and queenlike women thus neutralizes the potential exemplary power of Atossa: we examine the woman of the highest social degree in the nation and see that unnatural praise by incompetent zealots or flunkies makes unnatural women. Neither duchess nor queen is normative and each is shamed by the proper model of the humble, genuine, titleless lady to whom the poem is addressed, and whose portrait now is painted in all her mutable glory. For the only time in the ethic epistles a "middle-class" norm functions without aristocratic precedent, and it opposes the views of Atossa, the queen, and Juvenal's declining Roman family.

Specifically, Atossa's isolation contrasts with the lady's links to others. She is a friend, she has a heart to be touched, has a sister, daughter, husband, and adoring poet in her web of humanity. Since she is human, she is capable of change, and thus also contrasts with the "varnish'd" queen who is willing to be "The same for ever!" Hence she raises thoughts in others, and charms in herself; she disdains loss of lottery tickets or of youth, and now is a mother, as she once was a virgin. The portrait of the lady in her family life shows that she has learned the lesson Pope has taught—that being a queen in public life destroys women, whose proper sphere is private life. In so learning, the lady also becomes the female model of the *discordia concors*, of what Pope again, in his own note, calls "The Picture of an estimable Woman, with the best kinds of contrarieties" (p. 72 n.). She is both ruler and ruled as she manipulates the normal family squabbles for the family's advantage. She

> ne'er answers till a Husband cools,
> Or, if she rules him, never shows she rules;
> Charms by accepting, by submitting sways,
> Yet has her humour most, when she obeys.
>
> (Lines 261-64)

In the process, she also has improved man who, earlier in the poem, was attracted by the charms of the unreliable Calypso who debased rather than exalted her lover or spouse.

Reconciliation of opposites is especially appropriate for woman, since as Heaven's favorite and "last best work" (line 272) she is an amalgam of the best of both sexes. God takes

> Your love of Pleasure, our desire of Rest,
> Blends, in exception to all gen'ral rules,

196

Your Taste of Follies, with our Scorn of Fools,
Reserve with Frankness, Art with Truth ally'd,
Courage with Softness, Modesty with Pride,
Fix'd Principles, with Fancy ever new;
Shakes all together, and produces — You.

(Lines 274-80)

Even God is viewed with domestic spectacles in this fa-
milial vision, as "Blends" and "Shakes" suggest God the
chef following a recipe in the cosmic kitchen.[15]

Pope also suggests both normal human continuity and
the relationship between procreating poet and procreating
woman. We remember that in Juvenal's sixth satire the
poet was hostile to Roman woman, because she was pol-
luting the once strong Roman family that could no longer
trust her as chaste and nourishing mother. In Pope's ethic
epistle, the poet can be friendly to his educable woman,
because she is a source of British strength and an effective
model for her country's duchess and queen. The lady is a
happy mixture of contrarieties blended by God: "Be this a
Woman's Fame: with this unblest, / Toasts live a scorn,
and Queens may die a jest" (lines 281-82). Pope has defined
woman's true fame, shown the source of that fame, and
demonstrated an example of it in the world. He thus can
end his poem with an affirmation and with another stab
at the real or poetic Atossa. The lady's parents are charac-

---

[15] For instance, to make a "Sauce for Boiled *Ducks* or Rabbits," one
peels and slices onions, boils them in milk and water for twenty min-
utes and drains them in a colander. Then chop the onions, put them
into a saucepan, and "shake in a little Flour, with a little Cream, . . .
and a good Piece of Butter; stir all together over the Fire till the But-
ter is melted, and they will be very fine." Hannah Glasse, *The Art of
Cookery, Made Plain and Easy* (1747), p. 7. Pope's heavenly chef allows
a tone of benevolence not possible in a more secular, and more aggres-
sive, work that is an apparent offshoot of Pope's *To a Lady*. See *The
Mistakes of Men In Search of Happiness. An Ethic Epistle, To Mrs.
* * * * * * * (1761). The woman who seeks to rule her man evokes
debate, confusion, and "domestic strife." She must painfully learn that
"A WOMAN to be happy must Obey" (p. 11).

teristically human in wishing their daughter beauty and wealth. God is characteristically divine in giving her what is best:

> The gen'rous God, who Wit and Gold refines,
> And ripens Spirits as he ripens Mines,
> Kept Dross for Duchesses, the world shall know it,
> To you gave Sense, Good-humour, and a Poet.
>
> (Lines 289-92)

These last three divine gifts affirm the bond between the human and divine, art and life, man and woman. More specifically, our celebratory poet holds up his lady and her divine virtues as a norm for Britain and memorializes her in art.

Pope again has made his Horatian epistolary satire deal with controllable folly not uncontrollable vice. He triumphs over but does not annihilate that folly, for he knows it is irremediable by his secular force. As a Horatian, Pope bravely works with the materials of his world which, every poem in the epistles to several persons shows, is savable; it still has powerful forces working for it and, above all, still has God "incessantly turning the evils arising from the follies and vices of man to general good."

III: BEYOND HORACE

God the patriot, God the cook, God the architect; the king the builder, the patron, the inspirer of love and loyalty in his subjects; the satirist the muted enemy of folly in a world capable of reform and capable of defeating enemies of order and decency; the satirist part of a network of close personal relations extending socially below and above himself, to man and woman, king and God; the satirist in sophisticated dialogue with those who wish to have his wisdom and are capable of accepting his affectionate corrections: these are some of the components of Pope's attractive Horatian satire, which appears in its relative purity in the epistles to several persons. The imitations of Horace and dialogues *"Something like Horace,"* generally are harsher, different in aim and achievement, far more mingled in their use of satiric conventions, and thus heavily larded with Persian or Juvenalian strains foreign to poems like *Burlington.* These Horatian, ethic, epistolary satires show their genesis in comedy, a genre that tends to hold out hope for renewal and change, sees norms among ordinary non-royal persons, and seeks to give us pleasure in a recognizable world. Such a work may include fantasy and foolishness, as in the *Tempest*; but these are held together by the sane and shaping voice of Prospero, who knows that the world is neither brave nor new, but is so to the child he loves and who will restore the vernal while becoming autumnal as an adult ruler. Sadness and the potential for violence remain at the heart of things in much of the best comedy, whether *Twelfth Night, The Tempest, Tom Jones,* or *The Magic Flute,* as indeed it must if we are to appreciate the triumph of love, civilization, and renewal that the conclusion brings. Horace's "Journey to Brundusium" is either incomprehensible or vapid unless it is set against the years of bloody civil wars that seemed, finally, to be ending through the diplomatic mission of reconciliation Maecenas was undertaking. Comedy enshrines the myth of renewal and it is that renewal which Pope seeks to embrace in the four epistles of his system of ethics in the Horatian way, why he ends their collected form with lines from *Burlington* he must have suspected in 1731 and known in 1735 to be wish fulfillment—just, indeed, as Horace must have known that union between Antony and Octavian was wish fulfillment:

> Bid Harbors open, public Ways extend,
> Bid Temples, worthier of the God, ascend;
> Bid the broad Arch the dang'rous Flood contain,
> The Mole projected break the roaring Main;
> Back to his bounds their subject Sea command,
> And roll obedient Rivers thro' the Land;
> These Honours, Peace to happy Britain brings,

These are Imperial Works, and worthy Kings.

(Lines 197-204)

Such setting of goals to be reached is part of the beauty of
the epistles, for they look forward to a better world than
the one we inhabit in external reality, or even at the begin-
ning of the poem. In another age Timon's gross building
shall be replaced by productive farmland. God shall send
rain to balance the drought and reconcile extremes.

The satirist's ultimate placidity—often unseen or ignored
by Pope's enemies—was useful for the tones of the epis-
tolary satirist in the Horatian way. Other generic needs and
external circumstances awakened Pope from his dream of
"happy Britain," and so in other satires God the loving
creator who returns order in His leisurely fashion is meta-
morphosed into God the avenger, who had better return
order now, and with the angry satirist as His agent. By
1738 order can be restored only in the after life, and the
divine and earthly satirist are ineffectual in the face of
transcendent and unchanging corruption. As the 1730s
progress, Pope becomes more committed to and identified
with opposition to Walpole, is subject to threats more
ominous than those long present in pamphlet attacks upon
him, and sees less hope in writing to powerful allies who
might help the state. Pope's adaptation of the Horatian
epistle stretched its conventions to include some political
opposition and divine Christian benevolence. When the
form could stretch no further, he abandoned it in favor of
more satirically complex and modulated works that use
Horatian buildings, with Persian or Juvenalian rooms, and
furnishings by Lucilius. This process does not offer a neat
line of development, for it begins after only two of the four
ethic epistles were published and shows Pope continuing
to try the gentler as well as harsh mode until 1735; but
begin it does, and in Pope's first imitation of Horace, the
First Satire of the Second Book, to Fortescue (1733), a poem
quickly recognized for its satiric, un-Horatian traits.

░░░

CHAPTER 7

The Mingled Muse: Pope's *First Satire of the Second Book of Horace Imitated*

O NE POPULAR VIEW of Horace's sophisticated and confi-
dent satiric voice was offered by the Abbé Charles Bat-
teux, whose widely known and conveniently unoriginal
Course of the Belles Lettres appeared in English in 1761.
Horace's satire shows "the sentiments of a polite philoso-
pher, who is concerned to see the absurdities of mankind."
He sometimes "diverts himself with" those absurdities and
berates them through "general portraits of human life." If
he occasionally becomes particular it is not to offend but
"to enliven the subject, and put the moral . . . into action."
His characters normally are fictitious: real persons named
are those "only who were universally decried, and had no
longer any pretence to reputation." Horace's genius was
neither malicious nor morose, but that of "a delicate friend
to the true and the good; taking mankind as it found them,
and esteeming them oftener rather objects of compassion,
than of hatred or ridicule. . . . His style is plain, delicate,
sprightly, and full of moderation and gentleness; when he
corrects a fool, a fop, or a miser, he does it in so nice a
manner, that the wounded hardly feels any smart."[1]

At least some details of this portrait of Horace may be
seen in his first satire of the second book, an apologia that
Pope imitates, with significant differences, in 1733. Horace
begins by addressing the distinguished lawyer Trebatius,

[1] *Abbot Charles Batteux, A Course of the Belles Lettres: or, the
Principles of Literature. Translated from the French . . . By Mr.
Miller*, 3: 144. The article on satire (by the Chevalier de Jaucourt) in
the *Encyclopédie* (Neufchâtel, 1765), 14: 697-702, includes Batteux's
"Parallèle des satyriques romains & françois par M. le Batteux." See
Miller's translation, 3: 192-95, which substitutes Dryden and Young
for the French satirists.

a man who first was a friend of Cicero's and then a friend and advisor to Julius and Augustus Caesar. Augustus would in fact do nothing regarding law without consulting him.[2] Trebatius tells Horace that if he wishes to avoid charges of satiric brutality, he should either not write at all or sing Caesar's martial praises and gain appropriate rewards. Horace laments that he cannot produce the requisite epic poem, associates himself with his superior Lucilius as a satirist whose harsh verse defends Rome by attacking its enemies, and insists that whatever happens, even if death threatens him, he must write. To Horace's adamant "scribam," Trebatius offers a worldly and paternal "O puer" (line 60), a friendly warning of consequences, and a willing ear when Horace again asserts the Lucilian pattern of attack on the wicked—including leaders of the nation, if necessary—and praise of the virtuous. All the seeming outrage, however, never becomes Juvenalian. In Batteux's words, Horace is diverting himself, enlivening the subject and showing himself a friend of the good while being sprightly and moderate. The moderation is induced by Trebatius's own presence as a powerful muscle in the legal arm of the Augustan court, and equally powerful evidence that Horace does have the approval of the great as he claims (line 76). Trebatius thus says, in lawyerly evaluation of Horace's outburst, "I can't find anything to disagree with" (line 79). The satire ends with Horace's witty turn on Trebatius's final advice regarding "mala . . . carmina" (line 82)—that is, libelous verse. Horace ignores this as a legal description

---

[2] For some of the better known commentary on Trebatius, see André Dacier, *Oeuvres d'Horace en latin et en françois, avec des remarques critiques et historiques* (1681-89), 3rd ed. (Paris, 1709), 7: 21-22. "Il fut aussi en grande consideration auprès d'Auguste, qui ne faisoit rien sans le consulter" (p. 22). Trebatius was, of course, glossed and discussed in the other standard editions, encyclopaedias, and dictionaries. Subsequent quotations are from this edition of Dacier and are cited in the text. The Horace not from Pope's facing page is quoted from *Quinti Horatii Flacci opera*, ed. Ludovicus Desprez (1691), 7th ed. (1722).

and turns it, instead, into a qualitative matter. In the process he accepts Trebatius's earlier counsel, as he implied he would (lines 17-20), that he praise Caesar and receive his rewards. He wonders, What if I write good verses and Caesar's judgment praises them? And if I have only attacked those who deserve it, while being untainted myself? (lines 83-85). In such a case, Trebatius concludes, the legal slate will be wiped clean and Horace is free.

As the poem develops, it clearly supports the moral and governmental status quo. Horace's portrait of Lucilius, for example, now is very different from the portrait of the pre-Augustan rough versifier and vilifier in *Satires*, i. 4, and i. 10. He has become the friend of the great Scipio Africanus and Laelius, a testament to their worth, a companion of their private moments, and an ideal for Horatian life and letters. Moreover, the establishment's favorite lawyer, several unnamed but known aristocrats, and the princeps himself are, finally, friends of Horace and his satire. The enemy is routed, the general's tent is colored with imperial purple, and the satirist has shown the unbelievers that their prudence, if not virtue or taste, should suggest finding another opponent. This satire is a triumph of wit, threat, and dubiously moral suasion that helps both Horace's personal case and that of the government, here portrayed as guided by the exquisite hand of a martially unvanquished, poetically literate, and judicially wise emperor.

Eighteenth-century theories of imitation encouraged independent use of earlier models, a liberty that Pope's hostile readers often thought degenerated into license. William King argues that an imitator is not *"bound Prentice"* to his author, and far later the extremely free imitator of Juvenal's first satire describes his method as using "Juvenal only as English soldiers use a bastion, to fight with greater safety, but not to skulk behind constantly like a rifleman."[3] By

---

[3] King, trans., *The Art of Love in Imitation of Ovid*, p. xxxix; *XSMWPDRIBVNWLXY: Or, The Sauce-Pan* (1781), p. 25.

1733 Pope is neither an apprentice nor a skulking rifleman, and so his first imitation of Horace is very different from his original in tone, effect, and practical achievement, though certainly part of the world of convincing apologia that Horace had so brilliantly initiated. Pope uses the Horatian bastion while often being un-Horatian, and presses the appropriate Persian and Juvenalian conventions into his satiric army.

In the Advertisement (1735) to *Fortescue*, for example, he says that "An Answer [to his detractors] from *Horace* was both more full, and of more Dignity, than any I cou'd have made in my own person." He goes on to say that "the Example of much greater Freedom in so eminent a Divine as Dr. *Donne* [in his satires] seem'd a proof with what Indignation and Contempt a Christian may treat Vice or Folly, in ever so low, or ever so high, a Station." Both Donne and Horace "were acceptable to the Princes and Ministers under whom they lived"—Princes *and* Ministers, we note. Pope is largely aiming at the latter in his poem, since Walpole manipulated George II, as Maecenas did not manipulate Augustus. Moreover, Donne is placed under one of two politically acceptable rubrics. His satires first appeared in 1633, and so may have been considered spiritually Stuart, however much they attacked aspects of court life. If Pope thought them Elizabethan, as they were, the satires were nonetheless admirable because written under a monarch idolized by the opposition, one who, unlike George II and his minions, had the properly Britannic ability to smite the offending Spaniards hip, thigh, and mainmast in the bargain. A satirist can be safe under such a "free" political order—as indeed Pope himself was when he versified Donne at the request of the Earl of Oxford when he was Lord Treasurer, and the Duke of Shrewsbury who once had been Secretary of State, "neither of whom look'd upon a Satire on Vicious Courts as any Reflection on those they serv'd in" (p. 3). The political barbs and implied contrast with Walpole are clear; Oxford and Shrewsbury, serving under Queen Anne, were the last two men with the title Lord Treasurer, after which the offices were in part settled on the First Commissioner of the Treasury, which Walpole held from 1715 to 1717, and again from 1721 to 1742 under the Electors of Brunswick-Luneberg. In spite of the bastion of Horace, behind which Pope fights "with greater safety," the Advertisement quickly suggests a Juvenalian sense of looking backward for norms, of seeking another dynasty in which a satirist can function as he should. Pope must act impartially in his country's interest and attack knaves of whatever social or financial worth. "This," he tells Lord Hervey in a then unpublished letter, ". . . is rendering the best Service he can to the Publick, and even to the good Government of his Country"—a service for which he seems to get only abuse from His Majesty's court.[4]

Horace was leagued with his court and its values; Pope offers a Tory and Stuart, rather than Whig and Hanoverian, genealogy and indicates one of the serious consequences of the change in governments. Donne, the younger Pope, and Horace himself were not merely safe but encouraged under their dispensations; the older Pope is clouded with the vague but real threat of libel and, as the poem will show, physical attack for his virtuous satire. The new

[4] "A Letter to a Noble Lord. On occasion of some Libels written and propagated at Court, in the Year 1732-3," in *The Works of Alexander Pope Esq.*, ed. William Warburton (1751), 8: 208. "Libel" was one of the frequent charges against Pope. See, for example, the anonymous *Ingratitude: To Mr. Pope Occasion'd by a Manuscript handed about; under the Title of Mr. Taste's Tour from the Land of Politeness, to that of Dulness and Scandal, &c. &c.* (1733): "your *satirical* Pieces, as you are pleased to call them, are mere *Defamatory* Libels; for he that transgresses the Rules of *Satire*, whose Business is to expose and lash *Vice* with Severity, falls at once, either through *Ignorance*, or *Wilfulness*, into *Defamation*, whose scandalous Office is to attack and blacken the Reputation of Persons, though undeservedly" (p. 3). The author's judgment is as accurate as his attribution and as elegant as his taste. See the brief description of the frontispiece to this effort in chapter 5, n. 16, above.

world of princes and ministers is peopled by those of less than moral or intellectual excellence. As Pope says in the Advertisement, there is no "greater Error, than that which Fools are so apt to fall into, and Knaves with good reason to incourage, the mistaking a *Satyrist* for a *Libeller*;[5] whereas to a *true Satyrist* nothing is so odious as a *Libeller*, for the same reason as to a man *truly Virtuous* nothing is so hateful as a *Hypocrite*" (p. 3). Pope necessarily is on the defensive in his world of fools, knaves, and hypocrites eager to accuse him of libel. I suspect that Bolingbroke and Pope thought the legal issue, and not merely the flap about Timon, was relevant to Horace's case in his first satire of the second book. This similarity also helps to differentiate the two satirists and their poems: Pope will use Horatian conventions and "canvass" in his own way—for instance, in resolving the central issues of how to define satire and its relation to the government and great men, how harsh satire may be legally safe, and how satire differs from libel.

I: QUID FACIAM?

As Horace's poem opens, he and Trebatius are talking, perhaps in a neutral place, perhaps in Trebatius's home, perhaps in Horace's. We do not know the location, which is of

---

[5] By making this distinction, Pope was adapting a recognizable opposition argument, as exemplified in the *Craftsman*, No. 117, 28 September 1728, a reply to the administration's *London Journal*: "other Authors . . . have been commonly so modest as to distinguish between *Libelling* and *just Satire*; but the *Journalist* . . . confounds them together, and does not advance one Argument, which is not equally conclusive against them *both*." Satire, the *Craftsman* insists, is a supplement to the law and preserves decency and propriety through fear of shame. Libel calumniates and misrepresents "for vile, wicked and unjust Purposes." This number is a return of fire in the battle for a free rather than a licensed press. The Postscript to No. 122, 2 November 1728, continues the heated exchange, concludes with Horace's ringing defense of satire in *Satires*, ii. 1, and its final lines, with "OPPROBRIS DIGNUM"—he deserves abuse—in distinctive type. In this instance, at

marginal importance here; we do know that Augustus's
own lawyer is giving Horace advice. By publicly speaking
to Trebatius, Horace is defending himself with, not from,
the Augustan court. Pope, on the other hand, is topographi-
cally more precise and provides a change of venue necessary
for his changed purpose: he is in Fortescue's chambers,
whose walls are lined with law books in easy reach so that
Fortescue can, as the manuscript puts it, deal more easily
with what Pope calls "My case" and show specific laws and
cases (lines 147-49).[6] The legalistic, administration, cau-
tious lawyer in his chambers contrasts sharply with Pope's
later vision of the opposition, brilliant, intellectual envi-
ronment of his grotto: "if your Point be Rest, / Lettuce and
Cowslip Wine; *Probatum est*" (lines 17-18) versus "The
Feast of Reason and the Flow of Soul" (line 128). The
ostensible dialogue between Pope and Fortescue is set
against the superior backdrop of assumed dialogue be-
tween Pope and Bolingbroke. Each dialogue of course bears
its own symbolic weight and values.

Moreover, unlike Horace, Pope specifies those whom he
has offended—including Peter and Chartres, emblems of
Walpolean corruption, and the court poet whose verse pre-
sumably is as good as Pope's in quality and superior in
quantity. "The Lines are weak, another's pleas'd to say, /
Lord *Fanny* spins a thousand such a Day" (line 6), we hear,
without the detractor's hearing that if he is correct my
Lord Fanny produces a thousand more weak lines than
Pope. The satirist leaves that calculation to our own higher

---

least, Horace's poem hit the opposition's case in general and Pope's in
particular. The discussion of libel and its consequences, we shall see,
runs throughout Pope's imitation and its political and legal contexts.

[6] The extremely complex manuscript of the poem is in the Berg
Collection of the New York Public Library. Many of its readings, how-
ever, are reproduced in *The Works of Alexander Pope*, ed. John Wil-
son Croker, Whitwell Elwin, and William John Courthope (1871-89),
3 (1881): 289-300. "My case" appears on p. 289n. Subsequent references
to this edition are cited in the text as EC.

mathematics; but he guides us toward the object of his satire by naming Lord Fanny and by emphasizing a key word in the facing Latin: "Mille die versus *deduci* posse" (line 4). Hervey does not write but "spins" his verse, and already is made part of the subhuman and finally slight court entourage.[7]

Pope also sets off *Praescribe* in a similar way—a word Robert Ainsworth illustrates with this very line from Horace, and defines as *"To order, appoint, or ordain."*[8] Trebatius! What am I to do? Prescribe it! Though Trebatius now merely says "Quiescas" (line 4), he soon adds that Horace should praise Caesar (lines 10-12), advice that Horace agrees to accept at the appropriate time (lines 17-20); but for Pope such an order is impossible, and he is thus immediately in legal and physical danger, though he presents that danger in a playful way. "There are to whom my Satire seems too bold" (line 2) is in part a loose version of "Sunt quibus in Satyra videar nimis acer, & ultra / Legem tendere opus" (lines 1-2). Dacier merely notes that a nasty form like satire should be restrained, imitate the old comedy, and not take the horrible liberty of crying down all the world. Dacier (following Suetonius), Père Sanadon, and Desprez in the Dauphin's Horace, make clear what the penalties were for violating the laws of satire. "La loi des douze tables," Sanadon says, "portoit peine de mort contre ceux qui déchiroient la réputation des autres par des vers satiriques, & Auguste renouvela cette même loi, qui avoit beaucoup perdu de sa vigeur."[9] English satirists long feared

---

[7] Italics and Roman type have been inverted both from Pope's Advertisement and his facing Latin.

[8] Robert Ainsworth, *Thesaurus linguae latinae compendiarius . . . with Additions and Improvements By Samuel Patrick* (1736), 2nd ed. (1746).

[9] Sanadon, *Les Poésies d'Horace* (Paris, 1728), 2: 225; Dacier, *Oeuvres d'Horace* 7: 56, borrows from Suetonius, *Augustus*, 55, and quotes the words of the law; Desprez, *Quinti Horatii*, pp. 434n, 582n. R. E. Smith discusses "The Law of Libel at Rome" in the *Classical Quarterly*, 45 (1951): 169-79, especially pp. 177-79, for Horace and Augustus. For

trials for *scandalum magnatum*, and Pope himself knew
from many sources that the Roman penalty for libel was
death. In appropriately Augustan Britain, Walpole's
friends and Pope's enemies would gladly have reinstituted
that penalty on behalf of Pope and the opposition; the
government contented itself instead with threats of action
and punishment, an occasional exemplary arrest and trial,[10]
and its own, and sympathizers', responses that included
libel and brutality as well as reasoned arguments. Pope's
shrill remark at the end of his Advertisement thus is not
only a literary but an attempted, if useless, legal distinction
between legitimate satire and illicit libel, and an attempt to
forestall prosecution or worse.

For example, Pope's weighted figure of speech quickly

---

further discussion of relevant Roman law and its relation to literature,
see A.H.M. Jones, *The Criminal Courts of the Roman Republic and
the Principate* (Oxford: Basil Blackwell, 1972), and Michael Coffey,
Roman Satire (Methuen & Co., 1976), pp. 136-37, 231n. 83, and 248nn.
92-93.

[10] For further discussion of such government action, see Laurence
Hanson, *Government and the Press, 1695-1763* (Oxford Univ. Press,
1936); C. R. Kropf, "Libel and Satire in the Eighteenth Century,"
Eighteenth-Century Studies, 8 (1974-75): 153-68; Donald Thomas,
"Press Prosecutions of the Eighteenth and Nineteenth Centuries," *The
Library*, 5th series, 32 (1977): 316-18; and, among other sources, *The
Doctrine of Libels Discussed and Examined: A Treatise Shewing From
the best Authorities, what shall be deemed and taken for Defamatory
Writings, and how far the same are punishable by our Laws* (1728).
This treatise, which mentions the Roman penalty of death for libel
(p. 84), was later attacked by *The Independant Briton* (1742). Admin-
istration and opposition journals and pamphlets frequently exchanged
pleasantries regarding who was libeling whom. See notes 4 and 5 above.
Of course it was not always necessary to threaten merely legal action
in order to intimidate an opposition author. The poet of *A Friendly
Epistle to the Author of the State Dunces* (1733) appends this note:
"A Printer, who having been employ'd in Printing a certain Paper
some way reflecting on Mr. *Poultney* and his Family, was, by their
Emisaries and Allies, cudgell'd almost to Death, and were never pun-
ished" (p. 8n). This threat to Paul Whitehead was extended to Pope,
as *Fortescue*, and Lady Mary's and Lord Hervey's *Verses* make clear.

provides a context of violence not present on the facing page. When he says that he must write "for my Soul" (line 12), Fortescue, perhaps hoping to protect his client, answers: "You could not do a worse thing for your Life" (line 15). Pope both contrasts his own spiritual and Fortescue's temporal concerns, and draws out the implications of Horace's problem of appearing to go beyond the rules of the genre—a problem whose resolution must wait until the end of the poem. In the meantime, though, Pope's position is appreciably more dangerous than that of Horace, who bluntly says in response to Trebatius's directions —no, I cannot praise Caesar the great soldier because my talents are not along those lines. I shall not now praise him as wise and brave but (in the words of Creech),

> when Occasion serves my Muse designs
> To try that way, but my unpolish'd lines,
> Unless by chance a happy Time appears,
> Will never pass the judging *Caesar*'s Ears,
> Whom if you try to stroak, He's free from Pride,
> And kicks you off, secure on every side.[11]

Pope could not praise his monarch as a wise man and soldier without making an ass or a sycophant of himself. Horace fortuitously supplied exactly the right word for an attack upon Walpole's peace policy. "Nec *fracta pereuntes cuspide Gallos*" (line 14); there could be no fallen Gauls if Walpole decreed that the Gauls were not to be fought. As Joseph Warton says, "Pope has turned the compliment to Augustus into a severe sarcasm."[12] Moreover, Pope rejects Fortescue's prudent urging that he praise the monarch or the royal family; he even banishes his manuscript's original line that said, however ironically, "I'll take the first

---

[11] Thomas Creech, *The Odes, Satyrs, and Epistles of Horace* (1684), 2nd ed. (1688), p. 421. Subsequent quotations from this edition are cited in the text.

[12] *The Works of Alexander Pope* (1797), 4: 64n. Subsequent quotations from this edition are cited in the text.

occasion, I declare," to praise "the king" (p. 291n EC).
Instead, we see that

> They scarce can bear their *Laureate* twice a Year:
> And justly CAESAR scorns the Poet's Lays,
> It is to *History* he trusts for Praise.
>
> (Lines 34-36)

Horace's learned, proud, sensitive Caesar would rid himself
of a poor poet as quickly as the horse would kick an awk-
ward groom. Pope's Caesar dismisses the poet's in favor of
history's (presumably harsh) judgment. Furthermore, Pope
deftly clogs the bolt-hole that Horace just as deftly opened.
Horace will praise Caesar *"dextro tempore"* (line 19), at
the right time, in words Pope set in distinctive type. Since
Pope rejects the Caesarian option he must look elsewhere
for the subject of his proper moment of praise; like Horace
he offers it at the end of the poem, though for a very differ-
ent purpose.

Horace cleverly foreshadows his ultimate escape from
threats of punishment for his satire; through Trebatius he
also introduces a moral authority for his support of the
state. When Horace talks about the right time to praise
Caesar, he is responding to this direction from Trebatius:
"Attamen & justum poteras & scribere fortem, / Scipiadam
ut sapiens Lucilius" (lines 16-17)—Write of Caesar as just
and brave, the way wise Lucilius did of Scipio. This is the
first of three references to Lucilius, a sign that he will be
on the side of the new Caesar as of the old Scipio, and that
Horace will emulate him in this respect "when Occasion
serves." Pope at once says *no* to this uncharacteristic version
of Lucilius and as yet says nothing of his satiric predeces-
sors. Only Sir Richard Blackmore, Budgell, or the Laureate
Cibber would so glowingly praise George Augustus.
"What?" Pope says, as he later says "Alas!" (lines 23, 33) to
comparable advice.

These differences widen even more through Pope's lines
45-100, where we see his apparent efforts to be as docile as

he can, his signs that suggest the difficulty of such a role, and his realization that in the present Augustan world he will quickly be forced into the harsh satire he prefers to avoid, and for which he must now defend himself. We will, that is, see a progressively more Juvenalian posture as the imitation of Horace locates itself in a progressively more Juvenalian world.

The poem on Pope's facing page is of course very different. The need to write satire, Horace says, is inborn. He will follow Lucilius, who spoke openly to his book as to a trusted friend and recorded his good or faulty deeds there: "And hence his Books do all his Life explain, / As if we saw him live it o'er again" (p. 421). Horace also knows that Lucilius had his harsher side, that he himself might be attacked by others and thus must use his pen, his natural weapon of defense, to respond to the violence others initiate: "melius non tangere clamo" (line 45)—better not touch me, Horace warns. He finally is touched and responds with manly satire:

> whether I live long or no,
> Or Rich, or Poor, howe'er my Fortunes go;
> Live here at *Rome*, or banish'd take my flight,
> Whatever is my state of Life, I'll write.
>
> (P. 423)

Pope is both more and less restrained. He seems to try very hard indeed to be as pleasant as he can and to ally himself not with a satirist, even Horace's introspective and lyric Lucilius, but with men of political virtue or moderation, whose good actions are clear at once.

> I love to pour out all myself, as plain
> As downright *Shippen*, or as old *Montagne*.
> In them, as certain to be lov'd as seen,
> The Soul stood forth, nor kept a Thought within.
>
> (Lines 51-54)

Pope's own "soul" also stands forth in his works, and we recall that earlier Pope said that unless he writes "for my Soul I cannot sleep a wink"; later it is the "Flow of Soul" (lines 12, 128) that characterizes his talks with Bolingbroke. That soul is tinged with distinctly opposition colors, and so his example of Shippen foreshadows things to come, since that avowed but parliamentary Jacobite was an enemy of "faction" and a model of integrity whom Sir Robert himself praised and could not bribe. In 1726 he wrote a stinging attack on Edward Young's *Instalment* and its fulsome praise of Walpole; the title page of his *Remarks Critical and Political* even quotes a (fancied?) couplet from Pope on "*Venal Pens.*"[13] No wonder Pope originally wrote that such a man's soul "Stands boldly forth" (p. 293, EC). Pope avoids mentioning Lucilius or any other comparable guiding satirist, since Horace's Lucilius praises a major figure in the government and because here he is a private and not the public poet Pope is to become. When Pope introduces his version of Lucilius, it will not be such a man, but a recreation of the free, pristine satirist of the tradition of Juvenal and Persius in opposition, someone like Shippen, willing to tell the truth and suffer if necessary as Shippen did when sent to the Tower for telling Commons, among other things, that George I "was a stranger to our language and Constitution" (p. 293n, EC). Warburton disapproved

13 This work and an attribution in a contemporary hand are in the Bodleian Library. The title-page motto is: "*Some Venal Pens so prostitute the Bays, Their Panegyricks* lash, their Satires Praise. POPE.*" So far as I can tell, this couplet is not Pope's. Pope may have been indebted to Shippen for literary as well as political guidance, since his *Moderation Display'd* (1704) includes several foreshadowings of the *Dunciad*. See Frank H. Ellis, ed., *Poems on Affairs of State: Augustan Satirical Verse, 1660-1714 Volume 7: 1704-1714* (New Haven: Yale Univ. Press, 1975), pp. 23, 23n, 31, 31n. Shippen's *Faction Display'd* (1704), which Pope may also have in mind, is reprinted in volume 6 of *Poems on Affairs of State*, ed. Frank H. Ellis (New Haven: Yale Univ. Press, 1970), pp. 651-73.

of Shippen's politics, but he took part of Pope's point in the allusion. Shippen and Montaigne, he says, "had this, indeed, in common, to use great liberties of speech, and to profess saying what they thought" (4: 60n). Later in the century, Warton misses the rest of Pope's point, while noting his divergence from Horace. He scolds his author because "A poet, like Lucilius, ought to have been named, not a politician" (4: 67n). In fact, however, the politician predicts the direction Pope will take and suggests that Pope has placed his tongue firmly in his cheek when he claims to be "Tim'rous by Nature, of the Rich in awe" (line 7), and hopes to avoid embarrassing his betters. The compliant satirist seems almost willing to replay a form of Persian and Juvenalian silence, as expressed in each man's first satire. He will

> Publish the present Age, but where my Text
> Is Vice too high, reserve it for the next:
> My Foes shall wish my Life a longer date,
> And ev'ry Friend the less lament my Fate.
>
> (Lines 59-62)

> Papist or Protestant, or both between,
> Like good *Erasmus* in an honest Mean,
> In Moderation placing all my Glory,
> While Tories call me Whig, and Whigs a Tory.
>
> (Lines 65-68)

Like Horace, who has no comparable passage, but in a higher key and for higher stakes, Pope is responding to his earlier delicate legal situation. Lines 61 and 62 again suggest a threat to the poet's life; the earlier allusion to Shippen and, perhaps, the present rhyme of *Glory* and *Tory*, presuppose a temporary detour on the road of moderation. He only uses his weapons of satire "in a Land of Hectors, / Thieves, Supercargoes, Sharpers, and Directors" (lines 71-72)—that is, as Pope believes, the world of 1732-33 under Walpole's guidance. Hence when we see "touch me, and no

214

Minister so sore," we are not surprised also to see it fol-
lowed by "Who-e'er offends, at some unlucky Time / Slides
into Verse, and hitches in a Rhyme" (lines 76-78). Just
seventeen lines ago if the Vice was too high, Pope would
ignore it and publish posthumously; now an offender will
be "Sacred to Ridicule! his whole Life long" (line 79).
Pope must abandon moderation because moderation has
abandoned the world in which one must expect to be
hanged "if your Judge be *Page*," and to be "P—x'd by
[Sappho's] Love, or libell'd by her Hate" (lines 82-84).
These words again remind us of the legal situation with
which the poem began. Students of Pope normally concen-
trate upon the witty outrage of "P—x'd by her Love"; in
this context Pope was as concerned with Lady Mary's
"libel" of him, for it suggests both that he has been
"touched" and thus may attack in return, and that those
charging him with criminal acts are themselves criminal.[14]
  In any case, this section of the poem makes plain that
Pope's conceptions of his satiric art, its subject, and his own
and Fortescue's character are markedly different from what
they were at the beginning of this once lighthearted inter-
view with the lawyer from whom he asks free advice. In
the process of conducting the dialogue, Pope has learned
about himself, the forces with which he must contend, and
the risks inherent in being a satirist if the court he hopes to
reform wishes to destroy him (lines 15, 102, 104, 146). He
thus moves from a respectful request for help to insistence
regarding what he must do, whatever the consequence:
"Then learned Sir! (to cut the Matter short) / What-e'er
my Fate, or well or ill at Court" (lines 91-92), whether he
is to have a long life or already is dying—or conspired

14 For support of this conjecture, see Pope's letter to Fortescue, 8
March 1733, in response to his—and Walpole's—request that the offen-
sive couplet be expunged. Pope refuses, since that lady took "her own
Satisfaction in an avowed Libell, so fulfilling the veracity of my
prophecy." The *Correspondence of Alexander Pope* (Oxford: Claren-
don Press, 1956), 3: 354; referred to hereafter as *Correspondence*.

against?—"In Durance, Exile, Bedlam, or the Mint, / . . .
I will Rhyme and Print" (lines 99-100). Pope's fluid poem
has moved us from timidity to courage; from a willing dis-
regard of exalted vice for reasons of personal security, to a
willful exposure of vice with grave personal risk; from
Fortescue's "I'd write no more" (line 11) to his own "I will
Rhyme and Print" (line 100); and from acquiescence in the
needful caution of Persius and Juvenal, to greater bravery
in exposing his weak body to ministerial threats as he de-
fends virtue. The poem's "world" soon calls upon Pope to
test and act upon his new character, and to try to define
satire and libel in the moral terms of his Advertisement
rather than the putative legal terms of the administration.

II: THE DEFENSE OF VIRTUE

Pope's reactions are the opposite of those Fortescue advised
and hoped for. In the manuscript, Fortescue is even clearer
when, after line 68, he echoes the conclusion of Juvenal's
first satire: " 'Twere safer yet, you only lashed the dead, /
The heirs of such would hardly break your head" (p. 294n,
EC). He preserves the spirit of those lines in Fortescue's
mock-lament that his determined visitor will be killed if he
persists in his harsh satiric genre.

> Alas young Man! your Days can ne'er be long,
> In Flow'r of Age you perish for a Song!
> Plums, and Directors, *Shylock* and his Wife,
> Will club their Testers, now, to take your Life!
>
> (Lines 101-4)

Since Fortescue was both a friend and aid to Pope, he could
not be attacked directly, especially since he is trying to keep
his rash, non-fee-paying client from harm;[15] but he clearly

---

[15] The adversarius was not labeled "Fortescue" until Warburton's
edition of 1751, though Pope had his friend and attorney in mind
from the outset. See Pope's letter of 18 February 1733 in his *Corre-
spondence*, 3: 351. In April of 1733 he shows that he still thinks of

functions as the administration's prudent or amoral Persian Monitor and can see Pope's verse only as a mere song. His own predictions of conspiracy and murder do not trouble him as much as ridiculing taste, blaspheming quadrille, and laughing at peers (lines 38, 40). The hint behind his earlier "You could not do a worse thing for your Life" (line 15) emerges openly—and is the more damning, since it comes from a source presumably close to administration values and methods.

In so writing, Pope made a significant choice regarding the meaning of his parallel passage in Horace, a choice perhaps guided by earlier satiric practices or by the *Craftsman* for 2 November 1728, which cites the same lines and finds fatal meaning in them.[16] My boy, Trebatius says, I fear your days will be short and that some great friend will strike you with a freezing frost ("O puer, ut sis / Vitalis, metuo; & majorum ne quis amicus / Frigore te feriat": lines 60-62). The key words are "Frigore te feriat." Desprez says of Frigore: "Morte quae frigida est: vel, frigido ac fastidioso vultu"—either killed ("iced"?) or treated scornfully. Creech takes the former interpretation: "*Well, Sir, I see your Life*

Fortescue in terms reminiscent of the "F" of his imitation, whom he calls "my Council learned in the laws" (line 142). In this letter he says that if Fortescue is elevated to the bench, "Twickenham will be as much at the service of my lord judge, as it was of my learned council." *Correspondence*, 3: 364.

16 See part of this number reprinted in Maynard Mack, *The Garden and the City: Retirement and Politics in the Later Poetry of Pope 1731-1743* (Toronto: Univ. of Toronto Press, 1969), p. 176. Mack's discussion of the political background of these poems remains indispensable. Other writers used this ambiguity in Horace's poem for their own purposes as well. Hence the author of *The Second, Fourth, and Seventh Satyrs of Monsieur Boileau Imitated* (1696), has the dissuader in Boileau's fourth satire say:

Shun it . . . , for fear that one of those
Whom you in Satyr have decreed t' Expose,
Should some way take to cool thy raging blood,
And make thee write again if thou think'st good.
(P. 26)

then can't be long, | Some great Ones, faith, will stop your railing Tongue" (p. 423). Ainsworth, however, gives *frigus* the metaphorical meaning of "(5) . . . *Coolness of affection"* and cites Horace's line above. Philip Francis firmly straddles the fence: "Thy Days are short; some Lords shall strike thee dead / With freezing Look." His note to the line well exemplifies Horace's apparent ambiguity as perceived by several seventeenth- and eighteenth-century commentators who, Francis observes, "are much divided about the Meaning of these Words," some interpreting them to mean "*to put out of Favour,"* others "that *frigus* here signifies *Death.* . . . The Translator is very little certain that he hath chosen the best of these Opinions."[17] Whichever Horace meant— I suspect, with Joseph Warton (4: 73n), that he intended the freezing of his career and not murder—Pope has cut the knot with "you perish for a Song!" (line 102) and placed the words in the mouth of one of Walpole's legal advisors.

Fortescue thereby evokes his friend's noble defense of himself and virtue, lines which, Warburton wrote, are "not only superior to Horace, but equal to any thing" of his own (4: 67n, and Warton, 4: 74n). They also offer us Pope's version of the true satirist, the true Lucilius, and the true royal court. In the process, Pope characteristically borrows from Horace while making his own superior domestic investment with foreign capital.

We have seen Pope move from willingness to write but not publish, to determination to rhyme and print. Fortescue's warning forces him into a yet more vigorous role. He transmutes self-defense into Virtue's defense, as he becomes the active warrior whose stylus has become a stiletto, and whose opening words Benjamin Loveling found useful for his own imitation of *The First Satire of Juvenal* (1740, p. 20).

[17] Desprez, *Quinti Horatii*, p. 433n; Ainsworth, *Thesaurus linguae latinae*; Francis, *A Poetical Translation of the Works of Horace* (1747), 5th ed. (1753), 3: 175-77, 175n.

> What? arm'd for *Virtue* when I point the Pen,
> Brand the bold Front of shameless, guilty Men,
> Dash the proud Gamester in his gilded Car,
> Bare the mean Heart that lurks beneath a Star.
>
> (Lines 105-8)

Pope's final line shows the disparity between the external and internal quality of the relevant Knight of the Bath or Garter; it is also an Anglicized version of Horatian unmasking. This line faces us: *"Detrahere & pellem, nitidus, qua quisque per ora /* Cederet *introrsum turpis"* (lines 64-65). The ancient players' masks were made of skin and, when removed, could reveal the ugliness beneath—the star of knighthood covers the base heart and is as flimsy and misleading as an actor's mask. Pope not only is defending himself and virtue from knights and gamesters; he probably is attacking Walpole and virtually daring him to take the action for libel Pope feared at the beginning of the poem.

Specifically, "Bare the mean Heart that lurks beneath a Star" is at once general and particular. There were several starred villains Pope could have attacked, but "beneath" and "Star" would have evoked associations with Walpole. A star is the emblem of the Knights of the Bath, with which Walpole was honored on 27 May 1725 after persuading George I to revive the order with thirty-eight such places useful for political suasion. Of greater importance, Walpole resigned this knighthood on 26 June 1726 to accept the starred Garter, the first given to a commoner since 1660, and an elevation that caused anger among the nobility and shows of pride and position from Walpole. He had his bust sculpted by Rysbrack (ca. 1730), with a Roman toga nobly draping his shoulders and the star prominently engraved. He also had his portraits repainted with the order's George, star, and blue ribbon, and he was nicknamed both the knight of the Blazing Star and Sir Blue-String. Moreover, he also "had the Star and Garter plastered into the new ceilings and carved into the chimney pieces at Houghton," so that he quite literally was beneath a star.

J. H. Plumb has well documented these stellar pyrotechnics, as had many contemporary writers. Edward Young, for example, had a keen eye for preferment and in 1726 celebrated Walpole's elevation in *The Installment*. The world can see that

> all the scatter'd merits of his line,
> Collected to a point intensely shine.
> See, Britain! see thy Walpole shine from far,
> His azure ribbon, and his radiant star;
> A star that, with auspicious beams, shall guide
> Thy vessel safe through Fortune's roughest tide.

Young also notes the higher magnitude of the present star, which is worthily displayed because, among other good reasons, it "Confirms grown Virtue, and inflames the new." In 1733 a less devoted celebrant of the great man joins the many others in focusing on that offensive element. He depicts Walpole's defeat in the excise-scheme and shows him beshitten with fear as the opposition threatens to hang him, even though he has "A Paper in Form of a Star" placed "on his Left-Breast, or near there about." In the same year "Mr. Guthry" parodies *Fortescue* and has Pope say that he "Hated the Minister that wore *a Star*."[18] More than any

---

[18] J. H. Plumb, *Sir Robert Walpole: The King's Minister* (The Cresset Press, 1960), p. 101; Young, *The Works of Dr. Edward Young* (1783), 5: 211, 213. Walpole hangs in *The City Triumphant, Or, the Burning of the Excise-Monster. A New Ballad* (1733), p. 8. Guthry, "The First Satire of the Second Book of Horace, Imitated. In a Dialogue between Mr. Alexander Pope, and the Ordinary of Newgate," in *Mr. Pope's Literary Correspondence. Volume the Second* (1735), p. 89. For one of the numerous allusions to Walpole and his blazing star, see *Characters: An Epistle to Alexander Pope Esq; and Mr. Whitehead* (1739), p. 9. See also chapter 9, note 4, below. The first edition of *Fortescue* inadvertently drew further attention to "Bare the mean Heart" by printing "Bear the mean Heart"—as Thomas Bentley notes in his *Letter to Mr. Pope* (1735), pp. 8-9. For a parallel sort of satiric unmasking, see the de Silvecane *Traduction nouvelle des satyres de Perse* (Lyons, 1693), on Satire Four, line 44: "Il parle alegoriquement à Neron en la personne d'Alcibiade, & luy dit qu' il a des ulceres caché

other enemy's misnamed "honour," Walpole's conspicu-
ously displayed star was, for Pope and others, the mask that
hid a mean heart and had to be torn off for the sake of
truth.

The brave new Pope no longer needs Fortescue's advice
regarding what to do, though Pope will later ask his attor-
ney's opinion regarding the success of the case Pope himself
has been pleading. Pope defends himself by insisting that
he is not beyond the law, as the lawless potential murderers
would have it, but the protector and agent of law, for his
satire will "Brand the bold Front of shameless, guilty Men"
(line 106), some of whom have been libeling him. John
Chamberlayne reports the harsh punishments that libel
evoked, "but of late," he says, "we have left off the Cruelty
of cutting off Ears, severe Whipping, Branding on the Fore-
head, Boring the Tongue, and the like."[19] Pope will renew
an ancient punishment on his detractors' behalf. The law-
yer Fortescue, however, blandly accepts murder by offended
courtiers, and thus disqualifies himself from the noblest of-
fices of defense of virtue, or even of understanding the true
satirist's role: "Can there be wanting to defend [Virtue's]
Cause, / Lights of the Church, or Guardians of the Laws?"
(lines 109-10). The unspoken answer is *yes* if Fortescue ex-

sous son bandier doré, c'est-à-dire beaucoup de vices que l'éclat de ses
richesses & de son élevation cachent à la veue du peuple" (p. 212).

Furthermore, "the proud Gamester in his gilded Car" (line 107), if
not Walpole himself, as Maynard Mack suggests (*Garden and the City*,
p. 182), may well be the late Colonel Francis Chartres, the wealthy
and notorious gambler often associated with Walpole. Swift, for in-
stance, says that he himself "Despis'd the Fools with Stars and Garters,
/ So often seen caressing *Chartres*." *Verses on the Death of Dr. Swift*
(1731), lines 323-24; see also lines 189-96: *The Poems of Jonathan Swift*,
ed. Harold Williams, 2nd ed. (Oxford: Clarendon Press, 1958), 2: 565.
The previous norm of gartered knight was, in theory, somewhat higher.
See Elias Ashmole, *The History of the most Noble Order of the Garter*
(1715), p. 131.

[19] *Magnae Britanniae Notitia: Or, the Present State of Great Britain*,
33rd ed. (England), 12th ed. (Scotland, 1737), p. 194.

emplifies Walpole's justice.[20] As Warburton says of this line, "just *Satire* is a useful supplement to the sanctions of *Law* and *Religion*; and has, therefore, a claim to the protection of those who preside in the administration either of church or state" (4: 68n and see 4: 74n, Warton). Pope assumes the unmet claim in his definition of "just *Satire*"; in so doing, for the first time he mentions specific satirists of recent vintage, reflects upon Horace's version of Lucilius, and begins what will be the final break from his model.

Horace's own apologia draws upon Lucilius for the third time in the poem, as his Lucilius becomes the scourge of the wicked—including the *Primores* populi (line 69), presumably the praetors and consuls, when necessary. He is also the close friend of the noble Laelius and Scipio Africanus, with whom he would retire to private life and amusements, and neither of whom objected to his attacks upon corrupt leaders. Lucilius was a friend only to virtue and the friends of virtue (line 70). Horace knows that his social and creative positions are inferior to Lucilius's, but that nonetheless he too has lived with the great and that his envious detractors had better be careful, for they will find him harder to crack than they think. Horace, in short, rests his case upon his Lucilian nature, which excludes rough versification and includes wisely praising the praiseworthy established order, being open and frank, and lambasting even the mighty if they deserve to be lambasted. Such a poet is a model for Horatian life and letters, and

[20] An angry reader may have been responding to these and to other lines, especially in the *Epilogue to the Satires* (1738), when he claims:

> That Poet ever unregarded sings,
> Who in low *Scandal* deals, and trivial *Things*;
> Who wants to hear, *Attorneys* may be Knaves?
> Sing, "Kings are *Tyrants*: *Senators* are *Slaves*:
> "*Judges*, too partial, wait a great Man's nod;
> "And not a *Bishop*, that believes in GOD."

A warning of libel, loss of ears, and sustenance follows. See *The Art of Poetry* (1741), pp. 5-6.

an implicit warning to those who think they can "freeze" Horace.

Pope has no use for Horace's redefined Lucilius. He neither places himself below his satiric ancestors nor approves of their closeness to the courts of their rulers. Instead, he urges that he is superior to the courtly Boileau and Dryden and, by extension, to Lucilius and Horace. James Grainger praised Tibullus over Horace as "a true Patriot" for divorcing himself from the court[21]—that is precisely the praise Pope wishes to have. Horace says that Lucilius was a friend only to virtue, here exemplified by two great men in authority. As Pope's enemies were aware, Pope speaks that line of himself and in the process affirms his satiric genealogy of freedom, boldness, and absence of awe and servility. He also characterizes himself as engaging in important intellectual, spiritual, and political activity with his great friends, whereas Horace's Lucilius enjoys childish relaxations with his. Pope thus rejects his own satiric predecessors as too "Horatian" in their relationship with corrupt courts and draws himself as no longer fearful of law but as the agent of and supplement to law; and he is no longer fearful of death but willing to face death and thus make his potential murderers fear him. He will not restrain his satire against vicious foes "too high" (line 60), who now must tremble at the exposure they cannot stop. Pope rejects the safe bravado of the coddled Horace, transcends the caution of Persius and Juvenal, and contrasts Hanoverian in-

21 *A Poetical Translation of the Elegies of Tibullus; and of the Poems of Sulpicia* (1759), 2: 70. Somewhat earlier, Grainger insists that "Tibullus never could prevail upon himself to flatter those, whatever Affection they expressed for the Muses, whom his principles taught him to detest as the Enslaver of his Country. This, as Pope emphatically expresses it, 'kept him sacred from the Great,' who doubtless perceived with secret Displeasure (for Augustus and Maecenas well knew the Importance of having the Poets on their Side) that no Loss of Fortune, and no Allurement of Ambition could induce Tibullus to join in the general Chorus of their Praise" (1: xxxv). Pope's shade must have been pleased with such a remark.

timidation with Stuart and even Bourbon acceptance of satire.

> Could pension'd *Boileau* lash in honest Strain
> Flatt'rers and Bigots ev'n in *Louis'* Reign?
> Could Laureate *Dryden* Pimp and Fry'r engage,
> Yet neither *Charles* nor *James* be in a Rage?
> And I not strip the Gilding off a Knave,
> Un-plac'd, un-pension'd, no Man's Heir, or Slave?
> I will, or perish in the gen'rous Cause.
> Hear this, and tremble! you, who 'scape the Laws.
>
> (Lines 111-18)

Both Warburton and Warton note Pope's divergence from Horace in this passage, and Warburton adds that Pope, who refused to flatter, had to change Horace's intention of complimenting earlier times, since it was his design "to satirize the present" (Warburton, 4: 68n).[22] Indeed, in the manuscript he extended that satire to George II himself, as he describes his own "bribeless cause," and the very different court in which "with pride, a King may be a screen" (p. 297n, EC). The independent Pope, aware of his mortality, thus will attack the unworthy great "while I live," regardless of the world's commendation or indifference. The once timid man warns his well-connected antagonists that unless they are virtue's friends they are his enemies, and thus shall not "walk the World, in credit" to their graves (lines 119-20).

Fortunately, the satirist has his own version of Scipio and Laelius. While defining libel-free just satire, Pope has also come to define the true court as like the earlier one of his "Stuart" Advertisement in which he can thrive. Here the world's charges and threats are as calming as the gentle rolling of the sea, and we find the varied kinds of nourishment and order lacking in the minister's world. We also

---

[22] See also Warton, *An Essay on the Genius and Writings of Pope*, vol. 2 (1782), 5th ed. (1806), 2: 285.

find functioning norms and a vital countryside that re-
flects the best of civilizing man:

> Know, all the distant Din that World can keep
> Rolls o'er my *Grotto*, and but sooths my Sleep.
> There, my Retreat the best Companions grace,
> Chiefs, out of War, and Statesmen, out of Place.
> There *St. John* mingles with my friendly Bowl,
> The Feast of Reason and the Flow of Soul:
> And He, whose Lightning pierc'd th' *Iberian* Lines,
> Now, forms my Quincunx, and now ranks my Vines,
> Or tames the Genius of the stubborn Plain,
> Almost as quickly, as he conquer'd *Spain*.
>
> (Lines 123-32)

The facing Latin, however, helps to clarify both the
break from Horace and the political nature of Pope's norm.
"Quin ubi se a *Vulgo & Scena*, in *Secreta* remorant / *Virtus
Scipiadae*, & mitis *Sapientia Laeli*" (lines 71-72)—when vir-
tuous Scipio and wise and mellow Laelius withdrew from
the mob and the theater of life; that is, in the equivalent
of the highlighted words, when Bolingbroke and Peter-
borough joined him in his grotto away from the mob of
the court, the city, and the theater (in the sense of masking
internal meanness behind external glory [line 108]). Unlike
Horace's Scipio and Laelius, Pope's chief and statesman are
heroes of the opposition; and unlike Horace, Pope will not
praise Augustus as Lucilius praised Laelius (lines 16-20).
Pope's friendship in his grotto des refusés preserves the
lingering Stuart glories as we move away from Fortescue's
urban "Hanover" chambers to a nostalgic court in the
country. Bolingbroke is first minister, Peterborough is tri-
umphant general over the Spanish, and Pope is the cele-
brating poet who lives with his nation's true great men.
He is a friend to the worthy, a soother of turmoil, and a
confidant who respects privacy—precisely what he cannot
find in the world of Fortescue, Walpole, and George II; nor
even at the Horatian court of Augustus, for by 1733 that

prince often was regarded as a ruler only the blemished court poets would wish to sing. Warburton notes that "Horace makes the point of Honour to consist simply in his living familiarly with the Great. . . . Our Poet, more nobly in his living with them on the foot of an honest Man. —He prided himself in this superiority" (4: 71-72).

Pope is also more noble than his aristocratic attackers, for the end of this paragraph (line 142) concludes his reversal of roles. Already he has made his potential murderers tremble, become the defender of law that Fortescue should have been, placed the charge of libel on Sappho, and branded guilty men. He again picks his legal word and again attempts to show that his detractors are criminal, vulgar, and associated with the dangerous and unreliable urban masses who, late in the seventeenth century, were the tools of ambitious Whigs and frequently engaged in Pope-burning: "who unknown defame me, let them be / Scriblers or Peers, alike are *Mob* to me" (lines 139-40). The brilliant defense has properly turned the tables. The once supplicating client in the lawyer's chambers has become the rhetorical vindicator of the highest notions of law; he has also shown the deficiencies of the putative plaintiff and judge and, equally important, done so in part by means of their "own" words and inadequate deeds. But he must return from the world of his grotto and the Stuart shadow court to the world of Brunswick, Walpole, hanging judges, and uncertainty. The manuscript was clearer in its legal metaphor, possible chastisement of Fortescue, and overt attack upon his colleagues.

> The Courts are open to whoe'er show cause,
> And base attorneys will pervert the laws.
> This my plea, and this is my precedent,
> Unless my learned counsel shall dissent.
>
> (P. 229n, EC)

The printed version is appreciably muted in tone and trades hostility for a couplet that mingles declarative and interrogative sentences. "This is my Plea, on this I rest my Cause— / What saith my Council learned in the Laws?" (lines 141-42). What he says, and how the poet's remaining lines function, return us to earlier themes, earlier contrasts with Horace, and what may help resolve the fancied problem of whether Pope is, finally, triumphant or defeated in the poem and its immediate, real context.

III: Such as Sir Robert Would Approve

Trebatius hears Horace's similar question regarding his own case, thinks it a sound one, yet adds—"Sed tamen ut monitus caveas" (line 80): but nevertheless, let me warn you to beware, lest ignorance of our sacred laws gets you into trouble. If you write bad verses—"mala . . . carmina" —against someone, he can take legal action. Pope adapts the key sentence and places it in quotation marks and in distinct type throughout: *"Si mala conditerit in quem quis carmina jus est / Judiciumque"* (lines 82-83). He knew that these were the words of Augustus's reinstituted, potentially fatal, Law of the XII Tables (Dacier, *Oeuvres d'Horace*, 7: 56). Horace knows his way around this deadly trap, and so his reply to Trebatius fulfills his earlier promise to praise Augustus. What if I write good verses and Caesar approves of them? (lines 84-85). He is playing upon Trebatius's and the law's *mala carmina* with his own *bona carmina*, qualitatively good verses approved by Caesar. He evades the trap apparently by means of an amusing poetic quibble but actually by the quiet compliment to Caesar that affirms the close relationship between the poet and the throne. As Desprez notes regarding "sed bona si quis / iudice condident laudatus Caesare" (lines 83-84), "Augustus enim & versus faciebat interdum & quotquot bonos facerent amabat" (p. 434n): indeed, Augustus occasionally made verses and however many were made well he would love. Horace is appealing from one poet to another and flattering his master, as many of the commentators and translators remark. Sanadon observes: "je suis persuadé qu'il l'a mis à dessein, pour doner à entendre à ces censeurs qu'il se tenoit bien assuré de l'aprobation & de la protection d'Auguste. Le tour est modeste & adroit" (2: 232)—and it is devastatingly effective. "The old scrupulous Lawyer is at last convinced, more by the authority of Caesar than the weight of argument," William Boscawen says later in the century.[23] The Law of the xii Tables has only as much authority as its renovator Augustus wishes it to have; he will not level it against an excellent and loyal poet, a friend of Trebatius and the intimate of Maecenas, Pollio, and Augustus himself. Under such circumstances the hostile great men would not dare to "freeze" Horace, whatever their personal pique. Horace both justifies himself and his genre and warns his detractors that they will lose if they engage him in battle or legal contest. As Creech translates Horace's remark, "justly, mighty *Caesar* is his Friend, / He loves such Poems, and he will defend" (p. 424). There is harmony between the throne, the lawyer, and the poet; a nameless, foolish plaintiff who might pursue the case is left in the satiric lurch. "The foolish Action shall be turn'd to sport; / He laugh'd and jeer'd at, You discharg'd the Court" (p. 424).

Pope's own conclusion technically follows but morally and politically abandons Horace. Though Fortescue's response to Pope's question is approving, he cautions—"beware! / Laws are explain'd by Men—so have a care" (lines 143-44). Pope's plea may be good, but his life remains in danger, since the court can murder legally, however "honest" the victim might be.

> It stands on record, that in *Richard*'s Times
> A Man was hang'd for very honest Rhymes.
> Consult the Statute: *quart.* I think it is,

[23] Boscawen, *The Satires, Epistles, and Art of Poetry of Horace* (1797), p. 116. For further commentary on Augustus and the law, see Desprez, *Quinti Horatii*, p. 434n, Sanadon, *Poésies d'Horace*, 2: 231-32, and Francis, *Works of Horace*, 3: 178-79.

> *Edwardi Sext.* or *prim.* & *quint Eliz*:
> See *Libels, Satires*—here you have it—read.
>
> (Lines 145-49)

John Butt tells us that the penalty for libel in the laws cited was "imprisonment, until the originator of the libel was found," and that the "maximum penalty allowed . . . was imprisonment for life and loss of goods on the second offense" (p. 19n). Giles Jacobs's *New Law Dictionary* (1729), later supplemented by Blackstone, provides three folio columns of instruction on the definitions of libel in Britain (while also stating that the Roman penalty for libel was death), and coincidentally glosses Fortescue's "very honest Rhymes"—that is, truthful satire which still may be interpreted as libel and thus be actionable, as Colingbourne found at the end of a rope provided by Richard III, an analogue, Maynard Mack shows, for George II: "it is far from being a Justification of a *Libel*," Jacobs says, "that the Contents thereof are true, or that the Person upon whom made had a bad Reputation; since the greater Appearance there is of Truth in any malicious Invective, so much the more provoking it is." In addition, a libel "against the King and State" is highly actionable: "all Persons exposing any Books to Sale, reflecting on the Government, may be punished," and "a general Reflection on the Government is a *Libel*, though no particular Person is reflected on." Yet more, "the Contriver, Procurer, and Publisher of a *Libel*, are punishable by Fine, Imprisonment, Pillory, or other corporal Punishment, at the Discretion of the Court, according to the Heinousness of the Crime."[24]

---

[24] *New Law Dictionary*, 8th ed. (1742) s.v. "Libel"; Mack, *Garden and the City*, p. 140. The legal distinctions were not buried in law books. See David Morgan, *The Country Bard: Or, The Modern Courtiers. A Poem Inscribed to the Prince* (1739): "The *Athenians* (a much wiser People than we are) thought no Treatise, however severe, a Libel, if true. That Doctrine has been held for Law in *Britain*, 'till sacrificed to *Power* by *those*, whose Duty it was to preserve it" (p. 3n). The author of a *Letter to a Friend in the Country, Upon Occasion of the*

In spite of an increasing number of threats, there were few convictions for libel against the government in the 1730s; but Pope can scarcely be blamed for wanting to remove his satires from the class of libels and make them immune from legal action by the administration, and, improbably, even acceptable to it.

By line 150 and Pope's final speech, then, he has offered and perhaps won his plea before the impartial reader, and supported his good character before the reader prejudiced on his behalf; he has shown that he is the defender of law, religion, and a variety of other virtues. He has also painted his detractors with their own ugly colors of libel, defamation, conspiracy to commit murder, cowardice, and like charming traits. But as we have seen, Fortescue remains cautious and concerned with the problem that started the poem—Pope's satire may go beyond the laws of the genre and the land. Pope thus adapts an apparently Horatian verbal ploy:

> *Libels* and *Satires*! lawless Things indeed!
> But grave *Epistles*, bringing Vice to light,
> Such as a *King* might read, a *Bishop* write.
>
> (Lines 150-52)

"Might" is amusingly conditional, since George II had less than paramount interest in such illumination, and Pope has already shown that bishops do not defend the Church; if they did, the satire would not have to be written and Pope would not be the lonely Juvenalian defender of Vir-

---

many Scurilous Libels which have been lately publish'd (1743) agrees that libel is difficult to define, but is confident that attacks upon *"noble* Families" and *"Majesty* itself, are *Libels.* . . . If what they asserted was *true*, such Writings would still in all Law and Equity be deemed *Libels*; and how much more then, when in several Respects it is notoriously and evidently *false*?" (pp. 23-24). See also the unsigned *A Satire. Also, Imitation of the First Satire of Boileau* (1777): "Lawyers hold (we all love something new) / That *libels* are most *infamous* when *true*" (p. 6).

tue, Church, and Law. Furthermore, the manuscript origi-
nally had drawn Fortescue urging Pope, after line 28, to
praise some hero or statesman who had in turn read and
praised his Homer, whereas

> o'er epistles
> Of good and just and fit a great man whistles.
>
> (P. 291n, EC)

With this dangerous couplet expunged, Pope could claim
that he really hoped Sir Robert would approve of his grave
epistles, and thus could moot any argument regarding their
legality. That would be impossible if he had already shown
the court's attorney admitting that Walpole was contemp-
tuous of them (see *OED*, s.v. whistle, verb, trans., II, 7b, 9).
Even without the earlier disclaimer, however, the difference
between Horace and Pope here is substantial, as the former
closely ties himself to his presumed benevolent political
order, and Pope dissociates himself from his presumed
malevolent order.

Moreover, Horace has Trebatius break in immediately
after Caesar Augustus is mentioned; Pope has Fortescue
wait until Walpole rather than George Augustus is men-
tioned:

> Such as Sir *Robert* would approve——
> *F.* Indeed?
> The Case is alter'd—you may then proceed.
> In such a Cause the Plaintiff will be hiss'd,
> My Lords the Judges laugh, and you're dismiss'd.
>
> (Lines 153-56)

Fortescue's reply makes plain that ministerial and hence le-
gal permission are needed for Pope's satire to be safe; in
spite of his apparent triumph, on practical grounds he re-
mains a suppliant. Horace's triumph is genuine, if largely
tactical, and leads to a continuing, unintimidated, and suc-
cessful career; Pope's diminished triumph is internal to the
poem only, for he remains the sole defender of virtue, and

the administration rejects his position entirely. If Sir Robert does not approve, the case is not altered and Pope is back to "beware! / . . . have a care," and the threat of hanging. Sir Robert's approval replaces Augustus's, because he and not George Augustus is the real center of power, from which Pope dissociates himself. Horace can win by means of a pun because Augustus approves; Pope wins because as readers captured by his poem and its values, we approve and know that the administration disapproves. Though we accept his distinction between libels and grave epistles, Fortescue knows that such a defense has no basis in law, and he remains nearly the same prudent court lawyer at the end of the poem as at the beginning. Pope's plea may be morally good, but that is legally irrelevant, as the real Fortescue's polite silence in his letters to Pope may suggest. Sir Robert and his comparably disapproving friends were not so polite. "It is time for [Pope] to retire, for he has made the town too hot to hold him," Bathurst thus wrote to Swift shortly after the poem appeared.[25] If we look briefly at the central normative passage regarding virtue and Pope's grotto we can see that on "real," and even internal satiric grounds, Pope actually is making the best of a bad job.

As the last defender of Virtue, Pope is in an unenviable position: if he wins he is woefully outnumbered and beleaguered nonetheless; if he loses he will "perish in the gen'rous Cause" (line 117), leaving poor Virtue again in need of unavailable defenders. The grotto itself, though surely pleasanter than the hostile world of London and the court, is just as surely an emblem of what was, rather than what can be. Pope and his friends retreated to Twickenham to make a court there because they were unwelcome at St. James's—hence his "best Companions" are "Chiefs, out of War, and Statesmen, out of Place" (lines 125-26). Peter-

25 *The Correspondence of Jonathan Swift*, ed. Harold Williams (Oxford: Clarendon Press, 1963-65), 4: 131-32.

borough's great triumphs were in 1705 and 1706, and Bolingbroke's in 1713. The admirable peace of the grotto is implied criticism of the administration's policy of appeasement. Peterborough's genius is applied to gardening at Twickenham rather than to fighting in Spain. Bolingbroke's intellectual brilliance illumines the grotto's darkness, not George II's. When Pope calls Twickenham his "retreat" he is using that word to mean "Place of privacy; retirement. . . . Place of security." In the context the word also connotes a military "Act of retiring before a superiour force," and this is especially apposite for Peterborough.[26] The vision of country values at Twickenham is a sign not of triumph but of the neglect that Pope and his friends suffered and were to suffer in spite of the temporary optimism surrounding Walpole's defeat on the Excise Bill, and even after his resignation in 1742. Pope earns the reader's respect and admiration and triumphs in that personal sense; but on practical terms neither his case nor the case of the opposition was altered by this or any other verse satire.[27] The mean heart was bared but the power of the star lasted for nine more years, and Pope and his readers knew that, in Warburton's words, "as soon as Sir Robert, the Patron both of Law and Gospel," is named as approving, Fortescue "changes his note"—but only in the poem, and only under circumstances that could not exist outside of the poem.

That external world had rather a different view of Sir Robert's involvement with Pope, for it immediately applied *Fortescue* to the political context the poem hoped to influence. There were predictable hostile responses—of Lady Mary and Lord Hervey in their *Verses . . . to the Imitator*

[26] Samuel Johnson, *A Dictionary of the English Language* (1755).

[27] For fuller discussion of opposition verse and other attacks on the administration, see Bertrand A. Goldgar's valuable *Walpole and the Wits: The Relation of Politics to Literature, 1722-1742* (Lincoln: Univ. of Nebraska Press, 1976).

of . . . Horace (1733), and their threats to beat Pope with cudgels as they did with words (p. 6); of *An Epistle to the Little Satyrist of Twickenham* (1733), which quotes several of Pope's offending lines and concludes that he, like Bolingbroke, will live "An everlasting Monument of Shame" (p. 10); of *The Muse in Distress* (1733), which also attacks Pope's praise of Bolingbroke and harsh view of national politics and calls Pope a prostitute author in league with a traitor (p. 12). Other writers adapted Pope's legal metaphor for their own purpose, one that implicitly recognizes the un-Horatian gloom in the poem and shows Pope as the loser not the winner of his case, since Sir Robert disapproved.

For instance, on 26 February 1733, "Mr. Guthry" completed his "First Satire of the Second Book of Horace Imitated. In a Dialogue between Mr. Alexander Pope, and the Ordinary of Newgate." He invites the reader to compare it with Pope's effort of 15 February so that we will at once see that the matter has been settled—that Pope already is deservedly jailed, awaits graver punishment for his libel of mankind, yet still wishes to write more to purge his spleen. The Ordinary, replacing Fortescue but using his words, says, "*You could not do a worse Thing for your life*" (p. 83). Pope himself will reserve the praise of virtue, not the dispraise of vice, for the next age; he knows that "Both High and Low wish me the shortest *Date*" (p. 86), and that "hang'd I shall be, if my *Judge be* P——" (p. 88). Far from being the brave victor over death and misapplied law, Pope embodies the vile fury over which death and law must triumph. The Ordinary says:

> *Alas, young Man! your days can ne'er be long,*
> In Flow'r of Age you'll dangle for a Song.
> *Ralph, Cooke, Concanen, Henly*, and his *Wife*,
> Will club their Testers, now, to take your Life!
>
> (P. 89)

Pope, who hates Walpole (p. 89), knows that nothing can keep him from death—"Methinks I feel the Bow-String in *my Sleep*." Having already condemned himself from his own mouth, Pope could not have been surprised by the Ordinary's response to his *"What* thinks my Rev'rend Father of *my Cause?"* (p. 91). Very little. Pope will be hanged for his infamous poems:

> *Libels* and *Satires,—lawless Things indeed!*
> Had I been just, set Virtue's Deeds *to Light,*
> *Such as a* King *might read, a* Bishop *write,*
> Such as Sir *Robert* would approve——
>   ORDINARY
>   Indeed?
> *Alter'd* had been *your Case:*—But to proceed.
> Fated is now your Doom, you will be Cast,
> And your *first* Psalm, I fear, will be your *last*.
>   (P. 92)

Guthry has taken many of Pope's assumptions and conclusions and imitated *Fortescue* from a ministerial point of view. *"Alter'd* had been *your Case"* if Sir Robert approved, as Pope and the administration knew he would not, and as Guthry made clear on his poem's appearance on 2 March, just fifteen days after Pope's.[28]

28 For Guthry, see n. 18. This work also was printed as "A Just Imitation of the First Satire of the Second Book of Horace. In a Dialogue between Mr. Pope and the Ordinary of Newgate. With Achilles Dissected," by Alexander Burnet. The apparently pseudonymous Guthry may be Burnet, or perhaps Curll. On 8 March 1733 Pope writes to Fortescue regarding both this work and the *Sequel*: "There has been another thing wherein Pigott is abused as my Learned Council, written by some Irish attorney; & Curll has printed a Parody on my own words which he is as proud of as his own productions, saying, he will pay no more of his Authors but can write better himself." *Correspondence*, 3: 354-55. I have discussed some of the responses to Pope's poem in "Such as Sir Robert Would Approve? Answers to Pope's Answer from Horace," *Modern Language Studies*, 9 (1979): 5-14. The poems mentioned

Four days later, the pseudonymous Patrick Mc Doe-Roch published his *Sequel of Mr. Pope's Law Case: Or, Farther Advice thereon*, purporting to be from a fledgling lawyer who is aware that "The Point is not, Did you right,—or wrong?" (p. 8) but whether he knows "How stands the Great-Man? Does he appear? / (Not against, but for you: I mean, be sure!)" (p. 5). Pope's present lawyer is useless, since only if one can do a variety of legally irrelevant things, like "trot the long Dance" or talk nonsense, "There might be some Hopes,—to succeed" (pp. 6-7). The trial itself will be either a farce or "a bitter Jest," and will conclude with

Gaol or Pillory,
Unless Death or Money makes Matters easy.
A fine of Ten Marks by *P—pe* rich and great; ·
A Trifle back of his Subscription Cheat.

(P. 9)

Mc Doe-Roch's counsel is simple and glosses a key description of Pope's grotto as a retreat: "Take Advice,—indulge Retreat" (p. 9) and "spare the Great Man" (p. 10).

The only practical success or practical triumph that *Fortescue* had was as a self-contained poem that nobly upheld Pope's refusal to be intimidated or to be silenced by threats of law or violence from aristocratic criminals. In that sense it is a consoling effort for the writer and the neutral or opposition reader; but each understood that its scene of peace with a worthy and pleasable Walpole was a

---

there and above do not exhaust the replies and allusions to *Fortescue*. See for example, *A Friendly Epistle to the Author of the State Dunces* (1733), p. 9; *A Proper Reply to A Lady Occasioned by her Verses address'd to the Imitator of the First Satire of the Second Book of Horace* [1733]; *An Epistle from a Gentleman at Twickenham, to a Nobleman at St. James's. Occasion'd by an Epistle from a Nobleman, to a Doctor of Divinity* (1734), p. 6. J. V. Guerinot's useful *Pamphlet Attacks on Alexander Pope 1711-1744* (New York: New York Univ. Press, 1969) lists many of the hostile responses to Pope's career.

Horatian mirage in a Juvenalian world. In terms of printed response, the poem's amiable fiction was rejected within two weeks. To be sure, Sir Robert's friends and flunkies were annoyed to see him "approving" of attacks on himself; they would have been surprised to hear that they were defeated by so easily denied a misrepresentation; and equally surprised to see a distinguished lawyer won to a position without legal foundation. Pope is noble in defeat —but the hemlock is no less hemlock for being taken with dignity.

Pope's dual focus—hope for union and awareness of its impossibility—helps to explain *Fortescue*'s mingled Horatian and Juvenalian conventions. The framework, obviously from Horace, has his words facing us and highlighted to suit Pope's own purposes, and assumes an understanding of the two cultures and some of their similarities and differences. The ability of Horace to defend himself by means of a poet-emperor, for example, contrasts with Pope's monarch who remained ill at ease with English. The conversational tones, the civilized exchanges between country "squire" and court-attorney, the ability to moderate tone in accordance with the fluid relationship, the praise of a country retreat, and of course the passionate defense of satire and satirist, all have Horace as their spiritual father from whom they gain authority. That certainly is not the authority of imitating well in the limited sense of adapting one's ancient betters to modern inferior circumstances and talents; nor is it the authority one gains in identifying with the author imitated, since the opposite is more nearly true. It certainly is the authority demanded by the best eighteenth-century theory and practice of imitation—an emulation, a "contest of superiority"—as Gilbert Wakefield calls it,[29] with one's literary ancestor, which forces the modern's skills into play.

That contest also evokes the Juvenalian quality of the poem, for as we have seen, Pope rejects not only the Ho-

[29] *Observations on Pope* (1796), p. 248.

ratian political and moral framework but also Horatian
conclusions in several instances, for his world is one, not of
union with, but alienation from the court. Pope's adapta-
tion of Horace's Sabine farm thus is apparent rather than
real, for his grotto evokes past glories in a past dynasty and
suggests Juvenalian nostalgia for the unreclaimable na-
tional spirit and virtue; Horace, on the other hand, shows
his pride in the glorious if humanly fallible present. Hor-
ace's poem concludes with recognition that his world is one
governed by men not law, but that since his prince is a
supportive poet, all is well. Pope's governing men are hos-
tile to his poetry, and all is not well. Even in 1733 Pope's
Juvenalian world is in decline, rotten at its political core,
and no longer reliable at its highest levels—monarch, min-
ister, church, law, and trade are corrupt. The satire leans
upon its Horatian source and preserves its optimism, in the
poem at least, and illusion of an ongoing civilization still
capable of muddling through. Its conclusion can be read
not only as Fortescue's knowledge of Realpolitik, but of
Pope's willingness to share a joke with Walpole, of attrib-
uting to him enough good humor to accept the outrageous
notion that he could approve of so antipathetic a work.
Civility, in short, still has a chance, and institutions, but-
tressed by the friendly intentions, if not tones, of satire can
be useful in this world, if only to maintain needful myths
of survival. That is, I think, one reason why the poem is
often read as far more jolly a product than it is and why the
Juvenalian impetus, still lacking many of the dark tones
of its Persian cousin, is largely offstage.

But those dark tones are in fact there, if lighter than
they would be in five years. Persius, we remember, was more
concerned than Horace or Juvenal with declining literary
standards and achievement. His first satire shows a friend
or monitor urging him not to write because of the personal
danger involved. If he must write, "accommodate his Vein
to the Taste of the Times, and . . . write like other People."
Persius adamantly refuses so to accommodate himself and

shamefully to win a shameful audience. "The only Readers whose Applause he covets, must be Men of Virtue, and Men of Sense"[30]—men no doubt like Bolingbroke, Cobham, and Peterborough, whom Pope names as his allies. But the political and legal climate demand that he maintain some Persian "obscurity"; hence the protective ambiguity behind "Bare the mean Heart that lurks beneath a Star" (line 108); hence Fannius for Hervey. Each is decipherable and, if need be, legally defensible as a general statement. The need for defense in the cause of virtue, however, is yet another sign of the Persian mood, one that, in this case, is closely related to the perceived antiministerial coalition between Persius and Juvenal. Moreover, though Fortescue does admit some of the worth of Pope's case, he changes very little and is an improved offspring of the Persian uneducable *adversarius* of Satire One. The difference between "I'd write no more" (line 11) and "you may then proceed" (line 154) rests upon the fantasy that "*Sir Robert* would approve" (line 153).

Fortescue, then, may be seen as a Horatian satire that nonetheless quarrels with Horace, his poem, and culture at several points and invites us to see the new Augustan world as one becoming painfully like Nero's or Domitian's. Indeed, the prompt replies to *Fortescue* make plain that the poem's internal triumph was not sustainable in the external world, and that Juvenal and Persius might soon become dominant forces in Pope's mingling of satiric conventions. *An Epistle to Dr. Arbuthnot* (1735) continues and darkens the practice of mingling, and continues to show how less and less relevant Horatian values were in the Juvenalian world in which Pope was forced to live.

[30] [Thomas Brewster], *The Satires of Persius Translated into English Verse*, 2nd ed. (1751), pp. 5-6. The original is italicized.

CHAPTER 8

XXXXXXXXXXXXXXXXXXXXXXXXXXXXXXXXXXXXXXXXXXXXXX

An Epistle to Dr. Arbuthnot:
The Education of an Opposition Satirist

I: Through Time and Satiric Modes

Pope's *An Epistle to Dr. Arbuthnot* (1735) has been called "the most Horatian of Pope's original works" and one that shows him "most Horatian when he was being most fully himself." Such remarks are commonplace in the criticism of this poem, and though something may be said in their defense, more should be said against them. *Arbuthnot* shows Pope using the different satiric conventions but not, finally, settling upon a grimmer version of Horace, as he does in the earlier *Fortescue*. Instead, he abandons the remnants of Horatian epistolary satire and comments upon his own contemporary world thereby. We recall that in 1753 the Abbé Yart said that this poem offers "des morceaux admirables, écrits avec la force & la véhémence de Juvénal, la légèreté & la finesse d'Horace, la précision & la noblesse de Perse."[1] As I hope to show, the Persian and especially Juvenalian conventions establish themselves as necessary responses in a world increasingly dominated by dangerous and powerful enemies.

The differing uses of the word "please" in the Advertisement immediately make clear that *Arbuthnot* lacks the community of values between satirist and monarch essential for the solid base of Horatian epistle and satire. Pope would not have thought of publishing his poem "till it pleas'd some Persons of Rank and Fortune . . . to attack

---

[1] John Butt, ed., *Imitations of Horace*, p. 94 (original works); Reuben Arthur Brower, *Alexander Pope: The Poetry of Allusion* (Oxford: Clarendon Press, 1959), p. 293 (fully himself); *Idée de la poësie Angloise, ou traduction des meilleurs poëtes Angloises* (Paris, 1749-56), 3 (1753): 96.

240

... not only my Writings . . . but my *Person, Morals,* and
Family." The ceremonious and nasty pleasure of the aristo-
crats—including Lord Hervey, the Vice Chamberlain,
Queen's confidant, and one of Walpole's liaisons with the
throne—contrasts with the moral and literary pleasure
Pope seeks: "If [the poem] have any thing pleasing, it will
be That by which I am most desirous to please, the *Truth*
and the *Sentiment*; and if any thing offensive, it will be
only to those I am least sorry to offend, the *Vicious* or *the
Ungenerous.*" Since Pope generally does not name his foes,
"they may escape being laugh'd at, if they please."[2] On the
one hand we see pleasure behind the courtiers' malicious
and personal attacks upon Pope's writings, shape, and fam-
ily; on the other we see pleasure as the poet's externalized
desire to offer his verifiable truth and thoughts, and the
chance for his victims to escape public retribution by si-
lence. Pope is forced to respond and to attack members of
the court and administration, some of whom are vicious or
ungenerous.

Pope qualifies the genre of Horatian epistle while also
moving away from Horatian support of the government.
His correspondent is a more important citizen of the past
dynasty than of the present one, for as Pope reminds us,
Arbuthnot was physician to Queen Anne, and now is as
out of place as his friends Bolingbroke and Peterborough;
and, to Pope's sorrow, Arbuthnot was dead by the time the
poem in his honor appeared. That doctor himself is aware

---

[2] P. 95. Italics and Roman type have been inverted here. Compare
Pope's trinity of "*Person, Morals,* and *Family*" with this remark by
Thomas Cooke regarding Theobald's quarrel with Pope in *Shakespeare
Restored,* "in which he attacked Mr. *Pope,* regarding him only as the
Editor of that Author, without any Reflections on either his Person,
his Morals, or Family. This seems to me to be the principal Cause of
Mr. *Pope's* writing the *Dunciad*; of which Mr. *Theobald* is the Hero."
See "An Examination into the Controversy betwixt the Poets and Mr.
Pope," Letter 5, Saturday, 29 March 1729, in *The Letters of Atticus, As
Printed in The London Journal, In the Years 1729 and 1730, On Var-
ious Subjects* (1731), p. 34.

of the change in circumstances, and urges caution in dealing with a court and courtiers capable of threatening physical punishment and defamation of character. As Thomas Bentley notes, this epistle is thus harsher than its Horatian predecessors and most modern counterparts. The Abbé Yart also recognizes the vehemence in *Arbuthnot* and sees it, not merely as a conventional apologia with obligatory self-defense, but as a poem of outrage, anger, and frustration in a society increasingly unable to offer Horatian civilities.[3]

The frantic opening of the poem—"a burst of [Juvenal's] involuntary indignation," Gilbert Wakefield claims[4]—highlights Pope's frustration and the collapse of several kinds of values. The colloquial "Shut, shut the door, good *John*! fatigu'd I said" (line 1) shows the poet's home invaded both by a familiar Juvenalian horde of bad poets and by disrupters of hitherto stable personal and literary traditions. Such replacement of the good with the bad reaches its successful conclusion in the *Dunciad* of 1743. In the meanwhile, however, Pope is able to resist the visitations of the sacrilegious, insectile, and variously deranged intruders. Pope is concerned not only with their numbers and social and moral disorder, but also with their attempts to absorb him into their world by pleas, violent restraint, flattery, and bribes. In so doing, they pervert classical and literary history, attribute a form of solipsism to Pope, and help him to define himself as their opposite—a device of definition Pope will use throughout the poem.

For example, all the lunatic poets "Apply to me, to keep them mad or vain" (line 22); they seize and tie him down to force his aid (line 33); and they urge him to correct their works—"I'm all submission, what you'd have it, make it" (line 46). Though Pope extends sound advice,

---

[3] Bentley, *A Letter to Mr. Pope, Occasioned By Sober Advice from Horace* (1735), p. 14n; *Idée de la poësie Angloise*, 3: 98, 102n. Yart also discusses the difference between Horace's epistles and Pope's epistles in *Arbuthnot*: 3: 100n.

[4] *Observations on Pope* (1796), p. 227.

"Keep your Piece nine years" (line 40), such Horatian wisdom (*Ars Poetica*, 386-89) is of course useless in modern Augusta, and so he remains subject to the threatening, if comic, attack of the dunces. If he approves of a stranger's play, "Commend it to the Stage" (line 58); and if Lintot balks at the author's price why, he tells Pope, "Not Sir, if you revise it, and retouch" (line 64). Though besieged, Pope continues to keep away from such tainted offspring, happily finds an excuse to shut the door, as John apparently could not in time to have the proper effect, and thereby begins to be active in his own defense:

> All my demurrs but double his attacks,
> At last he whispers, "Do, and we go snacks."
> Glad of a quarrel, strait I clap the door,
> Sir, let me see your works and you no more.
>
> (Lines 65-68)

The Midas passage, which follows, modifies the anger and hyperbolic whimsy of this opening section and its apparent "légèreté & finesse d'Horace," for we there see a theory of causation that implicates Walpole and his king, and does so with an allusion to the world of monarchic judgment of letters: Midas receives his asses' ears for wrongly judging that Pan was a better poet than Apollo. This offense to the gods and to good taste was replayed in the British court's selection of Cibber as poet laureate, though the Queen's patronage of Stephen Duck (a named target in the manuscript) and Walpole's patronage and suborning of numerous literary hacks were likely to have been in Pope's mind as well. What has been called an abrupt transition to Midas actually is closely knit to the preceding lines.[5] The revelation of Midas's ears urged royal

---

[5] See William Warburton, *The Works of Alexander Pope, Esq.* (1751), 4: 13n. Joseph Warton, *The Works of Alexander Pope* (1797), 4: 13; Butt, *Imitations of Horace*, p. 100n. Warburton makes clear Pope's indebtedness to Persius, but is seduced by the myth of Persius's obscurity:

responsibility—*ad exemplum regis*—for the spreading of asinine taste and sounds, and also shows that the court is at the center of the literary corruption Pope is trying to avoid. Indeed, in the poem's holograph, Pope had originally complained that "folks thrust those Honors in my face";[6] that is, they thrust the (of course metaphorical) asses' ears or other awards received from the court. Moreover, a manuscript note recorded by Jonathan Richardson, Jr., but not printed in any edition, reproduces line 18 of Ausonius's twenty-eighth epistle to Paulinus; this is the only discussion of Midas Pope mentions that uses the Latin word "minister" to describe the servant who sees Midas's ears.[7] Pope indicates the relationship between bad letters

---

The Poet means sung by *Persius*; and the words alluded are,

Vidi, vidi ipse, Libelle!

Auriculas Asini Mida Rex habet.

The transition is fine, but obscure: for he has here imitated the *manner* of that mysterious writer, as well as taken up his *image*.

[6] The complex manuscript is divided between the Pierpont Morgan Library (MA 352) and the Huntington Library (HM 6006). This quotation is from HM 6006, which is subsequently so identified in the text. I am grateful for permission to quote from this manuscript, and for a facsimile of the Morgan manuscript. Parts of the *Arbuthnot* manuscript are printed in *The Works of Alexander Pope*, ed. John Wilson Croker, Whitwell Elwin, and William John Courthope (1871-89), 3 (1881): 241-74, notes. For further comments on the making of *Arbuthnot*, see George Sherburn, "Pope at Work," in *Essays on the Eighteenth Century Presented to David Nichol Smith* (Oxford: Clarendon Press, 1945), pp. 49-64, and John Butt, "Pope's Poetical Manuscripts," in *Proceedings of the British Academy*, 40 (1954): 23-29, and plates. J. Paul Hunter also makes good use of the manuscripts in his "Satiric Apology as Satiric Instance: Pope's *Arbuthnot*," in *Journal of English and Germanic Philology*, 68 (1969): 625-47.

[7] This is from Pope's *Works* (1735), p. 61, which Richardson annotated from Pope's own manuscripts. See *The Correspondence of Alexander Pope*, ed. George Sherburn (Oxford: Clarendon Press, 1956), 4: 78, and 4: 374. For the apparent genesis of the idea of the collation, see Jonathan Richardson, Jr., *Richardsoniana: Or, Occasional Reflections on the Moral Nature of Man* (1776), p. 264. The copy of the

and bad throne in the allusion to Midas (who, we shall
see, was both Nero and George II), and in his own com-
parable attitudes at court or country. When forced to offer
judgment at Twickenham, he "can't be silent, and . . . will
not lye" (line 34) about the wretched stuff before him.
When confronted with the biting and kicking asses of the
court, he is again forced to speak out, to reject Arbuthnot's
"Tis nothing," to tell "That Secret to each Fool, that he's
an Ass" (lines 78, 80), and to gain sleep through such
purgation. Pope establishes his own character as truth-
teller to foolish poet or monarch—for each is part of the
increasingly dangerous substitution of bad values for good,
against which Pope wishes to shut his door, and against
which he confesses himself ineffectual. The "smarts" in-
duced by his and others' laughter have no influence upon
the dim poet Codrus, borrowed from Juvenal's third satire.
As if to signal the topsy-turvy world to which Midas-like
values lead, Pope inverts the point of the Horatian lines
he is adapting.

> Let Peals of Laughter, *Codrus*! round thee break,
> Thou unconcern'd canst hear the mighty Crack.
> Pit, Box and Gall'ry in convulsions hurl'd,
> Thou stand'st unshook amidst a bursting World.
>   (Lines 85-88)

Works is in the Huntington Library, HM 6009, and is referred to here-
after as Pope-Richardson, *Works*. I am grateful for permission to quote
from these notes. The annotation reads:

> Depressis scrobibus vitium regale *minister*
> Credidit.
>   Auson. Paulino xx[v] iii

The Latin adds, ". . . idque diu texit fidissima tellus: / inspirata dehinc
vento cantavit harundo." The English translation, from the Loeb text,
is "To deep-dug pits a servant revealed his royal lord's deformity, and
long the earth hid the secret most faithfully; thereafter the reed
breathed on by the wind, sang the story." *Ausonius*, trans. Hugh G.
Eveleyn White (London and New York: Wm. Heineman, G. P. Put-
nam's Sons, 1919-21), 2: 110-11, lines 18-20. See n. 18 below.

The convulsions are those of laughter at Codrus's bad play, and of the spasmodic wrenching and collapse of the literary fabric, none of which trouble the playwright. As Pope says immediately thereafter, "Who shames a Scribler? break one cobweb thro', / He spins the slight, self-pleasing thread anew" (lines 89-90), until, spiderlike, he has recreated his own universe. Two characteristic weapons of Horatian satire—laughter and shame—are useless in this world.

Horace's third ode of the third book, and especially lines 7-8, is Pope's announced source for this section (p. 101n) and contrasts sharply with the new world of impenetrable and uneducable poet and king. Here is part of the design of the poem as earlier commentators taught it to Pope's contemporaries. The poet wishes

> to prevent *Augustus* from executing a Design of his Uncle *Julius*, who, it was said, intended to have translated the Seat of the Empire from *Rome* to *Alexandria* or *Troy*; from which the *Poet* apprehending very dismal Consequences might arise to the prejudice of the *Roman* Empire, he took this covered and ingenious manner of insinuating the Danger of such a Project to *Augustus*, whom it would not have been so safe to advise in a more open way. . . . He begins with drawing a beautiful Character of a just Man, who is endued with such Resolution and Constancy, that no Temptations or Fears from abroad can shake the inflexible Honesty and steady Purpose of his Soul.[8]

Such steadfast behavior will evoke Augustus's future deification; in the poem it evokes Juno's equally steadfast warning that even if Augustus rebuilds Troy three times, she will level that hated city.

Pope changes Horace's context, though like him he is covertly telling his Augustus of the dangers of transferring

---

[8] David Watson and Samuel Patrick, *The Odes, Epodes, and Carmen Secularae of Horace* (1742), pp. 228-29.

the seat of empire. Horace portrays a righteous monarch who gains external, divine approval of his acts by resisting pressure and preserving the rightly established order; Pope portrays a dunce who does not preserve but destroys his world of pit, box, and gallery. Horace's monarch would be secure in a falling world, for he is a stable man of good values and knows that the gods will reward him; Pope's dunce is secure because he is incapable of understanding his own and his literary world's depravity. Horace's Juno speaks with divine force and makes plain that she will destroy the hated competing empire; Pope's speaker makes plain that his Codrus is immune to destruction, and will both rebuild what satire destroys, and make himself king of his own universe. Pope's reference to the *Dunciad* a few lines earlier (line 79) suggests that a transfer of empire has already taken place under the new Augustus, as the flimsy modern world replaces the substantial ancient one:

> Destroy his Fib, or Sophistry; in vain,
> The Creature's at his dirty work again;
> Thron'd in the Centre of his thin designs;
> Proud of a vast Extent of flimzy lines.
>
> (Lines 91-94)

Divine vatic power in Horace becomes satiric impotence in Pope. "Whom have I hurt?" (line 95) he asks Arbuthnot. He has hurt no one because he is using the inappropriate tools of Horatian smarting ridicule and shame (lines 84, 89); he has also helped to demonstrate the irrelevance of Horatian literary values by showing the dunces' rejection of lengthy revision and by inverting the purpose of virtuous intransigence in the ode. The education of Arbuthnot himself is obvious in his poem; Pope too must be educated, however—to the need to hurt, to beat or flap before his satire can be effectual, as it must if he and his family are to escape the danger they are in. "No Names— be calm—learn Prudence of a Friend" (line 102), the agitated doctor urges, and hears Pope say, in part: "Of all mad Creatures, if the Learn'd are right, / It is the Slaver kills, and not the Bite" (lines 105-6).

Part of what is being killed, convulsed, burst, and cracked is the Greco-Roman historical past, which is being replaced by the tradition as viewed by flattering poets. They see in Pope not the culminating individual talent in a long tradition, but an epitome of physical aberration, distortion, illness, and death incidentally related to literature and history—the cough of Horace, the high shoulder of Alexander the Great, the long nose of Ovid, and a presumably piercing eye of undetermined ancestry (lines 116-18).[9] Pope illumines the true effect of such mindless and illogical flattery, again distances himself from it, and comments upon the besieging dunces' distorted view of the world.

> Go on, obliging Creatures, make me see
> All that disgrac'd my Betters, met in me:
> Say for my comfort, languishing in bed,
> "Just so immortal *Maro* held his head:"
> And when I die, be sure you let me know
> Great *Homer* dy'd three thousand years ago.
>
> (Lines 119-24)

The manuscript version of these lines makes even clearer the tactless intrusion into Pope's life and his classical inheritance. In the earlier effort he was courted by those who thought he was "thick & short" like Horace; Pope must have realized that the dunces were not quite so blind, and so changed his phrase to "though lean, am short." The original view of Alexander was not merely a shoulder but

---

[9] Compare [Peter Whalley?], *An Essay on the Manner of Writing History* (1746): improper imitation of earlier historians has induced even "stupidly transcribing . . . Defects and Failings: So that such a Resemblance of their Authors, may not improperly be compared to that with which the Courtiers of *Alexander* were ambitious to be distinguished, when they complimented that Prince by holding their heads aside" (pp. 6-7).

an entire "Back too high." The grotesque distortions thus spawned these rough lines:

> and make me
> Go on obliging Sir! ~~What joy to~~ see
>
> A ~~This~~ monstrous mixture of
> ~~All the defects of these great men,~~ in me.
> All that disgracd my Betters, met in me.
>
> Say, for my comfort when I'm sick a-bed,
> ~~Why not [?] comfort me wⁿ sick a-bed~~
>
> Just   ~~Say thus [?]~~ immortal
> So ~~Bacon yawnd, so~~ Maro held his head;
>
> (HM 6006)

The monstrous thing of the dunces' vision is bluntly stated, and finally submerged in the more polished "All that disgracd my Betters, met in me." By exiling Bacon, Pope preserves his focus upon the classical past and, the aptly named Alexander the Great obviously excepted, preserves his focus on poetry as well. The "monstrous mixture" is exactly what Pope hopes to avoid in his own personal and literary life—and is exactly what Sporus will be.

Thus far Pope has removed himself from those who would abuse him and the state—often the same men. As a formal verse satire, his apologia introduces positive values as well, values exemplified in his own conduct, that of his friends, and their recreation of a nurturing literary tradition in conflict with that of scribbling dunces. Specifically, the clerk who disobeys his father in order to write bad poetry and pester the adult Pope (lines 17-18, 21-22) is countered by the natural calling of the child at Binfield, who "No Duty broke, no Father dis-obeyed" (line 130). Those who publish only for money are countered by young Pope's publishing at the request of Granville, Walsh, Garth, Congreve, and Swift (lines 135-38). The beginning of Pope's poem shows him isolated in his attempt to resist the many ill-advised and aggressive imposers on his home, person, and literary inheritance; Pope's normative analogue of this section reverses the process, as he seeks the help of many others who are willing to open, not shut, their doors because of his talent, inborn ability to lisp in numbers, and willingness to give and take love. Moreover, as we are forced to see, most of the encouragers of proper poetry were relics of the Stuart dynasty or are the opposition against Walpole.

> The Courtly *Talbot, Somers, Sheffield* read,
> Ev'n mitred *Rochester* would nod the head,
> And *St. John's* self (great *Dryden's* friends before)
> With open arms receiv'd one Poet more.
> Happy my Studies, when by these approv'd!
> Happier their Author, when by these belov'd!
> From these the world will judge of Men and Books,
> Not from the *Burnets, Oldmixons,* and *Cooks.*
>
> (Lines 139-46)

Though posterity will judge rightly, in the meanwhile the world is dominated by the Burnets, and the St. Johns are out of place. Pope is eulogizing the past at least as much as he is chastising the present. He thus continues to describe the progress of his poetical career and moves from late adolescence—about age sixteen or seventeen, he tells us—to his appearance as a poet of innocent "pure Description" (line 148) in works like *Windsor Forest* (1713) and the *Rape of the Lock* (1714), when he nonetheless was attacked by Gildon and Dennis (lines 151, 153). The chronological sequence of this section is important: it is preceded by "Great *Homer* dy'd three thousand years ago," and begins with Pope as infant Achilles dipped in ink (lines 124-26). It juxtaposes life with death, and normal continuity with abnormal spiderlike creation from the self; it also transports us to a world in which the harmless and encouraged young Alexander Pope was gratuitously berated. He is not, that is, being bitten and kicked by opponents because he has bitten and kicked first—he always was defensive not aggressive.

Moreover, the time sequence serves as a backdrop for the depicted insanity with which the poem begins. Pope's early attackers are precursors of the madmen of 1734; but they did include "some more sober Critic" (line 157) from whom Pope could profit, and they did at least have a mite of intelligence that allowed them to set commas and points in their editorial labors on their betters: "Ev'n such small Critics some regard may claim, / Preserv'd in *Milton*'s or in *Shakespear*'s name" (lines 167-68). In spite of the many onslaughts, Pope is in control throughout this section—forgiving, condescending, confessing the rare proper hit, evaluating the exact degree of minuscule competence in the incompetent, and assuming that such men could be mildly treated because they were not threats to him, to letters, or the nation: "I wish'd the man a dinner" (line 152); "I never answer'd" (line 154); "If wrong, I smil'd; if right, I kiss'd the rod" (line 158); " 'twere a sin to rob them of their Mite" (line 162); "Pretty!" (line 169); "I excus'd them" (line 173); "I gave them but their due" (line 174). Hence,

> All these, my modest Satire bad *translate*,
> And own'd, that nine such Poets made a *Tate*.
> How did they fume, and stamp, and roar, and chafe?
> And swear, not *Addison* himself was safe.
>
> (Lines 189-92)

The world of Pope's young literary manhood is one in which modest satire is appropriate for unpleasant situations, and he need not fear the later invasions of the lion in his den. The satire on Atticus-Addison thus is sedate, sad, and decorous in its relationship between follies committed and punishments offered, one of which is laughter. "Atticus," in short, is a model of the Horatian satire once possible in Britain of the near-Stuart past, of 1715, when Addison's ungenerous response to the first four books of

Pope's *Iliad* evoked an early version of this portrait and Addison's submission.

The portrait looks back to two earlier parts of the poem, each of which reflects badly upon Atticus and well upon Pope. Addison was clearly worthy of the exalted role he had in British literary circles: he was warmed by true genius, inspired by fair fame, blessed with talents and arts to please, and, like Pope, "born to write." He was also born to "converse, and live with ease" (lines 194-96), and that is where he begins to reject the obligations of his office, and to contrast with Pope's affectionate and supportive line of wits and friends who "With open arms receiv'd one Poet more" (line 142). In contrast, Atticus wishes to have, not a republic of letters, but a Turkish autocracy; he wishes to encourage, not the friendship, approval, and love of Pope's older literary cousins-german, but scorn, jealousy, hate, leers, sneers, dislike, and the reluctance to appear what he is. He will "Damn with faint praise, assent with civil leer" and is "A tim'rous foe, and a suspicious friend" (lines 201, 206). Moreover, Atticus is also unlike Pope of the epistle's opening lines, when he had long replaced Atticus atop Britain's Parnassus. Pope wishes to escape from the many flatterers who were even worse than the highly placed enemies Arbuthnot feared would harm his friend (lines 101-4). Pope dislikes and punishes sycophants; Addison, "Dreading ev'n fools, by Flatterers besieg'd," does not shut the door, promises but never delivers, and is "so obliging that he ne'er oblig'd" (lines 207-8). In a comparable situation, an angry Alexander Pope says— "Go on, obliging Creatures, make me see / All that disgrac'd my Betters, met in me" (lines 119-20). He is seized and tied down, and must "sit with sad Civility" (line 37) while his flatterers demand their fee of kind words to wretched poems. Atticus, however, enthrones himself as the adored center of his own literary nation and will

> Like *Cato*, give his little Senate laws,
> And sit attentive to his own applause;

While Wits and Templers ev'ry sentence raise,
And wonder with a foolish face of praise.

(Lines 209-12)

Since this is the temperate, modest satire that once was possible, its final couplet returns us to a flawed but corrigible, or at least controllable, world in which satire genuinely is useful. "Peals of Laughter" (line 85) are ineffectual against Codrus in collapsing 1734, but in stable 1715 "Who but must laugh, if such a man there be? / Who would not weep, if *Atticus* were he!" (lines 213-14). As Pope told Spence regarding this internecine literary squabble, he sent Addison the first draft of this portrait. Consequently, "Mr. Addison used me very civilly ever after, and never did me any injustice that I know of from that time to his death."[10]

The transition to Bufo is significant for several reasons: for one, it continues the theme of Pope's dissociation from the offending hordes and shows him ignoring his name as posted and attacked on walls, shouted by hawkers, or rhymed in poems. For another, he differs from Atticus when he "sought no homage from the Race that write" and tried to treat his fawners with the same oriental distance with which Atticus treated him. He "kept, like *Asian* Monarchs, from their sight" (lines 219-20), and stayed away from the hacks now even more powerful and numerous than they were earlier, and now occupying the theaters. By avoiding these witlings, Pope refuses to contribute to a national illness, "To spread about the Itch of Verse and Praise" (line 224). Itch, Johnson tells us in his *Dictionary* (1755), is "A Cutaneous disease extremely contagious, which overspreads the body with small pustules filled with a thin serum, and raised, as microscopes have discovered, by a small animal. It is cured by sulphur." The

---

[10] *Joseph Spence: Observations, Anecdotes, and Characters of Books and Men Collected from Conversation*, ed. James M. Osborn (Oxford: Clarendon Press, 1966), 1: 72, 9 August 1735. See also Warburton, *Pope's Works*, 4: 27n.

insects, spiders, and other biting creatures, however, are im-
mune to Pope's medicine. He had first hoped that Arbuth-
not could supply a *"Drop* or *Nostrum"* to remove them
(line 29); he himself would "drop at last" (line 39) the use-
less, because not taken, literary-medicinal advice that they
keep their piece nine years. Sulphurless Pope refuses to
spread the contagion that he cannot cure; but he himself
gets sick nonetheless—as we see in the opening of the
poem, its plea to Arbuthnot, and the introduction of Bufo.
"But sick of Fops, and Poetry, and Prate, / [He] To *Bufo*
left the whole *Castalian* State" (lines 229-30).

"Bufo" not only evokes the decline of the aristocrat's
morals and literary taste apparent in Persius's first satire;
it also evokes the Juvenalian world of decline toward
which *Arbuthnot* is moving. Pope alludes to Juvenal *Sat-
ires*, 7, 36-78, and the patron there who, like Bufo, pays
poets with poetry rather than with the continuing support
possible in a better age. Juvenal's typical modern patron
is a poet himself and passionately fond of his own verse;
he will lend you a ramshackle distant house for your
recitation, will provide his freedmen and clients as
clacquers, but will not help you to pay for the rented
benches and chairs. For all that, poets go on with unprof-
itable writing because of the "scribendi cacoethes." The
successful poet, though, is free from inner and outer care,
is without bitterness, loves the woodlands, and can drink
at the spring of the muses. How can the pauper be a poet?
Horace was well fed when he wrote, and if Virgil did not
have his slave and a good roof over his head, there would
have been no *Aeneid*!

Pope may have laid the groundwork for the use of this
satire when he scolds the sycophants who were keen to
reassure him that "Great *Homer* dy'd three thousand years
ago." Juvenal's patron, who adores flattery, is so confident
of his own verse that "uni cedit Homero / Propter mille
annos" (lines 38-39). Gifford senses Pope's source here and
translates it appropriately in 1802: "if they yield to Homer,

let him know / 'Tis—that he liv'd a thousand years ago."
Gifford also sees that "The Bufo of Pope is shadowed out
in part from this animated passage" of Juvenal, and in his
own version he strains the Latin and has this patron, like
Bufo, "pay in kind" and assign his poet "A dry rehearsal."
Pope's "Itch of Verse and Praise" is probably a version of
Juvenal's "scribendi cacoethes," or as Gifford more lux-
uriantly has it, "insatiate itch of scribbling."[11] Juvenal's
fortunate Horace and Virgil are supported by their Au-
gustan patrons; his unfortunate modern poets are deprived
of food and opportunity. Pope's nurturing Stuart line of
Granville, Walsh, Garth, and others disappears under the
Hanoverians, who leave Gay to starvation and neglect.

The portrait of Bufo thus continues the chronological
advance and literary decline that begins after Pope's ado-
lescence. For example, Addison and Pope could have been
brothers jointly reigning in the republic of letters; Bufo
has the entire state of letters and is unworthy of it, as he
sits atop an Apollonian hill of his own making. The meta-
phors of ruling and replacement were clearer in two un-
printed versions. In one, Pope labels himself "A quiet
Prince, I slumber on my seat," while B—b absorbed "the
whole Parnassian State." In another, Bufo again replaces
Pope who "peacefull . . . lay Slumberg on my ~~Seat~~
Throne."[12] The hint of Pope's own irresponsibility is re-
placed by his patience and innocence in the poem's final
form, which insists more strongly on the world's collapsing

---

[11] William Gifford, *The Satires of Decimus Junius Juvenalis* (1802),
pp. 242-43. Compare Pope's line 224 with the fourth line, below, from
The Confederates: A Farce. By Mr. [Joseph!] Gay (1717), a parody of
the Arbuthnot-Pope-Gay *Three Hours After Marriage*, an attack on
Dr. Woodward:

> Go, Doctor, go; thy Patients' Pulses feel,
> Handle the Syringe, or in Purges deal:
> The Muses dwell not in thy Northern Air;
> And *Poetry*'s an *Itch* not catching there.
>
> (P. 4)

[12] Pope-Richardson, *Works*, p. 68.

values. Specifically, the Apollo to whom Pope implicitly bows when he invokes King Midas's asslike ears (line 69-82) was an active force in the ancient world and punished even a king if he displayed bad taste. Modern Bufo replaces that divine judgment with his own, as he is "Proud, as *Apollo* on his forked hill" (line 231). Pope despises flattery and avoids giving or receiving patronage; Addison unworthily accepts and encourages flattery but does not demand it; Bufo, "puff'd by ev'ry quill," is "Fed with soft Dedication all day long" (lines 232-33). Pope belongs to a proper nurturing literary tradition; Addison, presumably part of that tradition, disgraces himself by attempting to shut out a legitimate heir to it; Bufo is like the modern sycophants who replace the normative with their own aberrant tradition of coughing Horace and aquiline Ovid. Bufo's version of literary history leads to death, mindlessness, materialism, servility, and hunger, as he and Horace, "hand in hand in song," are associated with Bufo's library and its "Busts of Poets dead / And a true *Pindar* . . . without a head" (lines 235-36). Pope is asked for aid by the place-seeking Pitholeon, and is rejected; Addison's flatterers pestered him as well and found him "so obliging that he ne'er oblig'd" (line 208); Bufo received his wits to be fed by the flattery hitherto despised or too easily tolerated. His poets "first his Judgment ask'd, and then a Place" (line 238), while fawning over their hopeful patron, who sometimes rewarded them with food, wine, praise, or unnourishing theatrical chores. Bufo "To some a dry Rehearsal . . . assign'd" (line 243), whereas Pope neither went on errands for rhyme "Nor at Rehearsals sweat, and mouth'd, and cry'd" (line 227).

The sense of further decline and danger from Atticus to Bufo is made plain in the portrait's final lines. We recall that Pope's receptive literary guides included several who were "great *Dryden*'s friends before" (line 141), and that Pope contrasts his connection to this tradition with his divorce from the new distortion of it. We thus are not surprised to see that Dryden also divorces himself from Bufo—and pays for such worthy independence from the ominous man who sits atop "the whole *Castalian* State" (line 230).

> *Dryden* alone (what wonder?) came not nigh,
> *Dryden* alone escap'd this judging eye:
> But still the Great have kindness in reserve,
> He help'd to bury whom he help'd to starve.
>
> (Lines 245-48)

Unlike Atticus, Bufo is beyond satiric control and is dangerous to life and letters, for he encourages the bad, starves the good, and is a paradigm for the great of Pope's recent past, who followed Bufo's pattern, encouraged duncery, and ignored Gay. Pope himself tries to nurture Gay as Dryden's friends nurtured him, but finds that encouragement is not enough when one needs more of a return on a literary investment made on behalf of the nation:

> they left me GAY,
> Left me to see neglected Genius bloom,
> Neglected die! and tell it on his Tomb;
> Of all thy blameless Life the sole Return
> My Verse, and QUEENSB'RY weeping o'er thy Urn!
>
> (Lines 256-60)

After "Atticus," Pope tries to become indifferent to attacks on his name and reputation, and defines himself, in part, by being the opposite of his antagonist. He uses the same technique after "Bufo," as he pleads to be left to "live my own! and die so too!" (line 261), to be with his friends, avoid patrons, courts, and "great Affairs," (line 267), and even avoid poetry if he wishes. But Pope must pay the penalty both for his own eminence and for living after Gay's death in 1732, for that Hanoverian world is characterized by, one may say, the slimy Bufo not the diminished Atticus, and thus that world continues to displace the good with the bad and to distort literary and human perceptions. Pope sees Swift as a friend to serve and perhaps as an aid in saving his soul (line 274); his pestering antagonist ignores Pope's denials and sees such a meeting as a conspiratorial conclave to produce "something" (line 276), after which he "for mine obligingly mistakes / The first Lampoon Sir *Will.* or *Bubo* makes" (lines 279-80). Balbus, the perpetrator of this judgment, offends both Pope's poetry and politics in replacing his opposition satire with their administration libel. In spite of Bufo's (the toad's) influence on his world of Balbus (the stutterer) and Bubo (the owl), Pope remains detached, no longer laughing as he could with Atticus, but at least condescending in the face of vulgarity, and still trying to use civilized weapons of ridicule. "Poor guiltless I! and can I chuse but smile, / When ev'ry Coxcomb knows me by my *Style*?" (lines 281-82). Such a pose becomes impossible once we progress from Atticus, held in check by his own temerity and decency, and "Willing to wound, and yet afraid to strike" (line 203), to the near past of Bufo, who "Sate" and was "Fed" and "went" and "Receiv'd" and "pay'd," and now to the contemporaneity of "hurts," "Insults," and "wounds" (lines 287, 288, 292, 293). We have entered the world of 1733-34, of Sporus, of the court's immediate attacks on Pope's person, family, and morals. Pope finally realizes that this world requires, not detached and superior Horatian laughter or smiles, but the bitter fight to the death with a reincarnation of the Grand Antagonist himself, where only the savage indignation of Juvenalian satire is appropriate, and where even the prudent Arbuthnot—a representative of the neutral or skeptical audience—is provoked into satire and the satirist's cause.

The context of "Sporus" is extraordinary in its evocation of Pope's anger and his antagonist's traits; it also reinforces the poem's movement toward depravity as it moves through time. Pope is indignant, not merely at someone who hurts, but at one "who hurts a harmless neighbour's peace"; nor at a mere insulter, but one who "Insults fal'n

Worth"; nor at a mere liar, but someone "Who loves a Lye" (lines 287-89). Sporus is an active detractor under the guise of patron who "wounds an Author's honest fame" (line 292); he betrays, misrepresents, and misapplies, with "Lust" (line 301). Balbus's poor taste made him confuse Yonge's lampoon for Pope's satire; this new antagonist maliciously and consciously reverses the process and will "Make Satire a Lampoon, and Fiction, Lye" (line 302).

Pope's Horatian weapons once were suitable for the Addisonian world of modest satire. Pope has wrongly extended that "sad Civility" (line 37) to an age in which it is useless, and thus he says that "No creature smarts so little as a Fool" and asks "Whom have I hurt?" (lines 84, 95). This innocence is gone now, as Pope accepts the full implications of life under Midas-Nero-George II-Walpole and their court's luminaries who were pleased to attack his writings, *"Person, Morals,* and *Family."* Arbuthnot, who began his remarks to Pope with "Good friend forbear! you deal in dangerous things" (line 75), becomes Pope's ally in recognition and support, as he too changes from Pope's earlier notion that fools feel nothing—certainly not the smarts of laughter—to an awareness of the proper punishment for such men. Both Pope and Arbuthnot abandon detachment and accept the need actively to engage the enemy, who is also an enemy of the nation and God:

> A Lash like mine no honest man shall dread,
> But all such babling blockheads in his stead.
>   Let *Sporus* tremble—"What? that Thing of silk,
> *"Sporus,* that mere white Curd of Ass's milk?
> "Satire or Sense alas! can *Sporus* feel?
> "Who breaks a Butterfly upon a Wheel?"
> Yet let me flap this Bug with gilded wings,
> This painted Child of Dirt that stinks and stings.
> (Lines 303-10)

The earlier insect and biting imagery has been enlarged and extended beyond Pope, for Sporus stings and annoys the witty and the fair. More important, the queen herself is threatened, for her confidant Lord Hervey is a type of Milton's venomous spitting toad planting falsehoods in Eve's ear. Perhaps the queen of Midas can sleep now, but she nonetheless is in grave danger. Pope characterizes Sporus through an apparently endless series of offenses in this harshly Juvenalian catalogue of a creature with interchangeable roles who

> spits himself abroad,
> In Puns, or Politicks, or Tales, or Lyes,
> Or Spite, or Smut, or Rymes, or Blasphemies.
>
> (Lines 320-22)

Hervey's oxymoronic "florid Impotence" (line 317) amphibious sexual nature, toothless smiles, "corrupted Heart" (line 327), and destructive flattery—all are, in Johnson's definition, beaten "with a flap, as flies are beaten." Pope thus wishes to break the exemplar of hostile court literary and political methods nurtured by Walpole, for "as the Prompter breathes, the Puppet Squeaks" (line 318), or as a manuscript version had it, "When W——le blows, & bids yᵉ Puppet squeak."[13] All this heavy artillery is necessary because we have moved from squabbles about leadership in the republic of letters, to aristocratic patronage that dominates that republic and encourages the bad and starves the good, to the seat of administration and royal power "at the Ear of *Eve*" (line 319). The moral and political stakes are higher than they have ever been, as the contemptible toad Bufo becomes the satanic toad Sporus.

Horace's association with and authority from the court are as ineffectual here as his satiric laughter that assumes the possibility of shame in the victim. Persius's seriousness and opposition to his Caesar and court are useful guides; but his ultimate stoic equanimity and withdrawal are inappropriate, for unlike Persius, Pope is being attacked in

---

13 Pope-Richardson, *Works*, p. 73.

his family and person, not in his sensibility. Pope also seems to care more about the fate of his nation than does Persius. Once we reach Sporus, Pope is seen as a member of the characteristically embattled and shrinking minority, a citizen of a nation corrupt at its highest levels and hence further corrupted by subservient imitators; he is the hero willing to take chances while protesting the decay he knows he cannot stop but hopes to postpone, if only for the moment of the satire that he must write. Juvenal, indeed, was less brave than Pope, who has a more threatening opponent, and who attacks known members of today's court, not those long dead. The antithetical Sporus—the male whore of Nero—"Now trips a Lady, and now struts a Lord" (line 329). That bisexuality is an emblem of diabolical intrusion in a once benign world:

> *Eve*'s Tempter thus the Rabbins have exprest,
> A Cherub's face, a Reptile all the rest;
> Beauty that shocks you, Parts that none will trust,
> Wit that can creep, and Pride that licks the dust.
>
> (Lines 330-33)

Once again after a portrait, Pope defines himself by negatives; but now he avoids the quick return to detachment and relative tranquillity, and instead he remains in the contemporary world of the ominous stinging Sporus. Hence the fever pitch of self-definition and rejection of Sporus that lasts for thirty-three lines after the portrait itself; hence the poem's most vivid representation of battle; and hence the affirmation that, in spite of all trials, the effort has been worthwhile.

Pope's negatives recall and reject several of Sporus's traits. He himself is "Not . . . nor . . . / Not . . . nor . . . / Not . . . nor" (lines 334-36) a slave to fortune, fashion, money, ambition, pride, and servility. Unlike Sporus and his untrustworthy parts, Pope, for all the sexual mockery heaped upon him, "pleas'd by manly ways" (line 337). Sporus would lick the dust to gain and preserve the

courtier's position he wished; Pope fought "not for Fame,
but Virtue's better end" (line 342). He "stood the furious
Foe," and "the damning Critic," and "The Coxcomb hit,"
and "The distant Threats of Vengeance," and "The Blow
unfelt" (lines 343-49), and attacks upon all those matters
and persons outlined in the poem's Advertisement:

> The Morals blacken'd when the Writings scape;
> The libel'd Person, and the pictur'd Shape;
> Abuse on all he lov'd, or lov'd him, spread,
> A Friend in Exile, or a Father dead;
> The Whisper that to Greatness still too near,
> Perhaps, yet vibrates on his SOVEREIGN's Ear—
> Welcome for thee, fair Virtue! all the past:
> For thee, fair Virtue! welcome ev'n the *last*!
>
> (Lines 352-59)

Sporus has been poisoning Pope's reputation with his mon-
arch—and Pope has resolutely defended Virtue even while,
as Warburton says, "being forced to undergo the severest
proofs of his love for it, which was the being thought
hardly of by his SOVEREIGN."[14] Pope may again be recalling
the allusive context of Horace, *Odes*, iii. 3, 7-8, in which he
and not, say, Cibber, is the good man steadfastly resisting
external threats; he certainly is abandoning the world of
moderation and Arbuthnot's medicinal aid. He has learned
that his own punitive and destructive flaps are the only
effectual cures for today's illnesses. Indeed, Pope has im-
plicitly redefined his earlier annoying attackers, has recog-
nized that the fawning, bribery, and disruption of literary
tradition and honesty in the comic opening of the poem
are part of the world of political and moral disorder he
is now fighting. "*Sporus* at Court, or *Japhet* in a Jayl" are
equally knaves, as are "A hireling Scribler, or a hireling
Peer" (lines 363-64).

The repeated word "hireling" evokes the question, Hired

14 Pope's *Works*, 4: 41n.

by whom? and that, in turn, recalls the line which describes Sporus as controlled by his prompter (line 318). Pope is again offering a theory of causation, is attacking Sporus while implying that his actions are guided by the corrupter behind him. Surely it is no accident that Sporus as puppet appears immediately before Sporus as toad spitting forth his venom to the queen. John Butt has noted that "Some suggestions for the character of Sporus were taken from Caleb D'Anvers' [Pulteney] . . . *A Proper Reply To a late Scurrilous Libel; intitled, Sedition and Defamation display'd*, dated Jan. 20. 1730-1" (p. 119n).[15] Hervey is characterized there as writing in "little, quaint Antitheses" (p. 4), as "such a nice Composition of the two Sexes, that it is difficult to distinguish which is more praedominant," and as "a pretty Medley of the *masculine* and *feminine* Gender" (p. 5). He is a "little Master-Miss" who would be loath to lose his place "or even *another Tooth*" (p. 6); he tells fibs (pp. 5, 6, 31), is a traitorous flatterer (p. 15), and wrongly draws his "Grey-Goose Quill" against superior adversaries (p. 15). These suggestions are more extensive still, for the *Proper Reply* includes an attack upon Walpole and his relationship with Hervey, and predicts and provides some of Pope's language and rhetoric in *Arbuthnot*:

> I cannot . . . forbear admiring the Sagacity of your *Patron*, in chusing such a *Pupil* and *Advocate*. A Circulator of *Tittle-Tattle*, a Bearer of Tales, a Teller of Fibs, a Station'd Spy, even where you was admitted under the strongest of Pretences of Friendship, and under the strongest obligations to it, is a subject worthy his Care, and must be capable of making great Advances in these Mysteries of *political* Magick, into which He hath initiated you. (P. 6)

[15] For further discussion of the sexual context of Hervey-Sporus, see chapter 5, note 6, above.

The foreshadowed relationship between prompter and puppet is clear enough; but Pulteney makes another damning and abusive point. Walpole's political corruption is as much a violation of nature as Hervey's sexual corruption, and is indeed "a parallel Case" to it, though harder to punish because the corrupter of the state also acquires the power of the state. There is, Pulteney says, "a certain, unnatural, reigning Vice (indecent and almost shocking to mention)," which deserves severe punishment. There must be "*two Parties* in this Crime; the *Pathick* and the *Agent*; both equally guilty." The pathic generally has been "The Proof of the Crime," but "Evidence will not be obtained quite so easily in the Case of *Corruption*, when a Man enjoys every Moment the Fruits of his Guilt" (pp. 27-28). By simple extension ("I need not explain These any farther," Pulteney says [p. 27]), Walpole is Hervey's patron and prompter because they have similar natures and perversions: Walpole does to Britain what Hervey does to, or receives from, his chums. Both seducer and seduced are equally guilty, for Britain, as exemplified in its court, has allowed itself to be perverted. Hervey is worthy of his prompter's care and exercises his dictates, including "The Whisper that to Greatness still too near, / Perhaps, yet vibrates on his SOVEREIGN's Ear." Sporus at court is a projection of Walpole, who enjoys the fruits of his guilt while Pope is forced to defend Virtue with his few veteran troops. Pope does indeed please by manly ways.

Only after this virtual exorcism of Sporus, the man behind him, and the engagement in battle with other knaves, can Pope begin to soften the long crescendo and return to personal apologia and verifiable acts of aid, friendship, or silent tolerance for detractors—Dennis, Theobald, Cibber, Moor, Welsted, Budgell, and Curll. Only now, with Sporus defeated, can he return to an earlier chronological period and introduce his parents—not as the Horatian wise father, but as yet another instance of Pope's own education and the decline of the world from Stuart to Hanoverian dynasties. Why should he not have replied to Lord Hervey and Curll when they abused him?

> that Father held it for a rule
> It was a Sin to call our Neighbour Fool,
> That harmless Mother thought no Wife a Whore.
>
> (Lines 382-84)

Pope is substituting his literal for his literary ancestry, replacing the loving poetic with loving familial guides who provided a sound but, alas, charmingly archaic moral education. As the direction of the *Epistle to Dr. Arbuthnot* suggests, if it is sinful to call someone fool, it may nonetheless be necessary if he bites and kicks and defames even those like Pope's father. And as the *Dunciad* made and would make clear (1728, II. 173; 1743, II. 181), Curll's own wife was the whore who behorned him, and of course Lady Walpole was as noted for her gallantries as Sir Robert was for his. Pope's dead father and lingering mother are products of another age, one of secure Horatian contacts and modest satire; as babes in the wood of modern error, they need their son's protection, for they can offer none of their own with their naive and unfashionable ethic of goodness: "Hear this! and spare his Family, *James More!*" (line 385).

The manuscript again suggests some of Pope's intention in characterizing his parents—including his own legitimate and his opponents' illegitimate genealogy, and his parents' inability to understand the diminished world their son combats. Pope had to drop some of these earlier remarks, since they might have implied discontent with part of his inheritance. There the dunces' vision of the classical past made monstrous in Pope leads to four lines claiming that his lamentable body "came not from Ammon's Son, but from my Sire," and that his headaches, "which I could well excuse," came not from poetry, but "a married Mother." Pope could not risk a possible accusation that would sap the selfless and generous sentiments with which *Arbuthnot* finally ends, but we can see why he flirted with the first version when we see what follows:

> if He in whom their frailties joind
> Happy! ~~thrice happy had I heir'd as well~~
>
> Had heird as well ye Virtues of their mind.
>
> ~~The Christian Kernel, as the crazy Shell,~~
>   ~~He meek~~ my christian Father
> ~~Meek was my Sire, &~~ held it for a rule
>
> It was a Sin *to call our Brother Fool*;
>
> She, harmless Matron, judgd no
> ~~My Mother judgd no wedded~~ Wife a *Whore*;
> Hear this, & spare my Family, James M—re!
>
>   honest Sire unknown
> And couldst thou think ~~my Father wast un-~~
> Merely because thou dost not knowe thy own?
> Known he shall be! & lov'd, and honord long,
> If there be Force in Virtue or in Song.
>
>   (HM 6006)

Pope admits that his own Christian kernel and, in the revision, his own spiritual virtue, are less than his father's and that, strictly speaking, he himself is wrong to satirize his brother or neighbor and call him bastard—as much orthodox Christian doctrine would have argued.[16] Nonetheless,

---

[16] For one contemporary disavowal of satire, presumably based on religious conviction, see David Scurlock, Vicar of Pottern, Wilts., *A Caution against speaking Evil of our Governors and of One Another. As it was delivered in a Sermon Preached at St. Paul's Cathedral* (1733). Satirists with "an unChristian and malicious Spirit (p. 9) have libeled and maligned "our publick Ministers, our Nobles, our Bishops, and even *our King upon the Throne,* and his Royal Consort . . . in order to inflame the People into Sedition against them" (p. 12). This is done in spite of the apostles' command "to all *Men, Speak Evil of no Man*" (p. 19).

such a fall from innocence is necessary in the contemporary world. I hear some condescension when Pope writes "My Mother judgd no wedded Wife a *Whore*," and rewrites, "She, harmless Matron, judgd no Wife a *Whore*." The exclusion of "wedded" in both the second and the printed versions suggests that Pope is questioning, however affectionately, his mother's judgment; she cannot understand that "Wife" euphemistically also means "A kept mistress, concubine" (*OED*, 2c), as opposed to Mrs. Pope as "a married Mother." In tentative manuscript as in final poem, the world that Pope received is not the one his father sired, where being harmless meant, in turn, receiving no harm.

We normally think of the three hostile portraits in *Arbuthnot*; but there is a fourth, loving one, of Pope's father who, like his son, is defined by negatives. Unlike his diseased son, however, Pope's father remains healthy, perhaps because he is part of an earlier healthy environment. His fortune was his own, he had neither pride nor strife, neither marital discord nor rage, was not noxious, saw "No Courts . . . no Suits . . . / Nor dar'd an Oath, nor hazarded a Lye," was not learned, and "knew no Schoolman's subtle Art / No Language, but the Language of the Heart" (lines 392-99). The poem unites father and son by means of their negation of modern values, and connects Pope to his unpoetic, nurturing, real family that is even more important than the poetic family of great Dryden's friends. Pope's father is a model of life, not of literature, is part of the virtue Pope is honorbound to defend against any odds, and is superior to any royal model we have seen: "Oh grant me thus to live, and thus to die! / Who sprung from Kings shall know less joy than I" (lines 404-5).

The poem's final paragraph reinforces the sense of reversal of roles. Pope the son, for example, becomes the protector and resurrector of his mother, who had been dead for eighteen months when the poem was published. He will "rock the Cradle of reposing Age" (line 409); and like a parent he will "Explore the Thought, explain the asking Eye" (line 412). He now becomes a nonsatiric doctor, and "With lenient Arts" hopes to "extend a Mother's breath" (line 410); and he asks Heaven to preserve Arbuthnot, who had hitherto been seeking to preserve Pope. Finally, Pope returns to a calm that is possible only because his lashing satire has temporarily made the world, or at least the world of his poem, safe for gentleness, friendship, and the "social, chearful, and serene" (line 416) state he wishes for his friends. If one assumes that Arbuthnot speaks the final couplet—as Warburton did and the Twickenham editors do not—the conclusion also signals a return to spiritual order. As the poem opens, Pope is besieged everywhere and every day: "No place is sacred, not the Church is free, / Ev'n *Sunday* shines no *Sabbath-day* to me" (lines 11-12). Atticus was "Blest with each Talent" (line 195) but used them improperly, and Sporus was the reptilian Satan tempting Eve. In contrast, whether Pope's blessing for Arbuthnot "be deny'd, or given, / Thus far was right, the rest belongs to Heav'n" (lines 418-19)—to a Heaven confidently reinvoked and capable of joining its wisdom to the steadfast men who uphold its values. We have, that is, the harmony of poet, friend, family, and Heaven, and are reconciled to the grim world as we see a return to order and the triumph of virtue and its soldier. That surely is one reason why the *Epistle to Dr. Arbuthnot* is so popular a poem, and why it often is called Horatian, for it seems to conclude as we wish it to conclude in an epistolary world of manifold communication.

But the reconciliation lacks significant elements. There is no harmony between Pope and his nation as presently constituted; he has realized that his pose of detachment, laughter, and ridicule is no longer tenable; the exemplars of his congenial literary and genetic families are dead or dying, and their values and traditions have already been replaced by less attractive modern substitutes, so that Pope is far more isolated than he may seem. Arbuthnot has been rationally won over to his side, but he too is an aging Stuart relic and is helpless until he abandons the antique civilities of a lamentably antiquated world; Sporus has been broken (in the poem) but by main force not reason, and his malice regarding Pope yet may be heard by his sovereign (line 357). The rest belongs to Heaven, but Sir Robert's values still render this world treacherous. The triumph of goodness is real but muted, joyous but sad; it has the solemnity of a requiem and the colors of autumn leaves lovely because they are dying.

The mingled but finally un-Horatian *Arbuthnot* may be seen more clearly when it is set against the more Horatian *Epistle to Bathurst*. *Bathurst* deals with abstract matters like good and evil, competing ethical systems and the after-world; it insists upon the ultimate harmony between educating poet, educable man, benevolent God (the source of the poet's values), and the nation, still defeating internal threats and functioning within the protective confines of the *discordia concors*. *Arbuthnot's* dialogue considers personal, satiric, and familial matters, in which the poet is on the defensive, the adversarius urges silence in the face of powerful enemies, civilized discourse and modest satire prove progressively less useful, the integrity of literature, the family, and the throne are invaded, and the benevolent *discordia concors* becomes instead a "vile Antithesis." In the one the devil can be treated with amused contempt, since in spite of his apparent victory over Sir Balaam, he remains a dupe and shows that God orders the world for the best. In the other, the blaspheming devil-figure violates nature, must be treated with ferocity, evokes the reluctant but medicinal lashes of the converted adversarius, and requires the satirist's utmost efforts to defeat, rather than educate. At the end of *Bathurst* all of the poem's positive values are affirmed, active, and alive; at the end of *Arbuthnot* all of the poem's values are affirmed, some are active, and some are dead, and the reconciliation between the poet and the nation, as exemplified in its political administration, is gone. The Horatian has yielded to something else.

II: AN ANSWER FROM PERSIUS

Like so much of Pope's later poetry, *Arbuthnot*'s richness of texture stems in part from his blending of the varied satiric techniques available to him. The Abbé Yart insists that "en quelques endroits" Pope has borrowed the tone, dialogues, and mysterious and obscure air of Persius "pour dérober aux yeux de ses ennemis dangereux ou puisans, les traits qu'il leur lancoit." Indeed, Yart adds, when dealing with Pope one must remember that he was, among other things, "un Philosophe chagrin & sévère"—that is, the term that Boileau had used to characterize Persius.[17]

One of the Persian places that Yart may have had in mind here is the Midas passage, whose possible source is the accepted commentary on roughly comparable lines in Persius's first satire, which had long been regarded as an attack upon Nero, his tragedy, and his nobles for their collective abuse of poetry. Since such mockery could not go too far without an invitation to open veins in a warm bath, Cornutus prevailed upon Persius to change and to soften a key line that drew upon the familiar story of Midas, the king of Phrygia who was granted his wish that everything he touched be turned to gold. More important here is Midas's poor taste in music, for he preferred the music of Pan to Apollo, who promptly punished Midas by giving him asses' ears. Midas hid his shame beneath his cap, but his barber discovered the ears and, bursting with his knowledge, dug a hole in the earth, told it, refilled the hole, and both relieved his burden and kept the secret—he wrongly thought, for on that place a reed grew and whispered its secret to the world.[18]

---

[17] *Idée de la poësie Angloise*, 3: 96-97, 3: 240 (Philosophe).

[18] Pope himself glosses line 72 of *Arbuthnot*: "The Story is told by some [Ovid *Met.* xi 146 and Persius *Sat.* 1 121] of his Barber, but by

Persius revitalizes the second part of the myth. At line 8 he cries, "who is there in Rome who is not. . . ." He cannot yet say what demands to be said, and so waits until line 121, when he asks, *"Who is there who has not the ears of an ass?"—auriculas asini quis non habet?* According to the old scholiast, whose remark was broadly accepted by Pope's ancestors and contemporaries including Boileau, this line originally was *Auriculas asini Mida rex habet—*King Midas has asses' ears or, as Cornutus feared that everyone would understand it, Emperor Nero has asses' ears and thus has the taste, talent, and intelligence of the creature he resembles. For Romans the word *rex* was also a virtual synonym for tyrant, and so the line had to be generalized and made apparently unimperial in its attack. Students of Persius in Pope's generation probably would read the line about Midas's ears and recall both the Midas myth and Persius's putative original use of it as an attack upon Nero and bad poetry.[19] That being so, "Midas" in other satires hostile to a court probably would evoke that same association, especially if it is helped along by the word "king" and by a particular action that associates the modern king with an ass. Here is *Arbuthnot*'s conflation of Persius's Midas sections:

Chaucer of his Queen. See Wife of Bath's Tale in *Dryden*'s Fables [lines 157-200]." The information in brackets is John Butt's, *Imitations of Horace*, p. 100n. Dryden also clarifies the allusion in his own *Persius*, where we see that "By *Midas*, the Poet means *Nero*." The Works of John Dryden, vol. 4, *Poems 1693-1696*, ed. A. B. Chambers, William Frost, and Vinton A. Dearing (Berkeley and Los Angeles: Univ. of California Press, 1974), p. 279n. Dryden is following Casaubon: see the editors' note, p. 664, n. 240. See also Ludovicus Prateus, *D. Junii Juvenalis, et A. Persii Flacci Satirae* (1684), 7th ed. (1736), p. 234, n. 121, on *Auriculas asini, Mida rex habet*; Prateus adopts "Casaubonis, Lubinus, & alii."

[19] Pope apparently assumes such recollection of the myth in the *Dunciad* of 1743, when he has Settle happily proclaim of Cibber: "See, see, our own true Phoebus wears the bays! / Our Midas sits Lord Chancellor of Plays" (III. 323-24).

'Tis sung, when *Midas*' Ears began to spring,
(*Midas*, a sacred Person and a King)
His very Minister who spy'd them first,
(Some say his Queen) was forc'd to speak, or burst.
And is not mine, my Friend, a sorer case,
When ev'ry Coxcomb perks them in my face?

(Lines 69-74)

Arbuthnot dismisses Pope's plight with "Tis nothing," and hears the outraged echo, "Nothing? if they bite and kick?" (line 78). He then blurts out the secret that Persius held for 111 more lines, and that he would make even more overt in his imitation of Horace, *Epistles*, i. 1 (1737), where "a Minister's an Ass" (line 96):

Out with it, *Dunciad*! let the secret pass,
That Secret to each Fool, that he's an Ass:
The truth once told, (and wherefore shou'd we lie?)
The Queen of *Midas* slept, and so may I.

(Lines 79-82)

Pope is casting Arbuthnot in the role of the dissuading, protective, Cornutus, for as soon as Midas appears, the worried Doctor urges Pope to forbear and not "name Queens, Ministers, or Kings" (line 76). As "Out with it" may suggest, Pope is bringing the scholiast's meaning from its limbo of censorship, telling his adversarius that he will not be a docile pupil and abandon satire, and is bravely labeling King Midas an ass during his own lifetime and not thereafter. Indeed, to carry the Cornutus-Arbuthnot analogy one step further, when Arbuthnot himself becomes a satirist and lashes Sporus as a "mere white Curd of Ass's milk" (line 306), Pope's once friendly dissuader has become actively involved with the protection of virtue and battle against vice.

Moreover, as Maynard Mack has shown, the word "kick" connoted the fierce anger of George II and his "savage temper which could only be relieved by kicking somebody or something." Hence on 16 July 1737 *Fog's Weekly Journal* portrays Augustus Caesar, that is, George II, kicking a football and then his flattering courtiers. "This Impudent paper with its audacious parallel," as an eighteenth-century reader called it, goaded the government into arresting the printer.[20] Pope also incriminates Walpole (and Queen Caroline) by insisting that the first minister, and not a mere barber, sees the king's folly and no doubt shares it. In fact, since Midas gained his asses' ears for offending the god of poetry, Walpole emerges as an accomplice, as the man who brought bad judgment in poetry—the selection of Cibber as poet laureate for example—to the king. At the same time, however, Pope adopts Persius's prudence in the face of powerful enemies by veiling much of this meaning and having the possible recourse of claiming Boileau's ninth satire (1667) as an innocent analogue, for Boileau there writes that "Midas, le roi Midas a des oreilles d'âne" (line 224). If Louis XIV took no umbrage, surely, one might argue, George II should not either.[21] Pope also

[20] For Mack, see *The Garden and the City: Retirement and Politics in the Later Poetry of Pope 1731-1743* (Toronto: Univ. of Toronto Press, 1969), p. 130. See also p. 138 and "An Essay on Kicking" mentioned there, and pp. 297-98, describing an engraving of George II in a kicking mood. The remarks regarding the "audacious parallel" are written on the copy in the British Library's Burney Collection.

[21] This line of course is attacking not Louis XIV but Chapelain, as king of Boileau's literary enemies. Pope may be looking at Boileau through English spectacles. Compare this section from the 1712 translation of Boileau's ninth satire, with Pope's Midas section in *Arbuthnot*. This "Boileau" provides Midas, the choleric tone, and the ineffectual satirist useful at different places in *Fortescue*, *Arbuthnot*, and the *Epilogue to the Satires*.

> When his pretended Right [to high poetic praise] some Fools
>   proclaim,
> My Choler with Disdain is in a Flame.
> And if I durst not vent my raging Spleen,
> Or tell the World my Grievance with my Pen,
> Like the fam'd Barber I shou'd dig a Hole,
> And there discharge the Burthen of my Soul.
> There whisper to the Reeds that *Midas* wears

adopts at least part of Persius's printed, not censored, version by generalizing onto the literary world: each London and Roman fool is an ass, for in literary, moral, and asinine matters the principle of *ad exemplum regis* extends down the social scale. I believe that Pope bases his Midas passage on Persius's printed text and the commentary upon it, and he intensifies its impact by condensing, enriching, and making plain the theory of causation apparently implicit in Persius's *auriculas asini quis non habet*? Neither Persius nor Pope has such beastly organs, and both men become progressively more endangered and lonely in their normal states. The asses "bite and kick" as well as taunt Pope by perking their ears in his face (lines 78, 74); unlike their antique royal paradigm, they lack even a sense of shame for their ears and the reason for their presence. The world is worse than worst, it seems, under King Midas II. Pope's magnifying rage sees "a bursting World" (line 88) that demands satire, however ineffectual and dangerous it might be. In the process, he becomes the informing barber, the speaking reeds, the Persian satirist ("un Philosophe chagrin & sévère"), the tutor of Cornutus, and the British scholiast-hero undaunted by friendly or courtly pressures.

The *Epistle to Dr. Arbuthnot*, then, begins with a frantic scene and ends with a calm scene. The poet's earned resolution demands his education as well as that of his adversarius, an education regarding the efficacy of different kinds of satire appropriate for different times. He takes us to his secure literary familial childhood and adolescence and contrasts his nurturing, loving literary tradition with the aberrant new one now replacing it. As the poem progresses, he

---

Beneath his Royal Crown an Asses Ears.
What hurt has my impartial Satire done?
Its Talent is not baulkt, it labours on;
Folio's on *Folio*'s still are brought to light,
And *L——s* Garrets groan beneath the Weight.

The Works of Mons. Boileau. Made English from the last Paris Edition By Several Hands, 2nd ed. (London, 1736), 1: 244-45.

shows us his young poetic manhood and an age in which modest satire could in fact have its proper effect upon Atticus; he moves to the more ominous and more recent aristocratic patron Bufo, who encourages the bad and starves the good; and he settles upon one source of his poem, Sporus, who is the diabolical and malicious tormentor of himself, his family, and his sovereign. In passing through time, Pope also passes away from Horatian laughter and ridicule, into Persian gravity and hostility to the literary and political state, beyond Persius's timid tutor Cornutus, and finally into the yet more severe mode of Juvenalian violent lashing and flapping of immoral values at the heart of the nation. Having defeated his main antagonist and convinced the adversarius of the rightness of his cause, Pope then introduces the harmless family that Sporus and others had maligned—but introduces them to show their frailty, vulnerability, and the death of their values with their persons. By becoming so Juvenalian, Pope is adapting himself to the needs of his time; but he is also showing that his parents' values are as outmoded as modest satire and other presumably Stuart values and partisans. The courteous epistle *To a Lady* is Pope's only Horatian poem to follow *Arbuthnot* and its Pyrrhic victory. Thereafter, he would alternate or blend Horace with the more severe tragic masks of Persius and Juvenal, as his satiric needs required, and he would end his career by being dominantly Juvenalian in a poem that rejects Horace as a willing captive of the court.

CHAPTER 9

Pope: An Overview of Mingled Satires

I HOPE THAT THE UTILITY of such a notion as the mingling of satiric conventions is as clear to readers now as, I think, it was to Pope and others in the 1730s. His *Epistles to Several Persons* (1731-35) show a Christian, modified, but overwhelmingly Horatian ethic; his more mingled *Fortescue* (1733) significantly increases Juvenalian and, to a lesser degree, Persian elements; his *Epistle to Dr. Arbuthnot* (1735) shows the satirist moving through time and apportioning his chronological, political, and satiric youth to Horace, and his more mature, combative, and threatened years to Juvenal and Persius. Not all of Pope's formal verse satires can profitably be read with the criterion of relatively discrete or mingled satiric conventions. *Sober Advice from Horace* (1734) an imitation of *Satires*, i. 2, for example, seems to me largely punitive, with moral and political satire as a secondary goal. Both the sixth satire of the second book of Horace and the seventh epistle of the first book are out of Pope's usual heroic couplet mode and are subject in part to Swift's form, style, and needs.

Many of the other satires, however, can be illuminated by means of the notion of "mingling," though as the term denotes, rigid lines of demarcation are difficult to find, and unlike *Arbuthnot*, in these poems one sees an ebb and flow rather than progressive use of the different modes. I suggest a spectrum with three broad areas on which the other satires and epistles may be placed, with some variations depending on the individual reader's response: the dominantly Horatian with lesser Juvenalian or Persian suggestions and devices; the substantially mingled with Horace still important, but with threats of Juvenalian and Persian invasion; and the dominantly Juvenalian and Persian, with lesser Horatian suggestions and devices. Such an overview may be helpful in meeting one of Pope's own standards for reading his poetry. On 10 February 1733 he writes to Swift saying that "my works will in one respect be like the works of Nature, much more to be liked and understood when consider'd in the relation they bear with each other, than when ignorantly look'd upon one by one."[1] Both the imitations of *Satires*, ii. 2, to Bethel, and *Epistles*, ii. 2, to the "Col'nel," fall into the more Horatian family in Pope's related satires.

I: HORATIAN DOMINANCE

Bethel (1734) stems from a general and "philosophical" satire, one aimed at reinforcing the virtues of temperance and the folly of gluttony. Pope preserves much of those tones and in some ways enhances them through his own affectionately communal world. His poem begins in a pre-prandial setting, with several friends willing to share Pope's board, wisdom, and reported principles and practice of the admired Bethel:

> What, and how great, the Virtue and the Art
> To live on little with a chearful heart,
> (A Doctrine sage, but truly none of mine)
> Lets talk, my friends, but talk before we dine.
>
> (Lines 1-4)

Bethel's following sermon is not, at first, addressed to the aberrations of a particular court or man; it is opposed to gluttony, to the human fallibility that Pope's friends shared, for even they can be turned away from "sound Philosophy" by an abundance of food and drink (lines 6-8), perhaps to be supplied by Pope's own hospitality. Bethel is aware that "Preach as I please, I doubt our curious men / Will chuse a *Pheasant* still before a *Hen*"

---

[1] *Correspondence of Alexander Pope*, ed. George Sherburn (Oxford: Clarendon Press, 1956), 3: 348. Hereafter cited as *Correspondence*.

(lines 17-18). The world will not reform itself for his sake, and it is less good today than in the past—but Bethel continues his sermon as spoken by Pope to his friends. Both speakers assume that the effort is worthwhile, that the world has enough decency, shame, or desire to arrest its decline, and that at least those in Pope's circle will wish to restrain themselves.

Bethel does not, however, advise us only to avoid gluttony, since lean-shanked avarice is no better. The golden mean "Between Excess and Famine" (line 47) is his norm, for "He knows to live, who keeps the middle state, / And neither leans on this side, nor on that" (lines 61-62). Sordid penny-pinching is well illustrated in Avidien and his wife, who not only dine like animals "on rabbits and on roots" (line 52) but regard it as an equally lucky day when they find a bank-bill or lose a financial burden—when they "heard their Son was drown'd" (line 56).

Bethel's sermon, in contrast, is resoundingly social, and urges the value of harmony within man, family, friends, and past, present, and future. Without temperance, for example, man becomes a living tomb and "one intestine war" as his "Soul subsides" (lines 72, 79). In the days of our fathers, whose values Bethel hopes to preserve, hosts were "More pleas'd to keep [rank venison] till their friends could come, / Than eat the sweetest by themselves at home" (lines 95-96). These men are remembered with pleasure now and are norms for the future, whereas Lord Fanny, less ominous here than as Sporus in *Arbuthnot*, gourmandizes as part of his reward for courtly corruption, and shall be punished with isolation and danger for body and soul.

> When Luxury has lick'd up all thy pelf,
> Curs'd by thy neighbours, thy Trustees, thy self,
> To friends, to fortune, to mankind a shame,
> Think how Posterity will treat thy name;

And buy a Rope, that future times may tell
Thou hast at least bestow'd one penny well.

(Lines 105-10)

Bethel's social values infuse Pope's own following speech and spread to those around him. Early in the poem Pope says that Bethel's sage doctrine is "truly none of mine" (line 3); about halfway through that recitation, at the praise of temperance, Pope breaks in to say about "our Friend" that "what he said I sing" (line 68). When Bethel concludes, Pope identifies himself with his prolocutor and claims that "His equal mind I copy what I can, / And as I love, would imitate the Man" (lines 131-32).

That imitation takes several forms, as Pope becomes the living model of the preserved rural, antique past. Bethel, for instance, urges "a homely dinner" (line 12); Pope is "Content with little" (line 137). Bethel warns us to be prepared should "Fortune . . . change her mind" (line 123); Pope is as happy poor as when rich, and thus "Fortune not much of humbling me can boast" (lines 133-34, 151). Bethel characterizes a better age's hospitality to friends; Pope tells us that "ancient friends, (tho' poor, or out of play) / That touch my Bell, I cannot turn away" (lines 139-40). Bethel laments the collapse of Avidien's family ties; Pope characterizes a world in which an "ungracious Son / . . . cries, my father's damn'd, and all's my own" (lines 173-74). Pope himself shows only the highest respect for the sold forest, land, and house (lines 135, 155) his father hoped to pass on.

Moreover, the knowledge that Bethel communicates to Pope is, in turn, communicated to Swift, a nonce-adversarius who replays Pope's own temporary disclaiming of wisdom. Swift wishes that Pope owned his rented house, which could be left to a son or wife (lines 162-63). Pope denies the value of illusory and easily manipulated ownership and instead urges the value of Use (line 165). Property can change; man in harmony with himself and his environment exercises genuine dominion over the self. He thus tells Swift, who does not respond, but is likely to be sympathetic, "Let Lands and Houses have what Lords they will, / Let Us be fix'd, and our own Masters still" (lines 179-80).

And so the poem ends, having made clear the dangers of intemperance, the virtues of the golden mean, the values of Bethel that move to Pope, to Swift, and to the other friends and readers assumed to be at the nourishing table. The poem's proud declaration of mastery signals the inner advantages of Horatian retirement and shows us how the values of the past are transmitted to the present. Property "Slides" (line 178); Pope, Swift, and those of us who imitate them as we can, are fixed, masters still. In the poem folly and vice are defeated in spirit if not in Law ("Tho' double-tax'd, how little have I lost?" [line 152]); we thus hear the Virtue, and see the Art of modest, temperate, and successful retired life.

Bethel also includes harsher Juvenalian satire directed at significant, named, and known sources. As one would expect, the poem abounds with unfriendly references to Sir Robert and the Hanoverian court, and includes stabs at money, trade, power, and those who enjoy such worldly pleasures. The seven uses of the word "friend" suggest the approximate Horatian and Juvenalian proportions in *Bethel*. The word appears five times in positive ways and is associated with the speakers and their values. "Lets talk, my friends" (line 4), Pope says before he introduces his rustic spokesman, whom he later calls "our Friend" (line 68) and thus includes in the circle of present guests. Bethel himself refers to "Our Fathers" who kept their venison hanging until "their friends could come" (lines 91, 95). Pope returns to the same word and association with food and hospitality when he regains the podium, and he advises that his "ancient friends (tho' poor, or out of play)" (line 139) remain welcome at his home, where all things are "my own, / And yours my friends" (lines 156-57). Bethel's and Pope's friendship is intimately associated with the poem's norms—temperance, affection, retirement, hospitality, and preservation of ancestral values.

The two other uses of the term embody negative values. If one wishes to thrive in the modern political world, why

Let me extoll a *Cat* on Oysters fed,
I'll have a Party at the *Bedford Head*,
Or ev'n to crack live *Crawfish* recommend,
I'd never doubt at Court to make a Friend.
(Lines 41-44)

Similarly, Lord Fanny will be alienated from all decent men and future fame and will be "To friends, to fortune, to mankind a shame" (line 107). The court induces false friendships, inappropriate use of food, and ultimate loneliness.

This hostility to the values and occupants of the court produces the Juvenalian undercurrent in *Bethel*, whose specificity of causation deviates from its parent poem. Pope's satire shows more of a declining world than Horace's and locates many of the vices attacked, not in the human situation or the rich in general, but in the court that mirrors Sir Robert—who was known for his generous appetite, girth, and, the opposition claimed, wealth used tastelessly and for selfish ends. Crawfish evoke a friend at court; the Wortley Montagus (Avidien and his wife) are the avaricious "dog . . . and bitch" (line 50); "a Clergy, or a City, feast" (line 76) illustrates destructive gluttony; and Lord Fanny will sacrifice reputation for "fresh Sturgeon and Ham-pye" (line 103). The poet earns his equanimity in the face of the government's double taxation, religious bigotry, standing armies, and the loss of his patrimony.

The latter point suggests one reason Pope imitated this

poem in which Horace introduces the farmer Ofellus as his spokesman. David Watson borrows Dacier's analysis and says that "This *Ofellus* was one, who being stript of his Inheritance after the Battle of Philippi, when *Augustus* distributed the Lands of *Cremona* and *Mantua* among his Veterans, was yet sensible of no Change in his Condition, because in his Abundance he had accustomed himself to a frugal abstinent Life; and by that means put himself out of the power of Fortune."[2] By analogy, Pope too was stripped of his inheritance after his side lost, and he too was penalized by his Augustus. Unlike Horace's Ofellus, Pope is willing to blame his monarch and those around him. "What's *Property?*" the man deprived of his property asks Swift. "You see it alter / From you to me, from me to Peter Walter" (lines 167-68); or it may "Become the portion of a booby Lord," or it "Slides to a Scriv'ner or a City Knight" (lines 176, 178). Even the penultimate line of the poem may allude to the land of England, and the houses of Commons and Lords whose Lord and lord-maker was Walpole, and so, "Let Lands and Houses have what Lords they will" refers not merely to property but to the corruption of the political process itself. The Horatian dominance in *Bethel* allows the poem to end with its optimistic, if withdrawn and stoical, "Let Us be fix'd, and our own Masters still." But already the displacement of the country values (here of course a political totem) with city values is taking place; already the modern physical possession of ancient homes—"Hemsley once proud Buckingham's delight" (line 177)—is removing ancient values, just as ancient literary traditions are threatened in *Arbuthnot* of 1735, and are eradicated in the *Dunciad* of 1743. Even now the speaker's triumph requires a retreat into the self and one's encircling friends because happiness is progressively more difficult to find in such a world. Horace as exemplar

---

[2] David Watson and Samuel Patrick, *The Satires, Epistles, and Art of Poetry of Horace* (1743), p. 125.

of successful retirement in a social and philosophical world in which the middle, colloquial style is fitting, nonetheless now is in a satiric world in which the unshaken mind at least feels several vibrations—as it does in Pope's imitation of Horace's second epistle of the second book in 1737.

This imitation addressed to an unknown Colonel is an epistolary poem in which the poet objects to having been asked to write an epistolary poem. Time is a great ravager, and leaves Pope all too little of itself to polish and shape his life—a matter more important than the shaping of verse. Time has another essential function—the positive one of inducing loved memories, of transmitting and, for the right person, preserving culture. Hence Pope warmly tells his Colonel that "my Father taught me from a Lad, / The better Art to know the good from bad" (lines 54-55). Both father and son refused to be defeated by religious persecution, and the son, "thanks to *Homer*," prospers and is "Indebted to no Prince or Peer alive" (lines 68-69) but only to, say, the dead Hector, Achilles, and Agamemnon. Moreover, if Pope were to write, he would please very few, and if he were to visit London he would be in danger of losing his life and poetic identity. Pope now is able to introduce a comic, satiric scene that at first mocks bad poets and his own weaknesses, and then springs into an *ars poetica* affirming the painful but godlike process of making poetry. At the end of this passage, Pope uses his own *Essay on Criticism* (1711) as an affirming link between his youthful and mature roles in the critical and poetic processes.

Town poets behave embarrassingly like Sergeants at Law, who puff one another in order to be puffed. Thus, one versifier says to another, "Yours [is] *Milton*'s Genius, and mine *Homer*'s Spirit." Even Theobald becomes Shakespeare, and Cibber, in this dialogue between mutants, transcends all the muses. Such poets "take what Names we please" (lines 136-42), Pope says, including himself in the fallible poetic condition at the beginning as at the conclu-

sion of this overheard conversation, in which he both flat-
ters and courts the mock Horaces and Drydens among
whom he is placed.

> "My dear *Tibullus!*" if that will not do,
> "Let me be *Horace*, and be *Ovid* you.
> "Or, I'm content, allow me *Dryden*'s strains,
> "And you shall rise up *Otway* for your pains."
> Much do I suffer, much, to keep in peace
> This jealous, waspish, wrong-head, rhiming Race;
> And much must flatter, if the Whim should bite
> To court applause by printing what I write:
> But let the Fit pass o'er, I'm wise enough,
> To stop my ears to their confounded stuff.
>
> (Lines 143-52)

The passage provides both its own antidote and a useful
hint regarding the genesis of that antidote. Pope can di-
vorce himself from his weaknesses if he divorces himself
from the corrupt city, its Walpolean values, and the tinsel
knighthood or peerage implied in the self-crowned poet
telling his colleague to "rise up *Otway*." That parody of
kingship and power soon finds itself acted out, with signifi-
cant differences, in the following paragraph. Now we have
not the casual making of great poets by the mouthing of
names, but severity of proceeding, strictness of judging,
and execution of offending words (lines 157-59). The
image of law metamorphoses into an image of the divine
and regal. The genuine, withdrawn poet can "In down-
right Charity revive the dead" words of the language (line
164), "Or bid the new be *English*, Ages hence, / (For Use
will father what's begot by Sense)" (lines 169-70). That
couplet recalls Pope's pleasant relationship with his peda-
gogical father, which is transformed into the relationship
of poet to his verbal offspring. The controlling poet will
"Pour the full Tide of Eloquence" and make it "divinely
strong" and "Rich with the Treasures of each foreign
Tongue" (lines 171-73). The gift of tongues is joined by the

gift of prudent cutting necessary for the poet-gardener, who will "Prune the luxuriant, the uncouth refine, / But," in a return to the poet as judge—"show no mercy to an empty line" (lines 174-75). All this artful making, judging, bidding, polishing, pruning, reviving, and waking result in a work that "You think 'tis Nature" (line 177). Pope long had known what he reminds us of by quoting a version of lines 362-63 of his *Essay on Criticism*, twenty-six years earlier: "But Ease in writing flows from Art, not Chance, / As those move easiest who have learn'd to dance" (lines 178-79).

This self-referential ploy allows Pope to show his own unified poetic and critical life, as the young man fresh from Windsor becomes an authority for the middle-aged man tired in Twickenham; it also firmly dissociates him from the poets whose self-aggrandizing fiat can make him Horace or Homer as they please. Alexander Pope is Alexander Pope still by staying away from Walpole's city and court, where poets subject Shakespeare and Milton to their own whims. Pope's normative artist subjects himself to other poets and will preserve not his personal, isolated monument, but himself as part of a handsomely continuous tradition. He will revive "Words, that wise *Bacon*, or brave *Raleigh* spake; / Or bid the new be *English*, Ages hence" (lines 168-69). The social epistle includes "Friend" as the last word of its first line; it links Pope and the Colonel, Pope and his poetic language, the living and dead, sleeping and awake, and native and foreign words; it links Pope's early and late poems; and it projects itself into "Ages hence," so that the Time Pope so feared at the beginning of the poem is transcended through art—indeed, through the poem that had to be coerced out of Pope because he did not have the time to write. The death of culture was very much on Pope's mind in 1737, but it was out of place in the genre of the dominantly Horatian epistle.

Or largely so—for this epistle is not so optimistic or so protected as the ethic epistles, in which the Horatian world

is completed and reinforced by the intrusion of a benevo-
lent Christian God. In the epistle *To Burlington* of 1731,
for example, Timon's unharmonious villa is turned to
good in the short run and is merely a temporary drought
in God's productive scheme. The poor are fed and clothed
through Timon's luxury and their labor, and

> Another age shall see the golden Ear
> Imbrown the Slope, and nod on the Parterre,
> Deep Harvests bury all his pride has plann'd,
> And laughing Ceres re-assume the land.
>
> (Lines 173-76)

In this imitation, however, Pope banishes both an intrusive
God and the consoling overview He makes possible. Pope
keeps his cherished concept of "That God of Nature, who,
within us still, / Inclines our Action, not constrains our
Will" (lines 280-81); but that God stays within. Accord-
ingly, in lines that might almost be read as an answer to
those (and others) from *Burlington* above, Pope insists that
property is temporal and is a useless support for one's ego.
The national and spiritual pleasures Ceres evokes in *Bur-
lington* are sadly lacking in the *Colonel*'s comparable
scene, which deflates man and man's works. In the Hora-
tian *Burlington* the good landlord's "plantations stretch
from down to down, / First shade a Country, and then
raise a Town" (lines 189-90); civilization advances with its
architecture. In the *Colonel*, the paths of nourishment and
civilization lead to the grave.

> Join *Cotswold* Hills to *Saperton*'s fair Dale,
>   Let rising Granaries and Temples here,
> There mingled Farms and Pyramids appear,
> Link Towns to Towns with Avenues of Oak,
> Enclose whole Downs in Walls, 'tis all a joke!
> Inexorable Death shall level all,
> And Trees, and Stones, and Farms, and Farmer fall.
>
> (Lines 257-63)

Burlington's lines are followed by "Who then shall grace, or who improve the Soil? / Who plants like BATHURST, or who builds like BOYLE" (lines 177-78). The imitation of Horace, which urges one to live decently today, sees buildings and plans—whether "Villa, Park, or Chace"—and says mournfully, "Alas, my BATHURST! What will they avail?" (lines 255-56). This section is considerably more somber than the parallel passage on Horace's facing page; it has greater precedent in the often gloomy tones of the *philosophe chagrin* Persius was thought to be, and in Juvenal's retreat from Horatian confidence in the value of a social world. The added melancholy may be induced by Walpole's corruption of London, politics, and letters; it may be part of Pope's growing awareness of the limits of his pleasures and his life and the need to "Walk sober off" (line 324); or it may have a variety of other causes. Whatever its genesis, his imitation of the second epistle of Horace's second book darkens Horace's and Pope's own earlier Horatian vision. At least two other imitations include even weightier Juvenalian and Persian qualities.

II: THE TILTING BALANCE

Pope's imitation of the sixth epistle of the first book of Horace (1737-38) turns the shadowy Numicius into the better known Murray, and a generalized poem urging sophisticated mistrust of the world into a moral imperative to avoid the attractions of, among other things, a political life that must steal one from one's better self. Reuben Brower has observed that lines 69-76 of Pope's poem connect "Pope with Dryden, whose translation of Persius he is apparently recalling."[3] This connection with Persius can be extended to much of the poem's insistence that only the inner life is reliable in the face of declining political and moral virtue. One may have genuine peace in this world,

[3] *Alexander Pope: The Poetry of Allusion* (Oxford: Clarendon Press, 1959), p. 310.

which will end all too soon in any case, by looking beyond
"Stars that rise and fall"; be philosophical, and "trust the
Ruler with his Skies" (lines 6, 8). The hint regarding stars
as political rewards, and rulers who cannot be trusted in
their own spheres, is enlarged shortly thereafter. The em-
blem of the Garter and the royal power behind it are re-
duced to the same real value as the noise of an approving
mob. Should we admire

> Popularity, or Stars and Strings?
> The Mob's applauses, or the gifts of Kings?
> Say with what eyes we ought at Courts to gaze,
> And pay the Great our homage of Amaze?
>
> (Lines 14-17)

With suspicious eyes, the poem suggests in answer to the
final question; otherwise we fall into extremes, develop an
"unbalanc'd Mind," and lose our better self (line 25), we
may infer, either to the bad of the court with its power or
to the good of the opposition, whose own virtue can be-
come overzealous and thus dangerous to one's psychic peace
(lines 26-27).

Pope highlights the court's dangerous appearance of
power as he shows the servants' ostentation of "Our Birth-
day Nobles splendid Livery" (line 33), or the illusory con-
trol of the Privy Council, the rewards of which are over-
work, indigestion, and a dubiously "noble Wife" (lines
37-39). To behave in such a way, Pope tells Murray, is to be
unfaithful to himself, for he was born "not to admire, but
be admir'd" (line 41); and is not death the end of Murray
as of other highly placed men, whether Cicero, who was
murdered by Octavian-Augustus, whom he wrongly helped
to office, or Hyde, the historian of Charles I's murder and
its consequences? Even the norms in this Horatian epistle
are found not in the court, or in the relationship between
poet and patron, but in Cornbury, a peer who rejects the
court and its fools' gold when he rejects a pension and the
bribery and degradation it implies. "Be Virtuous, and be

happy for your pains" if you follow such a man (line 63).
Very few men in this world of decline can accept such
advice. We recall the *Colonel*'s amusing use of mock-
knighthood, as poet raised up poet with an elevated name.
Murray uses a similar device but in a more ominous way,
because the title is conferred by the crown, the Garter
king of arms will distort history to produce a family, and
the only basis for such elevation is City money. In London
"A man of wealth is dubb'd a Man of worth, / Venus shall
give him Form, and Anstis Birth" (lines 81-82). Corruption
extends as well to the peerage. Now, if one wishes for
power, place, and pomp, why "hire a Slave, (or if you
will, a Lord)" (line 99) to supply all the gossip and tittle-
tattle, all the ins and outs of the court's intrigues. Horace's
epistle makes clear that should Numicius surrender to ad-
miration he will deal with the tribes and their politics and
not with the still untainted court of Augustus. Pope, how-
ever, shows that unworthiness at the heart of his Augustan
court, alludes to the purchase of votes in Cornwall, and
shows the prisoner of power also becoming a hypocrite, as
vice leads to vice. The slave, or Lord, finds a willing pupil
as he tells

> Who rules in Cornwall, or who rules in Berks;
> "This may be troublesome, is near the Chair;
> "That makes three Members, this can chuse a May'r."
> Instructed thus, you bow, embrace, protest,
> Adopt him Son, or Cozen at the least,
> Then turn about, and laugh at your own Jest.
>
> (Lines 104-9)

The penultimate paragraph moves us yet higher up the
social and government scale, associates Francis Chartres
with sexual and culinary excess that transforms one to a
beast, and probably concludes with an attack on George II
and his affair with Madame de Walmoden (as she then
was), since the king's six months of Teutonic rest and
recreation with her in 1736 were a subject of manuscript,

printed, and engraved attack.[4] The king himself thus is the poem's last example of one option in admiration associated with the court, one with no precedent in Horace, and more than enough in Persius's many perceived attacks on Nero, and Juvenal's on Nero and Domitian. Will not such a man "for a Titled Punk, or Foreign Flame, / Renounce our Country, and degrade our Name?" (lines 124-25).

The placement of this hostile outburst accounts in part both for the poem's somber and marginally reconciled tone. That is, it comes in the next to last and not the rhetorically more important last paragraph, which returns to the polished, avuncular, even confident tones that much of the rest of the poem also includes. What Warburton called Pope's "warmth of affection" for Murray motivates the poem, includes advice that he not be depressed because his lady has rejected him, sees norms like Cornbury still active and resisting corruption, and also sees Sir Robert as someone who is the creature of a moment, a meteor who is destroying himself while briefly lighting the sky.[5] "What is Fame? the Meanest have their day, / The Greatest can but blaze, and pass away" (lines 46-47), Pope says, alluding to the great man as Knight of the Blazing Star.

The poet remains powerful enough, in the poem at any

[4] See Maynard Mack, *The Garden and the City: Retirement and Politics in the Later Poetry of Pope 1731-1743* (Toronto: Univ. of Toronto Press, 1969), pp. 298-99, and pp. 213, 304. See also Mr. W—— [that is —Lorleach], *The Muff, Or, One Good Turn deserves Another; A Court Tale. Humbly Inscribed to Madame de W—lm——n* (1740).

[5] *The Works of Alexander Pope, Esq.* (1751), 4: 124n. See chapter 7, n. 18, above, for discussion of Walpole and his ornamentation. As supplements to this, see an undated attack—perhaps from the mid-1730s—with this title: *A Letter from Ibrahim Bassa, Grand Visier To the late depos'd Sultan Achmet, Who was strangled at the Demand of the People, for Male-Administration. To Don Ruperto de Poli, Knt. of the Blazing-Star, Descended in a right Line from the renown'd Don Quixote de La Mancha, and Fac-totum to the Island of Utopia. With Don Ruperto's Answer; Wherein are laid down several Rules, which if any Minister observes, he will aggrandize both Himself and his Family.* In 1742 A. B. prints *The Farce is over; or, The Plot discover'd without an Enquiry, A poem. Dedicated to the Rt. Hon. R. E. of O——d.*

rate, to control and defeat his enemy. He does so in part
by placing him on a larger chronological spectrum, by pre-
serving his own deep affection for Murray, whom he hopes
to protect, by remembering that his restless ambition is a
human problem and not peculiar to Sir Robert's world,
though Sir Robert himself may be a particular example of
the general process. Nonetheless, men's minds, unlike their
bodies, "may be cur'd, whene'er they please," and Pope can
show us how to affect that cure and why it is in our self-
interest to do so: "Would ye be blest? despise low Joys, low
Gains" and be as virtuous as Cornbury (lines 59-62)—and,
by the end of the poem, as the four other men evoked for
a concluding affirmation:

> If, after all, we must with Wilmot own,
> The Cordial Drop of Life is Love alone,
> And Swift cry wisely, "Vive la Bagatelle!"
> The Man that loves and laughs, must sure do well.
> Adieu—if this advice appear the worst,
> E'en take the Counsel which I gave you first:
> Or better Precepts if you can impart,
> Why do, I'll follow them with all my heart.
> (Lines 126-33)

Pope elegantly cleanses Rochester's *Letter from Artemi-
sia in the Town to Chloe in the Country* (1679) and plucks
out its counsel of love; he banishes Swift's *saeva indignatio*
and enshrines his laughter in its place; and he yokes them
into one better thing, so that Murray sees both love and
laughter illustrated in the speaker and the poem before
him, and then hears himself praised as having the potential
for yet better advice, which his tutor will follow with all
his heart. Murray has transcended the tempting world of
illicit admiration and become a norm in his own right.
The poem begins with Pope quoting and altering Creech
translating Horace: "Not to Admire, is all the Art I know,
/ To make men happy, and to keep them so" (lines 1-2).[6]

6 See Thomas Creech, *The Odes, Satyres, and Epistles of Horace*,
2nd ed. (1688): "Not to admire, as most are wont to do, / It is the only

That art then is enhanced by the different wisdoms of Rochester and Swift, and by the possibility of "better Precepts" from the brilliant young man Pope is complimenting. We move from versions of Horace as an authority, to Rochester and Swift singly, to Pope's combination of them, and then to Murray as projected norm and Pope as his student, not Horace's. Here, as in other places, Pope's epistolary recipient functions as a silent adversarius and suggests why Warburton called this "the most finished of all his imitations," one that produced "the supreme degree of excellence" (4:124n). That judgment is arguable, but *Murray*'s consolation, friendship, norms, verbal polish, and awareness of the human situation allow Horace temporarily to limit the Juvenalian and Persian beachhead.

The *First Epistle of the First Book of Horace Imitated* (1737) shows that beachhead extended farther. Perhaps that is one reason Pope begins his imitation with "St. John," his friend's family name rather than with his title, which had been erased from the roll of peers in 1714. Whatever the reason, Pope's address to Bolingbroke was a deliberate provocation of the court and was so regarded by its *Daily Gazetteer* and other ministerial partisans. The poet invokes not the prime minister and exemplar of court values—like Augustus's Maecenas and George II's Walpole—but a shadow minister and exemplar of opposition values. St. John is associated not with the declining "Now" in which Pope is sick, even Cibber is retiring, and generals will not, or are not allowed to, fight for the king (lines 4, 6, 7), but with the past of Pope's and the nation's prime. The conversational, Horatian tones of the first paragraph suggest a Juvenalian resistance to the court and a nostalgic celebration of the dying past, not salutary present.

Moreover, the cautious adversarius in *Fortescue* and *Arbuthnot* has been internalized and, though called Reason's

---

method that I know, / To make Men happy, and to keep 'em so" (p. 487).

whispering voice (lines 11-12), shares a great deal with earlier, vocal, external speakers. "Friend Pope! be prudent, let your Muse take breath" (line 13) could have been spoken by either of his dissuading colleagues. Indeed, Pope uncharacteristically seems to be listening to that voice rather than converting it, though the silence it urges does not come until Pope has lambasted the same enemies who are lambasted in those works as well. *Bolingbroke* includes much of this satire in its long central, political passage.

Though Wisdom's superiority and voice are clear at once—"As Gold to Silver, Virtue is to Gold" (line 78), she says—she is unheard after London's rasping demand to acquire money, "And then let Virtue follow, if she will" (line 80). Pope goes beyond his Horatian analogue when he insists on the breadth of the notion and its ecclesiastical and regal sources; it is spoken in high and low church, court and cathedral, scrivener's and treasurer's offices, and is "the saving doctrine, preach'd to all" (line 81). Within such a doctrine the worthy but poor Barnard is denied his true value, and the unworthy but rich Duke of Kent ("Bug") receives yet more rewards for his wealth and his servility.

Even Pope's affirmation functions as an attack upon what Sir Robert lacks and what he has done. To have true honor is to be sinless, innocent within and thus externally armed. Let this armor of innocence be "thy Screen, and this thy Wall of Brass; / Compar'd to this, a Minister's an Ass" (lines 95-96). What Pope calls a "new Court jargon" is contrasted with "the good old song" and "The modern language of corrupted Peers," with "what was spoke at CRESSY and POITIERS" (lines 98, 99-100). In making this contrast Pope is not only inviting us to prefer the old to the new moral language, not only adapting the Juvenalian and Persian device of praising the past at the expense of a specific government today; he is also recalling his contrast of past and now with which the poem began, and is adding another reason he must stop writing: the good counsel with which the poem abounds may be unheard over the louder words of corruption and avarice when the new banishes the old. Pope ridicules the rewards based upon getting place and wealth by any means; and he makes clear that the consequent closeness to the king is morally inferior to the distancing from "St. James's air" (line 110) that comes if one can face down "Proud Fortune, and look shallow Greatness thro' " (line 108). The court is like a lion's cave that the wise fox avoids; or, with blunt speaking more typical of Juvenal than Horace, "Adieu to Virtue if you're once a Slave: / Send her to Court, you send her to her Grave" (lines 118-19).

The court is also the grave of good example, as its pernicious values filter downward to aristocrats, new families, and the humbler working classes. London's voice, one heard in St. James's, is "Get Mony, Mony still!" (line 79). The rest of the multifarious people are "Alike in nothing but one Lust of Gold" (line 124), as the vision of greed spreads to "our mightier Misers" (line 126) seeking to plunder their own or other nations, and "The rest" (line 128) who embezzle from charities, pick pockets in church, or do a variety of other unamiable chores that, as here presented, could have appeared in Juvenal's third satire rather than Horace's facing Latin:

> Some keep Assemblies, and wou'd keep the Stews;
> Some with fat Bucks on childless Dotards fawn;
> Some win rich Widows by their Chine and Brawn;
> While with the silent growth of ten per Cent,
> In Dirt and darkness hundreds stink content.
>
> (Lines 129-33)

Sir Job, presumably a City knight of recent vintage, embodies many of these traits and suggests a difference from the Christianized Horatian ethic of *Burlington*. The knight and his lady begin to build a Palladian villa at Greenwich and just as, in words describing both the house and its occupants, "Up starts a Palace" (line 140), the couple decide to abandon the shell and live in town. Instead of invoking a benevolent God to return the land to the productive genius of the place, Pope allows the landscape to remain littered with the façade produced by thoughtless use of money. The poor "have the same itch" (line 154) and restlessly change barbers, or garrets, or places and, Pope says while again suggesting causation, "once aboard [their sculler], / Grow sick, and damn the Climate—like a Lord" (lines 159-60). The negative use of *ad exemplum regis* permeates this poem affectionately addressed to that court's enemy.

Paradoxically, however, Bolingbroke's presence at the beginning, end, and by extension throughout the poem, helps keep Horatianism alive and marginally dominant. The poem's first exclamatory couplet epitomizes the relationship between Pope and his friend: "St. John, whose love indulg'd my labours past / Matures my present, and shall bound my last!" (lines 1-2). He does not reappear until the final long paragraph and is then affectionately chided for not chiding Pope, for correcting only his external not internal slovenliness. He thus is "Kind to my dress, my figure, not to Me" (line 176). Bolingbroke "loves me, and . . . ought to mend" (line 178).

This friendship has many functions: the most obvious is the preservation of norms and positive social contact lacking in more Juvenalian efforts. St. John's values remain active and, perhaps as a result, encourage other normative voices and actions to remain active, just as the implied dialogue between Pope and his guide allows a world with dialogues of other sorts. Pope himself, for example, engages his inner Reason "that whispers in my ear" (line 11). He also moves between several sound intellectual positions and is "Sometimes a Patriot . . . / Sometimes, with Aristippus, or St. Paul," while remaining "Still true to Virtue, and as warm as true" (lines 27, 31, 30). The voice of Wisdom is strong enough at least to offer an alternative of Virtue to London's moneyed voice (lines 77-78), and there still are wise children willing to lead and to tell the court, "Virtue, brave boys! 'tis Virtue makes a King" (line 92). The "good old song" of Britain's noble past (line 98) thus remains vocal and, if not able to defeat court songsters, still is not in the angry Juvenalian key of lonely, symbolic protest before the end of civilization. So long as Bolingbroke can intrude on Pope and receive intrusion in turn, so long will there be hope and communication of hope.

Pope even uses Bolingbroke's apparent inadequacies as a subtle defense for his own satire. One who loves his friend ought to correct him and make him better than he is. Pope loves his country and, in turn, seeks to correct its abuses, not of dress or style, but of spirit, government, and conduct of mind. In so doing, Pope is adapting other Horatian devices—the use of "general" satire and the inclusion of himself and those he cares for within the scope of satire. This process begins in the poem's transitional, penultimate paragraph, which moves us from specific attacks upon the court and its influence to a more inclusive view of the human situation. Sir Job and his whiggish money, rewards, and architectural taste surrender to "am'rous Flavio," who is singled out as the first wedding guest to marry, and promptly "longs to lye alone" (lines 148-49). The court is a particular instance of human fickleness, as indeed Pope himself soon is as well. His clothing is disordered; his proud ability to move from one school of thought to another is nothing but incoherence and an "ebb and flow of follies" (line 168); his own resolutely non-court-induced building nonetheless associates him with the changeable City knight. "I plant, root up, I build, and then confound, / Turn round to square, and square again to round" (lines 169-70). The generalized aspect of the satire is made clear when Pope tells Bolingbroke that "You think this Madness but a common case" (line 172)—as it is, but like political madness nonetheless must be corrected.

And each can be corrected in at least two ways other than listening to the words of Wisdom and the clever boys.

The first is through the poetry that Bolingbroke's own pestering has induced. "Know, there are Words, and Spells, which can controll / (Between the Fits) this Fever of the soul," Pope says as he softens the Renaissance medicinal satirist and becomes a Horatian aware of meliorative, not conclusive or punitive, art. And "Know," he says again, "there are Rhymes, which (fresh and fresh apply'd) / Will cure the arrant'st Puppy of his Pride" (lines 57-60). For such a cure, "All that we ask is but a patient Ear" (line 64) and the willingness to abhor Vice, be friendly to Philosophy, and accept the *nil admirari* preached in *Bolingbroke* (lines 75-76) as in *Murray*. The court is unwilling to have patience, be such a patient, or recognize that it is ill. Pope is willing to be the doctor and patient both—but urges his friend to correct him and to help him be like Bolingbroke personally and politically. John Butt reminds us that the poem's final lines refer to Pope, not the peerless St. John (pp. 292-93n). The ambiguity must be intentional, however, for the portrait includes much of what Bolingbroke already is or has overcome. The stern but exemplary and affectionate Guide, Philosopher, and Friend embodies many of the positive values praised; he is the opposite of the negative court values blamed in the poem, and

> ought to make me (what he can, or none,)
> That Man divine whom Wisdom calls her own;
> Great without Title, without Fortune bless'd,
> Rich ev'n when plunder'd, honour'd while oppress'd,
> Lov'd without youth, and follow'd without power,
> At home tho' exil'd, free, tho' in the Tower.
> In short, that reas'ning, high, immortal Thing,
> Just less than Jove, and much above a King,
> Nay half in Heav'n . . .
>
> (Lines 179-87)

Pope is able to deflate grand aspirations already approaching comic excess, and returns to the attractive fallibility that the poem also celebrates. Hence he will attain such heights "except (what's mighty odd) / A Fit of Vapours clouds this Demi-God" (lines 187-88). Pope does not, finally, urge us to imitate the inimitable. One of the reasons that satire should "be kind, and let the wretch alone" (line 135) is that Pope recognizes he too needs a cure for his feverish and fitful soul. Accordingly, he offers these self-referential lines that tell Bolingbroke about Pope's strengths and weaknesses: "Late as it is, I put my self to school," as he clearly needs to do, "And feel some comfort, not to be a fool" (lines 47-48), as he clearly has a right to feel. No longer will he be *Fortescue's* Juvenalian warrior braving death to fight evil, or *Arbuthnot's* noble protector of Virtue, his person, family, and country. "I'll do what MEAD and CHESELDEN advise, / To keep these limbs, and to preserve these eyes" (lines 51-52). Words like *keep* and *preserve*, together with their cousins *love, Reason, true, fit, Virtue, Wisdom, school, controll, cure, Philosophy, friend,* and those in the concluding lines regarding Pope and Bolingbroke—all are as representative of this imitation as is the central attack on Walpole's court and the deliberate affront to it by replacing Maecenas with Bolingbroke. Indeed, I suggest that Horatianism here ekes out its slender victory because Bolingbroke is Pope's present model of good. Such a satiric mode includes communication between the poet and the benevolent and powerful who are positive influences; the acceptance of human weakness when it is not malicious and destructive; inclusion of oneself and one's norms in "kind" satire; an insistence that moderation, wisdom, and virtue are attainable, and that a cure is possible between fits of human folly. Several of Pope's other satires, especially his two dialogues of *One Thousand Seven Hundred and Thirty Eight,* show him tilting the balance of mingled conventions yet farther from the Horatian side, so that Juvenal, Persius, and their elevated, tragic, solemn opposition and defeated voices gain the ascendance, even in poems that seem to declare their Horatian genealogy.

III: Juvenal and Persius in Triumph and Defeat

Pope's headnote to his versifications of John Donne's second and fourth satires appears to focus on style. It quotes Horace's *Satires*, i. 10, 56-59, which asks: "as we read the writings of Lucilius, what forbids us, too, to raise the question whether it was his own genius, or whether it was the harsh nature of his themes that denied him verses more finished and easier in their flow?" For our purposes, the second question is more important than the first, since by 1735 Pope is not merely polishing rough diamonds, as he largely does in his first unpublished version of Donne's second satire in 1713. Rather, he chooses to update Donne because Lucilius is the friend of virtue characterized in Horace's first satire of the second book, and the political satirist whose attacks upon highly placed corruption in the state were protected by yet higher governors. We remember that in *Fortescue* Pope appropriates the line Horace offered to Lucilius, and labels himself "To VIRTUE ONLY and HER FRIENDS, A FRIEND" (line 121). We remember, as well, that in the 1735 Advertisement to these imitations, Pope praises Horace and especially the "much greater Freedom" of Donne for his "Indignation and Contempt" toward vice or folly in whatever station. Like these satirists, Pope himself was protected by an understanding court, for the Stuart ministry encouraged his first versification of Donne, and neither Harley nor Talbot regarded satire upon "Vicious Courts as any Reflection on those they serv'd in" (p. 3).[7]

---

[7] The original is italicized. For useful comments on these versions, see William Ayre (Edmund Curll?), *Memoirs of the Life and Writings of Alexander Pope, Esq.* (1745): "Of these two Satires which he has moderniz'd from Dr. *Donne*, we shall only say, that under that Cover he takes the Liberty to say, what without the Doctor at his Back, he would not" (2: 201). Thomas Tyers reports that "Dr. Donne . . . does not afford Mr. Pope such opportunity of entertaining satires as Horace. The copy certainly pleases us more than the original." *An Historical Rhapsody on Mr. Pope*, 2nd ed. (1783), pp. 61-62. There are less interesting comments in Warburton's and Warton's editions of Pope. The translation of Horace is from the Loeb text.

Pope thus initiates his reader into Donne's world by evoking an image of the satirist as indignant enemy of vice in what is, nonetheless, a well-ordered state. The first part of this image is consistent with the perception of Renaissance satire; the second is consistent with the opposition's perception of Queen Elizabeth as friend to liberty and freedom at home and enemy to tyrants abroad. The *Craftsman* for 22 September 1733, No. 377, for example, includes "the immortal Queen *Elizabeth*" as one of "*the English Monarchs who were most indulgent to the Liberties of the People*," and who insisted on "*the Power of* Parliament *in limiting and binding the Descent, or Inheritance of the Crown, or the Claim to it*." Donne's freedom and combativeness thus remain in Pope's versifications, where they are emblems of his opposition loyalties. Since Pope also insists on Lucilius's well-fenced world, he evokes other points of comparison or contrast: namely, that unlike Lucilius-Donne, but like Juvenal, he is exposed and persecuted by his government; like Persius, he is in a world in which a poet bemoans the collapse of poetry; yet like Horace, he maintains some control over his environment and those he satirizes, and is able to see a world well away from its death throes.

Such Horatianism is a significant but small part of "The Second Satire of Dr. *John Donne*." For instance, in Pope's second *Dialogue* of the *Epilogue to the Satires* (1738), "Vice with such Giant-strides comes on amain" (line 6), that the worst one can say about today will be untrue because it will be too moderate tomorrow. In 1735, however, and not in the 1713 version, which lacks the term, there must be "One Giant-Vice, so excellently ill" (line 4) that all others seem pitiable by contrast. The nature of that vice is still partially veiled here, as it is not in Pope's final dialogues. Similarly, this world at least preserves the façade of satiric control of one's subjects of attack. Bad poets are "hardly worth your hate" (line 12), and the many false confessors and martyrs are contemptible here and will be punished hereafter: "Ev'n those I pardon, for whose sinful sake / Schoolmen new tenements in Hell must make" (lines 41-42).

On balance, though, this versification of Donne has far more non-Horatian than Horatian satiric traits and tones. The opening lines portray a Persian world of literary decline, in which most poets are inept; several are beggars in their poems to Lords; others write because it is the mode; and yet others, "far more wretched" (line 29), steal genuine wit and turn it into literary excrement. Peter Walter is a specific instance of the decadence based on the court's example. When Peter acts on your behalf, he betrays you and lies to God and peers "Like a King's Favourite—or like a King" (line 78).

Peter's behavior is characteristic of lawyers' morality in legal matters. "These are the talents that adorn them all" (line 79), we are told about a world enclosed in its own vice. Accordingly, such men continue to acquire, "Till like the Sea, they compass all the land" and, "Then strongly fencing ill-got wealth by law" (lines 85, 93), secure their own fortune while intentionally neglecting their clients' interests. The consequences for the land as physical object and as various institutions are fatal, as old values die with old estates and landlords. Much of this key passage also appeared in Pope's versification of 1713, but it is hard to resist the temptation that he now wishes us to contrast the new world of Peter Walter—"like a King"—with the old world still possible when the lords Burlington and Bathurst were seen building in the graciously hospitable epistles addressed to them. In *Burlington*, for example, the father's land was passed to the son, who continues the symbiotic relationship between land, lord, tenant, animals, and the present and posterity, as forests "future Buildings, future Navies grow" (line 188). In the versification of Donne, we notice the loss not merely of the forest and its products, but of architecture, positive emulation, and link-ing of classes through charity. The speaker himself offers an elegiac wish that the golden mean still could exist.

> The Lands are bought; but where are to be found
> Those ancient Woods, that shaded all the ground?
> We see no new-built Palaces aspire,
> No Kitchens emulate the Vestal Fire.
> Where are those Troops of poor, that throng'd of yore
> The good old Landlord's hospitable door?
> Well, I could wish, that still in lordly domes
> Some beasts were kill'd, tho' not whole hecatombs,
> That both Extremes were banish'd from their walls,
> Carthusian Fasts, and fulsome Bacchanals;
> And all mankind might that just mean observe,
> In which none e'er could surfeit, none could starve.
>
> (Lines 109-20)

Pope must wish for, rather than actually see, such a world, because "these works are not in fashion now" and will be adopted by "no man" (lines 122, 124). The virtually norm-less world that Pope draws concludes with a return to the causation we have come to expect. Pope disingenuously claims to trust that this satire will be received "without offence" (line 125). Donne's poem hopes that "none" (line 111) would report him to the law; Pope in 1713 hopes that "no captious Fools" (line 132) will do the same; Pope in 1735 demands that "no Court-Sycophant pervert my sense" and draw his poem "Within the reach of Treason, or the Law" (lines 126, 128)—that is, either within the power of the threatening *scandalum magnatum*, or the libel laws in general, or perhaps charges of Jacobitism. The tenuous but finally positive world of *Arbuthnot* ends with the word "Heav'n"; the declining Juvenalian world of the second satire of Donne versified ends with the word "Law."

This unhappy progress continues in Pope's "The Fourth Satire of Dr. *John Donne*. . . . Versifyed," in which Pope apparently was not anchored by an earlier version in a better age, and so he was free to carry out fuller relevant implications in his original. This poem has been called "Courtiers out of Horace";[8] that useful term wants modification, for if Donne's poem is out of Horace, it is by Juvenal and, after long gestation, produced its best foal in 1735.

Both Donne and Pope borrow much of the first half of their poems from Horace's *Satires*, i. 9, in which an impertinent social climber tries to use Horace as his entrée to the court of Augustus, is rebuffed by the modest Horace, and is finally arrested for debt; Apollo helps to preserve the purity of the Via Sacra, where the action takes place. Like Donne, Pope uses this framework, presents the personal voice of the moral, beleaguered speaker, and shows him triumphant over the intruder who is ridiculed from the speaker's reasonably secure vantage, which the audience is presumed to share. In Donne, however, the satirist escapes, not when the law as agent of the gods and state arrests the Impertinent, but when he begs the ransom of a coin; in Pope, the man runs off and joins the minister's train.

Even the first half of the poem is thus limited in its Horatianism, as Pope's Impertinent, more than Donne's, is a grotesque thing out of nature, who is at home in a court "fill'd with stranger things than he" (line 181; line 152 in Donne). In a reverse of Horace's pattern, this mock-courtier is marginally "better" not worse than those he emu-

---

8 See Howard Erskine-Hill, "Courtiers out of Horace: Donne's *Satyre IV*; and Pope's *Fourth Satire of Dr. John Donne, Dean of St. Paul's Versifyed*," in *John Donne: Essays in Celebration*, ed. A. J. Smith (Methuen & Co., 1972), pp. 273-307. For other works on Pope's imitations of Donne, see Ian Jack, "Pope and 'The Weighty Bullion of Dr. Donne's Satires,' " *PMLA*, 66 (1951): 1009-22; Erskine-Hill, *Pope: Horatian Satires and Epistles* (Oxford: Oxford Univ. Press, 1964), pp. 14-17; and Peter Dixon, *The World of Pope's Satires: An Introduction to the Epistles and Imitations of Horace* (Methuen & Co., 1968), especially pp. 95-96. For further discussion of Pope's version of Donne's second satire, see Aubrey L. Williams, "What Pope Did to Donne," in *A Provision of Human Nature: Essays on Fielding and Others in Honor of Miriam Austin Locke*, ed. Donald Kay (University: Univ. of Alabama Press, 1977), pp. 111-19.

lates, and in this sense he is different from them. The contempt that we have for the hopeful courtier is transferred to the larger court, where the poet, apparently subject to the devil's promptings, has also come. That court, indeed, is bad, though in the poem not yet diabolical. Its sins are the familiar ones of pride, a tendency to *"Ill"* and negligence of good, being in debt without intending to pay, vanity, idleness, and falseness (lines 19-23). This catalogue of conventional vice and folly is magnified when the Impertinent appears in his hyperbolic splendor. Adam would not have known what to call this creature; Noah would have refused him a place in the ark; he is more monstrous than the creatures born from African sun or Egyptian mud, or even than the stuffed oddities owned by the virtuosi Sloane and Woodward. His clothing is as bizarre as his person, and his exotic combination of languages is punctuated with court civilities that are actually flattering lies. The ensuing dialogue at least suggests the Persian as well as Horatian, for in spite of its quick pacing, play of wit, and satirist's verbal triumphs, Pope the satirist is ineffectual, and the foolish Impertinent remains unpunished by the state. The mocked creature accepts insults as praise and offers insulting praise in return—"Obliging Sir! for Courts you sure were made" (line 86). Though the satirist bluntly states that "the Court show *Vice* exceeding clear" and that "None shou'd, by my Advice, learn *Virtue* there" (lines 96-97), the amazed Impertinent insists that, on the contrary, "'tis the sweetest of all earthly things / To gaze on Princes, and to talk of Kings!" (lines 100-101). Nonsense, the satirist replies, borrowing the praise of the opposition's favorite kings fortuitously supplied by Elizabethan Donne. The only way one safely speaks the truth of kings is by being a guide to the tombs "Of all our *Harries*, all our *Edwards*" (line 105), for they are dead, cannot arrest one, and actually did heroic deeds against foreign enemies. Alas, the Impertinent refuses to be educated, and "You only make the Matter worse and worse" (line 121) by trying.

In Persius's first satire the uneducable adversarius implies
that Nero's court will threaten the satire and satirist it
finds offensive; he thereby defeats his own purpose and
confirms Persius's role in opposition. Here Pope's courtier-
adversarius performs a similar job by blithely telling of
what goes on in his court and confirming Pope's hatred of
the place. These lines in the Impertinent's mouth signifi-
cantly expand those in Donne and split entirely from the
strategy in Horace. This Impertinent is correct in his diag-
noses, though he wishes to contract the disease; Horace's
is wrong and is arrested for debt. Pope's courtier knows

> Whose Place is *quarter'd out*, three Parts in four,
> And whether to a Bishop, or a Whore?
> Who, having lost his Credit, pawn'd his Rent,
> Is therefore fit to have a *Government?*
> Who in the *Secret*, deals in Stocks secure,
> And cheats th' unknowing Widow, and the Poor?
> Who makes a *Trust*, or *Charity*, a Job,
> And gets an Act of Parliament to rob?
>
> (Lines 136-43)

Though Pope is sickened, "nothing can / Silence, or hurt"
(lines 159-60) his talkative adversarius, who goes on to at-
tack Sir Robert himself, becomes a speaking *Craftsman*
who "names the *Price* for ev'ry *Office* paid" (line 162), and
hints that the court connives at Spain's piracy and Dun-
kirk's illegal continuance as a port. Of course this man
does not understand the implications of his own words and,
when the just-maligned minister appears, rushes to join
him and his strange crew. The court and its gate-crasher
thus are nearly one:

> Away he flies. He bows, and bows again;
> And close as *Umbra* joins the dirty Train.
> Not *Fannius* self more impudently near,
> When half his Nose is in his Patron's Ear.
>
> (Lines 176-79)

Like Donne before him, Pope also flies as one who is bailed out of prison—and so the minimally Horatian part of this satire ends, with the prison metaphor given to the good man, not the bad, with the Impertinent an emblem of the court, not its opposite, and the adversarius both uneducable and, on his own terms, triumphant, while the satirist is on the defensive and fears the law that once protected his satiric ancestor.

This broken-backed poem sets itself in the court in its first section, and in the court by means of a dream vision in its second section, where we see truth unobscured by the gloss of day and the mockery of the Impertinent. The opening part, through line 183, now emerges as apparent, not real, and the laughterless dream reveals all in yet more elevated and grimmer tones. The nightmare vision of the damned thus alludes to several devices used in the versification's first section. There "The Poet's Hell, its Tortures, Fiends and Flames" (line 7) were as nothing when compared to the court's torture, which forces him to pay "for all my Satires, all my Rhymes" (line 6), and ultimately— with a clear reversal of Horace—to flee in fear of the law (lines 170-73). Now, not even Dante could have beheld the "Scenes of *Envy*, *Sin*, and *Hate*" at the court (line 193). The poet himself no longer will fear "One of our Giant *Statutes*" (lines 173), but he assumes the uncompromising blunt, Juvenalian role of enemy of corruption and friend of Truth. This satirist is not punished for his satire, but is the punisher of those deserving satire.

> Base Fear becomes the Guilty, not the Free;
> Suits Tyrants, Plunderers, but suits not me.
> Shall I, the Terror of this sinful Town,
> Care, if a livery'd Lord or smile or frown?
> Who cannot flatter, and detest who can,
> Tremble before a *noble Serving-Man*?
> O my fair Mistress, Truth! Shall I quit thee,
> For huffing, braggart, puft *Nobility*?
>
> (Lines 194-201)

306

Several lines later, Pope again recalls his earlier amusing section and rejects the laughter there implied. Then, he "Ran out as fast, as one that pays his Bail, / And dreads more Actions, Hurries from a Jail" (lines 182-83). Here in his dream showing reality, he quits the room "As Men from Jayls to Execution go" (line 273), as he sees before him the picture of what the court actually is—the Seven Deadly Sins in tapestry form and a fit image of what he as mere earthly satirist is confronting. Now indeed he realizes his own weaknesses and the limits of his abilities against such massive vice. Shaking with fear, he surrenders the satiric role—certainly to Dr. John Donne on the facing page, and possibly to his colleague Dean Swift, who is willing to join Pope in lonely battle:

> *Courts* are too much for Wits so weak as mine;
> Charge them with Heav'n's Artill'ry, bold *Divine!*
> From such alone the Great Rebukes endure,
> Whose *Satyr's sacred*, and whose Rage *secure*.
> 'Tis mine to wash a few slight Stains; but theirs
> To deluge Sin, and drown a Court in Tears.
> Howe'er, what's now *Apocrypha*, my Wit,
> In time to come, may pass for *Holy Writ*.
>
> (Lines 280-87)

The versification of Donne begins with a Horatian framework already modified by the Persian and Juvenalian urgings of the Renaissance; it adds Pope's own level of attack upon the specific aberrations of Sir Robert's court. In its second part it moves to a dream vision that denies even the frantic black comedy and satirist's weaknesses of its Horatian past; it elevates the satirist to the role of fearless enemy of what he has seen and is seeing; and it concludes with a vision of evil so great that the satirist must invoke divine aid to calm his shaking body (line 279) again aware of its frailty. This poem is "out of Horace"— very far out indeed, in spite of the Horatianism it initially seems to invite.

We again see such apparent Horatianism in one of Pope's most Juvenalian poems, his *First Epistle of the Second Book of Horace, Imitated* (1737), addressed to George Augustus as Horace's letter was addressed to Caesar Augustus. I have considered that poem at length elsewhere and so shall treat it only briefly here.[9] In *To Augustus* the power of court values is so great that Pope can gain an audience with his king only by appearing to be a court sycophant and seeking patronage for dreadful modern poetry. He shows the ongoing replacement of good literary values with bad, as the taste of mobs is now the taste of lords (line 311), and the king destroys rather than protects letters and kingship. "Old Edward's Armour beams on Cibber's breast" (line 319), and the sleep of the *Dunciad* is not far away (lines 400-401).

In considering the Horatianism of particular works, I have paid special attention to the recipient of the epistle and the real or implied speakers in the poem. Dialogue, communication, preservation of norms, all are present in other, positive poems. In *To Augustus*, however, such positive values are generally from the past; the values of the present are negative and the poet himself dons an ill-fitting Horatian mask in order to write to a monarch who would not appreciate the ironic leer behind this happy modernism:

> Tho' justly Greece her eldest sons admires,
> Why should not we be wiser than our Sires?
> In ev'ry publick Virtue we excell,
> We build, we paint, we sing, we dance as well,
> And learned Athens to our Art must stoop,
> Could she behold us tumbling thro' a hoop.
>
> (Lines 43-48)

---

[9] See *Augustus Caesar in "Augustan" England: The Decline of a Classical Norm* (Princeton: Princeton Univ. Press, 1978), pp. 182-217. See also pp. 243-52, for the *Daily Gazetteer*'s response to *Augustus*, and for some of the Irish background of lines 221-24, the praise of Swift.

Pope of course rejects such tone and content, but he lacks the support of his monarch, aristocrats, or even a powerful opposition figure. Overwhelmingly, the court controls the voices in *To Augustus*, in some cases even voices that talk of poetry. The clever boys in *Bolingbroke* spoke about how Virtue makes a king. Now, "What Boy but hears the sayings of old Ben?" (line 80). All full-grown critics seem to offer mindless commonplaces regarding Jonson's art, Shakespeare's nature, and the dubious virtues of contemporaries, so that the audience also sees only what the "pretenders to Criticism," as Pope calls them (p. 201n), wish them to see in an age where the king's own poet is Colley Cibber: "These, only these, support the crouded stage, / From eldest Heywood, down to Cibber's age" (lines 87-88). When Pope wishes to show a poet's utility for the state—that is, for the minister's court—he allows his speaker to trivialize his art and use it for teaching children songs and foreigners (like George II?) the language. At another time, he praises the unfortunate psalms of Sternhold and Hopkins (lines 230-40). When he breaks out of that misguided role, however, he immediately becomes bluntly hostile and invites us to see that Horace's facing page is blank:

> I scarce can think him such a worthless thing,
> Unless he praise some monster of a King,
> Or Virtue, or Religion turn to sport,
> To please a lewd, or un-believing Court.
>
> (Lines 209-12)

In this poem Pope is utterly distanced from both the person and the age he is addressing. Today, "(excuse some Courtly stains) / No whiter page than Addison remains" (lines 215-16). Addison died in 1719, and Swift, the more genuine norm, is praised for his opposition activities, especially in the *Drapier's Letters* of 1724: "The Rights a Court

---

Malcolm Kelsall also discusses "Augustus and Pope" and the fragment *One Thousand Seven Hundred and Forty*, in *Huntington Library Quarterly*, 39 (1976): 117-31.

attack'd, a Poet sav'd" (line 224). Pope could not have
been surprised that the Privy Council considered this line
actionable but "passed it by," as Alderman Barber told
Swift, and as John Butt reminds us, because the Drapier
wrote "in the late King's time" (p. 213n). Did the court
recognize that the isolated voice can be annoying rather
than politically dangerous? If so, it had also recognized one
of Pope's essential Juvenalian traits—the role of indignant
satirist who praises the past and lingering friendships now,
because so much of the public present induces outrage.
Pope must deal only with the shell of greatness, with, in an
obvious pun, "The Forms august of King, or conqu'ring
Chief" (line 391), and has no one in power to praise. "Oh!
could I mount on the Maeonian wing, / Your Arms, your
Actions, your Repose to sing!" (lines 394-95). *To Augustus*
is an epistle sent to the Dead Letter Office, though none-
theless someone was there to open and read it, as several
Gazetteer responses and the publicizing of select bits of
Privy Council discussion indicate.

One of those readers was the "Friend," an "impertinent
Censurer" (p. 297n) and exemplar of Walpole's political
and literary values in the two dialogues called *One Thou-
sand Seven Hundred and Thirty Eight . . . Something like
Horace.* These parents of other jeremiads whose spelled-
out year serves as a title, later were renamed the *Epilogue
to the Satires,* and with good reason, for they are the last of
Pope's formal verse satires; they carry his Juvenalian and
Persian mode to its farthest limit.[10] He substitutes the

[10] If not in fact, certainly in spirit, Pope's poem is the direct ancestor
of the satiric annual. This subspecies of formal verse satire deserves
study. Though it exists throughout the century, here are a few of its
earlier exemplars: [Bezaleel Morrice], *The Present Corruption of Brit-
ons; Being a Paraphrase On the Latter Part of Mr. P—E's first Dia-
logue, Entitled One Thousand Seven Hundred Thirty-eight* [1738];
[Thomas Newcomb], *A Supplement to One Thousand Seven Hundred
Thirty-eight. Not Written by Mr. Pope* (1738); *A Dialogue on One
Thousand Seven Hundred and Thirty-eight: Together with a Pro-
phetic Postscript As To One Thousand Seven Hundred and Thirty-*

harsh, unvaried, court voice for the benevolent, or prudent, or unspoken but implicitly sympathetic voice in all but the versifications of Donne and *To Augustus*.

Both displacement of good by bad values and reversal of roles are made clear at once in the first dialogue: the hostile Friend, rather than Pope, begins the poem, places Pope on the defensive, uses the court to determine aesthetic and satiric norms, and tries to make him the adversarius in need of conversion to the proper point of view. The Friend harshly says about Pope what in other places Pope tolerantly said of himself—as in the *Colonel*, where he admits that "There is a time when Poets will grow dull" (line 200). Now, the Friend says, "Decay of Parts, alas! we all must feel," and adds, "Why now, this moment, don't I see you steal?" from Horace (lines 5-6), who is both superior to and different from Pope. The court Friend claims that Pope is "too *Moral* for a Wit" (line 4); he thus is too moral to be associated with Horace and the court. The subsequent portrait of Horace is consistent with administration and opposition beliefs, and distances Pope from the author whom this dialogue is supposed to be *"Something like"*:

But *Horace*, Sir, was delicate, was nice;
Bubo observes, he lash'd no sort of *Vice*;
Horace would say, Sir Billy *serv'd the Crown*,
Blunt *could do Bus'ness*, H——ggins *knew the Town*,
In *Sappho* touch the *Failing of the Sex*,
In rev'rend Bishops note some *small Neglects*,
And own, the *Spaniard* did a *waggish thing*,
Who cropt our Ears, and sent them to the King.

---

nine (1738); *Seventeen Hundred and Thirty-nine. Or, The Modern P——s* (1739); *One Thousand Seven Hundred Thirty-Nine. A Rhapsody. By way of Sequel to Seventeen Hundred Thirty Eight: By Mr. Pope* (1740) ; [James Miller], *The Year Forty-One. Carmen Secularae* (1741); *Discord, or, One Thousand Seven Hundred Forty Four. By a Great Poet lately deceased* [1744]; *One Thousand, Seven Hundred, and Forty Five. A Satire-Epistle; After the Manner of Mr. Pope* (1746).

POPE: OVERVIEW OF MINGLED SATIRES

His sly, polite, insinuating stile
Could please at Court, and make AUGUSTUS smile:
An artful Manager, that crept between
His Friend and Shame, and was a kind of *Screen*.

(Lines 11-22)

Pope's alienation from the ideal Augustan poet is clear in
the contrast between line 2, where "the Court see nothing
in" Pope's satire, and line 20, where Horace "Could please
at Court, and make AUGUSTUS smile." Similarly, the *nil
admirari* preached in *Murray* and *Bolingbroke* is replaced
by the Friend's petulant query regarding the use of Pope's
reforming verse: "where's the Glory? 'twill be only thought
/ The Great man never offer'd you a Groat" (lines 25-26).

Pope is able to reply after twenty-seven and one-half
lines of court propaganda, and immediately begins to di-
vorce himself from it. The changed adversarial relationship
here is illustrated when we recall the end of *Fortescue*,
where Pope fantasizes that his "grave *Epistles*, bringing
Vice to light" (line 151) are "Such as Sir *Robert* would
approve," to which Fortescue says, in the same line, while
abandoning all objections, "Indeed?" (line 153). Five
years later Pope had learned better, and when the Friend
tells him to "Go see Sir ROBERT—" he completes his line
with a grumbling incantation and disclaimer: "See Sir
ROBERT!—hum—" (line 27). Pope is the one whose mind
must be changed, but unlike his attorney in 1733, he does
not surrender his own values upon mention of ministerial
power. Instead, he withdraws yet farther from Walpole's
court life and, we soon realize, demonstrates the wisdom of
nil admirari. Sir Robert, the fountainhead of power, is
happier in his social than public role, where he is encum-
bered with bribe seekers whom he dares not laugh at, and
where he must be artful and regard everyone as having his
price. Pope suggests his own moral isolation in such a
world when he asks the Friend: "Would he oblige me? let
me only find, / He does not think me what he thinks man-
kind" (lines 33-34).

The Friend, however, is content and urges Pope to ac-
commodate himself by satirizing many of the norms in his
other poems—the *Bible*, honesty, independent Whigs,
Patriots, and friends. In this reversal of roles, the Friend
also assumes the pose of ineffectual satirist that Pope occa-
sionally struck in *Fortescue* and *Arbuthnot*. These targets
"nothing hurts; they keep their Fashion still, / And wear
their strange old Virtue as they will" (lines 43-44). In fact,
he continues, dominating the dialogue and replacing Pope
as the defender and definer of satire, laugh at your friends,
not "at Fools or Foes; / These you but anger, and you
mend not those" (lines 53-54). According to the Friend's
apologia, court-sanctioned satire is as benevolently tooth-
less for the vicious, whom it should comfort, as hostile to
the virtuous, who are disturbers of the peace and should
be attacked. For example, after telling Pope to redouble
his hostile laughter at friends, the impertinent censurer of-
fers this administration *ars satirica*:

> To Vice and Folly to confine the jest,
> Sets half the World, God knows, against the rest;
> Did not the Sneer of More impartial men
> At Sense and Virtue, balance all agen.
> Judicious Wits spread wide the Ridicule,
> And charitably comfort Knave and Fool.
>
> (Lines 57-62)

Pope now appears to surrender the moderate and aloof
tones of his first reply and to blend his voice with the
Friend's. His first act as converted adversarius is to apolo-
gize for being so dense: "Dear Sir, forgive the Prejudice of
Youth: / Adieu Distinction, Satire, Warmth, and Truth!"
(line 64). The sedated part he plays demands kindness to
several of the men and values he has been scolded for
scolding. "Come . . . / Come . . . / O come" (lines 65, 66,
73), he says to "harmless *Characters* . . . / *Henley*'s Oratory,
Osborn's Wit!" (lines 65-66) and the like. Here indeed we
have matter that Sir Robert would approve and here in-

deed we have permission to write satire so benign that Pope might "sing without the least Offence, / And all I sung should be the *Nation's Sense*" (lines 77-78). Nonetheless, the converted Pope seems to lack full faith in ministerial infallibility; he is wholly aware of the consequences for his art, his nation, and perhaps for his soul, for though his new pose may be legally innocent, it is morally corrupt:

> So—Satire is no more—I feel it die—
> No *Gazeteer* more innocent than I!
> And let, a God's-name, ev'ry Fool and Knave
> Be grac'd thro' Life, and flatter'd in his Grave.
>
> (Lines 83-86)

The Friend is a patient proselytizer; he both corrects Pope's scruples and uses Pope's word "grac'd" for his own definition of satire and what should become of those not satirized. Specifically, Pope may satirize "the Greatest—in Disgrace" and "exactly when they fall" (lines 88, 90). This notion of one's personal relations is of course foreign to Pope's esteem for "Chiefs, out of War, and Statesmen, out of Place" in *Fortescue* (line 126). Since "the Greatest" may also refer to Walpole, however, Pope's Friend characterizes himself as his benefactor's potential predator, and thus as more of an enemy to that great man than Pope, who, we are to believe, satirizes in order to reform the minister. In the meanwhile, though, Pope must also learn whom not to satirize—those in power, and those therefore raised to the height of royal, ministerial, and by extension heretical divine power, so that all past pains and sins are forgotten in the world of saintly grace borrowed in part from Isaiah 25:8. Satire has no function in the putative spiritual world in which several forms of humanity are banished,

> where no Father's, Brother's, Friend's Disgrace
> Once break their Rest, or stir them from their Place;
> But past the Sense of human Miseries,
> All Tears are wip'd for ever from all Eyes;

No Cheek is known to blush, no Heart to throb,
Save when they lose a Question, or a Job.

(Lines 99-104)

Pope as temporarily corrigible adversarius answers, "Good
Heav'n forbid, that I should blast their Glory" (line 105);
but his itch to satirize and his concepts of *ad exemplum
regis* and a hierarchical structure of society remain alive,
and these allow him to use one of Swift's most effective and
complex devices, the rapid shifting of masks. Pope alter-
nately wears the mask of court devotee, as in the line just
quoted, and his own "mask" of outrage at the spreading
of vice. He saps and demolishes the Friend's presumably
secure ground, even while appearing to accept his assump-
tions regarding government and satire. In so doing, Pope
offers one of the two most strident outbursts in all of his
poetry, and looks back to and rejects the Horatian norm
of polite satire that pleases the Augustan court. So far from
being the screening political Manager for Walpole, Pope
is the indignant Juvenalian-Persian satirist who focuses his
theory of causation on the throne and court; and he
thereby answers and escapes from the Friend's narrow con-
fines of ministerially approved satire that knows "its Time
and Place" (line 87).

In the Horatian epistle to Bathurst, Pope made clear
that Virtue was not an empty word. Now, Virtue is both
"an empty boast" (line 113) and is sadly democratic, since
it "may chuse the high or low Degree" (line 137), either
a monk or, even, a king. The case is altered for Vice, how-
ever, and provides the basis for Pope's anger. Vice is the
special province of the great, of the king, minister, and
highest aristocrats: "*Vice* is undone, if she forgets her
Birth" (line 141). If the nation is to preserve its stability,
social privileges must be protected and the throne cleansed
of the emulation of riffraff. "Shall the Dignity of *Vice* be
lost?" (line 114).[11] Here is the voice of the court's new pro-

---

[11] Pope's state of mind regarding "Vice" is well recorded in this
poem and in his correspondence. On 6 July 1738 he writes to Ralph

POPE: OVERVIEW OF MINGLED SATIRES

tector, the man the Friend has weaned away from the morality of a Wit.

> Ye Gods! shall *Cibber*'s Son, without rebuke
> Swear like a Lord? or a *Rich* out-whore a Duke?
> A Fav'rite's *Porter* with his Master vie,
> Be brib'd as often, and as often lie?
> Shall *Ward* draw Contracts with a Statesman's skill?
> Or *Japhet* pocket, like his Grace, a Will?
>
> (Lines 115-20)

Pope claims to be the censurer's ally and stoutly insists, "This, this, my friend, I cannot, must not bear; / Vice thus abus'd, demands a Nation's care" (lines 127-28). "What's more, diabolical Vice has fallen from the angels "to the Dregs of Earth" (line 142) and, instead of being left in the filth she deserves, is embraced by "*Greatness* . . . and she's mean no more" (line 144). How unaccountable for the great man to violate the social hierarchy he should protect! The results are serious, for so many other dregs wish to be corrupt, corrupted, and protected by the great, that "All, all look up, with reverential Awe, / On Crimes that 'scape, or triumph o'er the Law" (lines 167-68). The great thus are

---

Allen: "I can but Skirmish, & maintain a flying Fight with Vice; its Forces augment, and will drive me off the Stage, before I shall see the Effects complete, either of Divine Providence or Vengeance: for sure we can be quite saved only by the One, or punished by the other: The condition of Morality is so desperate, as to be above all Human Hands." *Correspondence*, 4: 109. As numerous administration responses make clear—the *Daily Gazetteer* for 26 May 1738, in chapter 5, section II, above, is one—Pope's view was not universally accepted. It was indeed regarded as "carried to excess" and as one of the "groundless . . . prognostications of poets" by Joseph Warton. See his *Essay on the Genius and Writings of Pope* (1756), 5th ed. (1806), 1: 352. For a useful discussion of Virtue under attack in Pope's satires, see Paul Gabriner. "Pope's 'Virtue' and the Events of 1738," *Scripta Hierosolymitana*, 25 (1973): 96-119, and for further discussion of Vice, see Vincent Caretta, "Two More Analogues to Pope's Vice Triumphant," *Modern Philology*, 77 (1979): 56-57.

proper targets for satire because they are accomplices in their own degradation, and they must be protected from themselves or the "thronging Millions" (line 157) will demand the same pleasures of Vice that the great deservedly claim as their own. The process already is so far advanced that "Nothing is Sacred now but Villany" (line 170), and Pope's job as satirist who protects the court is painfully difficult.

So one voice proclaims, at any rate, without fooling any reader from Twickenham's grotto to St. James's drawing rooms, for this fervent passage is transparent in its veiled attacks on the court. Pope's "own" voice proclaims that "Avarice in Kings" (line 110) leads to the same trait throughout the nation and political persuasions: "In Soldier, Churchman, Patriot, Man in Pow'r, / 'Tis Av'rice all, Ambition is no more!" (lines 161-62). Dennis Bond and Peter Walter embezzle and cheat because they "pay their Debts or keep their Faith like Kings" (lines 122-23). The first minister is one step below the throne, and reflects and enlarges its doleful influence. Molly Skerrett, Walpole's mistress, and the woman who later would be the Countess of Orford, is protected and elevated by Sir Robert and made the reincarnation of the scarlet whore of Babylon, diabolical Vice itself, and perhaps a Roman imperator leading conquered enemies in triumph; but here the conquered enemies are Virtue in general, English past virtue in particular, and English institutions. As Sir Robert's whore, she is praised at court, blessed by bishops, has money to bribe churchmen and judges, sets a model of corruption for the nation, and destroys resistance to her vicious ways:

> Lo! at the Wheels of her Triumphal Car,
> Old *England*'s Genius, rough with many a Scar,
> Dragg'd in the Dust! his Arms hang idly round,
> His Flag inverted trails along the ground!
> Our Youth, all liv'ry'd o'er with foreign Gold,

Before her dance; behind her crawl the Old![12]

(Lines 151-56)

This dialogue, ancestor of a moral *Dunciad*, shows that "All, all look up" with reverence "On Crimes that scape, or triumph o'er the Law" (lines 167-68). Even the "Triumphal Car" (line 151) of exalted Vice finds itself reproduced in triumphal crime (line 168), while all positive values—"Truth, Worth, Wisdom"—are decried; Villainy is overtly sacred, as in the Friend's portrait of specific court beatification (lines 91-104) it was overtly villainous. We hardly could be further from the social, corrigible, or tolerable and norm-filled world of competent governors in Horace's satires and epistles, and even, in varying degrees, in Pope's. Reuben Brower has remarked that in Horace's poems one does not often sense a man on the attack.[13] In

[12] For discussion of Molly Skerrett, see James M. Osborn, "Pope, the Byzantine Empress, and Walpole's Whore," *Review of English Studies*, n.s. 6 (1955): 372-82. For other contemporary attacks on her, see *The Rival Wives. Or, the Greeting of Clarissa to Skirra in the Elysian Shades* (1738), and the yet harsher *Modern Quality. An Epistle to Miss M—W— On Her Late Acquired Honour. From a Lady of Real Quality* (1742). The poet urges that the "truly *Great* / Will scorn the sullied *St—r* and *C——t*." These are the rewards of Corruption "while *Freedom* starves." The author sadly concludes: "*Ruin* the Nation, if you would be *Great*; / You see which way you will an *E—ld—m* get" (p. 5). The Reverend George Lumley of Merton College, Oxford, writes a happier poem that celebrates Sir Robert's union with Molly Skerrett, but which easily could be mockery, and certainly would have angered Pope and the opposition. See *The Greatest Statesman and the Happiest Fair, A Pastoral Humbly Inscribed to The Right Honourable the Lady Walpole* (1738). Molly is courted and, finally, won by her languishing lover, who previously had "In BRITAIN'S WELFARE spent the live-long Day," but now "PEERLESS SKERRETT did his Passion move." Hence

> Thus each consenting, they in *Marriage Bands*,
> Did jointly pledge their *willing Hearts* and *Hands*;
> The KING, the NOBLES, COMMONS, ALL approve
> Their HAPPY NUPTIALS, and their HEAV'N-BORN LOVE.
>
> (P. 8)

[13] *Alexander Pope: The Poetry of Allusion*, p. 183. Peter Dixon offers some useful contrasts between such a Horatian satirist and Pope's later pose. See *The World of Pope's Satires*, pp. 202-4.

this first *Dialogue* of the *Epilogue to the Satires* Pope at-
tacks with the courage of despair, looks back at the heart of
darkness he has shown, and perhaps like Juvenal's indig-
nant Umbricius or Milton's more noble Abdiel, says: "Yet
may this Verse (if such a Verse remain) / Show there was
one who held it in disdain" (lines 171-72).

The protesting verse lasts for at least two months more
in 1738, when the same speakers reappear in the poem's
second *Dialogue*, which again is initiated by the Friend
oblivious to the moral basis of Pope's argument. He even
suggests that the court's reader of dubious publications
will seek legal action: " 'Tis all a Libel—*Paxton* (Sir)
will say" (line 1). Pope's tack in this poem, however, is
different from that in the more defensive first dialogue;
now he becomes overtly aggressive and confident, reduces
the Friend's role, and discredits him in several ways.
Forced to attack only in general rather than specific terms,
Pope orates against "Rev'rend Atheists." The exchange
that follows demonstrates the Friend's inability to accept
in practice his own theory of satire—and if he cannot,
surely Pope cannot. It also shows that he is inconsistent
and, like the court he represents, impossible to please:

Ye Rev'rend Atheists!—F. Scandal! name them, Who?
   P. Why that's the thing you bid me not to do.
Who starv'd a Sister, who forswore a Debt,
I never nam'd—the Town's enquiring yet.
The pois'ning Dame—*Fr.* You mean—*P.* I don't.
   Fr. You do.
   P. See! now I keep the Secret, and not you.
The bribing Statesman—*Fr.* Hold! too high you go.
   P. The brib'd Elector—*Fr.* There you stoop too low.
   P. I fain wou'd please you, if I knew with what.

                                     (Lines 18-26)

The contrast between the educable and uneducable adver-
sarius is striking and accounts for much of Pope's anger
and frustration when he cannot engage in rational dis-

course in a rational world. "Must Satire, then, nor *rise*, nor *fall?*" he asks. "Yes," the Friend responds, "strike that *Wild*, I'll justify the blow. / P. Strike? Why the man was hang'd ten years ago" (lines 52-55). Counselor Fortescue agrees that Pope's satire may have been morally justified but was legally tenuous; physician Arbuthnot becomes a satirist himself when his patient characterizes a sick world; the impertinent censuring Friend will not change in the face of sound reasons for change.

Indeed, as we read this *Dialogue*, we suspect that Pope, consistent with his letter to Swift on 10 February 1733, is inviting us to consider the relation it bears to several aspects of his other satires as well. The most obvious relation, we have seen, is to the first *Dialogue*, which includes actors, issues, and some lines repeated here. In the first poem, Pope claims that he is silent regarding "Who starves a Sister, or forswears a Debt" (line 112); in the second he offers the same line, as an example of his general satire— nonetheless unappreciated by the court. In the first poem the Friend tells him to "charitably comfort Knave and Fool" (line 62); in the second Pope rejects this advice with, "better sure it Charity becomes / To tax Directors, who (thank God) have Plums" (lines 48-49). In the first poem the Friend says, "You still may lash the Greatest— in Disgrace" (line 88); in the second, Pope asks, also recalling *Fortescue* and his frequent praise of Bolingbroke, does the court remove a worthy man? "That instant, I declare, he has my Love: / I shun his Zenith, court his mild Decline" (lines 75-76)—and follows with celebration of dead or rejected grandees. The first poem shows millions of all classes seeking to be defiled by Avarice; the second offers Pope's regrets that he never "Din'd with the MAN of ROSS" (*Bathurst*) or Sir John Barnard (line 99), also praised in *Bolingbroke* (line 85) and victimized by the court.

Norms in earlier poems also reappear in this *Dialogue*— Cobham, Lyttelton, and Bolingbroke, for example (lines 130-32 and others in lines 77-93). In the first poem the

Friend draws a scene in which court flunkies are "Silent
and soft, as Saints remove to Heav'n," are aided by a
"ministerial Wing," and are placed "for ever near a King!"
(lines 93-96); in the second, Pope despises "All that makes
Saints of Queens, and Gods of Kings" (line 225). In *Ar-
buthnot*, the ineffectual satirist complains, "Who shames a
Scribler? break one cobweb thro' / He spins the slight,
self-pleasing thread anew" (lines 89-90); here he threatens
the "tinsel Insects" (line 220) of the court—"Spin all your
Cobwebs o'er the Eye of Day! / The Muse's wing shall
brush you all away" (lines 222-23). There are other signs
of such relation of poem to poem, but only one more need
be mentioned here, and is immediately relevant to the anti-
Horatian quality of the *Epilogue* itself. We recall that in
the first *Dialogue* Horace was the writer of innocuous court
satire, the screener of vice and shame, and thus "Could
please at Court, and make Augustus smile" (line 20). In
the second *Dialogue* Pope both attacks and grudgingly
praises Virgil: "To *Cato*, *Virgil* pay'd one honest line"
(line 120). That line—in praise of the republican Cato
Uticensis, Pope then thought (and later changed his mind)
—was the one honest line in all of the *Aeneid*, a political
poem in support of Augustus by an author who, Pope tells
Spence, was "as slavish a writer as any of the gazetteers."[14]
Each poem rejects a distinguished Augustan author who
supported the usurping tyrant, and each is resolutely Juve-
nalian and Persian in its hostility to its own tyrant.

The second *Dialogue*, I believe, also asserts its satiric
allegiance by both beginning and ending with allusions to
Juvenal. Pope claims that his harsh poem is not a libel be-
cause it is true, but that unless he prints at once it will be
a libel because "better" not worse than the increasingly
criminal acts he describes around him:

[14] *Joseph Spence: Observations, Anecdotes, and Characters of Books
and Men: Collected from Conversation*, ed. James M. Osborn (Oxford:
Clarendon Press, 1966), 1: 299-30.

How shou'd I fret, to mangle ev'ry line,
In rev'rence to the Sins of *Thirty-nine*!
Vice with such Giant-strides comes on amain,
Invention strives to be before in vain;
Feign what I will, and paint it e'er so strong,
Some rising Genius sins up to my Song.

(Lines 4-9)

This insistence upon the literal truth of the apparently
farfetched recalls a comparable device near the end of
Juvenal's sixth satire, in which the example of the imperial
family provides a model for the decay of the Roman fam-
ily. Wealthy adopted stepsons had better be careful, since
their nourishing food may be poisoned by an avaricious
mother. Juvenal anticipates the incredulity in his audience
and tells us not to think that he is abandoning satiric for
tragic conventions; everything he says is not merely prov-
able but even minor in comparison with a documented
case, as Dryden's version tells us:

You think this feign'd; the Satyr in a Rage
Struts in the Buskins, of the Tragick Stage;
Forgets his Bus'ness is to Laugh and Bite;
And will, of Deaths, and dire Revenges Write.
Wou'd it were all a Fable, that you Read;
But *Drymon*'s Wife pleads Guilty to the Deed,
I, (she confesses,) in the Fact was caught;
Two Sons dispatching, at one deadly Draught.
What, Two, Two Sons, thou Viper, in one day?
Yes, sev'n, she cries, if sev'n were in my way.
Medea's Legend is no more a Lye;
Our Age adds Credit to Antiquity.[15]

Similarly, at the end of the second *Dialogue* Pope is at
his most isolated, insists that he holds "the last Pen for

[15] See The Works of John Dryden, vol. 4, *Poems 1693-1696*, ed. A. B.
Chambers, William Frost, Vinton A. Dearing (Berkeley and Los An-
geles: Univ. of California Press, 1974), p. 199, lines 828-39; Juvenal,
lines 634-44.

Freedom" (line 248), and hopes to praise the "Last of *Britons!*" (line 250). "Are none, none living? let me praise the Dead" (line 251). Now compare Dryden's translation of lines 170-71 of Juvenal's first satire: "Since none the Living-Villains dare implead, / Arraign them in the Persons of the Dead."[16] Juvenal arraigns the dead because it is unsafe to attack their living heirs; Pope praises the dead because he cannot praise their living heirs. The genre of formal verse satire requires praise that is the opposite of the vice attacked. In a world of such decline, it is not hard to predict where Pope's next satires would lead—either to the different genre of apocalyptic satire, as in the fourth book of the *Dunciad,* or to the silence suggested in the final note to the *Epilogue* as it appeared in 1751:

> This was the last poem of the kind printed by our author, with a resolution to publish no more; but to enter thus, in the most plain and solemn manner he could, a sort of PROTEST against that insuperable corruption and depravity of manners, which he had been so unhappy as to live to see. Could he have hoped to have amended any, he had continued those attacks; but bad men were grown so shameless and so powerful, that Ridicule was become as unsafe as it was ineffectual. (P. 327n)

Pope's fragmentary *One Thousand Seven Hundred and Forty* thus includes this bitter couplet: "The Plague is on thee, Britain, and who tries / To save thee in th' infectious office *dies*" (lines 75-76). In that poem the only hope is Frederick, Prince of Wales, and like his satiric praiser, he too is "alone, . . . alone" (lines 85, 89), and if "unministered" (line 89) may be able to offer "one man's honesty [to] redeem the land" (line 98).

This self-conscious Christological function had in fact been Pope's in 1738 and was of course as ineffectual then as it was for Frederick, who died in the same year (1751)

---

[16] *Poems 1693-1696*, p. 107, lines 257-58.

that Warburton's great edition of Pope appeared. Pope's eloquent defense of his satire includes a projection of his saving role not merely onto all of Britain but onto all humanity, as the transformation of *I* and *mine* suggests:

> Ask you what Provocation I have had?
> The strong Antipathy of Good to Bad.
> When Truth or Virtue an Affront endures,
> Th' Affront is mine, my Friend, and should be yours.
> Mine, as a Foe profess'd to false Pretence,
> Who think a Coxcomb's Honour like his Sense;
> Mine, as a Friend to ev'ry worthy mind;
> And mine as Man, who feel for all mankind.
>
> (Lines 197-204)

The expansion of sympathy signals two other important aspects of the *Dialogue*: Pope needs to feel for all because, he claims, no one else will, certainly not the court and its friends; as a corollary, he must seek support not in this but the next world, where "Distinction, Satire, Warmth, and Truth" (*Dialogue* 1, line 64) already had gone. The last forty-odd lines of the poem thus accumulate several references to the Divine, which functions not, as in the Horatian *Bathurst* or *Burlington*, in order to protect the world's decent sublunary tenants, but to punish the vicious and hollow inhabitants of modern Britain. Hence we hear about satire as Pope's "sacred Weapon," given to his "Heav'n-directed hands" and guided by "the Gods" (lines 212, 214, 215). Pope himself is "Rev'rent" (line 216) and opposes "All that makes Saints of Queens, and Gods of Kings" (line 225). Many of these uses of divine authority are combined and expanded in a paragraph that answers the Friend's sanctification scene in the first *Dialogue*. Sycophantic poets may uselessly overpraise monarchs and nations which history will judge harshly. Pope's role and results are different:

> Not so, when diadem'd with Rays divine,
> Touch'd with the Flame that breaks from Virtue's
> shrine,

Her Priestess Muse forbids the Good to dye,
And ope's the Temple of Eternity;
There other *Trophies* deck the truly Brave,
Than such as *Anstis* casts into the Grave;

. . . .

Let Envy howl while Heav'n's whole Chorus sings,
And bark at Honour not confer'd by Kings;
Let Flatt'ry sickening see the Incense rise,
Sweet to the World, and grateful to the Skies:
Truth guards the Poet, sanctifies the line,
And makes Immortal, Verse as mean as mine.

(Lines 232-37; 242-47)

As the final note to this poem suggests—one probably based on threats in the *Gazetteer* and elsewhere[17]—Pope needed the feeble protection of Truth and Virtue, since he was getting none from other sources, certainly not from the court, a presumed center of value. And here is where the *Epilogue*'s last couplet firmly links this poem to Persius and his first satire. After the noble concluding harangue of the first dialogue, the Friend says that the administration will think it a mere libel. At the end of this dialogue and its more noble relationship of opposition satire with Virtue, Heaven, and Truth, the Friend says, "Alas! alas! pray end what you began, / And write next winter more *Essays on Man*" (lines 254-55). Pope may as well have been speaking to a rock as to this man, who still wishes only optimistic, cosmic poems that deal with general issues in general terms. The Friend wishes Pope to deny the development of his career as a satirist, to banish the mingled and especially the heavily Juvenalian-Persian qualities of his final poems. In the process, the Friend confirms the need for the kind

[17] See, especially, the *Gazetteer* for 16 July and for 27 October 1738, and other hostile works cited in chapter 5, section II, above. As early as 18 March 1733 Pope—more bravely because earlier in the battle?—tells Fortescue that "[I] hope I shall have long life, because I am much threaten'd." *Correspondence*, 3: 357.

of satire Pope is writing by confirming ministerial power, and the Friend's uncomprehending sensibility, one analogous to that of the Monitor in Persius's first satire.

Pope surely was capable of using satiric devices without awareness of precedent; but one major point of this book has been that he came to know himself by knowing others, that the breadth of his vision allowed him to incorporate the usable satiric past into his own present body of work so that he could be *"Something like Horace"* in these dialogues that employ rapid-fire witty exchange, very much like Juvenal in the pose of nostalgic and lonely defender of the old order's values against the new, and specifically like Persius in using the uneducable adversarius. Pope also borrows Persius's concern with the decline of letters, and his use of the persona who is consciously and obviously made as a foil to the satirist; someone who, as Persius says, he has made to speak as an adversarius, but who then takes on a fictive life of his own ("Quisquis es, o modo quem ex adverso dicere feci" [line 44]). The opponent exemplifies the values of the hated Nero, who provided one of the many unpleasant historical parallels and labels that the opposition tacked on to George II and Walpole.

In at least one case the combination of these and perhaps other Persian traits led the printer Bettenham and the bookseller Cooper to place Pope's name on the title page of Thomas Brewster's collected *Satires of Persius* in 1741. Brewster's Argument to Persius's first satire could serve as a gloss for much of *Fortescue, Arbuthnot,* and the *Epilogue to the Satires* and suggests how congenial Persius could be for Pope. The Argument points out uses of personae, dialogue and conflict with the adversarius, an attempt to stifle satire, a divorce from the values of the debased and debasing court, the isolation of the satirist, and the collapse of modern freedoms as contrasted with the unshackled, thriving past. "We may suppose the Author to be just seated in his Study, and beginning to vent his Indignation in Satire. At this very Juncture, comes in an Acquaintance, who, upon hearing the first Line, dissuades him, by all Means, from an Undertaking so perilous; advising him rather, if he needs must write, to accommodate his Vein to the Taste of the Times, and to write like other People." Brewster goes on to say that Persius would not seek fame or patronage under such shameful terms, that he in fact exposes the wretched literary taste of Roman nobles and their followers, and that he laments how "he dares not speak out with the Freedom allowable in former Times, and practised by his Predecessors in Satire, *Lucilius* and *Horace.* He then concludes, expressing a generous Disdain for all worthless Blockheads whatever: The only Readers whose applause he covets, must be Men of Virtue, and Men of Sense."[18]

Brewster's gloss demands that we focus on the dramatic relationship between the moral satirist and his incorrigible opponent. That is one of Pope's essential devices in the *Epilogue* and has scant parallel in Horace and none in Juvenal. Persius's adversarius in the first satire describes the growling guard dogs at the great man's gate. A Mr. Dudley in 1739, perhaps himself influenced by Pope, well characterizes the administration's willingness to intimidate those it could not buy. The Monitor in Dudley's imitation of this satire makes Persius's dogs yet more ominous:

> Yet the Resentments of the Great are strong,
> And if they snarl, they snap before 'tis long:

[18] The line from Persius ("Quisquis es") is quoted from *D. Juni Juvenalis, et A. Persii Flacci Satirae* (1684), ed. Ludovicus Prateus, 7th ed. (1736), p. 313. For Brewster, see *The Satires of Persius Translated into English Verse*, 2nd ed. (1751), pp. 5-6. Italics and Roman type have been inverted in the text. Someone, perhaps an eighteenth-century hand, has tried to erase "By A. Pope" from the title page of the 1741 edition in the Princeton University Library.

One of Brewster's notes to Persius's fourth satire also supplies a rough parallel to Pope's legal situation. Though Persius attacks Nero for prowling the streets (disguised and protected by gladiators) in search of illicit pleasures, "the Poet (says [Casaubon]) designedly left the Words capable of another Construction; to the End that if he

Hold in your Hand, avert the pointed Sting,
Or you may chance to starve, if not to swing.[19]

The Persian adversarius is the unchanging voice of the government's values. He triumphs over the satirist in practical terms, for he is incapable of feeling the shame that might bring reform, and is quite capable of threatening him with physical force, loss of audience, and literary seclusion. As a result, Persius retreats into irony and appears to praise what he despises and to destroy his own satire—precisely what Pope appears to do in the first dialogue with a deaf man.[20] When the hostile Friend tells Pope to mute his satire and "charitably comfort Knave and Fool" (line 62), he is adapting the advice of Persius's Monitor in Satire One, and he evokes a similar response. Pope asks to be forgiven for his error, banishes "Distinction, Satire, Warmth, and Truth!" (line 64) in favor of banalities, and concludes that satire is dead and that the fools and knaves shall be graced through life and flattered in their graves. With the Friend's patronizing "Alas! alas!" (line 254) in the second dialogue, Pope again shows that satire soft or loud, general or particular, comic or tragic, is useless when addressed to the courts and courtiers of those who will cause him to "Fall, by the Votes of [the modern] degen'rate Line!" (line 253).

Such satire clearly lacks the political protection that Lucilius was thought to have; but that did not inhibit Pope from adapting one of his devices. In the second dialogue Pope's Friend aggressively demands: "Hold Sir! for God's-

should be accused of glancing at the Emperor, by Means of this Ambiguity he might elude the Charge" (p. 93n).

19 *The First Satire of Persius Translated into English Verse*, p. 25.

20 Francis Howes, following Warton, but with more reservations, observes that in *Dialogue* II. 128-30, Pope imitates Persius, *Satires* 1, 128, "one of the most witty passages in Persius." Pope will "comply" with the wishes of his adversarius and criticize his friends—Cobham, Lyttelton, Bolingbroke—for flaws they obviously lack. See *The Satires of A. Persius Flaccus* (1809), p. 85.

sake, where's th' Affront to you?" and "What's that to you
. . . ?" and "How hurt he you?" (lines 157, 163, 165). In
Book 30, lines 41, 49-50, Lucilius's adversarius insists and
asks:

> Quod tuas [nunc] laudes culpas, non proficis hilum.
>   [1021]
> Quid tu istuc curas, ubi ego oblinar, atque voluter?
>   [1019]
> Quid servas, quo eam, quid agam? quid id attinet ad te?
>   [1020][21]

Considering how little one can reclaim of the context
and structure of Lucilius's satires, any notion of influence
here must remain speculative. This section, however, is
strikingly close to the interrogatory practice of Pope's
Friend in the second dialogue and, if not its parent, is at
the least a blood uncle. George Converse Fiske translates
these lines and describes the section in which Lucilius
seems to develop "an indirect defence of the humor of
satire against the charge of indiscriminate, bitter, and ma-
licious assaults on human weaknesses, such assaults as . . .
are associated with illiberal jest." Most of such lines, he
continues,

> are apparently put into the mouth of an *adversarius*—
> possibly a comic poet in the case of certain lines—who
> advances boldly to the attack. Lucilius, he says, is the
> author of a *"suspectum genus"* who, though he injures
> and blames, accomplishes nothing (1021). Why, says an-
> other victim of the satirist's lash, are you concerned as
> to whether I besmirch myself (with vice) and wallow in
> iniquity? (1019). Why do you narrowly observe whither

---

[21] The Latin and the initial line numbers are quoted from *Censorini
liber de die natali. . . . et C. Lucilii satyrarum reliquiae* (Leiden, 1767),
pp. 429, 430-31, but without italics. The bracketed word and numbers
are used by Fiske, n. 22, below, and are from *C. Lucilii carminum
reliquae*, ed. Frederick Marx (Leipzig, 1904-5), 1: 69.

I am going, what I am doing? What is that to you
(1020)?[22]

If Pope is not echoing the parent of the nipping rhyme,
he instinctively falls back on one of his devices, and in so
doing he is continuing his later practice of adding non-
Horatian elements to his grim satires. The Lucilian-Per-
sian adversarius is questioning, angry, and critical; the Ho-
ratian general concern with how best to consider death as
part of one's humanity becomes the Juvenalian-Persian
assumption that the government will destroy the satirist
who crosses it; the poet lives in a world in which God is
the only reliable and powerful friend, and even He must
reward the deserving hereafter. With these poems formal
verse satire probably evolves to the farthest point on its
satiric spectrum—beyond this the genre changes, or changes
back, into something else.

[22] *Lucilius and Horace: A Study in the Classical Theory of Imitation,*
Univ. of Wisconsin Studies in Language and Literature, no. 7 (Madi-
son: Univ. of Wisconsin Press, 1920), p. 304. Aggressive questioning of
the efficacy of satire also was one of the responses to opposition satire.
See *A Friendly Epistle to the Author of the State Dunces* (1733), which
glances at Pope:

> Yes,—or to Faction and her Friends a Friend
> Thy Muse, audacious, would not thus offend.
> But can such ill-plac'd stingless Satire vex?
> Thy Mind's Intention only can provoke,—
> There's Murder in it: Thy Muse is but a Joke.
>   (P. 9)

Pope may have shared the eighteenth-century association of Lucilius
with republican liberty. For some of these remarks, see Weinbrot,
Augustus Caesar in "Augustan" England, pp. 139-40, n. 26. The same
association seems to have been made in imperial Rome. See William
S. Anderson, *Pompey, His Friends, and the Literature of the First
Century B.C.,* University of California Publications in Classical Phi-
lology, 19 (1963): 57-82, and Michael Coffey, *Roman Satire* (Methuen
& Co., 1976), p. 64.

CHAPTER 10

HHHHHHHHHHHHHHHHHHHHHHHHHHHHHHHHHHHHHHHHHHH

Conclusion

THE DIRECTION OF Pope's career as a formal verse satirist is from an essentially Horatian ethic epistle like *Burlington* (1731), to mingled satire with a variety of Horatian, Juvenalian, and Persian emphases, to the overwhelmingly Juvenalian-Persian elevation and gloom of the *Epilogue to the Satires* (1738). Both Pope's poems and his contemporaries' reception of them indicate that his career was progressively less, not more, of "an *Imitatio Horatii*," and that Horace's "place to stand" was progressively less, not more, attractive for him;[1] it was sapped and then replaced by the conventions of Persius and Juvenal, which Pope himself welcomed.

One may, however, raise certain questions regarding the satiric method I have attributed to Pope. Why did he continue to imitate the satirist he was supposedly rejecting? Should he not have imitated poems of Juvenal and Persius as well? Some answers to these questions have been implied in earlier discussions of the poems—imitating Donne's Horace, for example, is imitating a surrogate Juvenal. There are other answers as well, since in spite of Horace's several inadequacies, he and his special achievements were necessary for Pope's own purposes.

I: WHY HORACE?

Pope's imitations of Horace are part of his campaign to refine English verse. Early in his career he adapted the

---

[1] Reuben Arthur Brower, *Alexander Pope: The Poetry of Allusion* (Oxford: Clarendon Press, 1959), p. 165; Maynard Mack supports this description of Pope's career. See *The Garden and the City: Retirement and Politics in the Later Poetry of Pope 1731-1743* (Toronto: Univ. of Toronto Press, 1969), p. 234. Mack's study remains the most persuasive

CONCLUSION

Ovidian epistle and the Virgilian country poem, and as he matured he looked to the third member of that distinguished group to continue his task. Horace insisted that his own generation burnish the rusty knives of Lucilius; Pope had a comparable attitude regarding the satire of Donne and his successors. Horace also offered greater modulation of tone than Juvenal or Persius. Horace's varied voice sings secure retirement or refutes attacks on his poetry; it affectionately praises Maecenas as father or Horace's biological father; it considers literary traditions of which Horace is a part or political traditions of which Augustus is a part; and it engages in epistolary or present dialogue with the princeps or a servant. Such a persona suggests a practical pose of flexibility and mature wisdom rather than rigid patriotism or withdrawn stoicism, and it does so in a context of decent values in a decent state and, often, from a country retreat and *locus amoenus*.

This polished, complex voice offered Pope many advantages, including the few biographical and historical similarities that appeared to suggest a (tenuous) link between the two Augustan ages. Most obviously, the Sabine farm is paralleled in Twickenham, the circle of Augustus in Pope's eminent friends and Prince of Wales, postrevolutionary imperial Rome in postrevolutionary Britain taking its place among nations famous for arts and arms. Consequently, by putting on the mask of Horace, Pope could adapt him for satiric attacks upon the administration and attempt to make him a literary Trojan Horse. The sophisticated conversation appropriate between gentlemen might, however infrequently, bring Pope a hearing with those he wished to reform; by preserving the façade of civilized discourse, he briefly seemed a member of the club. Thereafter, he was freer to add intimations of political mortality that would have been rejected at once if he

---

and eloquent defense of Pope's positive Horatian and Virgilian contexts.

CONCLUSION

were too gloomy or elevated in angry monologue. Alternatively, Horace was useful for Pope's "patriot" ends, since the opposition's political program included the creation of a court of Bolingbrokean tincture at St. James's. Pope in his grotto could create a shadow cabinet or government in exile, in which his lowered voice would be listened to more intently. Cobham and Bathurst were no less peers for being in opposition, and no more likely than, say, the administration's Dodington to encourage what James Beattie called the "vindictive zeal of the unmannerly Juvenal."[2] The opposition program also was linked to the country and its landed gentry, and again found a sympathetic voice—if, ultimately, unsympathetic values—in Horatian respect for retirement and affection for rural rather than urban charms. Juvenal's country is a lingering enclave of otherwise moribund Roman virtues. Horace's country nourishes many of the best Romans and returns them to the city with renewed moral energy for the support of the thriving nation. Horace thus offered the norms of corrigible humanity, functioning government, and poets able to speak to their rulers in a manly and educational way. Much of this, Pope came to believe, was wishful thinking, or simple duplicity and collusion by Horace; but such mythology deserved preservation as a standard that Persius and Juvenal were less able to invoke as an active force in their own lives, cultures, or poems.

Horace could be invoked not only as a lost norm in *Arbuthnot* but as an inadequate norm in *Fortescue* and other poems. When Maecenas becomes Bolingbroke in Pope's imitation of the first epistle of the first book, Horace's union with the throne is, metaphorically, a noble ruin on the facing page; but the substitution also suggests that Horace lacked both moral and political judgment in sup-

[2] "On Laughter and Ludicrous Composition," in *Essays* (Edinburgh, 1766), p. 662. For a useful supplement to this remark, see Lord O'Hagan's words in chapter 6, note 8, above, where lords "hate a fervent tub thumper." London *Times*, 27 April 1978.

333

porting such a throne. Pope's Juvenalian implications are the clearer when placed in their Horatian frame. Hence Pope's rejection of Augustan tyranny is more striking when set against the flattery on the verso of the *Epistle to Augustus*; Pope's concern with licensing and government manipulation of the arts is more impressive when, in the same poem, we see Horace's willingness to accept and encourage such censorship; and Horace's insinuating voice is more dangerous when we see that in the *Epilogue to the Satires* it complies with the court's desire to turn satire into polite smiles and screening of corruption in the name of good manners. Pope is being consistent and commonplace when he says in his own epitaph, "Let Horace blush, and Virgil too" for profiting from flattery of their tyrant.[3]

The relevance of aspects of polished verse, modulated tone, miscellaneous devices, biography, politics, topography, and myths—these and the consequent opportunities for rejection, modification, and parody—all help to explain why Pope could imitate Horace and not necessarily identify with his values; in many cases hostility to those values is more nearly the case, as Pope's contemporaries often saw. We can add to these reasons the characteristic eighteenth-century wish to engage in a contest to excel the original, and the awareness that modern satire is a product of many individual talents within an evolving tradition. Though Horace was Pope's first companion in formal satire, he was joined by others who suggested different paths; he absorbed their several directions and arrived at a "place" far from the Sabine farm.

Perhaps this description of Pope's synthesizing muse will evoke related, useful speculation. The excellence of Pope's satires, for example, in part stems from the breadth of their form; they catch what Aaron Hill called both "the acrimony of *Juvenal*" and "the *Horatian* air of ease and se-

[3] *Alexander Pope: Minor Poems*, p. 376. The poem was published in 1738, and written at an indeterminate time—no earlier, I should think, than 1733.

renity," so that he is "raised and familiar at once." This complexity helps to recall the complexity of life—or so Samuel Johnson thought in 1765 when he praised Shakespeare's tragicomedies because they imitate nature, not critical rules. "The two modes of [dramatic] imitation, known by the names of tragedy and comedy," were so designed "to promote different ends by contrary means, and [were] considered as so little allied" that no Greek or Roman writer attempted both. Shakespeare, however, knew that "the mingled drama may convey all the instruction of tragedy or comedy . . . because it includes both . . . and approaches nearer than either to the appearance of life." His plays thus are "compositions of a distinct kind; exhibiting the real state of sublunary nature, which partakes of good and evil, joy and sorrow, mingled with endless variety of proportion and innumerable modes of combination."[4] Johnson's conception of Shakespeare's "mingled drama" at the very least parallels John Brown's, and others', conception of Pope's mingled satire.

Indeed, Johnson's "Prologue Spoken at the Opening of the Theatre in Drury-Lane, 1747" is also relevant for the study of evolving genres in the eighteenth century.[5] He characterizes Shakespeare as the coherent product of learning, imagination, truth, and passion; this fruitful union

---

[4] For Hill, see *The Correspondence of Alexander Pope*, ed. George Sherburn (Oxford: Clarendon Press, 1956), 4: 112, regarding the *Epilogue to the Satires*; for Johnson, The Yale Edition of the Works of Samuel Johnson, *Johnson on Shakespeare*, vol. 7, ed. Arthur Sherbo (New Haven: Yale Univ. Press, 1968), p. 66 (two modes), p. 67 (mingled drama), p. 66 (distinct kinds). Comparable evidence concerning the relationship of mingled literary forms and the complexity of life may be found in Collins's "Ode to Fear" (1746), lines 44-45, and "Ode on the Popular Superstitions of the Highlands" (1748?), and Horace Walpole's Preface to the second edition (1765) of *The Castle of Otranto*.

[5] Quotations are from The Yale Edition of the Works of Samuel Johnson, *Samuel Johnson: Poems*, vol. 6, ed. E. L. McAdam, Jr., with George Milne (New Haven: Yale Univ. Press, 1964).

allowed him personal immortality and his auditors instruction and pleasure. Thereafter, in the poem's chronology, Ben Jonson limits himself to academic learning, the Restoration wits imitate not nature but their own vice, early eighteenth-century tragedians use boring rules and declamation, and mid-century authors succumb to exotic farce and mere spectacle. Johnson begins his poem with Shakespeare's inclusive form and shows it atomized and decayed. The new theater, fortuitously opening with *The Merchant of Venice*, promises a new age which can return to Shakespearean nature and truth, communicated in a form that combines "useful mirth, and salutary woe" (line 60), and to a dramatic mode that imitated both real "many-colour'd life" and "imagined" life (lines 3-4). Shakespeare's practice signals comprehensive vision and successful mimesis; the debased or monolithic form signals meager and transient art that imitates the part rather than the whole.

Something like this unhappy progress in formal verse satire may offer one reason for the genre's lamented decline. I offer a tentative hypothesis, which requires abundant testing before it can be accepted, modified, or perhaps rejected—namely, that though Pope's influence is as varied as his practice, later formal verse satire tends to become either excessively Horatian or excessively Juvenalian, loses its modulation of voice and response, and suffers as a result. Such dissociation of satiric sensibility can even be useful for describing poems somewhat beyond the limits of formal verse satire, though of course it cannot "explain" all of the strengths and weaknesses of, say, Robert Lloyd's *The Progress of Envy* (1751), or Burns's "Holy Willie's Prayer" (1785, 1799), any more than it can "explain" Marvell's *Last Instructions to a Painter* (1667) or Rochester's "On Poet Ninny" (1680). Each of these, and numerous other satires between about 1660 and 1800, is different from classical models and Pope's amalgamation of them.

Extended speculation of this sort can take us beyond the

borders of this book and into realms of literary psychology and aesthetics, for which more than a tourist's visa is necessary. Johnson's remarks and their implications nonetheless suggest that Pope's satiric practice is part of an ongoing development in the relationship of modern to ancient literary forms and of art to reality, and that in his synthesis he was doing for his genre what Shakespeare and, in different ways, Milton had done for theirs. However that case may be, the perception and practice of Pope's unified satire has, I hope, been amply documented in earlier chapters. It remains to recall his varied influences and then to offer preliminary testing of the hypothesis of dissociation in later eighteenth-century verse satire.

II: Aspects of Pope's Satiric Influence

We have already seen that Pope's Horatian, mingled, and Juvenalian modes were adapted by other satirists eager to light their fires with flint from Twickenham's grotto. James Bramston's *Man of Taste* (1733) and William Thompson's *Sickness* (1745) suggest Pope's Horatianism; *Epidemical Madness: A Poem in Imitation of Horace* (1739) suggests the mingled Horatian and Juvenalian; the imitations of Persius, and Paul Whitehead's (?) *The State of Rome* (1739) suggest the blended Persian and Juvenalian; and *The State Weather Cocks* (1734) and Thomas Gilbert's imitation of Juvenal's first satire (1740) suggest more extreme Juvenalianism.[6] I shall call forth just one

[6] For these, see Bramston and Thompson, chapter 6, at note 3; *Epidemical Madness*, chapter 5, section v; Persius, chapter 4, section iv; *The State of Rome*, chapter 5, section i; *The State Weather Cocks*, chapter 5, section i; and Gilbert's *First Satire of Juvenal Imitated*, chapter 1, section iv.
Pope's dominant, immediate influence, however, was on the harsh side of the satiric spectrum, especially toward the latter part of the 1730s. Paul Whitehead thus insists that he will not "Leave to *Pope* the Poignance of the Pen," and that he will join Pope in "Poignance" and "gall some great *Leviathan* of Pow'r." See *Manners: A Satire* [1739], p. 12. Pope of course also inspired severe satires against him and his

more cousin from each branch of the family, the better to illustrate the power of Pope's fertilizing muse.

The poet of *An Epistle to a Friend, In Imitation of the Second Epistle of the First Book of Horace* (1739) has learned his Horace from Pope's gentler lessons.[7] The speaker tells his lawyer friend high truths regarding man's fall and redemption; but he does so in tones that are familiar, easy, pleasant, and unthreatening. Like Pope in *Bathurst*, the speaker turns his letter into a dialogue with an adversarius whom he tries not to tire, and toward whom he is both avuncular and self-depreciating.

> Enough of Sermons: I perceive you nod:
> You think me mighty wise, and mighty odd:
> Your Lips, I see, half verge upon a Smile——
> Dear Sir! observe the *Horace* in my Stile:
> Just such to Lollius, his young heedless Friend,
> He knew with decent Liberty to send,
> Beneath the Critique dextrous to convey
> Advice conceal'd in the best-natur'd Way.
> But you're no *Lollius* and no *Horace* I:
> Here is no Room sage Maxims to apply.
>
> (P. 6)

cause, one of the many of which is [Patrick Guthry?], *Candour: Or An Occasional Essay on the Abuse of Wit and Eloquence* (1739). Pope and his crew merely attack "Invented Crimes, and magnify'd offense"; the opposition has become "a publick Grievance" designed to "Subvert the State, and Anarchy restore" (p. 3). Pope himself earns this unhappy apostrophe, one based on the *Epilogue to the Satires* (1738):

> Oh Heav'n directed Muse! inspired Pen!
> To deal out Plagues, and wash the Leper clean!
> See the State-Cripple halt to touch thy Shrine,
> To rule in Senates, and in Courts to shine!
>
> (P. 5)

[7] This poem is apparently by Richard West. A version of it appears in Thomas Gray's manuscript Commonplace Book in Pembroke College, Cambridge, 1: 273-75, with these annotations: "Fav: from Epsome, before I went to France. in 1739," and "Horace. imitation of Epist: 2, L: 1. by R. West." I am grateful to the Master and Fellows of Pembroke College for permission to quote from these manuscripts.

CONCLUSION

Abrupt I finish, my hard Task is o'er:
Forgive me, *Pope!* I'll imitate no more.

(P. 14)

Pope's Horatian voice was often heard in such epistles and essays. That voice also could be infused with Persian solemnity, as in Thomas Beach's *Eugenio: Or, Virtuous and Happy Life. A Poem. Inscrib'd to Mr. Pope* (1737). This somber, melancholic effort uses generalized tag names, makes mild attacks upon the follies of the world, and quotes a few lines from the *Essay on Man* in support of Beach's points. The resolutely good, moral, and well-born Eugenio exemplifies his own satiric norm. He refuses to be depressed by painful questions regarding grand matters and is confident that history can lead to answers in a world still amenable to wisdom, to Burlington's and Cobham's successful buildings, and to instruction through Balaam's death and defeat. Beach implores the help of several "venerable Sages,"

But chiefly thou, O POPE, befriend my Lays,
No fancy'd Fame can bless me like thy Praise:
Believe for once, the Muse from Flattery free,
Who pants for Virtue, and wou'd copy thee.

(Pp. 5-6)

As we might expect, Pope's efforts that mingled Horatian with more Juvenalian conventions have the most variations and the most imitators. *The Modern Poet* (1736), or *The Patriot and the Muse* (1737), or *Plain Truth* (1747) are good examples, but another imitation of Horace is even better, for it shows that after 1733 imitating Horace often meant imitating Pope imitating Horace; and it also shows the poets' sensitivity to the difference between an epistle and a satire. The unsigned *First Satire of the Second Book of Horace Imitated* (1745) is a dialogue between a dissuading T—"Be silent," and "never, I beseech you, satyrize" (p. 4)—and J, the familiar courageous poet resisting oppression. The ambiguous suggestion that Horace might

339

be frozen if he satirized, had been interpreted by Pope and his friends as a threat of murder. J shares that reading and tells T that "If you want Rest; there are who may advise / A Draught of Laudanum to close your Eyes" (p. 5), and that "*Scand. Magnat.*—and then a Jail" (p. 6) may threaten him. Moreover, T continues, J will be rejected at court and may soon be killed, since an enemy "Can find a thousand Ways to heave you off" (p. 11). J refuses to surrender, and is not only as brave as Horace but as brave as the Pope whose resolute response in *Fortescue* he has in mind. For J, it is no matter whether the foolish world thinks him a knave or fool, "*Pope*'s Pupil, or of junior *Busby*'s School," since he will wage " 'Gainst Vice of every Kind, an honest War" (p. 9) and will write "In Spite of Harry, or his Grace, or *Colly*" (p. 10). These traditional targets evoke a traditional outburst and Pope's Juvenalian shade in his imitation of Horace. Is there an exalted enemy of virtue?

> He shall not 'scape, because the Knave is great,
> A Knave's a Knave to me in every State.
> *Pope* said (and *Pope* I'll copy as I can,
> For as I lov'd, I'd imitate the Man)
> When W——s sit Ch—f, is Justice to be sold?
> Must I still lose my Cause—without my Gold?
> Nor dare unmask him! dare not! I will dare,—
> I'll throw the venal Villain from his Chair.
>
> (P. 12)

In the face of all this, even the prudent T, still in a satiric world where suasion is possible, gives his modified assent, urges caution in attacking lords, and adds that the law remains a potential enemy (p. 19).

Pope's third influence is in overwhelmingly Juvenalian satires that find much corruption and little virtue in the declining nation. This mode was as uncongenial to Walpole's successors as to the great man himself. The author of *Power and Patriotism: A Poetical Epistle; Humbly inscribed to the Right Honourable H.[enry] P.[elham]* (1746)

laments that satirists wrongly have seen so much evil. These two paragraphs might be labeled "the Horatian epistle's answer to Juvenalian satires," and of course they place Pope on the bleak not the optimistic side.

> Ev'n **POPE** himself **APOLLO**'s fav'rite *Bard*,
> (To whom no *future Wit* shall be compar'd)
> In this too *err'd*——He thought that *Place* and *Power*
> Must Conscience *stifle*, Honesty *obscure*.
> That Statesmen knew no *Guides*——but *private Views*,
> That Int'rest's *Dictates* they could ne'er *refuse*.
> That *Pleasure, Power, Revenge*, or *Party-Rage*,
> Did *all* Mankind——but *most* the *Great* engage.
> And that *Self-Love* for *Social* to postpone.
> Was a *Greek* Virtue to this *Clime* unknown.
>   But though his *tuneful Muse* the World misled,
> To slight the *Living*, idolize the *Dead*.
> To think of *Greece* and *Rome* with awful Fear,
> And fancy none but *Knaves* and *Fools* born here.
> Yet You, Great Sir, ——You,——and your *noble*
>   *Friends*.
> Have made your *Country* and your *Age* amends.
> Taught us that *Patriot Virtue* still survives,
> And in bleak *Britain* as in *Athens* thrives.
>
> (P. 14)

Others before and after 1746 were not impressed with such an argument and thought that, so far from erring, Pope had hit his stride in his most accurate and vigorous satire. The title of Bezaleel Morrice's poem quickly announces its sympathies: *The Present Corruption of Britons; Being a Paraphrase on the Latter Part of Mr. P—E's first Dialogue, Entitled One Thousand Seven Hundred and Thirty Eight* (1738). Since the "genuine Aim of SATIRE is the *Redress of Evils*" it must "be bold, impartial and severe," as well as indignant, just, and a deterrent to vice. The ancient Greek and Roman satirists exercised a "manly Freedom" not permitted to moderns; yet surely, Morrice continues in his Preface, one must have that freedom if one wishes to protect Reason and Truth and to correct the many abuses that the law cannot reach (p. 5). Pope's "noble . . . Indignation at the present reigning Enormities" guides Morrice in this paraphrase, which condemns nearly all levels of society, especially the great men responsible for the care of the nation. The speaker is embattled but does have an ally whom he can trust when confronting Britain's innumerable corrupt potentates, and so he repeats many of Pope's lines and charges.

> Our Youth (in Liveries of foreign Gold)
> Before [Vice] caper, creep *behind the old*;
> See—to th' imperious Idol, *Millions run*,
> *And offer Country, Parent, Friend, or Son*;
> Hear her black Trump audaciously proclaim
> Thro' wretched Albion—that Desert *is shame*,
> And vile Corruption—no disgrace, or blame;
> *In Soldier, Church man, Courtier, Man of Pow'r*
> All other Prospects, Hopes of Wealth devour.
>
> (P. 8)

These are a very few further instances of Pope's disciples in his three kinds of formal verse satire: the dominantly Horatian, the Horatian mingled with the Persian or Juvenalian, and the dominantly Juvenalian, each adapted for its relevant moral or political end. John Brown's "ev'ry Poet's Pow'r in *One*" and "Each *Roman's* Force adorns his various Page" are, I think, descriptions Pope's eighteenth-century followers readily would have accepted.

III: Dissociation of Satiric Sensibility

Several of these followers did try Pope's mingling of modes,[8] but they could not scale his steeps, nor incorporate

---

[8] We recall, for example, that in *The Progress of Satire* (1798) William Boscawen says of Pope: "Each graceful form the Sons of Satire choose / Springs from thy various, thy accomplish'd Muse" (p. 10). See chapter 5, at note 10, above.

his model as Pope incorporated and altered Horace's, Persius's, and Juvenal's; instead, they generally turned to and exaggerated one or the other of Pope's chief models. Perhaps this is to be expected. *Paradise Lost* is the culmination and graveyard of traditional epic poetry, though few would have seen that at the time; a similar remark may be made regarding the offsprings of Pope's satires from 1731 to 1738. Much formal and some other verse satire after Pope's tends to be either Horatian or Juvenalian in the worst sense—either socially elegant with the satirist in control of an essentially trivial satiric subject, or bloated, hyperbolic, and rhetorical in a world of monsters whom the satirist hopes to knock down with his loud voice. One reason for Pope's malleable satire is his malleable speaker, who allows his tone to be determined by his satiric object. In *Arbuthnot* alone, we recall, he adapts himself to Horatian, Persian, and Juvenalian targets. Many of Pope's successors reverse that process, allow their predetermined tone to define their satiric object, and banish complexity of form with complexity of response. They either refuse to see dangers or see only dangers, and in either case they eliminate the attractive and varied voice both within and behind Pope's poems. As Donald Taylor observes, for example, Chatterton as a satirist engages in "a search for evil commensurate with his anger."[9] We can see some of this dissociated satiric sensibility in the later eighteenth century by contrasting the "mingled" attack on homosexuality in Pope's *Arbuthnot* with the trivializing Horatian attack in Garrick's *Fribbleriad* (1761), and the extravagant Juvenalian attack in Churchill's *The Times* (1764). Garrick's poem is not, strictly speaking, a formal verse satire, but it is

[9] *Thomas Chatterton's Art: Experiments in Imagined History* (Princeton: Princeton Univ. Press, 1978), p. 260. See also pp. 182, 199-200, and 211-12 for useful comments on the continuity, or lack of it, between eighteenth-century satiric kinds and generations, and particular satirists, especially Pope, Churchill, and Chatterton. What Donald Taylor calls "Churchillean" I prefer to call "Juvenalian," in celebration of roots.

sufficiently and consciously linked to Pope to qualify for its pseudo-Horatian role, and thus suggests that some traits of formal satire were carried into other satiric species.

We remember that Sporus, the male whore of Nero, is unnatural, a violator of the divine order, and demonstrably satanic as a tempting toad "at the Ear of *Eve*" (line 319). Pope so wishes this allusion recognized that his note in 1735 drew the reader's attention to Book IV, line 800, of *Paradise Lost*. The corruption of Eve is the corruption of Queen Caroline as ordered by Walpole who breathes the venom that puppet Sporus finally spits abroad. The portrait transcends its genesis in Hervey's personal insult and Pope's punitive satire, and reaches the highest moral fervor. In punishing Sporus, Pope wields the revealing, now satiric, spear of Ithuriel (*PL* IV. 811-13) and defends his readers as he defends himself against the forces of disorder; he is the ally of God's original plan and the lingering decency of His world, which is threatened by agents of darkness near the throne. The name Sporus also suggests a shift from the Augustan and Horatian to the Neronian and Persian. Protection of the satirist is replaced by hostility to the satirist, especially if he opposes the sexual deviance that is an emblem of political deviance. The poem that was Pope's own "Bill of Complaint" becomes an effort to stop the sodomizing of Britain; it can do this only with abandonment of desired Horatian satire in "Atticus," and with acceptance of Juvenalian indignation and Miltonic and Christian allusion in the service of the nation's unappreciative governors. Pope is only a small reason for his apologia, and Sporus's Master-Miss ambiguity is vile not before Pope alone but before God.

Garrick's *Fribbleriad* is an attack upon Thomas Fitzpatrick, called Fitzgig, for his hostile pamphlet *An Enquiry into the Real Merit of a Certain Popular Performer* (1760).[10] Garrick knew the *Epistle to Dr. Arbuthnot* and

[10] *The Fribbleriad* is quoted from *The Poetical Works of David Garrick* (1785). The word "fribble" also is used in William Kenrick's

clearly was aware of Pope's precedent in this sort of attack. The Fribble is "like a toad" who vents his "venom" (lines 42-43), and the speaker asks his muse to "Say for what cause these Master-Misses / To Garrick such a hatred bore" (lines 98-99). The poem also imposes a Miltonic frame—but there the similarity ends. Indeed, the use of Milton suggests a major difference from Pope. Garrick's *Fribbleriad* is both a mock-epic and a mock-Horatian poem in which the satirist controls a fool who mistakenly attacked his better and is punished with severe but amused contempt. Fitzgig remains Garrick's enemy, not Britain's, and the guiding structure of the council scene in Book II of *Paradise Lost* accentuates the piddling rather than ominous quality of the person and his sexual preference. The scene is held at a noisy public room of a declassé inn, is dubbed Panfribblerium in lieu of Pandaemonium, and includes mincing, dainty, stereotypical characters with names like Lord Trip, Sir Cock-a-doodle, Baronet, and of course Fitzgig, who, poor fellow, is elected Satan to attack the god Garrick. The hero is drawn "With stretch'd-out fingers, and a thumb / Stuck to his hips, and jutting bum" (lines 211-12). Pope's symbol of political and moral corruption, whose name and character both were attacks on the court, here is metamorphosed into an Irish upstart who is the "COCK FRIBBLE" (line 405).

The difference between Pope's concern with genuinely threatened institutions, and Garrick's concern with his undeservedly attacked but secure reputation, is made clear in lines Sir Cock-a-doodle speaks of Fitzgig himself:

"Would you have one can smile, be civil,
"Yet all within a very devil—
"Lay pretty schemes, like cobwebs spin 'em,

anti-Garrick poem *The Town. A Satire* (1748), p. 7, and in [Nathaniel Lancaster], *The Pretty Gentleman: Or, Softness of Manners Vindicated From the false Ridicule exhibited under the Character of William Fribble, Esq.* (1747). The work is dedicated to Garrick. Garrick included a "Beau Fribble" in his *Miss in her Teens* (1747).

"To catch your hated foes within 'em,
"Let him a thousand times break thro 'em,
"The *ingenious creter* shall renew 'em.

(Lines 199-204)

The antithetical smiling devil probably comes from Pope's
Sporus, or at the very least is analogous to him in the
comic way of the *Fribbleriad.* The cobweb image also
comes from *Arbuthnot,* and also suggests the difference be-
tween public and private concerns. Pope laments that he
cannot adequately destroy the bad poet; the laughable Sir
Cock mindlessly praises Fitzgig for being an industrious
bug—whom Garrick finally does destroy. Pope speaks to his
friend:

Who shames a Scribler? break one cobweb thro',
He spins the slight, self-pleasing thread anew;
Destroy his Fib, or Sophistry; in vain,
The Creature's at his dirty work again;
Thron'd in the Centre of his thin designs;
Proud of a vast Extent of flimzy lines.

(Lines 89-94)

Fitzgig aims at mischief (line 205); Sporus aims at God's
plan. Garrick deals with an impertinent who, in the way
of this Horatianism, he seems easily to manipulate and de-
feat. Pope deals with a force so ominous that he must
abandon modest satire and collect his harsher talents to
flap, break, and expose the great adversary. For one satirist,
homosexuality is a silly and superficially elegant aberra-
tion; for the other it epitomizes national decay at its pre-
sumed center of value.

Garrick's personal, "Horatian" poem was shaped by the
fragmented presence of Pope and Milton. Churchill's poem
exemplifies the hyperbole of a poet who ignores the sati-
rist's concern with his function in society. Churchill's knowl-
edge of varied satiric modes and his choice of the one most
suitable for his temperament is clear in his *Apology* of

1761.[11] Heaven designed the satiric muse's role as one "To please, improve, instruct, reform mankind" (line 315) and to make oppressed Virtue rise above "splendid Vice" (line 317). The task of subduing Vice to Virtue is not one for those who speak softly or tickle gently:

Now arm'd with wrath [the muse], bids eternal shame;
With strictest justice brands the villain's name:
Now in the milder garb of Ridicule
She sports, and pleases while she wounds the Fool.
Her shape is often varied; but her aim,
To prop the cause of Virtue, still the same.
In praise of Mercy let the guilty bawl,
When Vice and Folly for Correction call;
Silence the mark of weakness justly bears,
And is partaker of the crimes it spares.
                                        (Lines 320-29)

Like many earlier satirists, Churchill insists that he will not polish his vigorous lines for the sake of softness and sound. "Perish my Muse," he orates, "If e'er her labours weaken to refine / Th' gen'rous roughness of a nervous line" (lines 352, 354-55).

This satiric manifesto suggests that for Churchill satire's varied shapes were irrelevant, for he saw his life as a series of encounters with different persecutors, none of whom could humble him: "Ne'er will I flatter, cringe, or bend the knee, / To those who, Slaves to ALL, are slaves to ME" (lines 274-75), he claims in the *Apology*. The generalized sense of outrage often seems unearned, monotonous, excessive, and, perhaps above all, to lack an enemy who is a threat to anyone but the speaker's career and consequent self-image. That image is related, not to the harmonious working of the poet within the order of divine, social, and poetic institutions, but to the poet as his own subject.[12]

---

[11] Churchill is quoted from *The Poetical Works of Charles Churchill*, ed. Douglas Grant (Oxford: Clarendon Press, 1956).
[12] Thomas Lockwood emphasizes the mid- and later eighteenth-cen-

CONCLUSION

Churchill incorporates Juvenalian rage for apparently personal slights; he lacks the theory of causation that made Pope's satires so impressively urgent; and he cannot accept the mellifluence of Garrick's, or even Pope's, verse, since that would imply an enemy whom one can defeat without benefit of "Virtue's awful frown" (line 319). Excess is the bone and marrow of Churchill's satire, and is well illustrated in one of his own attacks on the presumed decline of heterosexuality, *The Times* (1764), a poem far more concerned with the outraged satirist than with the outrages to the nation that Juvenal saw in his second and ninth satires on a comparable subject.

The opening of the poem immediately establishes the angrily nostalgic contrast of past and present that soon discloses its grandparents' lineaments. "The Time hath been," and "Time was," and "Time was" (lines 1, 13, 33) that all virtues were active and vices controlled, when the shunned vicious at least tried to hide their shame and exalted scoundrels could be reformed because no one could be bribed to help them. Now, in this infinitely corrupt age, all this is reversed, and Churchill adapts the final paragraph of Juvenal's first satire to help find a model for his world:

---

tury examination of the self as a subject. "The characteristic subject of Churchill's satire," he observes, "is the satirist himself, or the satirist in relation to the world." Lockwood rightly extends this remark to Peter Pindar. See *Post-Augustan Satire: Charles Churchill and Satirical Poetry, 1750-1800* (Seattle: Univ. of Washington Press, 1979), p. 22. Donald Taylor's discussion of Chatterton's satire (note 9, above) is consistent with this paradigm of one kind of formal satire. Discussions of "Post-Augustan" and "Romantic" satire have flourished, especially for that interesting "transitional" satirist Byron. For some of these, see Jerome McGann, "The Non-Augustan Nature of Byron's Early 'Satires,'" *Revue des langues vivantes*, 34 (1970): 495-503; Mary Clearman, "A Blueprint for *English Bards and Scotch Reviewers: The First Satire of Juvenal*," *Keats-Shelley Journal*, 19 (1970): 87-89; Frederick L. Beatty, "Byron's Imitations of Juvenal and Persius," *Studies in Romanticism*, 15 (1976): 333-55; and Robert F. Gleckner, "From Selfish Spleen to Equanimity: Byron's Satires," *Studies in Romanticism*, 18 (1979): 173-205. Gleckner offers a useful summary of the recent critical trends.

We begin,
Where our Sires ended, and improve in Sin,
Rack our invention, and leave nothing new
In vice, and folly for our sons to do.
                              (Lines 105-8)

He quickly reconsiders a key word in that last line. "Sons"
denotes procreation, which denotes the coupling of male
and female, which seems no longer to be performed in a
nation so uniformly depraved (lines 109-18). Britain robs
the world to import and perfect foreign vices, and per-
forms sins beyond the reach of God's grace (lines 265-66).
In Pope's final satires he was the agent of an angry God;
Churchill is the master of God, as he declares:

Be Grace shut out, be Mercy deaf, let God
With tenfold terrours arm that dreadful nod
Which speaks them lost, and sentenc'd to despair;
Distending wide her jaws, let Hell prepare
For Those who thus offend amongst Mankind,
A fire more fierce, and Tortures more refin'd.
                              (Lines 273-78)

The monsters who control Sodom must be punished here-
after, since "On Earth, alas! They meet a diff'rent fate"
(line 280), and are forgiven their sins, or are joined in them
by hordes of like-minded chums.

A simple paraphrase of the remaining dreadful conse-
quences indicates Churchill's method. Hard-working
whores cannot earn a decent living anymore. Woman, who
excited the normal male till his "whole body [was] tingling
with desire" (line 326), is discarded in favor of some beastly
Ganymede or Hylas (lines 332-33). Women waste their
luscious youths as men seek male whores. Apicius, an aging
aristocrat, behaves like a lovesick adolescent who loses his
appetite. Why? Not because he lusts after a reluctant
wench, or because his wife remains unfaithful, or for any
other reason compatible with traditional upper-class de-
bauchery: "His cause of grief behold in that fair Boy; /

349

CONCLUSION

Apicius dotes, and Corydon is coy" (lines 429-30). Poor child—if only he could be saved from his vanity and leave Apicius's service, for that atheist lord surely will seduce and abandon him. But where can he go? The churches, the academies, the young, the old, the seeming rake, the married man—all are Apicius with different masks:

> Would'st Thou be safe? Society forswear,
> Fly to the desert, and seek shelter there,
> Herd with the Brutes—they follow Nature's plan—
> There's not one Brute so dangerous as Man.
>
> (Lines 495-98)

On the other hand, if you wish to live in society, "Amongst the monsters of Augusta's breed" (line 508), dress like a woman, "Put off the Man, from Men to live secure" (line 510). Being a transvestite for virtue's sake is better than being one for vice's sake. At least that way you won't be propositioned in the street, though you may be beaten. Women themselves no longer have to be careful, as in the good old days when only a castrated priest would be allowed into the house that included daughters. Now, even if females wished to be whores, there isn't a man around "Who thinks it worth his while to make them so" (line 536). Propagation is in danger (line 554). All the well-known studs are dead or dying. Pimps and whores have nothing to do. Concupiscence and lechery are in disgrace. Wise mothers pray for daughters, who, though rejected by men, will at least keep her company, whereas a handsome boy will become a pathic's plaything by the time he is sixteen. Want to keep him sound? Tell the world "That He is coarse, indelicate, and brown" (line 622) or Sodom's hordes will get to him. And of course keep male servants, tutors, priests, brothers, and even his father away from him. No one who is male can be trusted. Surround him with pretty, young, and willing maids, and count yourself lucky, and be indulgent, if "He chance to get some score . . . with child" (line 654). After all, "To have a bastard is some sign of grace" (line 658)—a grace the sodomites were refused.

I suspect that I am not alone in finding this hyperbole comic and therefore not likely to rouse my alarm or fears for the future of the race. Like Churchill's contemporary reviewers, however, I do not think most of the humor intentional. After the last tirade, Churchill offers the conventional Juvenalian apologia and a Persian insistence on telling the truth about Midas. Here the poet must speak out all the more in order to associate himself with the stallion, not the gelding or mare.

> Born in such times, should I sit tamely down,
> Suppress my rage, and saunter thro' the town
> As one who knew not, or who shar'd these crimes?
> Should I at lesser evils point my rimes,
> And let this Giant Sin, in the full eye
> Of Observation, pass unwounded by?
>> (Lines 659-64)

> Born in such times, nor with that patience curst
> Which Saints may boast of, I must speak, or burst.
>> (Lines 679-80)

Churchill concludes with regrets if he has offended the Fair, an assurance that he actually is writing for them— "The Cause of Woman is most worthy Man" (line 688)— and insistence that he will continue to write so long as a single sodomite prowls the land. He will track down and banish such deviants, until either God destroys them and their loathed city, or they reform, beg pardon of women, "And learn to honour them, as much as I" (line 702).

The moral ambiguities of the poem hardly need elaboration. For example, whether one wishes to hold up even the tainted norms of lechery, pimping, whoring, and bastardy on behalf of the beloved, luscious female sex is perhaps doubtful. The oceanic verbal virility of the poem helps one temporarily to overlook those blemishes while reading.

One does not overlook the incessant anger, improbable solutions, lack of focus, absence of specific causation, usurpation of the divine function, and the paucity of recognizable particulars which allow us to believe that a genuine enemy has performed genuinely offensive acts, that he is part of a larger coherent pattern of demonstrable corruption, and that he must be punished for the sake of the commonweal. The modern reader is likely to join the reviewer in the *London Chronicle* who said of Churchill's effort: "every one must applaud the Poet's indignation; but it would certainly have had a stronger effect, had it been less indiscriminate and *outré*" (Grant, p. 550). Garrick is so civilized that his satire causes twitters rather than concern; Churchill is so strident and excessive that in spite of his announced affection for the sex with which he prefers to copulate, we discount his claims and may not put on skirts to save our manhood. Pope is the most successful of the three in part because of his native talent, and in part because that talent—as in *Arbuthnot* and "Sporus"—was benevolently synthetic.

I do not wish either to ride the Horatian-Juvenalian hypothesis too hard or to insist that it offers the sole paradigm for the development of formal or other satire after mid-century. Both Johnson's *Vanity of Human Wishes* (1749) and Arthur Murphy's *Seventeen Hundred and Ninety One: A Poem in Imitation of the Thirteenth Satire of Juvenal* illustrate a redefined Juvenal without Churchill's lack of proportion. Garrick's *Fribbleriad*, however, suggests that the devolution of satiric kinds also may illumine some of the weaknesses in later satires different from Pope's, for here too we often see extreme Horatian or Juvenalian modes that actually abandon their neglected parents. When Pope does reemerge as a model, he becomes a source not for mingled but for grimly Juvenalian satire.

The Horatian impetus may be seen in the satires of Richard Owen Cambridge. Their frugal meal includes several imitations of Horace, adaptations of his techniques, and an affinity with satire's comic mask. In one poem that alludes to Pope's *Epilogue to the Satires* Cambridge uses Horatian dialogue to indicate that Horatian satire itself is unmannerly and suspect—that is in "The Danger of Writing Verse; A Dialogue between a Young Poet and his Friend. Addressed to Sir Charles Hanbury Williams, Knt. Occasioned by his satirical Ode upon Mr. Hussey's Marriage with the Duchess of Manchester; which gave so much personal offence" (1746). As in many satiric dialogues, the Friend tries to dissuade the Poet from writing satire. For Cambridge, however, the dissuader is not an arm of the ominous state, or an aristocrat offended by attacks, or a court hireling deaf to the song of virtue; instead, he is the exemplar of civility who hopes to aid society and the poet by blunting satire's barbs. The satirist's friends, for example, fear that his unforgiving foes will harm him and that the satirist soon will attack them. Indeed, Horace himself is generally enjoyed not merely because of his excellent verse but because his antiquity makes him safe for us. In any case, satire is read by the malicious, who enjoy seeing their fellows attacked. That is not the way human beings should deal with one another, the Friend insists, and he concludes with the salutary admonition that were Horace alive, "I should think it, tho' loth, / My duty to give this advice to you both."[13]

In this mid-century dialogue the Friend-and-adversarius embodies not the wrong but the right dissuasion from satire, deservedly has the last word, and rejects Horace because his satire offends. That Cambridge was not alone in recommending a subdued form of subdued satire, one ultimately traceable to certain Horatian devices and assumptions, is made clear in Christopher Anstey's *New Bath Guide* (1766), which reached its twelfth edition in 1784, and which in many ways embodies popular and amiable satiric flaccidity.

[13] The poem is quoted from *The Works of Richard Owen Cambridge, Esq.* (1803), p. 60.

CONCLUSION

The *New Bath Guide* is written in a series of epistles with some precedent in Horace.[14] The writer and recipient, however, are not Rome's polished satirist and powerful aristocrat but the naive members of the well-connected B[lunde]R[head] country family writing to their audience at home. The poem's tones and intention appear in Miss Jenny's first letter, which praises the "wholesome satire" that "much enhances / The merit of our best romances" as well as modern plays. The other letters in the series are also opposed to the "base and unjust accusations" that "Arise from the malice and spleen of mankind" (p. 78), as Mr. Simkin B–n–r–d puts it in Letter 12. Only "the meanest" of the poetic band take "satire's thorny road" (p. 110).

Nonetheless, there is satire aplenty here, though it is so gentle that in 1771 Smollett's *Humphry Clinker* takes many of the same scenes and, from Matt Bramble's point of view, puts them in a hostile Juvenalian perspective of the decline of civilized values. But for Anstey, the only relevant model is a wholly toothless satirist with a significantly altered but recognizable lineage. The first line of Anstey's "Epilogue" below probably comes from Horace's first satire of the second book and Pope's *Fortescue*; the second comes from Anstey's apparent desire not to cause any alarm by invoking those walkers among thorns; the third and fourth show that he is dealing with the most unthreatening sort of weaknesses in unthreatening folk:

> There are who complain that my verse is severe,
> And what is much worse—that my Book is too dear:
> The Ladies protest that I keep no decorum
> In setting such patterns of folly before 'em.
>
> (P. 105)

Anstey's version of a defensive Horace need not fret about his adversaria in such a world, since she—the change is

---

[14] Quotations are from *The Poetical Works of the Late Christopher Anstey, Esq.* (1808).

worth noting—is simply a creature of the fashionable mo-
ment and not an offended grandee able to bruise one's
corpus of bones or words. The satirist-Guide argues that he
never intended any harm to religion or virtue and that,
like Horace, he is imitating nature. As in Cambridge's ear-
lier poem, this Horatian apologia is found wanting because
it is found unfriendly—now by a judge perhaps less than
fully informed. The Second Lady rejects even Horace of
the *Ars Poetica* if he justifies satire at all.

> Prithee don't talk to me of your HORACE and FLACCUS,
> When you come like an impudent wretch to attack us.
> What's *Parnassus* to you? Take away but your rhyme,
> And the strains of the bell-man are full as sublime.
>
> (P. 107)

The women in this epilogue remain unconvinced and,
like their male counterparts in Horace and Pope, continue
to urge an end to satire—but now with a major difference.
"Pray," the Guide says to the ladies, "tell a poor poet
what's proper to do." The First Lady knows the answer:
"Why if thou must write, thou hadst better compose /
Some *novels*, or elegant letters in prose," and do so "In
epistles like PAMELA's chaste and devout— / A book that
my family's never without." The other women request an
appropriate hero with delicate feelings, taste, passion, and
"some incidents" in an amusing and pleasurable novel "Fit
for modest young ladies" (pp. 116-17). Earlier synthesizing
or Juvenalian satirists associated hostility to satire with hos-
tility to culture, decency, and exposure of evil. Anstey sees
the death of satire in the call for novelistic amusements
and is annoyed rather than apocalyptic. In earlier battles
for satire's life, Horace conjured up Lucilius, and Pope
adapted Lucilius, Horace, and Juvenal. Anstey raises the
shade of the actor Quin, an adversarius willing to justify
the satiric urge. "I come not to accuse / The motley la-
bours of the mirthful Muse" (p. 119), he reassures the
quaking mortal. Quin finally gives the Guide full permis-

sion to write on and to "Take the mask from [woman's]
d–mned hypocritical face" (p. 122). The Guide, helped by
the ghost whose harshness to women he cannot accept,
gives his own speech in defense of satire:

> Come on then, ye Muses, I'll laugh down my day,
> In spite of them all will I carol my lay;
> But perish my voice, and untun'd be my lyre,
> If my verse one indelicate thought shall inspire:
> Ye angels! who watch o'er the slumbering fair,
> Protect their sweet dreams, make their virtue your care!
> Bear witness, yon moon, the chaste empress of night!
> Yon stars, that diffuse the pure heavenly light!
> How oft have I mourn'd that such blame should accrue
> From one wicked letter of pious Miss PRUE!
>
> (P. 123)

Pope had elevated the apologia that Anstey diminishes.
In *Fortescue* Pope tells his lawyer that, whatever the odds,
he will "strip the Gilding off a Knave" or "perish in the
gen'rous Cause" (lines 115, 117); in *Arbuthnot* he tells his
doctor that "Curst be the verse, how well soe'er it flow, /
That tends to make one worthy Man my foe" (lines 283-
84). Pope's Juvenalian anger is transmogrified into Anstey's
laughter; his "perish" as death becomes "perish" as polite
satiric voice; his man of moral worth becomes a woman of
fashion. In *Fortescue* that lawyer says "if you needs must
write, write CAESAR's Praise" (line 21), and implies that the
king remains an active source of reward. Anstey's woman
says, "Why if thou must write, . . . compose / Some novels."
Pope justifies his satire with moral imperatives borrowed
from Horace and given backbone by his brother-satirists.
Anstey justifies his satire by rejecting even mild Horace and
insisting that—in the proper sort of female at Bath—virtue
already is guarded by angels. In such a comfortable world,
no wonder that the Second Lady can insist, "don't talk to
me of your HORACE and FLACCUS," for Anstey anticipates

her sternest demands and removes the arrows that the comic satirist once used.

Apollo, no doubt aware of the principle of *discordia concors,* saw fit to redress that balance and gave those barbs to Juvenal's later heirs. John Wolcot's invention of his generally raucous Peter Pindar well illustrates the other one-note version of satire that scarred the later eighteenth century, and which Peter himself called "volcanic."[15] Peter's satire includes energetic vulgarity, amusing scandal, and appealing abuse. Much of it has the compromised and compromising charm of a Rowlandson or Gillray print, in which the world seems to be populated by grotesques of whom we disapprove, but by whom neither we nor the artist are threatened. We laugh at such verbal cartoons in which the superiority of contempt replaces the insecurity of isolated outrage. Instead of Pope's ominous George II, we see Wolcot's ridiculous George III. The *Lousiad* (1785-95), for example, shows the king falling from his horse during the hunt: "all the Nobles deem'd their Monarch dead; / But luckily he pitch'd upon his head" (line 196). Wolcot abounds with this vivacious and surly wit; but he also abounds with hostility to the corrupt powers, fear of collapsing institutions, and, as Britain reacted to the French Revolution, fear of suppression or worse. His satire thus burns, scalps, kills, tears, blasts, lashes, cannonades, and pierces. It performs these acts with a sword, tomahawk, cannon, whip, or other weapon suitable for the blunt additive art of Peter's satire, which is "eagle, falcon, kite, / Hawk" (1: 404). Peter of course subjects much of his nation to his lash; in the process he incorporates several other genres in his broad net. Odes, elegies, jeremiads, mock-heroics, and epistles share approximately the same waspish tones, and so, as Peter says in an ode, he must praise the

15 Quotations in volume 1 are from John Wolcot, *The Works of Peter Pindar, Esq*[r] (1794); quotations in volume 5 are from *The Works of Peter Pindar, Esq.* (1801) . See 1: 86 for "volcanic."

virtuous abroad "Because I cannot find them . . . *at home*" (1: 439). In the gospel according to Peter, Horatian satire is not sly, polite, and insinuating, but is once again the product of rage, as it was thought to be in the Renaissance: "As brother Horace has it—*tumet jecur*: / Nor in her angry progress will I check her" (1: 89). Consequently, when Peter adapts the *nil admirari* tradition of Horace's sixth epistle of the first book, he turns away from modest disclaimer of the world's attractions and toward his own more vigorous attack—here upon Bishop Porteus and Hannah More.

There are several reasons for Peter's anger. One is that he waves a banner inscribed with Juvenal's *facit indignatio versum*: "Shock'd at th' abuse, how rage inflames my veins! / Who can help swearing when such wights he sees?" (1: 90). Another is that Wolcot's admittedly egotistical persona (5: 173) frets about how the world treats him. His "Jeremi-Ad," for instance, "pathetically lamenteth the fallen state of ONE of OUR MOST *admired* POETS, *videlicet*, MYSELF!" (5: 62). He also offers the commonplace that the British character demands ferocity, "truth," and repudiation of flattery, courts, and kings. In one ode, "Satire" asks the receptive Peter: "Where is the glorious freedom of our Isle, / If not permitted to call names?" (1: 86). In another poem, Peter talks with the laureate Thomas Warton, who grouses that Peter does not fear kings, whom he regards as "merely *common* folks" (1: 434). Peter himself rejects all "crouching courtiers, that surround a throne" (1: 440) and tells Warton that he must turn his back on a king who would "disgrace thy lay," must be like a bristling porcupine, and must not trade his soul for mere sustenance (1: 442).

Anger and satire are predictable when Peter looks at this apparently unredeemable world in which his poetic weapons slay fewer than he hoped and endanger himself. Accordingly, in "Liberty's Last Squeek," Peter complains that because of Pitt "there is death in the joke / That squinteth

at Queen or at King" and folly must therefore "go *free*."
Such freedom means political and satiric slavery:

> Yes, FOLLY will prattle and grin
>   With her scourges OPPRESSION will rise,
> Since Satire's a damnable sin,
>   And a sin to be virtuous and wise.
>
> (5: 70)

In the second part of his poem, his "Ode to Jurymen,"
Peter hopes that his persecutors will not invoke "Dame
INJUSTICE," throw him in jail, and hang him (5: 80). And
in "Out at Last" he envies the poet Isaiah, who freely
satirized "the Babylonian Monarch"; but "Were *I* to talk
so of a *British King*, / What were my fate? Alas! a string!"
(5: 115).

By the end of the eighteenth century, Wolcot's Peter
Pindar comes to live in a world even more rigorously hos-
tile than that of Juvenal, who was merely banished, not
executed, for his impertinence to the court. Peter turns to
Pope for what may be his most eloquent response to that
world, and makes his own George III and Pitt as dangerous
to civilized Britain as Pope's George II and Walpole. Wol-
cot's title announces his genealogy and foreshadows his
intention, as we recall Pope's two dialogues of *One Thou-
sand Seven Hundred and Thirty Eight* in Wolcot's two
dialogues of *One Thousand Seven Hundred and Ninety
Six*.

Wolcot indeed echoes several of Pope's satires and de-
vices in this poem. In *Bathurst*, for example, Pope writes
that after the unworthy Balaam is knighted, "lo! two pud-
dings smoak'd upon the board" (line 360); in Wolcot's sec-
ond dialogue Peter says that "The JUDGES' venison smoak'd
upon the board!" (5: 29). Pope's second epistle of Horace's
second book characterizes London poets' displacement of
their betters: "Call *Tibbald Shakespear*, and he'll swear the
Nine / Dear *Cibber*! never match'd one Ode of thine"

(lines 137-38): Wolcot's Tom claims, "Call MASON, SHAKE-SPEAR; *Mister* HAYLEY, POPE / Their jaws with sudden inspiration ope" (5: 18). Such examples can be multiplied; but they are most significant, not as evidence to support one's intuitive response to Wolcot's poem, but because in certain ways they undergo a sea-change and significantly darken Pope's shading. Thus in *Arbuthnot,* Pope insists that "Curst be the Verse, how well so'er it flow, / That tends to make one worthy Man my foe" (lines 283-84). Wolcot's bitterly Juvenalian Tom sees no good man at all and turns Pope's couplet against a flatterer: "Curs'd be the period, whether verse or prose, / That round a worthless head a glory throws" (5: 17). Similarly, Arbuthnot asks "Who breaks a Butterfly upon a Wheel?" (line 308), but Tom sees a larger creature who needs rough strokes: "Who with a velvet lash would flog a Bear?" (5: 30). This depraved world offers no support from the throne or its aristocrats. Pope told Burlington that he could "Erect new wonders, and the old repair," and "Jones and Palladio to themselves restore" (lines 192-93). His ideas inspire the kings who will "Bid Harbors open, public Ways extend, / Bid Temples, worthier of the God, ascend" (lines 197-98). In Peter's normless world the satirist himself must assume the royal mantle, fantasize that if he had "GEORGE's millions" (5: 15) or, better still, if he were king, "palaces should rise," not for court sycophants, as now, but for lab'ring GENIUS" and Taste. He would renew the world with great artists and "Bid . . . Palladios spring" (5: 15).

Wolcot's effort in the genre of the satiric calendar enlarges Pope's scenes in another grim way. *One Thousand Seven Hundred and Thirty Eight* shows that even in its decadent world the satirist wields God's "sacred Weapon" (*Dialogue* II. 212), and that ultimately Vice shall be known and labeled and Virtue loved and protected—if only in the hereafter, where Virtue's "Priestess Muse forbids the Good to dye, / And ope's the Temple of Eternity" (lines 234-35). "Truth guards the Poet" and sanctifies his verse

CONCLUSION

(line 246), because whatever happens during this age, God will not let His servants be thwarted when all books are closed. For Pope, a distant "success" is possible so long as God is possible. In Wolcot's resolutely secular poem, wit and liberty are dead, the arts are in disgrace, and omnivorous ministers devour the country.

All this gloom is placed in a frame of energetic, sometimes clever exchange between Tom and Peter. Tom is a young college-bred satirist yearning to inflict himself upon the many who deserve his falchion, thunder, lightning, broadsides, and comparable weapons from the magazine of outrage. Peter is the jaded satirist cast in the unfamiliar role of dissuading adversarius and apparent advocate of Horatian ridicule. This heightened exercise in Pope's dialogue form is a virtual confrontation between apparently competing approaches to satire, and it shows that in so unhappy a time both rage and ridicule are useless. Unlike their poetic predecessors, Wolcot's satirist and adversarius agree regarding the need to punish those responsible for the malign world about them; and unlike their predecessors, his satirist and adversarius have only one another to speak to and are ignored by Pitt's minions, who nonetheless can destroy them. Hence when Tom fumes that he will "make a charming little *hell* for Courts," Peter replies with "Heav'ns! Tom, be cooler; take advice" (5: 13), and later, "Fie, fie, Tom—really you are too severe" (5: 30). Tom, in turn, scolds with "For shame!—by *ridicule* you ward each stroke, / And make the Ruin of the State a *joke!*" (5: 32), and "Misplac'd indeed is all your ridicule, / That means to thwart my plans by calling *fool*" (5: 33). Since the speakers are friends and share the same dark vision of the world, they finally agree and Tom is finally educated. He realizes that Peter's rough laughter is a good man's attempt to protest the world he cannot defeat.

TOM

So, then, you laugh at hopes of *Reformation?*

361

CONCLUSION

PETER

PITT finds a tame old *Hack* in our *good* NATION:
Safe through the dirt, and ev'ry dangerous road,
The BEAST *consents* to bear his galling LOAD;
And, spite of all that we can *sing* or *say*,
FOOLS will be FOOLS, and MINISTERS—*betray*.

(5: 35)

This is the ridicule of despair, not the ridicule of the satirist confident that laughter is appropriate in a nation whose ministers, like Maecenas, reflect a benevolent poet-prince to whom a poet-citizen can speak and expect to be heard.

This poem also shows a government potentially fatal to the satirist. From the start, Peter warns Tom that Truth is dangerous and cannot screen him: "The MUSE that tells plain truth, with edge-tools sports" (5: 8), that his song's "note is *death*" (5: 9), and that, perhaps alluding to Juvenal's banishment, Horace's *Satires* ii. 1, or both, Tom can succeed no better than a more famous opponent of Pitt's:

But what says PITT? will PITT thy rage allow?
Believe me, TOM, the blunderbuss of Law
Makes a long shot—an engine form'd to *awe*—
By this has many a bird of Satire bled—
Be prudent, therefore, and revere the *lead*.
Think of thy banish'd *Namesake*!

(5: 24)

Horace had used a comparable scene to argue on the authority of Lucilius—if he then was protected by the state in his just satire, so should Horace be now; Pope adapted this to argue that if the sycophants Boileau and Dryden could satirize freely then, so should Pope now. In Wolcot's scene, the argument on authority is an argument on punishment—Tom the satirist shall, he thinks, gain strength from the example of opposition punished by the court:

What! TOM PAINE?
I *like* the Man—should boast to *hold his train*:

CONCLUSION

TOM PAINE speaks boldly out; and so I dare
Strike at Court Slaves, nor sex nor order spare;
Spread o'er my quarry VICE, my eagle wings,
Nor dread the conflict, though opposed by *Kings!*

(5: 24)

Thus far we have seen Wolcot elevating scenes or devices from Horace, Juvenal, and Pope. He does the same with Persius. We remember that in his first satire the court's dissuading Monitor warned Persius that there is a snarling dog guarding the great man's door if he approaches. Pope may allude to this when, in *Bathurst,* Old Cotta's "gaunt mastiff growling at the gate, / Affrights the beggar whom he longs to eat" (lines 197-98). Wolcot's Tom may be alluding to both, and again heightening both, when he laments the decline not of hospitality but of aristocratic patronage in general, and the contempt with which art is held by the court:

How is fair ART, and SCIENCE, in disgrace!
What Patron meets them with a smiling face?
See, like a shadow, GENIUS, limping, poor,
In supplication at a GREAT MAN's door!—
And see with insolence his lacquey treat him;
And were he fat enough, the *Dog* would eat him.

(5: 23)

Though Peter immediately begs for Taste and Reason to return to Britain, he knows this is impossible so long as George III, Pitt, and their minions continue to reject and starve art and the satirists who hope to correct them: "Ere long [Pitt] leaps on PETER's dove-like strains; / And should the MUSE be ravish'd, what remains?" (5: 25). Like Pope before him, Wolcot exaggerated the dangers to the resilient nation and confused the discomfort of the part with the ruin of the whole. Along the way, however, he reflected and contributed to the process of bifurcation that formal and some other satire were undergoing through much of the later eighteenth century. Wolcot is most at home strutting and raging among ruins, and would be least at home in Pope's social, "artificial" grotto and gardens, where affection induces belief in anger, and literary form tries to suggest the complexity of human response.

The monist satiric practices of Cambridge, Garrick, and Anstey on the one hand, and Churchill and Wolcot on the other, highlight Pope's own plural or mingled formal verse satire; this (relatively) new kind, as Johnson said of Shakespeare, and Dryden said of Milton, improves on the ancient patterns because it includes their separate strengths. Pope used Horace, Persius, and Juvenal in the proportion his occasion demanded. His ability to combine every poet's power in one would have been lessened without his eclectic imagination and ability to compartmentalize, to accept and adapt certain literary devices and political postures in these poets while rejecting others. Pope's character, individual talent, and historical moment, including the prior example of Boileau, offered the perfect receptacle for the satiric traditions he inherited. Others thereafter tried to follow both his separate and synthetic roads; but they did so with less distinction and, more often, I believe, took the disparate paths that leave Pope's comprehensive achievement as impressive in its way as *Paradise Lost* is in its. Each is a monument to the highest level of a composite art shaped by a personal voice.

Translations of French Passages

34 15   A poet much superior to Horace, and whom all the wise men of Europe have celebrated with unanimous accord.

34 20   I was walking with Homer, Tacitus, and Lucan, and would not have left them to talk with you, if like so many others you had only intended to ornament antitheses.

37 14   A free soul elevated above the baseness of common opinions, to which constraint, servitude, complaisance, and flattery are unknown. It appears that in this Juvenal has surpassed Horace.

37 19   He spares no one, and . . . an intrepid warrior, he comes boldly to combat.

47 18   It is always the fault of the poet when he undertakes a subject which he can not treat politely.

84 15   And *Juvenal*, with Rhetorician's Rage,
Scourg'd the rank Vices of a Wicked Age.
Tho' horrid Truths thro' all his Labours
     Shine,
In what he Writes there's something of
     Divine:
Whether he Blames the *Caprean* Debauch,
Or of *Sejanus* Fall relates th' Approach;
Or that he makes the trembling Senate come
To the stern Tyrant, to receive their Doom;
Or *Roman* Vice in coursest Habits shews,
And Paints an Empress reeking from the
     Stews:
In all he Writes appears a noble Flame.

[Quoted from *The Works of Monsieur Boileau. Made English from the last Paris Edition, By Several Hands*, 2nd ed. (1736), 1: 103-4.]

84 28   Of these wise masters Regnier, clever disciple, alone among us formed [himself] on their models.

87 11   You are my Horace, my Persius, my Juvenal, and I find you alone in these three men!

87 18   When Boileau adapts Persius and Juvenal, he imitates the precision of the one and the energy of the other.

88 11   Suppose—that this was true, *learned* responds admirably to Persius, *Gay* to Horace, and *sublime* to Juvenal.

88 14   With notes, and above all with the comparison and the parallel of the places of Horace and Juvenal.

89 3   This satire is completely in the taste of Persius, and marks a gloomy philosopher [or thinker], and one who cannot bear the vices of men.

89 9   I have often heard it said to the author that in all he had taken from these three poets, nothing succeeded better than that which he had imitated from Persius.

97 1   He said sometimes in speaking of these sort of imitations, *This is not called imitating; it is to joust against his original.*

97 19   The case of impassioned satire is wholly different, as in Persius and Juvenal. These two poets, given over to their gloomy humor, preferred to imitate the philosophers or the sophists in their vehement invectives against vice, rather than to march, like Lucilius and Horace, in the steps of the ancient Greek comic dramatists.

98 3   Despréaux has not outdone Juvenal. The Latin expression has quite as much energy as the French expression; and the merit of our poet is to have changed the nature of what he borrowed from Juvenal, and to have turned an extremely serious idea to a witty, even a very witty, one.

102 31   There is nothing richer; there is nothing which can be more fruitfully cultivated, and which offers so vast a field for reflection: see how his beginning [of Satire Eight] is dry, insignificant, and even trivial:

Of all the Creatures which *Earth*'s Surface tread,
That fly i'th' Air, or in the Sea are bred,
Throughout the Globe from *Paris* to *Japan*,

PAGE/LINE

The arrant'st Fool in my Opinion's *MAN*.

[*Works of Monsieur Boileau*, 1: 209.]

103 6   Oh! how the Juvenal of England, Oh! how the impetuous Rochester enters his subject with a livelier manner when he treats the same subject.

Were I (who to my cost already am
One of those strange prodigious creatures, man)
A spirit free to choose, for my own share,
What case of flesh and blood I pleased to wear,
I'd be a dog, a monkey, or a bear,
Or anything but that vain animal
Who is so proud of being rational.

(Lines 1-7)

[*Satyr against Reason and Mankind*, in *The Complete Poems of John Wilmot, Earl of Rochester*, ed. David M. Vieth (New Haven: Yale Univ. Press, 1968), p. 94.]

103 13   Compare these two satires, M. le Marquis; in this one you will see overflow all the spleen of a sublime misanthropy, and such a one that ordinarily inspires the passion of virtue in vigorous hearts; you will see in the other, *that a goat has a better formed spirit than a man; that a doctor, even of the Sorbonne, is less learned than an ass,* and a hundred other commonplaces expressed, I confess, in very harmonious and very precise verse, but which leave nothing in the head nor the heart.

103 22   There is our genuine satirist! There is our Lucilius, our Juvenal, our Rochester!

112 24   In most of the books which had been written on matters either of theology or of metaphysics.

113 17   Called by some the English Juvenal . . . are in truth quite strong and even violent, but there is a great lack of skill and correctness, so that the English themselves do not classify him among poets of the first order.

113 24   Dedicated to a lady, and destined to divert the fair sex.

TRANSLATIONS OF FRENCH PASSAGES

113 32   More familiar in England than in France, or at least envisaged differently. The form of government renders lawful in the one, sometimes even useful, a kind of writing justly proscribed and scorned in the other.

114 16   There are sections in Shakespeare, in Milton, in Addison, in Pope, in Swift, in Gay, in Thomson, which are as deserving of our esteem as anything that antiquity ever produced.

114 n8   Pedantry, and singularity, or . . . they use vulgarity and expressions considered too common and low in France to be subject matter in literature.

115 7   Their country is the refuge of satire; there liberty almost always degenerates into unbridled license; each week is marked by newspapers of every kind, in which religion, or government, princes, magistrates, the clergy, are attacked without discretion.

115 16   That they contain many things that have never entered the human mind.

115 19   That the English language allows an author as elegant as Pope to insert these low words in his poem.

115 25   Is so exaggerated, that it is not permissible for me to cite more than six strophes out of sixteen.

115 32   English aversion for their kings and ministers. For a long time they bore the yoke of authority with repugnance; not content to have changed the fundamental laws of the kingdom under each reign, they submitted only reluctantly to those which they established a century ago. They attributed, often without scrutiny, to their kings and ministers projects of ambition, usurpation, and tyranny; and their poets, such as those whose works have been printed in an immense collection entitled [Poems on] Affairs of State, yet stir their nation's pride and love of independence.

369

TRANSLATIONS OF FRENCH PASSAGES

PAGE/LINE

116 19   Their poets, witness Pope and Gay, are more inspired than ours by love of their country, a passion which alone, after religion, can evoke the sublime. Let us therefore pass by the faults of their manners and of their style in favor of their heroic virtues and their noble ideas.

129 23   See translation for p. xii/13.

        More judicious and more chaste than Lucilius [Horace] holds the middle ground between the boiling invective of Juvenal and the obscure brevity of Persius.

154 16   Does it not seem that it is Juvenal who turns these thoughts of Horace to his own manner?

154 22   Has almost always this ardent, brusque, and passionate tone, which is so original and so natural.

155 1   Is almost always excessive.

155 2   A bitter and severe thinker, an ardent and excessive poet; in a word, an Englishman.

155 5   In the decadence of taste, the rhetorician Juvenal, nourished by hyperbole and exaggerated figures, . . . substituted a hard and bitter tone, a pedantic grandiloquence, for the politeness and urbanity of the favorite of Augustus; and satire, born from comedy, no longer preserved any trace of its ancient origin.

155 18   Some admirable sections, written with the force and the vehemence of Juvenal, the delicacy and the finesse of Horace, the precision and the nobility of Persius. In several places M. Pope seems to have appropriated not only the tone and the dialogues of this last poet, but even his mysterious air and his obscurity, in order to hide from the eyes of his dangerous or powerful enemies the darts that he aimed at them.

170 16   He works to uproot vice; and . . . in the second he strives to uproot errors and false opinions.

TRANSLATIONS OF FRENCH PASSAGES

170 18   He strives to give there some precepts for virtue, and to kindle in our hearts the love that it deserves.

170 n2   The subject of this piece is fine; but it is more fitting for a *Satire* than for an *Epistle.* . . . The *Moral Epistle* is properly a didactic work which it is necessary to embellish and that one can enliven, but of which the ground must necessarily be a collection of philosophic remarks expressed with sufficient vigor. That is what one seeks in vain here.

191 15   He has not written, like Boileau, with the intention of imitating Juvenal and of offending women: he has no other plan than to illumine nature.

208 24   The Law of the XII Tables bore the death penalty against those who defamed the reputation of others through satiric verse, and Augustus renewed this same law, which had lost much of its vigor.

220 n18   He speaks allegorically about Nero in the person of Alcibiades, and tells him that he has hidden sores under his golden robe, that is to say, many vices that the glitter of his riches and his exaltation hide from the view of the people.

228 1   I am convinced that he has put it there intentionally in order to make his censors understand that he considers himself thoroughly assured of the approbation and of the protection of Augustus. The trick is modest and skilful.

240 15   See translation for p. 155/18.

270 8   See translation for p. 155/18.

Index

INDEX

Bacon, Francis, 249, 285
Balaam, Sir, 177-79, 339, 359
Barber, Alderman John, 310
Barclay, Alexander, 5
Barnard, Sir John, 293, 320
Barrett, Stephen, 33
Bassus, Caesius, 64
Bathurst, Allen, Earl, 175-77, 183, 187, 192, 232, 287, 301, 333
Bathurst, Henry, 119
Battestin, Martin, xvii, 188n
Batteux, Abbé Charles, 17, 23, 47, 48, 69, 201, 201n, 202
Bayle, Pierre, 63, 287
Beach, Thomas, 339
Beattie, James, 22, 25, 26, 28, 333
Bentley, Thomas, 140, 143n-44n, 157, 160-61, 173, 220n, 242
Bernard, Jacques, 112
Bethel, Hugh, 277-83 *passim*
Bettenham, James, 326
Bible, 313
Bidle, John, 10n
Biographia Classica, 130
Blackmore, Sir Richard, 118, 128, 211
Blackstone, Sir William, 229
Blackwell, Anthony, 23
Blackwell, Thomas (the younger), 48, 110
Blondel, François, 17
Blount, Martha, 175
Blount, Sir Thomas Pope, 8
Blunt, Sir John, 311
Boileau-Despréaux, Nicolas: adversarius in, 94-95; on ancients and moderns, 98; *Art Poétique* translated, 85-86; and Augustus, 101-2; borrowings by, 89, 91-96; British dislike, 4, 99-101, 115, 128, 140; British imitate, 8, 96, 100, 102-3, 217n; British praise, 86, 120; Casaubon influences, 97; causation

in, 91, 95; Dacier influences, 97; dialogue in, 93, 95; editions of, 86; epistles criticized, 170n-71n; *Encyclopédie* on, x; French dislike, 101-4; on Horace and Juvenal, 18, 24, 101; Horatian, xii, 89-102 *passim*, 104, 168, 217n; Juvenalian, 88, 89, 92-94, 97-98; not Juvenalian, 80, 92-93, 95-96, 97-98, 100-1, 103-4; and Lucilius, 84; mixed satire of, xii, 4, 8, 86-87, 91-97, 105, 129, 364; Oldham translates, 96; on Paris, 92-93; on Persius, 69, 88, 89, 94-96, 270; Pope on, 168, 223-24, 362; and Regnier, 84-85; and Rochester, 96, 101-4, 103n; as Walpole ally, 168; Yart on, 87, 115, 191
    works cited: Art Poétique, 84-86; epigram, 88, 88n; *Epistles, III*, 89-91, 95, 170n; *VIII*, 98-99; *Ode sur . . . Namur*, 100, 104, 115; *Satires, I*, 89; *II*, 89, 217n; *III, IV, V*, 89; 92, 97-98; *VII*, 8, 89, 95, 96, 217n; *VIII*, 95-96, 97, 102; *IX*, 89; *X*, 89, 93-95; *XI, XII*, 89
Bolingbroke, Henry St. John, Viscount: and Arbuthnot, 250; attacks upon, 157, 163, 164, 173n, 234, 292; and *Fortescue*, 206, 207, 213, 225, 233; as Maecenas, 164, 292, 298, 333; on Persius and mingled satire, 131; Pope praises, 173n, 292, 295, 297, 320, 328; Pope's ally, 157, 162, 173n, 239, 241, 292-98, 333; Pope's poem to, 292-98
Boscawen, William, 25, 30, 153-54, 168, 228, 342n
Bowles, Thomas, 33
Bramston, James, 171-72, 171n-72n, 337

374

INDEX

Francis, Philip, 21, 218
Frederick, Prince of Wales, 323-24, 332
Fundanius, Horace's, 56

Garrick, David: adapts *Arbuthnot*, 345; Horatianism of, 344-46, 364; *Fribbleriad* and homosexuality, 343-46, 345n, 352; mellifluent verse of, 348
Garter, Knights of the, 219-21, 220n-21n, 288, 290, 290n. *See also* Walpole, Sir Robert
Garth, Samuel, 132, 249, 255
Gay, John, 20, 114, 116, 132, 255, 255n, 257
Gay, Joseph, pseud. for Breval, John Durant, 255n
Gazetteer, The Daily, 127, 292, 308n, 310, 316n, 325, 325n
George I, King, 213, 219, 310
George II, King: as Augustus, 18, 43, 164, 211, 247, 273, 289, 308-11 *passim*, 356; in *Bathurst*, 178; as builder in *Burlington*, 187, 187n, 188; as Domitian, 290; English of, 237, 309; as Midas, 243-44, 245, 259, 272-73, 274; as Nero, 123, 127, 148, 259, 290; Pope opposes, 51, 98, 165, 168, 222, 233, 246, 247, 289-90, 357, 359; in Pope's MSS, 224; as Richard III, 229; and Mme de Welmoden, 289-90; and Walpole, 149, 204, 232, 292
George III, King, 357, 359, 360-61
German Acta Eruditorum, 8
Gibbon, Edward, 34, 37, 39
Gifford, William, 25, 36, 37n, 38-39n, 49, 60, 66-67, 245-55
Gilbert, Thomas, 41, 117, 119, 119n, 146, 337
Gildon, Charles, 14, 18, 29, 250
Gillray, James, 357

Gould, Robert, 10-11, 26, 83
Grainger, James, 223, 223n
Granville, George, Baron Lansdowne, 249, 255
Gray, Thomas, 338n
Greene, Edward Burnaby, 24, 33, 39, 50, 60, 66, 67, 110
Gurges, Fabius, 78, 78n
Guthrie, Patrick, 158-59, 338n. *See also* Guthry, Mr.
Guthry, Mr., 220, 220n, 234-35, 235n

Hall, Bishop Joseph, 8n, 10
Hall, William Henry, 25, 133
Halsband, Robert, 122n, 146n
Handel, George Friedrich, 107
Harte, Walter, 28, 32
Hawkins, Sir John, 36n
Hayley, William, 360
Hector, Homer's, 283
Heinsius, Daniel, 8, 9n, 13
Henley, John, "Orator," 124, 313
Henry IV, King, 304
Hervey, John, Baron: attacks Pope, 158, 159-60, 210n, 233-34, 241, 265; and Caroline, 194; as Fanny, 207-8, 239, 278, 281, 305; homosexuality of, 145-46, 146n, 261-64, 269, 344, 346; Persian satire of, 122, 122n; Pope's letter to, 205; Pulteney attacks, 263-64; as Satan, 260, 268, 269, 275, 344; as Sporus, 258-65, 268-69, 272, 275, 278, 344, 346, 352; and Walpole, 194, 241, 260-64; Yart on, 154
Hesiod, x
Heywood, Thomas, 309
Higden, Henry, 19-20, 25
Hill, Aaron, 131, 150, 334-35
Hill, "Sir" John, 38, 133
Hodgson, Francis, 28, 36n, 42-43, 50

INDEX

Holyday, Barton, 9, 27, 28, 31, 60, 63, 68

Homer, x, xi, 34, 107, 248, 250, 254-55, 283

homosexuality: and Alcibiades, 74; Churchill on, 348-52; Garrick on, 343-47; and Hervey, 145-46, 146n, 261-64, 269, 344, 346; and Horace, 145-46, 145n-46n; and Nero, 74, 261, 344; Pope on, 145-46, 261, 264, 269, 344; Pulteney on, 263-64; Smollett on, 145, 145n-46n; Spence on, 146

Hopkins, John, 309

Horace, Quintus Horatius Flaccus, and Horatian satire: Anstey adapts, 353-57; attacked, xvi, 37-39, 40-44, 333-34; and Boileau, xii, 8, 24, 89-102 *passim*, 104, 168, 217n; British commentators on, 6, 9, 19, 22, 27, 39, 48, 105, 111-12, 128, 134, 140, 150; Cambridge adapts, 352-53; Creech translates, 19, 217-18, 228, 291; Dryden on, 8, 9n, 19, 28, 31-32, 31n, 38, 47, 110; French reactions to, 14-18, 37, 82, 114, 201, 240; Garrick adapts, 344-46, 352; and government, 49, 51-58 *passim*; homosexuality of, 145-46, 145n-46n; imitations of, 85, 108, 117, 137-39, 147, 173, 337, 338, 338n, 339-40; and Juvenal, 18, 19, 50, 81, 95-96, 121, 132, 254-55, 284; Juvenal inferior to, 12, 14, 15-22, 34, 36-37, 97-98, 130, 155; Juvenal and/or Persius equal to, 8, 22-26, 61-62, 133; Juvenal superior to, 5, 6-9, 17, 23, 26-43 *passim*, 110, 111-12, 130, 131; and Lucilius, 31, 46-49, 51, 72, 129, 131, 133,

202, 203, 211, 212, 213, 222, 299, 355, 362; and Maecenas, 51-58 *passim*, 73, 75, 162, 186, 199, 228, 332; mingled satire of, 130, 133-34; and odes, 8, 20-21, 27, 43; and opposition, 5, 40-42, 126, 148; and Persius, 50, 72-73, 81, 95-96, 129, 131, 327; Renaissance harsh satire of, 6-8, 6n, 12; reputation of, xiii, 5, 11, 18, 19, 44, 82, 110, 139; Rigaltius on, 25; satire and the age, 26, 27, 28, 258; his satire defined, xiii-xiv, 174, 176; his satire not unified, 30, 36; his satire not real satire, 31, 32, 35, 43; and Trebatius, 48, 73, 82, 201-3, 202n, 208, 210, 211, 217, 227-28, 231; Vossius on, 14

and Augustus: ally of, 40, 43, 98, 131, 157, 275, 311-12, 315; defended by, 73, 231, 232, 237, 238; Horace pleases, 155, 315, 321; Horace praises, 41, 51, 53-54, 57-58, 227-28; Horace writes about, 57, 71, 75, 77, 101, 140, 157, 168, 208, 210, 211, 246, 259, 303, 308, 332; praise of attacked, 333-34

conventions of, x, xvi, 105; adversarius, 95; comic, laughing, smiling, etc., xiv, 8, 9, 13, 15-17, 26, 27, 28, 30, 34, 130-31, 134, 165; conversational, 292; dialogue, xiii, 66, 95; family of, 54, 57, 265, 332; epistolary satire, 90, 105-9, 170-71, 174, 240; low or prosaic style, 14, 31, 32-33, 43; personal voice, 108; polished verse, 332; retirement, 56-58, 333; self-mockery, 96; union with decent court and society, 18, 37-39, 49, 51-58 *passim*, 105, 106, 107, 238,

379

INDEX

25, 28, 31-32, 31n, 38, 110, 190;
facit indignatio versum adapt-
ed, 116-21, 154, 358-59; French
reaction to, xii, 16-18, 34, 37,
82, 88-89, 92-95, 97, 100-1, 102-
4, 112, 114, 155, 240; and
Gould, 10-11, 26, 83; govern-
ment persecutes, 300; and
Horace, 18, 19, 50, 81, 95-96,
121, 132, 254-55, 284; Horace
inferior to, 5, 6-9, 17, 23, 26-43
passim, 110, 111-12, 130, 131;
Horace and/or Persius equal
to, 8, 22-26, 61-62, 133; Horace
superior to, 12, 14, 15-22, 34,
36-37, 97-98, 130, 155; imita-
tions of, xiv, 11-12, 19-20, 25,
36n, 40, 41, 40n-41n, 92, 119,
128, 218-19, 337, 352; limited
voice of, 332; and Lucilius, 46-
47, 49-51, 58, 133; mingled
satire of, 129-34; mode of
proceeding in, 76-81; model
of satire, 34, 35, 43, 44, 85;
moral satire of, 28; and Old-
ham, 11, 26, 83, 113, 117, 146;
and opposition to Caesar's
tyranny, xvi, 28, 42, 58, 81, 91,
93, 101, 290; and opposition
to Walpole, 5, 40, 41, 123, 124,
213; patrons in, 254-55; and
Persius, 58, 59, 75, 81, 95-97,
101, 121, 123-29, 131, 148, 168,
174-75, 239; and Pindar, 31;
and Pope, xii, xiii, 4, 43, 67n,
110, 122, 139, 151-54, 155, 212,
237-39, 240, 260, 275, 280-81,
292, 295-96, 298, 340; and
Renaissance satire, 5-8, 7n; re-
publicanism of, 96; on Rome,
xiv, 80-81; on Roman family,
196, 197, 322; his satire defined,
xiv, 174-75; satirizes the dead,
323; Vossius on, 14; Wolcot

adapts, 358-59; on women, 27n,
76-80, 94-95, 189, 190
   conventions of: angry, blunt,
harsh, indignant, severe, etc., 5,
28, 37, 38, 82, 100, 116-21, 130,
131, 132, 258; catalogue, xiv,
27-28, 94, 119; elevated, epic,
tragic, sublime, etc., 25, 30-34,
38, 75, 97, 126, 131-32; isola-
tion of speaker, 75, 118-21,
174, 230; monologue, xv, 95,
174; musical or sweet versifica-
tion, 21-22, 32, 34, 130; unified
arguments, 30, 131
   works cited: xiv, xiv n: *Sat-
ires*, i, 20, 20n, 46, 60, 80-81,
117, 125, 132, 148, 203, 218,
323, 337, 348; ii, 348; iii, 81,
92, 148, 245, 294; v, 81; vi,
76-80, 93, 177, 197, 322; vii,
40n, 148; viii, 98, 148; ix, 81,
132, 348; x, 132, 352; xiii, xiv,
19-20, 25, 352

Kelsall, Malcolm, 309n
Kenrick, William, 344n-45n
Kent, Henry de Grey, Duke of,
   293
King, William, xi, 203
Knox, Vicesimus, 86, 111, 130,
   140

Labeo, Persius's, 71
Lactantius, 45
Laelius, Lucilius's and Horace's,
   203, 222, 224, 225
La Fontaine, Jean de, 114
La Harpe, Jacqueline de, 114n
La Harpe, Jean François de, 102
Law of the XII Tables, 164, 166,
   166n, 208, 208n-9n, 209, 227,
   228
Le Monnier, Abbé, xii, 63, 129
Le Noble, M., 23

INDEX

Lepidus, Marcus Aemilius, 78, 78n
Lerenbaum, Miriam, 179, 180n
Letter to a Friend in the Country, A, 145n
Le Verrier, Pierre, 88
libel: administration on, 205, 205n, 230, 258, 325; convictions for, 230; definitions of, 229, 229n-30n; and grave epistles, 230, 232; and Lady Mary, 215, 215n, 230; laws of feared, 302; Pope on, 215, 215n, 226, 319; punishments for, 221, 222n; and satire, 206, 206n-7n, 210, 210n, 224, 230; truth of, 229n-30n. *See also scandalum magnatum*
Lipsius, Justus, 8, 9, 17, 27, 31
Lloyd, Robert, 336
Lockwood, Thomas, 347n-48n
Lodge, Thomas, 7
London Chronicle, The, 352
London Journal, The, 105-6, 157, 163, 206n
Longinus, Dionysius, x, xn
Lorleach, 150
Louis XIV, King: and Augustus, 15, 39, 82, 98, 105; and Boileau, 95, 98, 99, 100, 273, 273n; and English, 82; and Midas, 273
Loveling, Benjamin, 126-27, 218
Lubin, Eilhard, 45, 46
Lucan, Marcus Annaeus, 34
Lucian, 14, 23, 111, 112, 132
Lucilius, Caius: and administration, 126, 167-68; adversarius in, 328-30; and Augustan age, 46, 48-50, 72, 73; and Boileau, 84, 86; comic satire of, 97; French critics on, 47-48, 97, 103; friend to virtue, 46, 223, 299; government protection of, 48, 50, 300, 329; harsh satire

of, 8, 13, 46-47, 81, 130, 299, 329-30, 332; and Horace, 31, 46-49, 51, 72, 129, 131, 133, 202, 203, 211, 212, 213, 222, 299, 355, 362; and Juvenal, 46-47, 49-51, 58, 133; and Loveling, 128; mode of proceeding, 46-51; parent of satire, 6, 45, 129, 330; and Persius, 46, 49, 50-51, 58, 73, 133, 327; and Pope, 4, 200, 213, 218, 223, 299, 328-30, 355, 362; republicanism of, 49, 330n; reputation of, 5, 44, 45-51; specific attacks by, 46; and Warton, 214
Lumley, George, 318n
Lupus, in Lucilius, 46, 47
Lyttelton, George, Baron, 140, 142-43, 328n

Mack, Maynard, xvii, 180n, 217n, 221n, 229, 272-73, 331, 331n
Madan, Martin, 25, 34, 60
Maecenas Caius: and Augustus, 51, 55-56, 98, 204, 223n, 292, 362; and Bolingbroke, 162, 164, 298, 333; and court poets, 223n; and Horace, 51-58 *passim*, 73, 75, 162, 186, 199, 228
Magic Flute, The, Mozart's, 199
Maidwell, Lewis, 58, 58n
Man of Honour, The, 119
Manwaring, Edward, 74, 81
Marston, John, 10
Martial, Marcus Valerius, 36
Marvell, Andrew, 336
Mason, William, 360
Mathias, T. J., x, 49, 86-87, 120-21
Maupetit, M., 34, 38, 93
Mc Doe-Roch, Patrick, 236
Mead, Dr. Richard, 298
Messala, Marcus Valerius Corvinus, 70, 74

382

INDEX

Ovid, Publius Ovidius Naso, 248,
284, 332
Oxford, Edward Harley, Earl,
176-77
Oxford, Robert Harley, Earl,
178, 204-5, 299
Ozell, John, 85-86, 96

Pacuvius, Marcus, 13
Page, Sir Francis, 215
Paine, Tom, 362-63
Palladio, Andrea, xiii, 184, 187,
294-95, 360
Palmézeaux, Chevalier Michel
Cubières de, 102-4
Party-Satire Satirized, 140-41
Paulinus, Caius Suetonius, 244,
244n-45n
Paxton, Nicholas, 319
Peacham, Henry, 341
Perrault, Charles, 98
Persius, Aulus Persius Flaccus,
and Persian Satire, x, xii, xvi,
105; and Augustan age, 72;
and Boileau, 83, 88, 89, 95, 96;
and Brutus, 68; Casaubon on,
61-62, 62n, 66, 327n-28n; com-
mentors on, xii, 6, 14, 16-17,
25, 59-70, 69, 74, 88-89, 95-96,
97, 130, 131, 240; and Dryden,
32, 49-50, 65, 83, 287; equal to
Horace and/or Juvenal, 8, 62;
and Horace, 50, 72, 73, 81, 95-
96, 129, 131, 327; imitations of,
60-61, 60n, 68-69, 121-28, 148;
inferior to Horace and Juvenal,
32, 59, 61; and Juvenal, 58, 59,
75, 81, 95-97, 101, 121, 123-29,
131, 148, 168, 174-75, 239;
limited voice of, 332; and Lu-
cilius, 46, 49, 50-51, 58, 73, 133,
327; mingled satire of, xii, xv,
82-83, 129, 130-31, 133-34; mode
of proceeding by, 70-76; op-

poses Nero, xvi, 4, 42, 62-65,
67, 70-76, 91, 101, 126, 271,
271n, 305, 326; opposes Wal-
pole, 5, 40, 59, 121-29, 213; and
Pope, 4, 5, 64-65, 67, 67n, 110,
148, 151-52, 155, 238-39, 240,
260-61, 270-74, 275, 287, 292,
298; translations of, 25, 60-61,
110, 130-31, 154, 287, 326-27,
327n-28n; and Wolcot, 363
conventions of, 170, 174-75,
270-74; adversarius or monitor,
7, 67, 69, 71-75, 95, 137, 239,
305, 325-28, 365; bravery, 62,
68-69; coherent argument, 30,
131; contemplative, 121-22;
decline of letters, 30, 63-65,
124-28, 238-39, 273-75, 301, 326;
dialogue, 66-67, 70-71, 73, 122-
23, 125-26; elevated, or tragic,
14, 97; harshness, 5-6, 59, 64,
69, 121-28; irony, 67-68, 73;
isolation, 74-75, 126; obscurity,
59, 62-63, 82, 130, 131, 239,
270; persona, or disguise, 65-66,
67-68; political opposition, 62-
70, 70-75, 121-29, 260, 270-71,
275; prudence, 62-63, 69, 271-73;
solemnity, 25, 69, 82, 104, 122-
23, 138, 275, 287; stoicism, 122-
23, 260
works cited: Satires: Prologue,
60, 65; i, 46, 48n, 60, 65, 66,
69, 71, 124-28, 148, 238-39, 254,
270-74, 305, 325-28; ii, 70; iii,
60, 122; iv, 60, 65, 67, 70, 123-24,
148, 327n-28n; v, 70, 71; vi, 67,
70
Peter, John, 7n
Peterborough, Charles Mordaunt,
Earl, 225, 232-33, 239, 241
Phillips, John, 132
Pindar, Peter, *see* Wolcot, John
Piscus Grammaticus, de Satyra, 6

384

INDEX

INDEX

Howard D. Weinbrot is Professor of English at the University of Wisconsin, Madison, and is the author of *Augustus Caesar in "Augustan" England: The Decline of a Classical Norm* (Princeton, 1978).

Library of Congress Cataloging in Publication Data

Weinbrot, Howard D.
  Alexander Pope and the traditions of
formal verse satire.

  Includes index.
  1. Pope, Alexander, 1688-1744—Criticism
and interpretation.   2.   Satire—History and
criticism.   I.   Title.
PR3634.W4   821'.5   81-47957
ISBN 0-691-06510-1   AACR2